ADVANCE PRAISE FOR *CRITICAL SITUATIONS: A RHETORIC FOR WRITING IN COMMUNITIES*

"*Critical Situations* is a smart, provocative, truly original approach to the writing classroom that demands students take writing seriously. By emphasizing the workings of rhetoric on the national scene and in the local peer group, it enables students to see that words matter."

Melissa Ianetta
University of Delaware

"The approach to writing here is one that many of us who teach writing as citizenship greatly respect but rarely can see in a textbook. There are, of course, lots of textbooks that treat the subject of community and citizenship, but most treat those as hypothetical concepts and make the classroom a place to talk about what one might do, rather than a place where we discuss what we are doing. . . . In that way, this text has figured out [how to support] a course's work if the course's work isn't text based."

Dominic Delli Carpini
York College of Pennsylvania

Critical Situations "makes rhetoric available to students without burdening them with too much of the history and theory. It also refuses to make rhetoric prescriptive [and] . . . consistently invites us to consider how to use rhetoric in whatever critical situation we find ourselves."

David Coogan
Virginia Commonwealth University

"*Critical Situations* has a number of qualities that make it distinctive from other writing textbooks I've seen. First, its historical rhetorical approach infuses the book without overwhelming students with terminology they can't understand or use. . . . Second, its strong emphasis on situated writing allows students to have a say in aspects of their lives in which they most need to find an appropriate forum and craft an appropriate voice. . . . Third, the flexible organization should allow different sorts of teachers to use the book in the ways that make sense for their own classes. I am very impressed."

Libby Miles
University of Rhode Island

"I see the text as wonderfully distinct and special in its content, scope, and approach. . . . For example, the sustained attention to context, ethics, and evidence are presented through rich discussions supported by careful attention to the support work writers are asked to produce. Workshops that prompt writers to consider group work as significantly as these do, for example, indicate to students that group work is a serious, scholarly, and context-specific activity. I believe the text offers a new approach to teaching writing and provides students (and teachers) the tools and scaffolding needed to [understand] writing as context-specific inquiry."

Lee Nickoson-Massey
Elon University

CRITICAL SITUATIONS

A Rhetoric for Writing in Communities

SHARON CROWLEY
Arizona State University

MICHAEL STANCLIFF
Arizona State University

PEARSON
Longman

New York San Francisco Boston
London Toronto Sydney Tokyo Singapore Madrid
Mexico City Munich Paris Cape Town Hong Kong Montreal

Acquisitions Editor: Lauren A. Finn
Senior Supplements Editor: Donna Campion
Senior Media Producer: Stafanie Liebman
Senior Marketing Manager: Sandra McGuire
Production Manager: Eric Jorgensen
Project Coordination, Text Design, and Electronic Page Makeup: Electronic Publishing Services Inc., NYC
Cover Design Manager: John Callahan
Cover Photos: Jane Sterrett/Images.com
Photo Researcher: Clare Maxwell
Senior Manufacturing Buyer: Alfred C. Dorsey
Printer and Binder: RR Donnelley & Sons Company
Cover Printer: Phoenix Color Corporation

Library of Congress Cataloging-in-Publication Data

Crowley, Sharon, 1943-
Critical situations: a rhetoric for writing in communities/Sharon Crowley, Michael Stancliff.
p. cm.
ISBN-13: 978-0-321-24653-0
ISBN-10: 0-321-24653-5
1. English language—Rhetoric—Study and teaching. 2. Report writing–Study and teaching. 3. Critical thinking—Study and teaching. 4. Reasoning—Study and teaching.
I. Stancliff, Michael. II. Title.
PE1404.C759 2008
808'.0420711—dc22

2007038278

Please visit us at www.ablongman.com.

ISBN 13: 978-0-321-24653-0

ISBN 10: 0-321-24653-5

1 2 3 4 5 6 7 8 9 10—DOH—10 09 08 07

CONTENTS

PART III WORKSHOPS 209

GLOSSARY 277

PART IV READING ROOM: A SELECTION OF WORKS REFERENCED IN *CRITICAL SITUATIONS* 279

PREFACE

OUR APPROACH

Critical Situations: A Rhetoric for Writing in Communities was inspired by our students' ingenuity and eloquence over the years using language to solve problems and meet goals. We might never have realized the power of student writing had we not allowed students themselves to decide which problems and goals were worth addressing in the first place. Rather than prescribing rules for writing, we began posing questions about what successful writing might look like across the countless contexts in which writing matters. We call these writing challenges "critical situations" because of the *essential importance* they hold for student writers and also to suggest the habit of *critical thinking* that is the intellectual approach necessary for successful rhetorical work. Rather than asking students to *practice writing*, this book challenges students to undertake the *practice of rhetoric* by writing and speaking as a means of taking action. This idea that writing is a form of social action is a core premise among varied rhetorical traditions.

This book challenges students to take charge of defining "good writing" in the context of self-designed projects, in which they must come to terms with the criteria for successful writing as these necessarily emerge in the specific contours of rhetorical situations. As they research, read, and write, students learn about the possibilities open to them as communicators, about the parameters of public discourse surrounding their chosen project focus, the most persuasive arguments circulating, and the history of the situation itself. In this way, *Critical Situations* attempts to make good on advice given by teachers across disciplines to put student interests at the center of the curriculum. Students arrive at writing classrooms with a wide range of experience, interests, and strongly held commitments in the communities in which they live and work. While more traditional approaches to writing instruction ask students to check these experiences and interests at the door, so to speak, the approach we take in this book grounds instruction in the energy and particularity of students' lives. *Critical Situations* seeks to empower students to approach writing and speaking as integral life practices, not an academic exercise. No curriculum we could design would offer the kind of rich learning opportunities that emerge when a room full of people with greatly varied interests share their experiences navigating the constraints and possibilities of language work.

We take quite seriously the idea that all communication is a form of action and thus a medium for movement. All serious writers and speakers have places to go and things to do. *Travel, exploration, navigating, mapping, following paths, and reaching destinations*—these are among spatial metaphors that guide the instruction you will encounter in *Critical Situations.* Using this book, we hope students will see the classroom community as a point of departure.

DISTINGUISHING FEATURES

The Project Model

At the heart of our approach is what we call the project model. Over the years, our students have written workplace proposals, made informational fliers, launched letter writing campaigns, built Web sites addressing a variety of issues, made training videos, written mentoring manuals, written articles for a host of public forums, designed PowerPoint presentations, staged performances, and written scholarly essays. In every case, the project was grounded in community-based commitments and proceeded from rhetorical intentions students themselves articulated. In the project model, students take ownership of their work, defining key issues, developing an agenda for research and analysis, identifying important audiences, constructing the best possible arguments, revising, and ultimately, planning for publication in the broadest sense of bringing their work to the most meaningful audiences. Perhaps the greatest challenge of using *Critical Situations* is overcoming our own habits of imposing limits on curriculum, on the work of the writing classroom, and on rhetoric itself. We believe there is much to gain in transgressing these limits.

This project work becomes a laboratory for rhetorical education. To achieve this sense of a practicum, the workshop sequences integrated with major chapters of *Critical Situations* facilitate a collaborative and dialogic learning environment. In the project workshop, individual writing challenges illustrate core rhetorical principles for the group. In our experience, the project model results in an exciting classroom where people get real work done and learn sophisticated rhetorical principles as a matter of direct interaction with the social ground of their chosen project. Students learn from one another's challenges and insights as they work towards often radically different ends.

Mapping Communities

Helping students reconceive the communities in which critical situations emerge as rhetorical as well as social spaces is an important early step in the project model. The first two chapters of the book culminate in the process of community mapping, an extended reflection on the social commitments that orient our definitions of community. Rather than offering any single definition, we ask students to catalog their community involvement developing their own collective designations for community groups. Students chart the ground of their community involvement and the commitments, challenges, problems, activities, and common concerns that give communities definition and demand rhetorical action. For each community graphed onto the map, students pose questions that are in each community context critical. As we explain in Chapter 2 , the goal is to capture on paper the questions that hold communities together or create divisions within and among communities. We provide a variety of student examples to suggest the range of possible social commitments and approaches to the assignment.

The Invention Journal

At the core of the book are eight chapters on invention, that core rhetorical activity by which writers and speakers find and adapt the best arguments for the moment at hand. Once students have decided on a project focus, these chapters provide the framework and instruction for a rigorous process of rhetorical invention. Throughout the process, students record their thinking and planning in an Invention Journal modeled after the ancient commonplace book. The Invention Journal provides students with in-depth heuristics for developing arguments responsive to the demands of their chosen project work. The journal contains the bulk of students' intellectual work, as they refine their thinking and generate a wealth of ideas and arguments. Each student project becomes at once an opportunity for self-directed rhetorical action and also a rigorous course in critical reading, writing, and research. In other words, we adhere to the old adage that people learn best through application, by "doing." Fundamental rhetorical practices are presented with detailed instruction and many examples. Through the course of rhetorical action, students work toward general principles for locating and connecting to audiences, articulating lines of reasoning, using evidence, framing appeals within community beliefs, navigating conventions, and developing authority across writing contexts among other core rhetorical practices.

The Workshops

Within the chapters, students are directed to a collection of workshops, all of which are gathered in the third section of *Critical Situations*. These workshops are an archive of learning activities and thought experiments we have developed over the years and adapted from the work of the teachers we admire most. Integrated into each chapter, and organized so that teachers and students can choose those most appropriate for their classrooms, the workshops provide structure for a collaborative practice. Many of the workshops are intended to support student projects as they move towards completion and publication. Others provide individual and collaborative projects meant to slow down the process and to facilitate exploration of a variety of practical and theoretical aspects of composition. The workshops cover a wide range of issues, among them: the process of moving from invention to drafting; organizing and maintaining a productive collaborative environment; rhetorical research methods; summarizing key texts, arguments, and ideas; strategizing publication; reading carefully and critically; setting up classroom debates; and interviewing strategies. A series of workshops also address ethical issues of communication. These workshops on ethics, like all the others, emphasize writing and speaking as decision-making processes. Students learn more about the many activities subsumed under the term "writing," and experience greater agency as writers when it is broken down into a broader spectrum of thinking and action.

Case Studies

Linking all the chapters are two historical case studies. Illustrative discussions treat major events and figures of the nineteenth-century abolitionist movement and key texts written in response to the events of September 11, 2001. The case studies make a powerful complement to student project work, and throughout the book, students are encouraged to read actively and to consider the power of rhetorical craft to shape realities and influence history. Locating the invention and composing processes in the complexity of these historical case studies, students encounter dramatic and diverse illustrations of rhetorical endeavor. Many student projects are integrated into the chapters, allowing students to walk through their peers' thinking and writing processes, further enriching the spectrum of rhetorical practices students can consult as examples.

Both case studies consider moments of national crisis in which a range of issues were and are hotly contested and in which a broad range of political and philosophical positions have animated the public sphere. These dramatic differences and the manifestly high stakes of arguments about policy and ethical standards have proven compelling for the students in our courses. Established and maintained at the podiums and presses of the eighteenth and nineteenth centuries, the abolitionist movement was a grand project of the rhetorical imagination. Examining the speeches and writings of Norman Mailer, Sojourner Truth, Frances Ellen Watkins Harper, Frederick Douglass, and others, students encounter eloquence that helped change political history as well as our understanding of the public sphere and the history of rhetoric itself. The political and rhetorical conflicts engaged in the wake of 9/11 compare interestingly to the abolitionist context, as many of the same arguments regarding policy, ethics, social difference, and national definition are at play. Even six years after, we are still very much in a "post-9/11" world. While students will all have some familiarity with 9/11 sound bites and flashpoints, the deeper look at relevant arguments and the vast scope of the impact of 9/11 provide students with compelling reading in which to consider the practice and theory of rhetorical work.

Talk/Read/Write

In addition to the Invention Journals, collaborative exercises under the heading, "Talk/Read/Write" recur throughout the chapters. These compel students to think more about the rhetorical principles presented in each chapter. The questions and prompts of the "Talk/Read/Write" sections can be used as in-class exercises or as the foundation for freestanding assignments. All of which is to say that *Critical Situations* offers a wealth of material to instigate and structure daily classroom activities.

Instructor's Manual

As a supplement to *Critical Situations*, we offer an Instructor's Manual rich with resources for day-to-day teaching plans and with multiple frameworks for organizing courses as a whole. A variety of syllabus outlines and assignment and workshop sequences are provided. A detailed first chapter offers a holistic re-orientation for teachers with little or no experience using a project model.

MyCompLab (www.mycomplab.com <http://www.mycomplab.com>)

MyCompLab is a Web application that offers comprehensive and integrated resources for every writer. With MyCompLab, students can learn from interactive tutorials and instruction; practice and develop their skills with grammer, writing, and research exercises; share and collaborate their writing with peers; and receive comments on their writing from instructors and tutors. Go to <http://www.mycomplab.com/> to register for these premier resources and much more!

ACKNOWLEDGEMENTS

Michael thanks Sharon Crowley for the inspiration of her scholarship, her camaraderie during the troubling times that both intruded upon and motivated this writing, and her patience with his often-meandering sentences. Heartfelt thanks also to Sharon Kirsch for the example of her teaching and her brilliant (and multiple) readings of every piece of this manuscript. Gratitude also to Lauren Finn for her editorial guidance and good humor. And thanks to Scott Hitchcock of Electronic Publishing Services Inc. for his guidance and support throughout the production process. I acknowledge also my colleagues far and wide whose teaching practices, integral to my own, have become part of the pedagogical structure of this book. To all the students whose work graces these pages and to all the rest who have given this writing purpose, I offer my greatest thanks.

Sharon wishes to acknowledge Michael's amazing skill and resourcefulness as a teacher, qualities that shine through nearly every page of this book. Michael is also an able and gracious collaborator. The bagel place at the union allowed us to monopolize a table while learning about abolitionism and reconstruction, and while Michael resisted my readings of the events of 9/11. I also wish to thank Lauren Finn for editorial guidance. Finally, as always, I am grateful for my furry companions, who sleep at my elbow as I write.

We both thank Dominic Delli Corpini, York College of Pennsylvania; Margaret Whitt, University of Denver; Sue Carter, Bowling Green State University; David Coogan, Virginia Commonwealth University; Linda C. Macri, University of Maryland; Adrian Wurr, University of North Carolina Greensboro; Libby Miles, University of Rhode Island; Glen McClish, San Diego State University; Lee Nickoson-Massey, Elon University; Rolf Norgaard, University of Colorado at Boulder; Melissa Ianetta, University of Delaware; Beverly Wall, Trinity College; Jane Fife, Western Kentucky University; David Jolliffe, University of Arkansas.

SHARON CROWLEY

MICHAEL STANCLIFF

PART I

MOTIVATED CRITICAL CHOICES

1

CONTEXT IS CRITICAL

ON THE BUS

During a typically hot summer in Tempe, Arizona, near the campus of Arizona State University, a breathless young man and woman scramble onto a Valley Metro bus. Both peer anxiously out a window as the bus pulls away from the curb. Through the windows passengers see another young man sprinting after the bus, shouting and wildly waving his arms for the driver to stop. The couple explains frantically to the driver that the man in pursuit is very dangerous and means them great harm. "He'll kill my boyfriend!" the woman pleads. Her partner vigorously nods his head in agreement. The driver continues on, pretending to ignore the furious pedestrian running in the street. Regular passengers exchange glances that communicate relief over an unpleasant incident apparently averted.

But city buses move slowly picking up and dropping off passengers. With each stop, the young couple becomes increasingly uncomfortable, speaking in low but urgent tones. At a major intersection, the coming and going of a sizable group of passengers gives the pursuer time to catch up. As he draws closer and finally runs up alongside the bus, some passengers hear a stream of obscenity. As the driver begins to pull away from the stop, the angry young man leaps onto the steps of the bus and begins pounding on the doors, demanding to be let on. The young couple stands, as if to prepare themselves for whatever will happen next. The driver stops the bus. She radios in to report the situation and to request police intervention. She turns from the radio speaker to the would-be assailant, her tone shifting from controlled professionalism to angry warning. Unexpectedly, the young woman charges toward the door, shouting and cursing.

Passenger reaction on the bus varies as the man pounds on the door. Across the aisle, a mother shelters her two young children on the side of the seat farthest from the aisle. Another woman quickly stuffs items into her backpack and watches intently as the scene unfolds. An older man and woman move out of their front seats—a place reserved by custom for senior citizens—and walk toward the back of the bus. Outside, a man who is perhaps on his way home from work seems on the brink of taking things up with the agitated young man, who is now attempting to pry open the bus doors. On the sidewalk, yet another man has a look of pleasant expectation on his face as if this were the climax of a movie or television show. Even inside the bus, some passengers seem more or less amused. But another passenger raises her voice above the others beseeching the driver to "just drive away, drive away!" Someone asks the young couple, "Do you know if he has a gun?" The young man answers distractedly, "I'm not sure. I don't think so." Others bury their faces in magazines, pretend to sleep, or otherwise avert their gaze. In the back of the bus, a group of high school students talking seems somehow not to have noticed the events transpiring at the front of their bus.

At this point, a police cruiser arrives on the scene, and the would-be assailant disappears through an adjacent parking lot before the officers can set foot on the sidewalk. After the police officers ask a few questions, the bus is once again on its way. A mile later, the young couple steps warily off the bus.

The events that occurred on a city bus that hot summer day quickly became what we call a **critical situation**, in the sense that every action taken, and possibly every word spoken, became potentially important in determining what would happen next. Consider the complexity of this situation. Although all those present occupied the physical space of the bus, everyone involved did and did not share a single experience. Understandings of the reality and importance of the event shifted from seat to seat based on each person's perceived stake in the circumstances: those seated closest to the door and to the angry young man had more at stake than the students seated in the back rows, who seemed unaware that anything unusual was happening. For some passengers this was a moment of crucial importance, perhaps of life or death; for others it was literally a nonevent. A reporter who interviewed everyone present that day might ask each one to recount what had happened, why it was important or interesting, and what their main concern was in the moment. Passengers and witnesses would make very different assessments of what had been at stake and of the volatile dynamics that had played out before their eyes. The reporter would no doubt hear people talk about safety, fear, inconvenience—all the factors that motivated or failed to motivate them in the moment.

Reporters and police officers know that when a group of people are asked to explain the facts or the truth of any given situation, their accounts will vary. Eyewitnesses to events can seldom reach consensus about what happened. This is especially true of dramatic or traumatic events. Take, for example, eyewitness accounts of the crash of a hijacked aircraft—United Flight 93—in rural Pennsylvania on September 11, 2001. People who were nearby offer wildly varying accounts of what they saw and heard. Some witnesses say that they heard an explosion before the plane descended into view, while others say that debris from the plane began falling to the ground well before it crashed, as far as eight miles away from the crash site. These accounts suggest that the plane was coming apart prior to the crash, perhaps as the result of an explosion on board. Still other eyewitnesses attest that the aircraft seemed to be intact but its wings were rocking back and forth as it neared the ground, while others claim that it was flying upside down.

Eyewitness accounts vary because our sense of what is important, of what is real, is largely determined by where we are standing when the events in question occur. The phrase "where we are standing" is meant both literally and figuratively here; its meaning can be enlarged to include the positions we take on all matters that concern us. Our life experiences, the cultures we hail from, and the cultural presuppositions that make up our differing versions of common-sense knowledge, all determine who we are and what we believe; that is, they determine the positions from which we view issues that are important to us. Our stake in a given situation—what we imagine we will lose or gain—also influences how we view facts and ideas. Perhaps this seems obvious and hardly worth mentioning. If you think so, we ask you to suspend that judgment for a moment as we consider the profound implications of such differences of perception and opinion.

The inevitability of differences, of conflicting perspectives and experiences, makes up the basic landscape of a critical situations. Learning to respond as a writer or speaker to the disagreements and the differing social perspectives entailed in any critical situation gives you more options for composing in that **context**. This will be true whether you are researching a proposal for your workplace, trying to settle an ongoing dispute with a neighbor, or writing a research paper for your history class. Here we define *context* to mean the diverse beliefs and arguments that circulate around any position you take up—whether that position be pro-life, antiwar, or any of innumerable other possibilities. *Context* also refers to the lived experience and history that give rise to beliefs and arguments. Like it or not, war is a practice carried on by nations against one another; the practice of war produces histories of wars; the practice also gives rise to political, moral, and religious beliefs about war-making; and these beliefs in turn generate a host of arguments for and against war, both in general and concerning specific wars. All of this is part of the context of war.

Careful thought about context is nearly always necessary if you want to succeed as a writer or speaker. "Context is critical" is in fact one of our primary mantras. Writers and speakers who would address any issue need a working knowledge of the context surrounding it. Relevant contexts can include: the history of the issue, the communities that are discussing it, what participants stand to lose or gain, and all of the arguments that have defined how people understand the situation. Without a strong understanding of these dynamics, pitfalls await speakers and writers. Without careful study of the critical situation that surrounds an issue, a speaker or writer may make an argument that has long been discredited, or present unreliable evidence, or use an argument that offends an audience, all of which might damage your credibility. Such a speaker or writer will not be aware of all the arguments made available by a critical situation, will not know who are the most authoritative voices and which are the most persuasive lines of reasoning.

The chapters that follow present strategies for researching and analyzing the arguments that are available in any critical situation. As you read the chapters and work through the invention exercises that follow, we encourage you to think of research as a kind of analytical travel and the context surrounding your project as the terrain that must be navigated if your project is to be successful.

COMMUNICATION AND COMMITMENT

Communication of all kinds is the result of some kind of **commitment**, a dedication to a set of outcomes, ideas, or people who reside in communities that are impacted by a particular critical situation. Some of the commitments that motivated people on the bus to speak or act are obvious—commitment to one's children, to safety, to the right to travel to work without fear of violence. Others remain hidden at first glance. What was the dispute between pursuer and pursued? We don't know, but we can guess: the pursuer is a spurned lover, is owed money, etc. Our guesses include reasons that might motivate us or people we know to pursue a city bus for a mile, on foot, alongside a busy street on a hot day. We can guess about the pursuer's commitments because values and desires are shared among members of communities and cultures. In fact, we might say that shared values and motives define communities and cultures; at the very least they are part of the glue that holds such groups together.

Methodical and goal-driven communication—the kind we encourage in this book—results from commitment. The first three chapters are dedicated to helping you understand the commitments that motivate you to speak or write. Any person or group that has taken up a committed position within a critical situation is a **stakeholder**. We use this term because it acknowledges that writers and speakers have ownership in a situation. You can become a formidable writer or speaker only if you come to understand the commitments made and the positions taken up by others who have a stake in the situations that interest you. You are more likely to gain access to the discussion and to be heard within it if you can discover the interests that motivate other participants in the argument.

The chance occurrence on the bus was not a one-time event but part of a larger social picture. The situation of the bus itself evokes issues that are of perennial interest to people who live in large cities: the costs and benefits of public transportation, the scope of civic duty, and the potential for violence, to name just three. The situation raised questions about our responsibilities toward the **communities** in which we live. For our purposes here we define a community as any group of people who are interested in a situation because they have a stake in its outcome. Because all members of a community have interests or stakes in communal events and discussions, speakers and writers bear certain responsibilities toward them. And so we must ask: amidst our busy lives and individual concerns, how do we understand and weigh our responsibilities to one another? Had the angry young man indeed waved a pistol as he stood in the doorway of the bus, no doubt passengers would have tried to protect themselves, and perhaps some would try to protect the driver or the children as well. What community commitments demand our attention? Some passengers ignored the incident altogether, perhaps because they were busy with other tasks or because urban dwellers are used to this sort of thing. Set within these contexts, the potential conflict on the bus can be understood as emblematic of larger realities experienced by millions of people around the world every day. We can seldom decipher a final truth about this or any critical situation, but we can acknowledge complexity as the inevitable condition of community situations and thus of community-based communication.

For all our differences of commitment and perception, events often do place us into communities of common interest. Even the oblivious students in the back of the bus would have shared a real stake in the events if, say, the would-be assailant had gained access to the bus or had produced a gun. Stray bullets cut across social lines such as generation, race, gender and class. The bus is a powerful symbol of social systems and human interaction, in motion through civic spaces, the scene of carefully scheduled exchange and endlessly random encounters.

A special concern of this book is the ethical implications of this diversity of commitments and perspectives. Because we encourage you to take up communication as a way of gaining agency in the world, we feel we must remind you that there are always serious ethical implications entailed in writing and speaking publicly. One former student found herself hesitant and procrastinating just as she was about to upload a Web site she had designed. The site offered information about alternative methods of cancer treatment. As she designed the site, our student asked herself and others a number of ethical questions: What if visitors to the site altered the course of treatment prescribed by their doctors because of something they found on her Web site? What if her Web site served to further complicate the already complex and daunting experience of cancer patients? These questions led this student to a very careful reconsideration of her project. We applaud her willingness to think carefully about the impact her work might have on others, and we hope that you also move away from a purely individualist perspective on issues—if that is your primary lens on the world—as you work through this book. We argue, in fact, that the complexity of a situation cannot be understood productively unless you consider yourself as a fellow traveler whose life and fortunes constitute part of a larger social body. Like it or not, all of us are always already on the bus.

KEY CONCEPTS AND PROCEDURES

The following section defines key terms that guide our discussion. We encourage students and teachers to spend some time discussing these terms. Test our definitions against your own experience of composing and more generally of living in the world. As a group, you may decide to modify or replace these terms, but we believe that a common vocabulary helps greatly in establishing a productive community of learners. This is the goal of this chapter.

Committed Choices

The first step involves committing to a project. This book was written for writers and speakers who have a stake in their project, in other words, for people who care about the work they are doing. While writing this book we discussed examples of the most powerful communication we know and determined that there is at least one common denominator shared by all. That common factor is commitment. Communication that makes a difference, be it an internationally publicized political address or a workplace proposal, begins with committed choices made by people with a real stake in the issue at hand. As we worked on this book, we often recalled the work of our own students, who have so moved and impressed us with their commitment to composition as an important social practice. Almost without exception, the most impressive work was done by students who pursued issues that had great meaning for them outside of the classroom. Most teachers we know agree that their students work best when pursuing research and composition that connect to high-interest areas of concern—family and community issues, professional worries, political commitments, and on plans for further study.

One of the major complaints we hear from students in writing or speech classes is that they don't care about their topics, that they feel unmotivated. All of our experience leads us to believe that people don't learn much from unmotivated composing. Certainly, it doesn't inspire their best work. Like many other teachers, we think that students should choose and design their own composing projects. This is one way to address that perennial problem associated with learning to write or speak in school: lack of motivation. In our experience, students welcome the opportunity to take responsibility for designing and pursuing their own projects. We hope you will, too.

However, sometimes students do struggle when asked to choose their own direction for research and composition. It is not always easy to finish this sentence: "I really care about ________." Generally, we care about so many things that it is difficult to prioritize among them, and until we begin to research and think carefully, it can be very difficult to imagine how communication can make a difference in a given situation. Most writers and speakers are not entirely free to select and design their own projects, particularly if they work in academic contexts. Many of us have been trained through years of traditional schooling to feel much more comfortable with assigned topics and predetermined formats. Because of this, it may require a bit of practice to acquire the habit of discovery, which is to say, the habit of taking responsibility for the direction of our work.

Community

One powerful way to get past this initial block and locate meaningful places to work is to begin investigating the issues that link us to others in the communities that are most important to us. Look carefully at the places where you live and work. What are the key issues that crop up every day for your family, friends, neighbors, and coworkers? Ideally, your project will emerge from your own observations of and questions about daily life within a community that you consider your own. The people in these communities will be your audience, those people you want to inform, persuade or move to action.

But what exactly does *community* mean? In this book we define **community** as the place where our strongest commitments lie. It is where we have our closest connections, our greatest pleasures, and our most serious problems. Our earliest community consists of immediate family, and later, of other relatives and friends. Friendships are formed through proximity at first—as children we play with the kids next door rather than those living across town—but friendships can also form when we begin to associate with larger groups or communities: first grade, Sunday school, the street corner, the playground at a nearby park. As we grow older the communities to which we commit ourselves expand to include more structured groups: the chess club, the football team, band, debate, fans of the White Stripes or *Lost*, sororities, other members of our sociology class, and so on. Workers join unions and forge commitments both to other workers and to the goals of the union. If we enter a profession, we consider those who are in it with us to be colleagues whether we like them or not. Like other workers, professionals can be committed both to a group of colleagues and/or to a practice and its ethics: medicine, law, teaching, and so on. We adopt religious belief, or not, and it might be said that our fellow believers in Lutheranism or Wicca or atheism form a community of sorts. We adopt a politics or not, and it might be said that Republicans, Libertarians, Democrats, and Democratic Socialists each form a like-minded community. Members of the United Nations come there from all over the world, and often their loyalties to their home countries conflict with the community formed by membership in the United Nations. Nonetheless they agree to abide by the practices and beliefs of the UN, in the interest of contributing to the common good of all the peoples of the world.

Critical Situations

Consider three definitions of the word *critical*, the first of which we want to dispense with at the beginning. If someone is said to be a critical person, this is rarely a compliment. The common sense seems to be that people who are critical are rude, judgmental, and obnoxious. Children complain that parents and teachers are too

United Nations Assembly
Member nations across the globe send representatives to the United Nations assembly. Often, the loyalties and commitments of one nation conflict with those of other nations. Nonetheless, members remain committed ideally to pursuing the common good of people around the world and not simply to their own national concerns.

critical. Employees complain that their bosses are too critical all the way up the chain of management in any business or corporation. Critical people are thought to be picky, intrusive, and often wrong about whatever it is they are criticizing. This definition of *critical* is probably the most commonly used, but it will be of little help here.

A second definition of *critical* is "that which is too serious or important to ignore." Sometimes a critical situation entails life-or-death connotations. Critical patients are monitored constantly by hospital staffs. Political situations become critical when large numbers of lives and/or power and influence are at stake. To miss a critical point in a complicated explanation might well mean that you'll never truly understand the concept in question. This definition of *critical*, like the first, is often a matter of perspective or location within a community. One person's critical situation is another's dinner conversation. For football fans, third down in the red zone when the score is tied is a critical situation; for people who know nothing about football, such a situation looks just like many others that occur during a game.

We must all make determinations about what is and is not critical. We sincerely hope that the project you are undertaking is not a matter of life and death. However, we realize that at some point in life, everyone faces situations that can't be ignored. Recently, one of our students wrote an informational flier meant to educate Arizonans about the tragic deaths of Mexican immigrants attempting to enter the United States on Arizona's southern border. Another designed a Web site to chronicle the annual toll of those who drowned in Phoenix swimming pools. Other students address more pervasive national and international issues. Michelle Holtz, for example, researched the disturbingly dehumanizing images of African Americans that appear in popular culture, a problem she feels is compounded by the mistaken belief that as a society we have moved beyond racism. In both of these projects, the writers understand that the stakes are too serious to ignore, that is, they are *critical* in our second sense.

Our final definition of *critical* is "the practice of inquiry and analysis." Maybe in school you have been told that it is important to think critically about issues, not to simplify them, and to consider "both sides" (this is a misleading simplification, because most issues have many "sides"; that is, numerous positions can be taken up on any issue). All of this advice is easier to give than to follow. We want to specify the meaning of critical analysis just a bit: for us, critical analysis is the practice of investigating the relationship between knowledge and power, between events and their representations, between ideas and proposals. Negatively put, critical analysis is resistance to common sense. As we suggest throughout this book, skepticism is an important habit of mind for serious writers and speakers.

The process of critical analysis can change from one situation to another. The unquestioned assumptions and untested facts you face in a given critical situation will have their own history. You may have occasion to question a powerful social bias or the validity of some local wisdom, as did our student who studied advertisements in order to show that the culture has not moved as far past racism as is widely believed.

Because of the complex relations that obtain between events, ideas, and beliefs, we hope you develop the habit of thinking contextually. The philosopher William James claimed that "truth happens to an idea." He meant that assertions and arguments gain and lose power over time depending on any number of social factors. Take concern about global warming, for example. The problems caused by global warming seem to most people to be too big and too far away in time to merit serious attention. In fact, global warming makes the front pages only when a powerful figure, such as former Vice President Al Gore, draws attention to it in a compelling way. Because issues are tied to social concerns, critical analysis requires careful thought about the processes by means of which truth is produced. In the context of your project, critical analysis requires you to understand the factors that have generated the issue you are addressing as well as those factors that cause people to perceive it in the ways that they do. That is, you must investigate the history of the issue as well as differing attitudes about it.

- *Critical*, then, describes the level of importance of the situation you are engaging as well as your intellectual approach to research and composition. As we suggested in the first section of this chapter, a critical situation is both the circumstances that motivate your response and the perspective you take as a participant in those circumstances. Strategies outlined in this book will encourage you to examine what may seem at first to be strictly local terrain but which resonate within broader forces of power and influence at work in relation and international events. Alexis Cozombolidis, a student planning a career in broadcast journalism, was appalled by reports of sexual encounters between football recruits and undergraduate women "volunteers" who were ostensibly responsible for informal hosting during on-campus visits at her university. Cozombolidis's research into this local situation led to the realization that inappropriate behavior occurring during recruitment of college athletes was a national problem. Cozombolidis decided to compose an open letter to college football coaches, intended for *Sports Illustrated.* Another of our students, Soren Kest, made a dramatic discovery during his critical analysis: as he researched the process by means of which security cameras were installed at a local outdoor mall, he wrote, he learned that "what I thought was just a local problem turns out to be the kind of issue people across the country are debating in terms of privacy and security. There are a lot of different arguments on all sides of this privacy/security issue, and I still need to figure out who is saying what and why." Kest discovered, in fact, that installation of surveillance devices at the local mall was done in order to comply with the Patriot Act, which was itself a response to the events of 9/11. His critical analysis of a local situation uncovered many precedents elsewhere, and he also discovered that a number of protest strategies are available for those who oppose this sort of surveillance, and protest is the shape his project ultimately took. In short, this student's inquiry into a local issue developed into a rich engagement with America's current political climate. As a result, he came to understand his work not as an isolated effort but as related to a bigger piece of the world.

TALK READ WRITE

1. As a group, discuss the following questions: What are your initial reactions to our discussion of committed writing? Have you ever engaged in committed, goal-driven communication? If you have, share your

accounts of this activity with others. As an example of this kind of communication, you might even recall a disagreement you have had with friends, family, or coworkers in which you felt you had something important to lose or gain. Look for common threads and/or differences in the experiences reported by others.

2. Again working with a group, answer these questions. With which of the suggested three definitions of *critical* are you most familiar? In what context? Are there other definitions we should consider?
3. Discuss our definition of community with your group. Can you develop other definitions? How do these agree or disagree?
4. Now, working as a large group, discuss the commitments and issues that make your class a kind of community.

Rhetorical Invention

The finding or generation of arguments is called **invention**. In Latin, this term meant "to find" or "to come upon." Invention entails a process of searching for the arguments made available by the community who discusses an issue. To date, arguments about global warming can be found in scientific forums and in the work of people who oppose the science of global warming for political and religious reasons. These two communities both generate and circulate the arguments that are available for use on this issue, and that is where anyone who wants to join the conversation must look for them. Modern usages of the word "invention" suggest the creation of something that has not previously existed. For example, the Wright brothers invented the airplane; Edison invented the light bulb, and so on. The older definition that we are interested in resuscitating means nearly the opposite. In our usage, to *invent* is to discover all of the options for speaking and writing that are available to you in any given critical situation. These options already exist as possibilities because issues are in circulation among the communities concerned with them. The scope and depth of your invention depends on the complexity of the issue you are addressing, the attitudes of the audience you are addressing, and the time in which you reach that audience. We believe that writers and speakers must undertake a rigorous process of invention if they want to complete a successful project and to become a thoughtful member of the community in which their project is located. Accordingly, much of this book catalogues resources for rhetorical invention that are available to anyone who wishes to produce arguments that can intervene in critical situations.

Given the complicated and changeable nature of most critical situations, and given the complicated questions of interpretation, audience, and conventions they raise, how does a writer or speaker develop strategies for effective language use? What words will work? One of our students had firsthand knowledge about the wage gap that exists between men and women because she was a low-wage worker. She had also taken a Women's Studies course that alerted her to the fact that women are generally paid about two-thirds as much as men for doing similar work. In spite of her knowledge and personal experience, she struggled to find a way to address this problem. Could she address her employers without risking her job? Or should she try to motivate or organize other people who might be interested in this issue? If so, who? Who and where was her audience? How could she reach them? What were her options in terms of format or genre? Our student was particularly conscious of widespread cynicism about feminist politics, and this awareness became a complicated rhetorical problem for her. Looking for effective responses to such challenges is part of the work of navigating a critical situation.

Critical situations happen within systems, institutional networks such as neighborhoods, reservations, towns, and governments. Interests are often so closely intertwined that it is sometimes difficult to distinguish one network from another. One of our students, Trevor Boone, disapproved of a reading requirement recently instated in his high school alma mater because he believed it to be redundant and ineffective. His research into the rationale for the policy led quickly to links with the No Child Left Behind Act passed by Congress in 2000, which mandated the reading requirement. The local situation, as it turned out, could not be clearly understood without consulting the national context, and so Boone became informed on the current national debate about the president's educational policy. However, a decision made at a local high school might even be implicated with global politics. Then-Secretary of Education, Rod Paige, labeled the National Education Association a "terrorist organization" because the teachers' group had been critical of No Child Left Behind. Thus, Paige linked their opposition with that of people who want to harm Americans and instill fear. Thinking in terms of larger systems of policy and power gave Boone a much broader understanding of what was at stake for whom in the critical situation of his project. Schools are often politically volatile institutions, and it is likely that policy matters at a local school are playing out in the context of national education policy. So, even if you design a project around a local issue in your neighborhood or workplace, you may find it necessary to acquire knowledge about other, broader contexts in which this issue is also being discussed. Such knowledge will enhance your understanding of the matters at hand and will give you more options as a writer or speaker.

Much of the work in your project, then, will involve mapping out the social and rhetorical context of the circumstances or situation that have captured your concern. Situations are made up of contending voices, contradictory sets of information and the inevitable range of different perspectives that characterize the diverse social life of nearly any community. A rigorous process of rhetorical invention requires careful reading and researching, conversation, interviewing, taking notes, drafting arguments, and other strategies that will help you to understand the terrain in which you are working.

TALK READ WRITE

1. Pick several local issues, perhaps things that have become controversial on your campus or even in your classroom. As an exercise in examining multiple contexts, try to explain the larger debates and issues of which the local issue is just a component. For example, plagiarism, an issue in

many writing classes, is actually part of the larger issue of academic honesty. It could also be described as part of the larger context of copyright law or "intellectual property" rights. Property rights could be drawn out into the very broad context of the publishing industry or even of capitalist society. Think of as many broader contexts as you can.

2. Break the class into groups. In each, imagine that your teacher has assigned a 30-page research paper (one that was not on the syllabus) with three weeks remaining in the course. Brainstorm ideas for a meeting at which you will try to persuade the teacher that the assignment should be cancelled. Groups may also think of other audiences to address on this issue. Keep a list of all the ideas for research, argument and presentation that are suggested as you prepare. Then, make your case to the class.

The Invention Journal

Figuring out what project you will pursue is hard work. Choosing a project will challenge you intellectually, while the time and energy consumed by the legwork of research can be considerable. We think that all this effort results in writing and speaking that will actually interest readers and listeners, that will inform and perhaps move them.

In subsequent chapters of *Critical Situations*, you will frequently come across directions for making entries in an **Invention Journal**. As we have suggested, invention is the heart of motivated writing and speaking. Since antiquity, speakers and writers have kept journals and commonplace books in which to record, organize, and prepare for some action as a speaker or writer. They wrote down ideas that came to them while doing other things, and they copied lines of prose or poetry that they wanted to remember and imitate.

Your Invention Journal is the place where you will record your research and analyses. More specifically, the Invention Journal is the place where you will:

- Generate ideas for a project that addresses the situation at hand.
- Analyze lines of reasoning and ways of thinking that are important within that situation.
- Analyze your audience and your own perceptions of your audience.
- Record and plan further research.
- Plan for and analyze interviews.
- Record your own personal reactions to the issue you are addressing and the progress on your project.
- Begin organizing and composing your project in the form it will ultimately take.
- Record the feedback of your workshop partners.

The Invention Journal is meant to be the place where you generate ideas and arguments and also a bridge between your process of investigation and analysis and

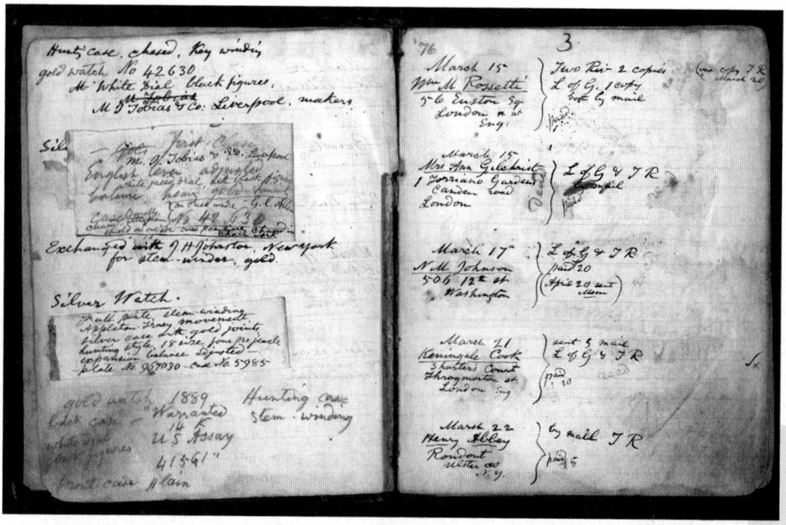

Walt Whitman's Commonplace Book
Keeping a *commonplace book* is an ancient practice. These volumes are places to collect ideas, relevant arguments, key pieces of evidence, notes on your audience, etc., for further use, and provide a record of your composition process. Pictured here is the commonplace book where Walt Whitman developed the poetics of his epic *Leaves of Grass*.

the final version of your project. If you are diligent in keeping an invention journal, you may find that much of your final project can be cut and pasted directly from it.

We suggest that you spend some time thinking about how you want to organize your Invention Journal. Once you start reading, researching, and discussing, you will find that keeping track of your thoughts and your records becomes increasingly more challenging. Whatever system of record keeping you decide on, it should help you to organize and focus your intellectual energies on your project. For convenience, we can subdivide invention journaling into three general categories: *collection, source analysis,* and *composition.*

Part of carrying out a successful project involves building an archive of relevant sources that will ultimately help you be an effective writer or speaker. Depending on the constraints on your work schedule, you may not have time to develop exhaustive knowledge about a critical situation. Nevertheless, we recommend that you aim toward comprehensiveness. It is also important that you have easy access to important documents from your critical situation. Students studying post-9/11 legislation, such as the Patriot Act or the constitutionality of a local renting restriction, should acquire hard copies of these documents, or bookmark their locations on Web sites where they are available, and/or save the URL in a separate file or notebook. It is also crucial that you record the location of sources while you are reading or producing them so that you have the citation information ready whenever you need it.

Computer files alone may not be adequate for collecting and organizing your source base. Sometimes data consists of photographs or other images. At other times it may include testimony from witnesses. Interviews may be an important source of information for you, and so tape recordings may be included in your Invention Journal. For instance, photographs that document the actual conditions of the neglected common area of an apartment complex might become important evidence of a landlord's failure to do adequate repairs and upkeep. Anyone who has dealt with insurance hassles after car accidents or in-home damage knows how important a good photographic record can be. It is quite possible that you will need to keep hard copy records in file folders to supplement your electronic archive.

Data, testimony, information, images, and statistics are not ordinarily persuasive all by themselves. Throughout this book, we encourage you to do original critical research. This means you must undertake serious analysis of all your source material. Once again, context is crucial. From what stakeholder position has a particular source been derived? What are the writer's commitments within the context of this critical situation? What persuasive strategies do you see at work in these documents? How is evidence used? What is emphasized and what is left out? How is one source supported or contradicted by others? Answering these and other questions as you gather and read research material will prepare you to compose a successful project and render the process rich in learning potential.

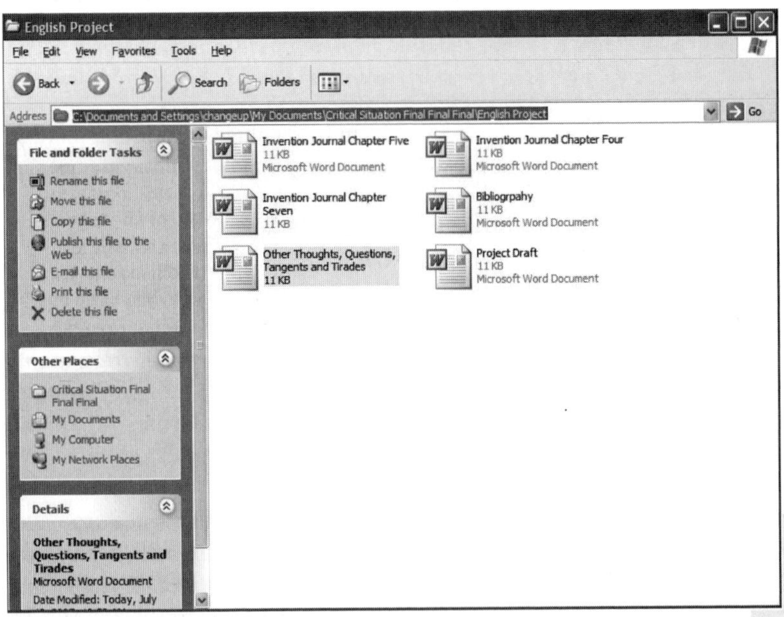

Screen Image of a Computer Filing System

A thorough invention process is meant to generate a great deal of written material. Keeping that material organized saves time and frustration along the way. Create a folder dedicated to your project. Within that folder, keep a file for each Invention Journal you work through, one for an ongoing draft of your project, one for a bibliography, and others for other relevant material.

As you work through the processes of research and invention—collecting information, analyzing and developing lines of argument and strategies of communication—you will begin to have ideas for how to put your project into its final form. Sentences will occur to you. As you decide on an audience, you will begin to think of convincing ways of addressing that audience. Careful study of your situation may lead you to the realization that a proposal is the most appropriate form for your work. Or, your research and invention may suggest that an article, a Web site, a presentation, a talk, or a letter may be more useful. In short, once you have done sufficient research and invention, you will find yourself ready to begin composing. It is likely that you will be able to cut and paste sections from entries in your Invention Journal as your project becomes more focused and as you begin thinking about how you might organize the presentation of your work.

However your composing process works, we recommend that you open a computer file titled "Project Draft" early in the process. Whenever the spirit moves you, or when prompted by something in your Invention Journal, go to this file and get your thoughts down on paper. Ideally, your project in its final form will emerge from your Invention Journal in just this way. However, professional writers and speakers often say that the most important composing occurs during revision. First drafts may marshal ideas and supporting information, but several more drafts may be necessary to tease out nuances and to refine expression. It is important, then, that you reserve time near the end of your composing process to draft as many versions of your project as are necessary to make it clear and persuasive.

About the Workshops

Throughout *Critical Situations*, you will be encouraged to participate in a variety of workshops. Many of these workshops are designed to help you complete your project work. Others are intended to *slow* the composition process, offering exercises to increase your skill and effectiveness as a reader and researcher. Others offer opportunities to explore the ethical dimensions of communication; we include these because like any other human activities, writing and speaking are decision-making processes in which we can make decisions about our own intentions and the potential impact our actions can have in a social context. Still other workshops provide a framework for in-class exercises and events meant to generate ideas for research and writing. Most of the workshops include assignment options that your teachers may or may not ask you to complete.

Overall, the workshops encourage you to pursue your projects as collaborative work. The serious writers and speakers we know often hit a

WORKSHOP 17: What are Your Collaborative Habits?

What does it mean to collaborate anyway? The exercises in this workshop will help familiarize class members with one another's working habits and allow you to begin building the foundation of a strong collaborative effort.

WORKSHOP 1: Agreeing on Workshop Guidelines

Productive collaboration doesn't happen on its own. This workshop makes recommendations for workshop guidelines and helps you through the process of deciding together on a set of guidelines and procedures on which everyone can agree.

point in their process when they say something like, "I need another brain to think about this," or "I need another pair of eyes to read this." The point of both comments is that no matter how broad our experience or how expansive our thinking, our individual perspectives have definite limits. Hearing firsthand accounts of situations that differ from your own is a great way to gauge possible audiences, to collect evidence and anticipate possible objections. In the context of the workshop, argument can happen in its best sense, as a cooperative process of inquiry and of reaching sound judgment about important problems and questions.

OUR CASE STUDIES

We can look to history for vivid examples of committed composition. We have both spent a lot of time studying critical situations that arose in recent and not-so-recent history. As teachers of rhetoric, we remain mindful of the insights of generations of writers and critics whose work has made a difference in the world. We have been drawn again and again to historical situations that no reasonable person would deny were of critical importance to a large percentage of the United States population and indeed to the world. We have chosen to highlight two of these transformative situations, using them as case studies to illustrate the rhetorical principles and practices we forward in the book. Our case studies are: the anti-slavery or abolitionist politics that emerged in America during the eighteenth and nineteenth centuries, and the events of September 11, 2001, and their aftermath. Both of these historical moments offer rich examples of historic critical situations and will provide valuable lessons and inspiration as you work on your own projects. For instance, David Walker's "Appeal to the Colored Citizens of the World" has much to teach us about saying the right things at the right time. Walker, a prominent African-American abolitionist, electrified public debate over the issues of slavery in the United States when he delivered this speech in 1829. The same could be said about people whose voices emerged forcefully in the wake of 9/11, such as New York City mayor Rudolph Guiliani or war critic Noam Chomsky. Through comparison we can also see how skillfully (or not so skillfully) each writer or speaker has rooted her or his text in the current moment, struggling against the constraints and helping to draw the conceptual map of the critical situation at hand. As such voices echo and intermingle through this book, they dramatize the power and importance of public discourse.

Finally, we make reference to a broad selection of student projects that we think are particularly interesting and instructive. We include the work of our own students as part of this historical perspective because we think that all intellectual work plays out in some larger context or contexts. We hope that these case studies encourage discussion of the ethical implications of community-based composition. We presume that for many users of this book, writing and formal speaking have been divorced from social reality; they have been, rather, a school exercise, a university requirement, a hoop to jump through. But composition can be much more than that if it is committed, goal-driven, and critical in our senses of that term. The case studies help us think through the ethical implications of our own participation in community issues.

The Abolitionist Era

The subject of our first case study is the struggle to abolish African-American slavery and to secure civil rights for African Americans before and during the Civil War and Reconstruction. This struggle is arguably the most important defining moment in United States history. As many abolitionists pointed out, it was a historic moment in which this country would or would not make good on its claims to democratic principle. We have found that students have often studied the Civil War but have been taught very little about the decades of protest that proceeded and followed the war. Even less is generally known about the brilliant and often controversial means of persuasion and publicity used by abolitionists in their projects of resistance and liberation. The words and actions of these committed activists changed the face of political discourse in the United States, and in studying that work, we confront a dramatic example of how a social movement is invented.

Consider the following excerpt from this 1859 editorial written by the prominent African American orator and poet Frances Ellen Watkins Harper:

> A hundred thousand new-born babes are annually added to the victims of slavery; twenty thousand lives are annually sacrificed on the plantations of the South. Such a sight should send a thrill of horror, through the nerves of civilization and impel the heart of humanity to lofty deeds. So it might, if men had not found a fearful alchemy by which this blood can be transformed into gold. Instead of listening to the cry of agony, they listen to the ring of dollars and stoop down to pick up the coin. (qtd. in Foster, 101)

Harper skillfully invokes the most powerful anti-slavery arguments of the day. Her description of the economics of slavery as a "fearful alchemy," conceiving of

NORTH STAR.

FREDERICK DOUGLASS, Editor. RIGHT IS OF NO SEX—TRUTH IS OF NO COLOR— GOD IS THE FATHER OF US ALL, AND ALL MEN ARE BRETHREN. JOHN DICK, Printer.

VOL. III. NO. 9. ROCHESTER, N. Y., FRIDAY, FEBRUARY 22, 1850. WHOLE NO. 113

Images of Abolitionist Newspaper Front Pages *(continued)*

THE LIBERATOR.

VOL. I.] WILLIAM LLOYD GARRISON AND ISAAC KNAPP, PUBLISHERS. [NO. 21.

BOSTON, MASSACHUSETTS.] OUR COUNTRY IS THE WORLD—OUR COUNTRYMEN ARE MANKIND. [SATURDAY, MAY 21, 1831.

THE LIBERATOR IS PUBLISHED WEEKLY AT NO. 10, MERCHANTS' HALL.

WM. LLOYD GARRISON, EDITOR.

EMIGRATION.

THE BLACK AT CHURCH.

MEETINGS IN GREAT BRITAIN,

SECOND MEETING IN EDINBURGH.

SLAVERY AND THE SLAVE TRADE.

Images of Abolitionist Newspaper Front Pages

The abolitionist movement was a effort of prodigious political imagination and sustained, skillful argument. Newspapers such as the *North Star* and the *Liberator* kept the goal of abolitionists in the public eye and helped to form a community of those opposed to the slave system. Editorials took slaveholders' white supremacist ideology to task and created a forum for fugitive slaves and others dedicated to the destruction of the slave system.

human beings only as potential profit wrung from laboring bodies, would have resonated strongly with her audience. The image of children in slavery affirmed widespread outrage over slavery as a crime against the family, and her mention of enslaved children allowed a more general consideration of the innocence of all the millions held in bondage. Indeed, as a nineteenth-century woman, Harper was all but obligated to frame her comments as a concern for the well-being of families; denied voting or property rights, women were thought to be incapable of speaking publicly about anything else. In addition, the potential for "humanity" to carry out "lofty deeds" towards liberation trades on a popular nineteenth-century idea about freedom and equality as inevitable historical forces. Indeed, common wisdom held that the progress of a society or culture might be measured by the degree of freedom and equality allotted to its citizens.

Reading and discussing the work of powerful speakers and writers like Harper can help us reflect critically on the opportunities and the constraints at work in our own critical situations. How do people think about the situation in which you are involved? How does such thinking constitute a rhetorical terrain you must navigate? Approaching texts with questions like these can turn your reading into a practice of rhetorical invention.

September 11, 2001

We decided on our second case study as we were preparing to sign the publishing contract for this book on September 10, 2003, one day before the second anniversary of what has come to be known as "9/11." These numbers have become a symbol of tragedy as well as signifiers of national resolve. As most Americans are aware, on that day four commercial aircraft were hijacked by 19 people who violently wrested control of the planes from their crews; they then flew three of the planes into the World Trade Center, in New York City, and the Pentagon, in Washington, D.C. Both towers collapsed about an hour later, as did the façade of the Pentagon where it was struck. The fourth plane, which was apparently on its way to the nation's capitol, crashed instead in a field in Pennsylvania. Evidence suggests that passengers on this plane stormed the cockpit in an attempt to retrieve control from the hijackers.

Norman Mailer, an admired but controversial American writer, was in Provincetown, Massachusetts, on 9/11. His daughter Maggie was staying in his apartment in Brooklyn Heights while he was away. The windows of that apartment open onto lower Manhattan, and they afforded a clear view of the Twin Towers of the World Trade Center. Mailer writes of his daughter's horror as she watched events unfold:

> Maggie had witnessed the first attack and was terribly affected by it. Then, while we were on the phone, the second plane hit the other building. I'm still watching on TV. In Brooklyn, Maggie and her friend are both seeing it through the window as well as viewing it on TV. That was a considerable shock. Why? Because the one thing TV always promises us is that, deep down, what we see on television is not real. . . . Now there are exceptions. The shooting of Lee Harvey Oswald by Jack Ruby was one; the second plane striking the second Tower; the collapse of the Towers. TV at that moment was no longer a coat of insulation between us and the horrific. When broken, the impact is enormous (8).

The Twin Towers Falling
Images of the World Trade Center collapsing became iconic very quickly after the event. Even years later, the images still shock us and remind us of the scope of the tragic events of what is now simply referred to as "9/11."

Mailer's daughter was among the relatively few people who actually saw the first plane strike the north tower of the World Trade Center between its ninety-fourth and ninety-eighth floors. Television coverage began a scant two minutes after this plane crashed into the building, as CNN's cameras began to broadcast images of the burning tower and the appallingly large plane-shaped hole that had appeared in its side. A little more than fifteen minutes later a second aircraft smashed into the south tower, and this time millions of people saw the crash on television. As Mailer suggests, the impact on viewers was enormous.

Later, Mailer was able to meditate on the meaning of 9/11. He argues that the events of that day challenged a powerful myth called American exceptionalism—the belief that this nation has a world-historical mission to achieve political or social perfection. In *Why Are We At War?* Mailer details his delayed reaction to 9/11:

> What in God's name was happening? It is one thing to hear a mighty explosion. It is another to recognize some time after the event that one has been deafened by it. The United States was going through an identity crisis. Questions about our nature as a country were being asked that most good American men and women had never posed to themselves before. Questions such as, Why are we so hated? How could

> anyone resent us that much? We do no evil. We believe in goodness and freedom. Who are we, then? Are we not who we think we are? More pressing, who are they? What does it all mean? (10–11)

These are proactive questions, and Mailer does his best to answer them in his book. His work shows how critical situations can stimulate invention; his experience of 9/11 led him to ask questions about America's role in world events and about the reactions of the world's peoples to American foreign policy.

The horrible events of 9/11 are regularly invoked as a rationale for legal and military initiatives that have been undertaken since that day. As we write, American soldiers are committed in Afghanistan and Iraq, where suicide bombings and other bloody events occur almost daily. Within our own national borders, debates about security, civil liberties, and the allocation of government money are framed as responses to 9/11. There is little in our national public discourse that does not bear the mark of these events. As a people, Americans are still affected by the events of 9/11, and these effects are entangled with many critical situations that are linked in complicated ways. The challenge of sorting through this rhetorical complexity offers us the opportunity to think carefully about the power of language in context and about the political culture of the United States at outset of the twenty-first century.

Student Projects

For those of you for whom the project-oriented approach to composition is unfamiliar, the examples of student projects in this book should be particularly helpful. They offer examples of motivated and skillful language use that are, perhaps, closer to home for new users of this approach. We make reference to a range of projects—Web design, magazine articles, political fliers, editorials, informational pamphlets, workplace writing, and traditional research essays. We looked for a range of motivating factors as well—the awful job, the need for childcare, a lack of adequate lighting in the public areas of an apartment complex, a local no-smoking law, an honors engineering project, a Supreme Court nomination, and many others. We hope examples of careful critical thought will inspire you and suggest the general usefulness of the rhetorical action. Such is the case with the work of Alexis Hucchochea, who wrote a pamphlet to be distributed to middle schools and high schools in her own city. Her intention was to inform young women about the controversial Safe Haven Program, which established drop-off sites where new-born babies could be left by mothers unable or unwilling to raise the children to whom they had given birth:

WORKSHOP 3: Different Values and Respectful Conflict

Arguments are inherently matters of conflict. Rather than trying to avoid such conflict, we recommend approaching it as a powerful learning opportunity and an intellectual resource. This workshop provides the framework for sharing our own value-based positions in a productive and respectful manner.

> Over half a million U.S. teens give birth each year. 83% of these teens are poor or of low income. The fact that numbers are so high in poor areas shows that these students

need to be educated on the options they have when dealing with pregnancy, mainly because it is something that is constantly in their faces, it is an unavoidable issue. I attended school in a poor area, and I can remember that as early as sixth grade, girls were getting pregnant. Those girls never thought they had any options and so they ended up being mothers at the young ages of 12 and 13. I know that a few of my 14-year-old sister's friends have had some close calls with pregnancy and whenever that happened they never thought they had any options outside of parenthood. Instead they worried about how they would take care of a child, if they were going to have to do it alone, and what they would tell their parents. I am aware that many teen's religious beliefs as well as values would prevent them from getting an abortion, but by giving the child to a safe haven the child would not only get a chance at life, but a chance to have a family that cares and loves the child.

WORKSHOP 18: What Do You Want to Learn about Composition?

We hope students will not simply produce successful projects using this book but also take away life-long lessons about what makes powerful writing and speech. The heart of this workshop is the "Writer's Inventory," which will help you clarify your learning goals and identify your strengths and weaknesses as writers.

Whatever your own feelings about such a program might be, we ask you to consider the good sense the author shows in choosing and addressing an audience. Notice also how her commitment to a community led Hucchochea to her act of advocacy. Motivated by her experience with young women who are trying to cope with unplanned pregnancies, she stuck consistently to the goal of providing these women with an option they might not have considered.

You too may find that part of making a strong argument is trying to persuade an audience to understand your critical situation in a particular way. Although the questions you ask and the positions you eventually take may not be as controversial or as important as those Harper or Mailer or Hucchochea investigated, you may find that you too will unearth alternate points of view. But if your invention process is thorough, you should be able to devise strategies for dealing with any perspectives you encounter, whether they resist or accept your point of view.

TALK READ WRITE

1. Compare the excerpts from Frances Ellen Watkins Harper's editorial, Norman Mailer's essay, and Alexis Hucchochea's Safe Haven pamphlet. Do you sympathize with these authors' positions? Why? Why not? As you compare and discuss, consider the key terms presented in this chapter: committed choices, critical situation, community, and invention. How does each writer's work exemplify these concepts?
2. Take some time to discuss the issues raised by our case studies. What do you know about the history of abolitionism? About government policy

since September 11, 2001? Write letters to your class explaining how either series of events has impacted your life and those of people who live in your communities.

3. Review "On the Bus." Plan and carry out a series of interviews with participants in some local situation or event where you live, work, or go to school. Work collaboratively to develop questions about the situation. Write out a transcript of the interviews and write an analysis of the different perspectives on the event.

LIST OF WORKS CITED

Harper, Frances Ellen Watkins. *A Brighter Coming Day: A Frances Ellen Watkins Reader.* Ed. Frances Smith Foster. New York: The Feminist Press at the City University of New York, 1990.

James, William. *Pragmatism: A New Name for Some Old Ways of Thinking.* New York: Dover, 1995.

King, John. "Page Call NEA 'Terrorist Organization.'" CNN.com. 19 April 2007. http://www.cnn.com/2004/EDUCATION/02/23/paige.terrorist.nea/.

Mailer, Norman. *Why Are We At War?* New York: Random House, 2003.

Walker, David. *David Walker's Appeal to the Coloured Citizens of the World, but in Particular, and Very Expressly, to Those of the United States of America.* New York: Hill and Wang, 1995.

2

CHOOSING A CRITICAL SITUATION

Ordinarily, people are moved to action because they are stakeholders in some critical situation; that is, they or members of their community have something to gain or lose in that situation. Accordingly, this chapter asks you to answer these questions about communities and stakeholders: what situations and discussions are important enough to you, or to your community, that you are willing to do something about them? What commitments motivate you to move from the role of spectator to that of participant, to move from interest to action?

Quite possibly, you can't fully answer these questions right now. The values and commitments that drive our actions often remain hidden from us until we examine the structure of our beliefs with some care. On the other hand, you may feel that your commitments are so obvious to you that examination seems unnecessary. In either case, you must be willing to grapple with your commitments and those of the communities of which you are a part in order to research, design, and finish a successful composing project. This chapter makes a start by challenging you to make a careful analysis of your commitments.

For those of you who knew long before opening this book what situations motivate you to write, this chapter will help you focus your interests and intentions and to develop the most effective strategies for written and spoken action. You may know exactly what change you want to effect—you want your boss to buy new tools to replace the decrepit ones you and your coworkers use every day; you want a speed bump on the street where your family lives; you think that the requirements of your major are insufficient or inflexible; you want a local no-smoking ordinance repealed or expanded; you want to support a candidate for local or national office, and so on. As clear and specific as these goals are, actually enacting them can be complicated and difficult. The shortest distance between two points might be a straight line, as mathematicians have taught us, but moving from commitment through a problem-solving process to effective communicative action is rarely simple or straightforward.

COMMITMENT AND SOCIAL CONTEXT

Even if your project concerns only your personal life, the social landscape through which you move every day is an important place to begin thinking about your critical situation. The things that move us to write are often fundamental needs, things that hit us in the gut and charge our emotions, and as we have suggested, this is the kind of writing most worth doing. There is a big difference, however, between feeling some desire for change and actually following through in language. Think of a time you felt you should have protested but did not. Think of the letter to the editor you didn't write (or the one you wrote but didn't send). Even if that letter is still sealed in an envelope somewhere in a desk drawer, your stake in the discussion may remain strong.

Communities are held together by a set of common concerns, needs, goals, beliefs, or problems. These are the places where arguments are generated and where their outcomes are decided. You have a chance to use language skillfully, to your advantage, within a community whose members are also concerned about your project. You may recall from the previous chapter that we define *community* as any group or groups of people who have a stake in a common critical situation. In what contexts do you find yourself confronted with situations that capture your attention? For many of us, conditions at work or issues important to the neighborhoods where our families live are an acute source of commitment and motivation. Such conditions generate what we call *issues*. An issue is any thing, event, or idea about which members of a community may disagree. It is in the nature of issues, as we define them here, to be controversial. That is, issues arise within or between communities when members of those communities disagree about some event, idea, thing, or practice. The disagreement may be internal, that is, it may exist among community members, or it may be external, as when members of two or more communities disagree with one another. In the cities in which we live, for example, people often form communities with others who live on their street or cul-de-sac, even though they have no other reason to know or care for one another. Because of their physical proximity to one another, internal issues often arise among people living in such communities. Ordinarily, these issues have to do with the appearance of the homes and yards on the street: for example, is everyone who lives on the street obligated to pick up trash from their yard as soon as it lands there? Should everyone who lives on the street put up holiday lights? But neighborliness can involve more than the appearance of properties. Other issues can arise in a neighborhood: Do the occupants of one or some houses party too late or too often or too loudly? Does someone let a dog or cat run loose and unsupervised? Do children tear up lawns or gardens while at play or trespass in some other way? A neighborhood issue can be far more serious, as well. Our students regularly write for their neighbors and elected officials as a means so addressing the impact of drug sales, violent crime, police harassment, and other difficult situations.

We belong to many different sorts of communities, and different issues circulate in each one. If you belong to a fraternity, for example, your group might have concerns about the condition of its house, about who will be pledged, and about the group's relation to the university at large. For teachers like us, whose work communities include students, teachers, administrators, and taxpayers, a list of key issues might include funding for schools, access to teaching resources, safety and privacy for students and teachers, appropriate testing methods, graduation standards, and so on. Issues such as these demand our attention because they emerge as thorny situations in the communities where teachers are committed. Our students and our colleagues have much at stake, for instance, in the amount of money allotted to support our university by the state legislature. When classrooms across the country become involved in a debate over free speech or academic freedom, we pay close attention because we know that precedents may be set or that new and powerful arguments may emerge regarding what can be said in a classroom. And some issues, such as war and the environment, can affect a nation or the entire world. Whatever issue you choose to pursue, understanding the people, events, institutions, and ideas that define the issue is the only way to speak and write with any authority about the issue at hand.

WORKSHOP 3: Different Values and Respectful Conflict

Arguments are inherently matters of conflict. Rather than trying to avoid such conflict, we recommend approaching it as a powerful learning opportunity and an intellectual resource. This workshop provides the framework for sharing our own value-based positions in a productive and respectful manner.

WORKSHOP 4: Ethics in Writing and Speaking Inventory

This workshop helps generate thinking and conversation about ethical issues in public writing and speaking. Working through the inventory individually or as a group, you have a chance to work towards ethical practices of communication.

TALK READ WRITE

1. Imagine that you and a group of your classmates belong to one of the following communities: a celebrity fan club (you pick the celebrity), a fraternity that has been put on probation by the university, a soccer team that loses all its games. Or choose some other group to which you can imagine you and your classmates might belong.
2. Now, ask yourselves: what concerns would we have as members of this group? List these. Would these matters be of concern to you if you were not members of the selected group? For example, would you care if the fraternity next door to yours were put on probation by the university? Why or why not?
3. As members of the same college or university or even of the same class, it could be argued that you and those enrolled with you make up a community, one of learners, or more specifically of writing or communications students. Working together, brainstorm a list of issues that emerge from your classroom, college, or university community.

COMMITMENT IN HISTORICAL CONTEXT—TROUBLE IN TRANSIT

> I would like to be known as a person who is concerned about freedom and equality and justice and prosperity for all people.
>
> *Rosa Parks*

As you begin to sort through your own commitments and motivations, consider the following committed writers in their historical contexts. Whether or not you are reading the full texts or the excerpts printed here, each of the following statements about motivation, interest, passion, and community commitment are very instructive. The writers and speakers quoted here were caught up in moments of extreme political turmoil and social change that would have ramifications well beyond their present moments and local sites. But for each, the immensity of the problem at hand brought their personal motivation clearly into focus. Your own emerging critical situation is likely very different from those recounted below, but you should read with an eye for details that may be sufficiently like it to be of use within your project. Debates about the theory and practice of democracy are still very much with us, for example. What issues or values are at stake for these committed writers that are still resonant today, perhaps in your own life and project research?

For many writers, commitment and choice of issue are crystal clear. Ida Barnett Wells was born a slave at the end of the Civil War near Memphis, Tennessee. Following the emancipation of African American slaves, Wells gained an education and became a teacher, newspaper editor, writer, and nationally recognized leader of the early civil rights movement. Wells is perhaps best known for leading what she called the "anti-lynching campaign," which exposed the scope of white supremacist vigilantism in the South. She launched a scathing critique of the rationales that cast lynch law as "justice." Raised in a family and community committed to extending democratic rights in the United States, Wells's career as an activist began when she defied state segregation laws by riding on a train car reserved for whites and was physically removed. Wells sued the railroad for damages, and though she won her case, the decision was later overturned by the Tennessee State Supreme Court. Consider the following excerpt from Wells's 1935 autobiography, *A Crusade For Justice,* in which she recounts the incident. Think of it as an account of the kind of commitment that grounded one of the most remarkable careers in American politics:

> I secured a school in Shelby County, Tennessee, which paid a better salary and began studying for the examination for city schoolteacher which meant an even larger increase in salary. One day while riding back to my school I took a seat in the ladies' coach of the train as usual. There were no jim crow cars then. But ever since the repeal of the Civil Right Bill by the United States Supreme Court in [1883] there had been efforts all over the South to draw the color line on the railroads.

Ida B. Wells

Ida B. Wells exemplifies the passionate commitment of a writer working for social change. Wells carried on her anti-lynching campaign despite numerous threats on her life.

> When the train started and the conductor came along to collect tickets, he took my ticket, then handed it back to me and told me that he couldn't take my ticket there. I thought that if he didn't want the ticket I wouldn't bother about it so went on reading. In a little while when he finished taking tickets, he came back and told me I would have to go in the other car. I refused, saying that the forward car was a smoker, and as I was in the ladies' car I proposed to stay. He tried to drag me out of the seat, but the moment he caught hold of my arm I fastened my teeth in the back of his hand.
>
> I had braced my feet against the seat in front and was holding to the back, and as he had already been badly bitten he didn't try it again by himself. He went forward and got the baggage-man and another man to help him and of course they succeeded in dragging me out. They were encouraged to do this by the attitude of the white ladies and gentlemen in the car; some of them even stood on the seats so that they could get a good view and continued applauding the conductor for his brave stand.

Written nearly forty years after the incident on the train, this prose bristles with anger. Wells remained committed to securing the African American civil rights that were still withheld in the Jim Crow era of segregation and common-place racial oppression. Wells's act of civil disobedience was just the beginning of a long battle waged in print and at the orator's podium, a battle she would never give up. In fact, when Wells died, in 1935, she was finishing her autobiography in which she continued to make all of her powerful arguments for social justice. For Wells, the era of Jim Crow segregation and legal racial discrimination was depressingly similar to the situation of the post-Reconstruction United States of her youth.

WORKSHOP 13: Readers Responding

This workshop offers powerful strategies for approaching reading as serious writers do, with a critical eye for the most important arguments and ideas. Following the strategies presented in this workshop, you will gain skills as an engaged reader and become more able to put what you read to work in your own writing.

WORKSHOP 16: Summarizing Arguments, Ideas, and Texts
Writers regularly present the work of others as building blocks for their own work. This workshop offers strategies for writing strong summaries to incorporate into your own writing.

WORKSHOP 8: Following Pathways: A Metaphor for Critical Reading and Research
Reading and research are like travel. They take us into the territory of new ideas and arguments. The exercises in this workshop will help you identify unfamiliar ideas and references and approach them as opportunities for learning, or in other words, "pathways" to knowledge.

Wells would not be the last, nor was she the first, African American woman to make principled trouble in transit. Decades before Wells's struggle with the conductor, abolitionist and feminist writer and orator Frances Ellen Watkins Harper used her experience of being expelled from public transportation to explain a larger political situation. Harper was part of the political fight to put the Fourteenth and Fifteenth Amendments and the 1875 Civil Rights Act into place.

At the National Women's Rights Convention in New York in 1866, Harper saw clearly that her argument for voting rights could not be the same as that made by her white counterparts, who were represented by important early feminists such as Elizabeth Cady Stanton and Susan B. Anthony. Harper's career is a fascinating record of negotiating often conflicting commitments and community interests together, of refusing to let the problems of racial and gender oppression to be thought of separately. This excerpt from her address is taken from the transcripts of the New York Women's Rights Convention:

> Today I am puzzled where to make my home. I would like to make it in Philadelphia, near my own friends and relations. But if I want to ride in the streets of

Frances Ellen Watkins Harper
Frances Ellen Watkins Harper delivered addresses and wrote poems, stories, articles, parables, novels, and correspondence in the service of abolitionism, women's rights, and other social causes. Only now is her work gaining the critical attention it deserves.

> Philadelphia, they send me to ride on the platform with the driver. (Cries of "Shame.") Have women nothing to do with this? Not long since, a colored woman took her seat in an Eleventh Street car in Philadelphia, and the conductor stopped the car, and told the rest of the passengers to get out, and left the car with her in it alone, when they took it back to the station. One day I took my seat in a car, and the conductor came to me and told me to take another seat. I just screamed "murder." The man said if I was black I ought to behave myself. I knew that if he was white he was not behaving himself. Are theirs not wrongs to be righted? (219)

Like Wells, Harper explains issues that motivate her, the "wrongs to be righted," as situations at the borders of multiple communities—in this case, Afro- and Anglo-Americans, men and women, enfranchised and disenfranchised, citizens and noncitizens. Though the attempted eviction from the train took place in Philadelphia, at this national conference Harper links the incident to national issues and to national and universal communities. We invite you to read the full text of the address, "We Are All Bound Up Together," and to consider the variety of strategies Harper uses to present a vision of a universal community.

Rosa Parks wished to be remembered as an advocate for universal "freedom and equality," and it seems that her wish will be granted by history. In 1955, Parks's refusal to give up her seat on an Alabama bus to a white passenger was a catalytic event in the civil rights movement. Her brave actions on the bus sparked the Montgomery Bus Boycott, which brought redoubled energy and attention to the African American struggle for social justice. Parks is an icon of the twentieth-century civil rights movement in the United States. When she died at the age of 92, her body lay in state in the rotunda of the United States Capitol. She was the first woman ever to be so honored. Her example of commitment to democratic principle resonates across our national political culture. Like many

Rosa Parks
When Rosa Parks died in October of 2005, public figures across the country eulogized her as a national hero. Parks's refusal to obey segregation laws remains a testament to the power of one person's commitment to justice.

peaceful protesters before and after her, Parks's simple but courageous act was to embody a refusal of unjust law and to put herself on the line. As a result, she became a touchstone for a social movement.

TALK READ WRITE

Read the full text of Harper's address and the first chapter of Wells's *Red Record.* Discuss similarities in the way these women define community and express their commitment to the cause of social justice.

COMMITMENTS GENERATED BY SEPTEMBER 11, 2001

From the moment the first plane hit the first tower of the World Trade Center in New York City, it might have been predicted that this single day would be remembered as a historical watershed. Many current debates are now explained in relationship to horrific events of that day. The war in Iraq, the state of civil liberties in the United States, the findings of the 9/11 Commission, and foreign policy issues such as the Israel-Palestinian conflict—all these pressing situations can be understood as connected to 9/11. Political repercussions from the event have been so great that almost anyone anywhere in the world could count themselves as stakeholders in the post-9/11 moment. Terrorist acts have taken place in England, Jordan, Morocco, Egypt, Saudi Arabia, the Phillipines, and Spain. Leaders of European countries disagree with their parties and their peoples about whether they should participate in the war in Iraq. Community divisions that existed prior to 9/11 are much more starkly drawn since, and new alliances have emerged that might have seemed unlikely before these events occurred.

Questions of commitment and community were foregrounded in the immediate wake of the attacks. The heroic actions of New York's firefighters and police officers achieved legendary status almost immediately as examples of commitment to the safety and well-being of the community as a whole. The outpouring of grief and support for the families of the victims worldwide suggested the possibility of a worldwide community committed to the well being of all citizens. Confusion, fear, and disbelief among many Americans were fueled by questions about the attackers' identity and motivation.

Many Americans asked what kind of commitment would inspire "them" to do this to "us"? Indeed the strong sense of a national "us" that many Americans felt after the attacks gained strength and definition from visions of a murderous "them," even before anyone mentioned Al Qaeda or Osama bin Laden. In his address to the nation on the evening of the attacks, President George W. Bush

Firefighters in NYC on 9/11
The heroism of New York City civil employees, including the firefighters pictured here, earned the respect and admiration of people worldwide. Their heroic actions have been described as a model of patriotism and selfless devotion to one's fellow citizens.

sought to express the commitment of a people and at the same time define a national identity and destiny:

> Today, our fellow citizens, our way of life, our very freedom came under attack in a series of deliberate and deadly terrorist acts. The victims were in airplanes or in their offices—secretaries, businessmen and women, military and federal workers. Moms and dads. Friends and neighbors. Thousands of lives were suddenly ended by evil, despicable acts of terror. The pictures of airplanes flying into buildings, fires burning, huge structures collapsing, have filled us with disbelief, terrible sadness and a quiet, unyielding anger. These acts of mass murder were intended to frighten our nation into chaos and retreat. But they have failed. Our country is strong. A great people has been moved to defend a great nation. Terrorist attacks can shake the foundations of our biggest buildings, but they cannot touch the foundation of America. These acts shatter steel, but they cannot dent the steel of American resolve. America was targeted for attack because we're the brightest beacon for freedom and opportunity in the world. And no one will keep that light from shining. Today, our nation saw evil, the very worst of human nature, and we responded with the best of America, with the daring of our rescue workers, with the caring for strangers and neighbors who came to give blood and help in any way they could. After all that has just passed—all the lives taken, and all the possibilities and hopes that died with them—it is natural to wonder if America's future is one of fear. Some speak of an age of terror. I know there are

dangers to face. But this country will define our times, not be defined by them. As long as the United States of America is determined and strong, this will not be an age of terror; this will be an age of liberty, here and across the world.

(CNN.com 09/11/2001)

This speech, delivered in a moment of great uncertainty, offered the audience a chance to reaffirm their commitment to what are popularly held to be America's national values—resolve, caring, freedom, and opportunity. The President repeatedly distinguished between caring, freedom-loving Americans and the enemy, who is represented as evil, as "the very worst of human nature." This dichotomy, separating "us" from "them," presaged the worldwide conflict and division that was to follow America's response to the 9/11 attacks.

TALK READ WRITE

Read the full text of President Bush's address delivered on September 11, 2001. Share your own memories of 9/11. Discuss your sense of how the world has changed since then. Discuss how the aftermath of 9/11 has influenced your sense of community belonging and social commitment.

FROM COMMITMENT TO ACTION: MAPPING COMMUNITY

Map (verb):
1) To plan or devise (a course of action, etc.); to project.
2) Of a landscape: to be spread out to view like a map.

From definition of "map," *Oxford English Dictionary*, 2nd ed. (1989), edited by Simpson, J. & Weiner, E. By Permission of Oxford University Press.

The primary invention activity of this chapter is to make a map of the communities in which you are a stakeholder and to chart the key issues that concern each of those communities. We use the term *map* as a metaphor, of course. A map is a tool used to navigate unfamiliar spaces, to find our way through strange surroundings. We consult maps when we are lost or uncertain of locations and coordinates. Why, then, is a map necessary for discovering the communities and issues that concern us the most? We argue that the most familiar places sometimes hold the most unknowns exactly because they are so common that we take them for granted. Mapping can be a powerful way to bring these unknowns to light. Choosing and focusing your issue through an analysis of social context should lead you to acknowledged experts and authorities in the situation you are investigating. This process will also help you find the right audiences and to begin cataloging the major perspectives and arguments you must contend with as you go forward with your project. Mapping can begin to make the history of an issue more accessible, thus enriching our understanding and resources as writers or speakers.

Here are two maps(see pages 38 and 39) that attempt to make sense of a complicated social situation. W. E. B. DuBois, the renowned African American writer, made this map as part of his study of African American Philadelphia, published as *The Philadelphia Negro: A Social Study* (1898). DuBois was convinced that if he could make people understand the social and economic situation in American cities, he could make inroads into fighting racism and the poverty plaguing urban African Americans. The "7th Ward" map attempts to offer a snapshot of the racial and economic breakdown of the ward. The second map (see page 40) charts the locations of murders of African Americans during the New York City Draft Riots of 1863. Sparked by the institution of a military draft, by competition between Anglo- and African American laborers and by racial animosity, the Draft Riots resulted in death, injury, and property destruction in New York's African American community. Notice how the spatial divisions of each map try to make meaning of what were incredibly complicated social dynamics.

Now, let's look at some student maps. Maria Rosales organized her social life and social concerns this way:

Student:
—Why is tuition being raised again?
—Should I apply to the Barrett's Honors College?
—What law schools should I apply for?

Daughter:
—What could I do to help my parents out more?
—How do I balance my sanity while making my parents proud of my academic achievements?

Girlfriend:
—How do I make more time to spend with him?
—Is he the one I want to marry in the future?

Best friend:
—What will it be like when she leaves for the military?
—Will we be best friends for life?

Sears sales associate:
—Should I find a new job that will be better for school?
—Should I find a new job that pays more so I can work less and get paid about the same?

Feminist:
—What programs could I volunteer for/join that supports women's rights?
—Will I have time to support the feminist groups?
—What do I think or do on a daily basis that makes me a feminist?

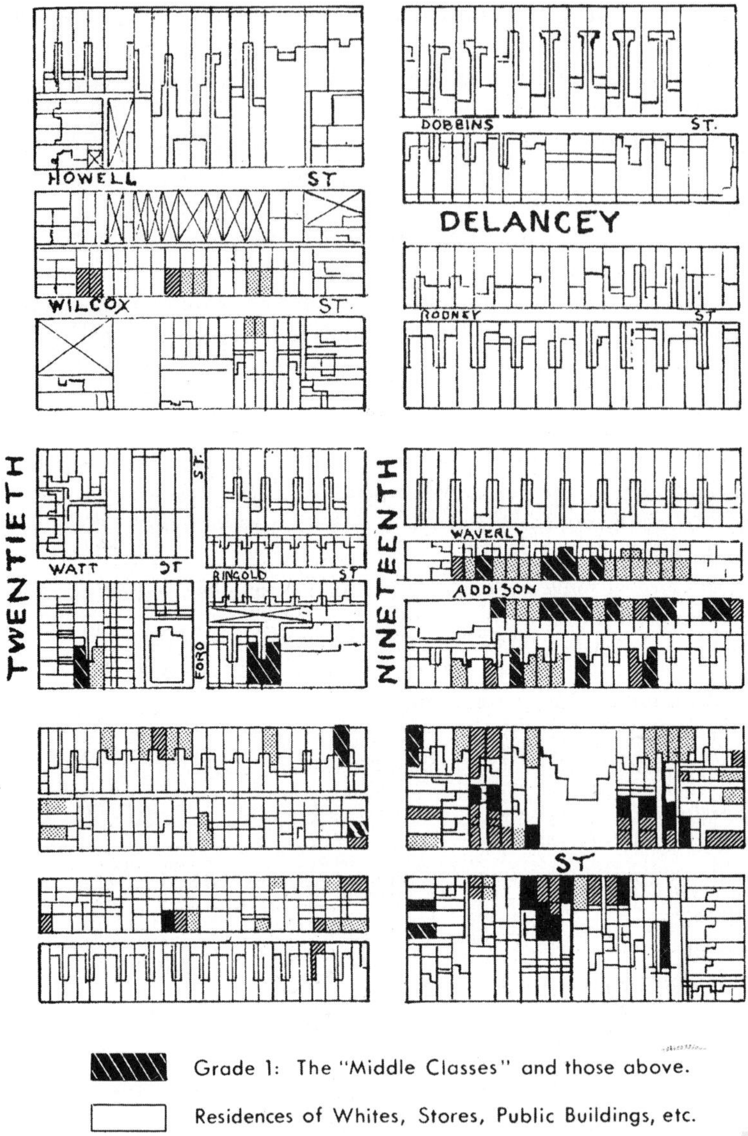

Map of Philadelphia's Seventh Ward in 1895, taken from W. E. B. DuBois's *Philadelphia Negro* (1899) *(continued)*

Hispanic woman:

—Will I be paid less because I am a woman even though I have the same credentials as a man?

—How many other Hispanic women have become lawyers?

—Will I have as much courage and determination as my grandmother did and become successful in life?

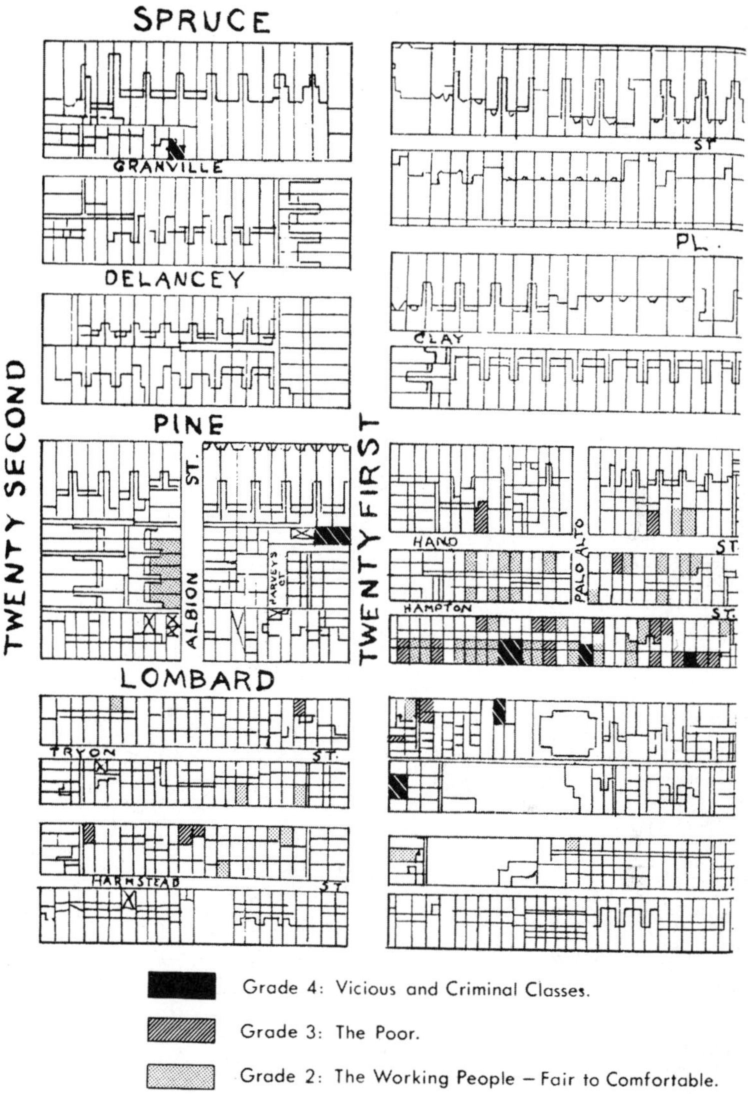

Map of Philadelphia's Seventh Ward in 1895, taken from W. E. B. DuBois's *Philadelphia Negro* (1899)

A pioneer of sociological study, W. E. B. DuBois believed that if politicians and the public understood the realities of impoverished African Americans in cities such as Philadelphia, more egalitarian policies would surely follow. DuBois's map of Philadelphia's Seventh Ward was one portion of the persuasive evidence he compiled in his classic *Philadelphia Negro: A Social Study.*

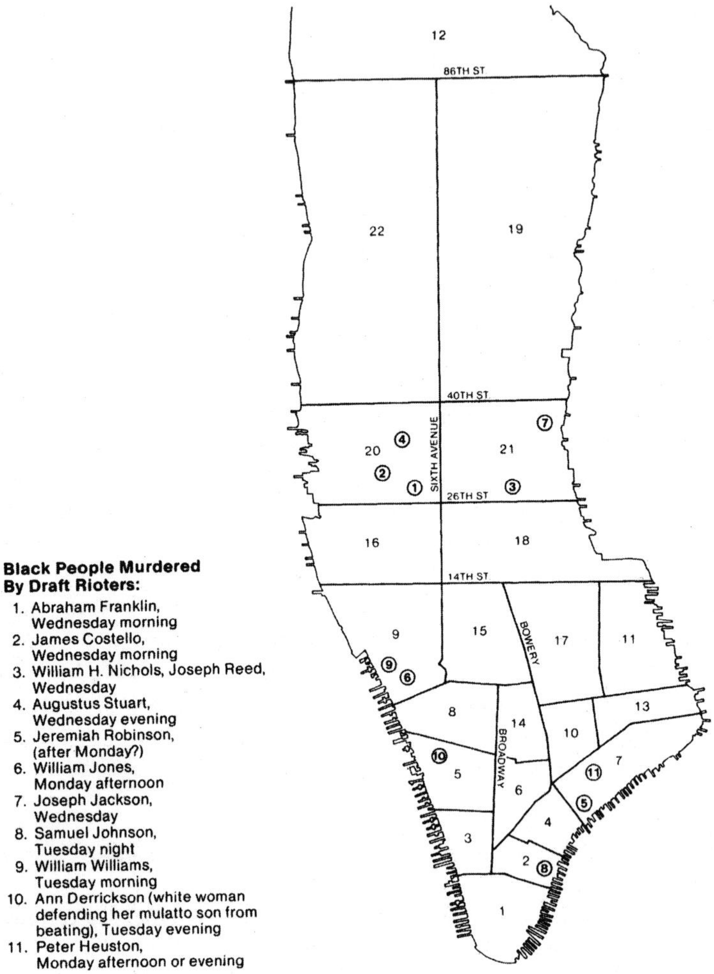

Map of the Sites of African Americans Murdered in the 1863 New York City Draft Riots

This map made by the New York City police following the so-called "Draft Riots" of 1863 indicates the locations where African American New Yorkers were murdered by white rioters. While the map doesn't come close to capturing the full tragedy and terror of the riot, it demonstrates how maps can be used to make sense of complicated, and in this case horrific, social situations.

U.S. citizen:
—Was the recent war necessary?
—School education—why hasn't it improved?

Student loan holder:
—How much will I owe at the end of my college career?
—Should I apply for scholarships to same money?
—Should I cut back on classes to work more to save money?

Driver:
—Why do people over a certain age still drive?
—Why are gas prices so high?
—Why is there no solution for traffic?

As you can tell, Rosales's concerns, captured in the form of questions, run a range of personal and political issues. We could even say that rendered in the interrogatory form of questions, her map demonstrates that no clear boundaries exist between personal and political. Ultimately, Rosales chose to write about salary disparities between men and women, but her questions raised many other important issues that could become useful projects

Amber Zaidi made the following map in a course dedicated to inquiry and analysis of issues of social justice. Like Rosales's map, Zaidi's locates intersections of private and public concern. Notice also that her questions range from very broad to very specific. We think it is particularly useful that Zaidi avoided "yes-or-no" questions, which tend to close down discussion, opting instead for open-ended phrasing that sends us out into discussion of all the possibilities:

Citizen of the world:
—What responsibility do I have to people of the world that I will never come into contact with?
—What about nuclear weapons? Do we have the right to limit what countries can have them? Should anyone be allowed?
—What about genocides across the world? Hutu and Tutsi? Kashmir? North Korea? Chechnya? What does justice mean after genocide?
—What can be done about poverty? Women and children.
—What can be done about child labor?
—What about women's rights in third-world countries?

United States citizen:
—Are the wars we're involved in (against terror, against Iraq) just?
—Do these people really want our help?
—Are we spreading democracy or causing new animosity to be built up?
—Global police? Shouldn't we be more concerned with what's going on in our own country? Do we really need to be telling everyone else what to do?
—What can be done about religious intolerance? Here and in the world?
—What about universal health care?

—What else could have been done in the wake of Katrina? Did it matter that the victims were mostly poor black people? Coastal rebuilding? Why doesn't the government spend on the Gulf Coast—what about the pollution-cancer connection?
—Racism—where does it still exist?

Pakistani American:
—How to adjust in an American society with a very different cultural upbringing?

Muslim:
—Women's rights in your religion? What's granted? How are they being suppressed? Is it religious or cultural?
—Living as a Muslim in America? What about our civil rights? How are we treated?

Daughter:
—What responsibilities do I have to my family? To be a good role model? To obey? Where do my own thoughts come in?

Student:
—Am I ever going to graduate?
—What do I really want to do with my life?
—How important are the things that I'm learning?
—What about education for the poor? Does the government do enough to help?

Arizona resident:
—How do we protect our environment from the pollution caused by all the new residents?

Friend:
—What are my responsibilities towards them?
—What is their influence in my life?

Future biologist:
—Ethics? Is research involving animals ethical? What about stem cells?

Muhajir:
—What does this mean? How does it affect my role in society?

We hope you will agree that these maps demonstrate social complexity as well as personal commitment. Now it is time to work on your own map

Invention Journal: Your Community Map

Using any manner of graphic representation, make a map of the communities in which you live and which are important to you. Be broad in your definition of community membership. Is your place in the community geographic? (I'm from the Northeast; I'm a Californian.) Civic? (I'm a U.S. citizen. I vote in school board elections. I'm from the tenth ward in Chicago). Political? (I'm a feminist, a Republican, a Democrat, a socialist, an anarchist.) Historical, racial, or ethnic? (I'm African American. I'm Israeli. I'm Mexican American. I'm Arab American. I'm

Native American.) Religious? (I'm Catholic, Muslim, Jewish, Quaker, Episcopalian, Buddhist.) Based on gender or sexuality? (I'm a woman. I'm heterosexual). Based on profession or vocation? (I'm a UAW member, a lawyer, a potter, a truck driver, a musician.) Based on school? (I'm a college student, a business major, a freshman). Social? (I belong to a sorority, the chess club, a square-dancing group)

Some of us are visual learners, and some are not. We suggest you choose the mapping format that comes most easily to you and that will be most helpful as you explore your own community life. The "cluster" format is perhaps the easiest kind of map to make, though there are many other possibilities: make an outline; make a list or a series of lists; make a chart. A group of intersecting circles might work well for you. A cluster of concentric circles might make sense. If you compose your map on a computer, you might use a series of text boxes or a spreadsheet program or even a database. Perhaps you will draw an actual map, complete with cities, territories, mountain ranges, rivers, and oceans that represent the social and rhetorical landscape you navigate every day. As more food for thought, consider David Sedgewick's map. Notice the wealth of connection and commitment represented on it.

You can probably imagine the kinds of work that could come from an exploration of the important questions that emerge on Sedgewick's map. In the end, Sedgewick researched what he felt were the unethical advertising techniques used by credit card companies to entice young people to spend beyond their means.

WORKSHOP 14: Reflecting on your Commitments

This workshop provides a framework for writing a personal reflection on the life events that make you a part of the communities to which you belong. This kind of writing can allow you to think more carefully about the rhetorical terrain of you community involvement and can provide you with a rich testament to your own community commitments.

CRUCIAL QUESTIONS: DECIDING ON A SITUATION FOR YOUR PROJECT

Once you have mapped the communities to which you belong, you can list issues that interest members of these communities. In order to discuss this part of the invention process, we need to define two more terms: *position* and *claim.* Because people are committed to communities in different ways and to varying degrees, they take different positions on the issues raised in those communities. One of the meanings of the word *position,* then, is: the place where a person is located in relation to others. Here, *position* means "a relationship to an issue," because issues are always located within critical situations, which are themselves produced by and within communities. For example, some neighbors may be annoyed by loud parties while others may be so busy they don't notice the noise. The neighbor who is annoyed has taken up a position on the issue of noisy parties, and if he puts this position into language, he might say: "I've had it up

David Sedgewick's Community Map

United States Citizen
Is the Iraq war just?
Presidential election—who to pick?
What can be done about gas prices?

Commuting Student
How should we deal with road ragers?
Why can't the university be more accommodating in terms of scheduling?

Environmentalist
What can be done to convince the public that water is a finite resource?
Why aren't we investing more in alternative fuel sources?

Father
How do I protect my children from media influence?

Political Independent
How can I help independent political candidates get a fair hearing?

Person Carrying Big Credit Card Debt
What can I do about my credit record?
Should I file for personal bankruptcy?
To what degree are credit card companies to blame for the debt epidemic?

Divorced Middle-Age Man
Is there love after divorce and addiction?
How do I meet people now that I don't go to bars?
Can we hope to find love on the Internet?

Sober Alcoholic
How can I stay "dry"?
How do I talk to my kids about addiction?

Member of Community Theater
What do we do with members who don't work their volunteer hours?
Why can't we stage less mainstream productions?

Caucasion
To what degree do I assume white privilege?

to here with those loud parties across the street." Thus he makes a claim. A claim is a statement that expresses its author's position on some issue.

We ordinarily ask students to phrase their issues as questions at first. Phrased as a question, an issue can be recognized more clearly as arising within a situation, a field of social dialogue that demands answers and in which stakeholders contend with one another. Here is a list of issue-questions generated by our students in the spring of 2003, in a course focused on science writing and communication. If you skim the list, you will see that many of these questions persist as sites of concern and conflict. Notice that some students focused on local situations, and that others were concerned about national or international situations.

- Is the public sufficiently aware of the activities of scientists?
- What is the ethical status of human embryo cloning?
- To what extent is human activity responsible for global warming? To what extent can human activities slow global warming?
- Is "missile defense" a worthy investment for this country?
- Are genetically engineered foods dangerous?
- How important is biodiversity to the future of our own species?
- What should be done about low science test scores in our schools?
- What is the best way to deal with the periodic controversy over the teaching of evolution in our schools?
- Should Tempe's Town Lake be stocked with trout?
- Should Arizonans be concerned about nuclear waste passing through the state on the way to Nevada?
- Is the delay of destruction of smallpox safe or risky?
- What is nutrition? What is nutritious?
- Who owns science, public corporations, and government?
- Were there design flaws in the World Trade Center that contributed to the 9/11 disaster?
- Should marijuana be legal for medical purposes?
- Does the development of Phoenix affect our water needs? Should preventive measures be taken?
- Should there be more restrictive rules for patenting genes?
- Body tissues are not regulated as organs. Cases of threatening infections have occurred during tissue transplants. Should new regulations be implemented?
- What kinds of stigmas are still associated with the AIDS virus? Why is science not moving faster on a cure?
- In terms of cancer research, how effective is the magnetic field therapy used to implode cells and why is it only offered outside the United States?
- Should experimental treatments be available for all of those individuals who desire them?

- What can be done for antibiotic resistance in hospital patients?
- Are investigations like the biosphere and space station realistic for future societies?
- Are we ethically responsible to provide AIDS drugs to African countries?
- Are solar and wind power realistic alternatives?
- Are we overusing antibiotics? Overprescribing? In livestock? Handsoap?
- What will be the environmental impact of construction at the proposed Arizona Cardinals Stadium site?
- Should Arizona drain Lake Powell as the Sierra Club is arguing?
- Should post offices reconsider their methods of profiling mail?
- Should California back off enforcement of environmental laws? Of laws against the destruction of rainforest?
- Urban sprawl—does it equal destruction of desert?
- What is the quality of the coverage of "scientific issues" in the *Arizona Republic* and in the press generally?
- Should HMOs cover alternative medicine such as herbals and the like?
- Is sustainable urban sprawl an oxymoron?
- What are the legal rights of animals? Who should regulate experimentation on animals?
- Is waste water being used properly?
- Lee's Ferry, Grand Canyon—should fishing rights be considered more important that fears of a dwindling native fish population? What if fishing and other factors eliminate native fish species in the Grand Canyon?

WORKSHOP 9: Gathering Information through Interviews

Because you are a member of the communities in which you are planning a writing project, it is likely that you know personally people with detailed information about pressing community matters. This workshop helps you prepare interviews to access that information.

Students sometimes found it difficult to decide how to phrase these questions because they took different positions on the issues raised by them. For some members of the class, to raise some of these questions was already to engage in argument (and we did argue!).

Once a community member has decided how to answer any of these questions, she can phrase this answer as a *claim.* The claim represents her position on the issue. Take this question from the list generated by our students, for example: Were there design flaws in the World Trade Center that contributed to the 9/11 disaster? Two obvious claims are made available by this issue: "Yes, design flaws in the WTC towers contributed to their destruction," or "No: the towers were designed to withstand the impact of a Boeing 757. So, some other reason must be found to explain their collapse." Other, more complex claims are made available by this issue as well, such as: "Even though the Towers were built to withstand the impact of a Boeing 757, its designers could not anticipate that even larger aircraft, such as the

767, would one day be built and deliberately flown into the Towers." (To see more such claims, and to read arguments made by engineers about this issue, check out the many Web sites devoted to the events of 9/11.)

Here is a second example taken from our students' list of issues:

—An issue phrased as a question: Should marijuana be legal for medical purposes?

—Possible claims (positions) made available by this issue:
 —Marijuana should not be legalized for any reason.
 —Marijuana should not be legalized for medical purposes.
 —Marijuana should be legally available to anyone who wants it.
 —Marijuana should be legally available for medical purposes.

Many other more complex or nuanced positions are made available by this issue as well.

TALK READ WRITE

1. With other members of your class, try to figure out how a few entries on the lists above suggest the communities, stakeholders, and social commitments entailed in each. Take the second entry, for example. Who is interested in cloning? In the ethical questions it raises? What communities are not interested? What are the stakes of those who oppose cloning? Who favor it?
2. Discussion of the legal status of marijuana abounds on the Internet. If you are curious about the communities who care about this issue, and about other possible claims made available by it, find a few Web sites devoted to marijuana use and look for the positions taken up and the claims expressed there.

Invention Journal: Further Mapping

We can't offer much advice about making a final choice among the issues located on your map. Discussion can help, but the choice must be yours. Think carefully again about the issues that keep you up nights and occupy your conversations and thoughts during the day. Consider ways in which you might work as an advocate for a given position with a community group. Consider all of the issues that emerged on your community map. Here are some questions to get you started thinking about these issues in a social context, which is to say, as part of a critical situation:

1. Look at each of the communities you charted on your Community Map. Take some time now to think and write about the situations that hold these communities together. Look back at David Sedgewick's or Amber Zaidi's map as a

guide. See how particular questions have a clear link to the definitions of community these students mapped. For each of your communities, make a list of at least three questions. If at all possible, avoid "yes-or-no" questions, phrasing them instead as open-ended exploratory questions.

2. What is the range of popular opinion about these questions (situations) within the community? List as many possible responses for each question as you can. Which positions do you agree with? Disagree? Why? It might be very useful at this point to share your list of questions with your workshop group members or even the whole class.
3. Conduct some preliminary research on any of the issues using Internet search engines such as Dogpile, Yahoo!, or Google. Collect some newspaper articles about any of the issues in local or national daily papers or through general news indexes such as Ebsco Host or Lexis-Nexis. Do members of other communities think that your issue is important? List other groups of people that are concerned with these questions. How do opinions and attitudes about the issue differ outside of your community?

WORKSHOP 18: What do You Want to Learn about Composition?

While deciding what work you will take on in your project, you can also make decisions about how this rhetorical effort will provide you with a laboratory for the serious study of reading, writing, and research. This workshop challenges you to organize your own agenda as a student of serious composition and thus to be an active rather than a passive learner.

Once you have decided, a mini-celebration is in order! You've just taken a major step in doing serious work by pursuing situations and issues to which you are truly committed. After your celebratory moment, take some time to write about your goals for the project. What do you hope to achieve through serious writing or speech? What are the ideal outcomes, and what small changes might you effect through your work?

ASSESSING SOCIAL AND RHETORICAL CONFLICT

Difference and conflict are the inevitable state of things—this is a rhetorician's baseline assumption. Examples abound. When we were first writing this chapter, the Massachusetts Supreme Court has just found the state's ban on gay marriage to be unconstitutional, opening the possibility for gay and lesbian couples to marry. Conservative politicians and community leaders at the state and national level have responded by renewing their demand for a Constitutional amendment prohibiting gay marriage. Issues can cause bitter division because they involve beliefs and values that are intimately tied to both individual and communal identities, and they can create critical situations because the available positions on them can be in conflict. In the early months of 2003 those who supported the American invasion of Iraq were bitterly opposed to antiwar protests that emerged all over the country. Conflicts such as these occur because our individual and community identities are wrapped up with those of the nation. In fact, communities are often connected as strongly by their conflicts and disagreements as they are by the commitments that members share. The state of the national economy is another contested issue that can hold Americans together as a national "we." But each of us will take up very different positions on this issue depending on own economic standing, whether we are poor, affluent, or just getting by.

But we don't need to consult the national or international stage for examples of social difference and conflict. They surround us all the time. It can be difficult

Pro- and Antiwar Demonstrations
War always excites staunch support and dogged criticism. Throughout history, disagreements about military action have been among the most heated political conflicts.

to think in rhetorical or social terms about issues that you've always thought of as "personal" or "private." Some of our students have been surprised to discover, for example, that issues about body image, which for them are tied up with identity and self-worth, are topics of discussion in the mass media. Some have subsequently researched and designed projects around media representations of body image. It is almost certain, in fact, that the issue you mull over alone and that you experience as specific to your own life is actually a matter of widespread concern, public discussion, and conflict. As a rule of thumb, it's probably a good idea to consider that your experience of conflict, no matter how individualized it seems, is almost certainly shared by many others. Making a jump from personal or private consideration to an inquiry into issues in context is crucial if we are to conceive of a critical situation—the rhetorical and social ground where we can plan and carry out meaningful projects.

Some community conflicts break down along lines of gender, race or ethnicity, economic class, sexuality, age—a host of social differences with long histories in the world's societies. Rosa Casas found the motivation for her project as she moved from one community to another, from the South Phoenix neighborhoods in which she grew up to the campus of Arizona State University, where she earned a bachelors' degree. Casas was surprised to experience culture shock just several miles from the place she called home. The following excerpt is from her reflection on the community map she made as she began her project.

> I found myself being judged and stereotyped every time I mentioned the fact of being from South Phoenix. When talking to my friends I found I wasn't the only one. They also had been through the same experience. We spent our time together talking about how people react to the words "South Phoenix." They acted as if it was the worst place you could live. They called it the bad side of town and made comments about the crime and violence. We were suddenly looked at like the bad apples when most of us had been our whole lives the good kids; most of us attending school on merit scholarships . . . While my friends and I chose to laugh and joke about people's ignorance, I found myself bothered deeply . . . Attending ASU has changed the way I look at myself . . . I always knew that Mexican-Americans are considered a "minority." The funny thing about all this is I just started feeling like a minority these past few weeks. In my neighborhood I find myself being part of the majority. At my high school I felt like everybody else and I fit in. Walking onto the ASU campus Monday morning August the 25, I found myself feeling alone, different.

Many people have this experience of what we might call insight through dislocation. Often we need to be outside of our home communities before we can see clearly how we are perceived by others. These perceptions were a real motivator for Casas. She quite rightly understood that the biases of race and class had real social stakes, that they assumed limits on people from the "bad side of town." As she searched for the sources of such perceptions, she began to catalogue media images of South Phoenix in the local press. In the Phoenix area, if South Phoenix appears in the newspaper or television news, it is almost always the subject of a crime report. Casas believed, and her research verified, that such images could have strong impact on public opinion. We applaud her commitment to her home community and to taking responsibility within a situation that troubled her. Perhaps you can recognize this other-side-of-the-tracks phenomenon in your own community.

Mapping can also reveal instances in which we have separate commitments that are at cross purposes. Caryn Bird wrote this community map when she was a first-year student at Arizona State University. Her cross-referencing technique used here is particularly useful in locating conflicts and contradictions. Even viewing this abbreviated version of Bird's map, you can see how she found her project at the borders between different communities:

Mapping Communities

Early Childhood Development (Academic Major)

Parent Education

Child Safety

Child Protective Service Effectiveness

See also: Driver, Two-Parent Home, ASU Student

Two-Parent Home
—Married Parents as Oddity
—What makes a family?
—Financial impact
—Impact on worldview

See also: ASU Student, Politically Conservative, Socially Liberal

Gay, Lesbian, Bisexual, Transgender Community (GLBT)
—AIDS Education
—Programs for youth
—Gay marriage, not "civil unions" (No separate but equal)
—Gay parenting/adoption rights
—Community education to end hate crimes
—Gay television craze
—The movement (Stonewall)

See also: Child Advocate, ASU Student, Socially Liberal

ASU Student
—GPA
—Education
—Future
—Work
—Balancing workload
—Reputation of school
—Transportation/Parking

See also: Fatty, Socially Liberal, Politically Conservative, Bicycle Rider

Socially Liberal
—Gay Marriage
—Sexual Liberation

Politically Conservative
—Fiscally Conservative
—Separation of government and personal life
—Proponent of indirect aid

See also: Socially Liberal, ASU Student, GLBT Advocate, Child Advocate

Fatty
—Acceptance
—Health
—Self-esteem

See also: ASU Student

Biker
—Car traffic
—Safety
—Pedestrian traffic on campus

See also: ASU Student

Bird's map represents a careful process of exploring the social ground of commitment. Mapping helped her to think more carefully about a contradiction she had already acknowledged in her own political self-definition. How did she reconcile her "politically conservative" commitments with those that inspired her as an advocate for the gay, lesbian, bisexual, and transgender community? In our current political moment, many political conservatives have rallied around an opposition to gay marriage, calling in some circles for a constitutional amendment to prevent marriage rights for gay couples. Research led Bird to the work of people who are strongly partisan, favoring gay rights. She also discovered voices that defied political expectation, for example, those of gay Republicans and liberal homophobes. She spent a semester studying all these perspectives in an attempt to retrieve a gay-friendly conservatism as a legitimate position on the political spectrum.

Invention Journal: Finding Other Stakeholders on Your Map

Social and rhetorical conflicts arise when differences and disagreement emerge among stakeholders in a situation. Such conflicts can take the form of war or physical domination of one group over another, but with luck, communication can sometimes alter the situation to accommodate some mutually satisfying solution. We concede that this ideal seems hopeful in a dangerous world. However, we are committed to it. Aristotle claimed that rhetoric is a means of finding "the available means of persuasion." Rhetoric is crucial for reaching sound judgments among stakeholders. Argument or critical exchange is not good simply for winning points but for drawing out the best ideas that the members of a community as a whole can muster. We ask that you consider both functions of rhetoric as you proceed with your project. You might gain power through careful speech and writing, and you might also find common ground with other people who have a stake in the issue that is important to you.

At the university where we teach, like most others, tuition has recently been raised (again), and in response, we have seen a number of student projects attempting to address this issue. Some students have organized letter-writing campaigns in protest, and some have crafted proposals for alternate means of increasing the university's profitability. Others have simply made arguments for a clearer explanation from the university administration about how all the new money will be allocated. Who would you list as the stakeholders in this issue? How would you describe the nature of their stake in the tuition question? Students concerned about this situation might easily develop the following list of stakeholders:

In-state students

Out-of-state students (for whom the tuition increase was higher)

Prospective students considering whether or not to attend the university

Parents or anyone else helping students with tuition

University administrators

University faculty and staff who might benefit from the increased profit

Local community colleges (whose enrollment might increase as a result of students being priced out of the university)

What other stakeholder groups might be included on this list? Who are the stakeholders in the situations you are most concerned about?

1. Make a list of as many stakeholders as you can think of in the situations that most interest you. Name stakeholder groups—organizations, local communities, institutions, professions. What does each party have to lose or gain and why?
2. Do preliminary research through Internet searches and by searching recent editions of local or major national newspapers such as the New York *Times*, the Los Angeles *Times*, the Boston *Globe*, the *Wall Street Journal*, and the Washington *Post*. Write down the names of high-profile spokespeople, politicians, administrators, and community leaders who have expressed a position on your issue. Summarize the arguments of each, and then write your responses to each one.

3. Imagine a dinner party attended by a few members of all the communities represented on your map. How would the conversation go? Would there be arguments? About what?

NO PERFECT MAPS: DEALING WITH ASSUMPTIONS ABOUT COMMUNITY

> Interests are embodied in the map as presences and absences.
>
> *Denis Wood*

Students in our courses have rightly pointed to a possible problem with the process of mapping communities. It is all too easy to fall into generalizations and stereotypes when we conceive of boundaries in the social world. Just because one person claims belonging within a community, that does not make it so, at least not beyond question. For instance, an advocate for children living in poverty may or may not be a part of a community of people living below the poverty line. Conversely, some communities claim us, whether we want them to or not. There are family communities, neighborhoods, and civic situations we could do without. Communities are shaped by historical events beyond our control, and so belonging is not always a choice. Survivors of the September 11 attacks, for instance, did not ask for the tragic sense of belonging that many now feel. We encourage you to think of the community map as a living thing, a document of identity and belonging that you might rethink as time passes, perhaps even before you finish your project.

The assumption that members of a community share the same attributes and concerns is all too common in the social world. Prejudice based on gender, race, sexuality, economic class, nationality, age and other factors are the most violent manifestation of assumptions about community. One of our students explained the anti-Muslim assumptions that impacted the lives of those in his community. He realized early on in his project that he could not assume that all American citizens were reasonable enough to recognize media distortions of Muslims when they saw them. Nor could he assume that more than a few people in this country had even a rudimentary knowledge of the Quran or of Islam.

The most vile justifications for racial slavery have been based on assumptions about communities. During the nineteenth century, American slaveholders and their sympathizers claimed that enslaved peoples were immoral, criminal, and animalistic. On the other hand, the abolitionist leader David Walker could not assume that all African Americans would agree with his call to action and resistance in "Appeal to the Colored Citizens of the World." Near the beginning of his text, he acknowledged that a number of his "brethren"—African Americans living in the Northern states, outside of slavery—benefited from complacency and political inaction and would thus curse his name for rocking the boat.

Very rarely are communities homogenous or as uniform as is sometimes assumed. Politicians in this country are fond of invoking the interests and concerns of "the American people," and as we suggested in the last chapter, nationality is one way to define community. We hope, though, that calling "we the people" together is a rhetorical strategy that will be apparent to you. How many people can justly claim to speak on behalf of some assumed collective called "the American people?" How do you feel when a politician claims to speak for you in this way, particularly if you disagree with the position being forwarded? During abolition, African American speakers and writers pointed out that the national imagination of one common people was exclusive in terms of race and gender. The collective "we" to mean "all Americans" is as much a political mythology as a social reality, and any claim that assumes such a "we" should be approached critically.

Avoiding assumptions about community is also crucial for thinking about audience. Caryn Bird, for instance, thinking about how to address gay issues with a conservative audience, found more variety of opinion than she had imagined before her research began. Not every Republican is antigay, as it turns out, just as not every gay person is to the political left of the Republican Party. In our classes, students from outside local Hispanic communities have at times been surprised when prominent leaders inside those communities make strong arguments for tougher immigration policies or against bilingual education in public schools. It is similarly unwise to assume that people adhere to particular ideas or act in certain ways based on their gender.

Of course, the multiplicity of community need not be thought of only in antagonistic terms. Americans have for centuries talked about diversity as a national value, and there is good reason to celebrate the rich network of social differences in this country. We agree that social diversity can be a strength for democracy; the situations of diversity and difference are, after all, where our greatest ethical and civic questions might be answered. It's tempting to imagine a world without the difficult borders of difference and communities in conflict because competing claims, misunderstandings, and clashes of perspective can be intimidating and frustrating. Even having a classroom discussion about social difference and conflict can be difficult because a range of stakeholder positions is likely to operate in any group. But history demonstrates that our differences cannot be ended, only negotiated for better or for worse.

TALK READ WRITE

1. Working together, develop a list of communities that are distinguished by age, gender, race, class, ability, and the like. Now, develop a list of stereotypes that people on the outsides of these communities buy into. Share ideas about where these stereotypes originate. Discuss how they are used in arguments.

2. Drawing from your own experience, discuss times and places in which you've been stereotyped as a part of a particular community. Discuss the effects of this stereotyping.

LIST OF WORKS CITED

Bernstein, Iver. *The New York City Draft Riots: Their Significance for American Society and Politics in the Age of Civil War.* New York: Oxford UP, 1990.

Bush, George W. "Statement by the President in his Address to the Nation." whitehouse.gov/news/releases/2001/09/2001091116.html. Accessed December 6, 2006.

DuBois, W. E. B. *The Philadelphia Negro: A Social Study.* Philadelphia: Pennsylvania UP: 1996.

Harper, Frances Ellen Watkins. *A Brighter Coming Day: A Frances Ellen Watkins Reader.* Ed. Frances Smith Foster. New York: The Feminist Press, 1990.

Wells, Ida B. *A Red Record. Southern Horrors and Other Writings: The Anti-Lynching Campaign of Ida B. Wells, 1892–1900.* Ed. Jacqueline Jones Royster. 73–157. New York: Bedford/St Martin's, 1997.

Wood, Denis. *The Power of Maps.* New York: Guilford Publications, 1992.

PART II

CRITICAL QUESTIONS:

Reading, Research, and Invention

3

ASKING THE RIGHT QUESTIONS

Remember the incident on the bus described in the first chapter? Imagine that two passengers riding on that bus discuss the event after it is over. The first passenger might say something like "Wow—that was really scary." The second might respond by saying "Nah—I wasn't scared." Each of these people has expressed a position, and hence they are engaging in **rhetoric**. An ancient teacher of rhetoric named Aristotle defined rhetoric as the ability to find the available arguments. That is, Aristotle defined rhetoric as the art of invention—finding or discovering the claims and evidence that circulate in critical situations.

Aristotle taught us that people who use rhetoric want to achieve many different goals—for example, they may wish to solidify their membership in a community by praising or blaming people or events that are important to that community. More often, though, those who use rhetoric want listeners or readers to change beliefs they hold or actions they undertake. This is true even when students speak or write for teachers. Although they may not be primarily interested in persuading teachers to change their minds about issues raised in their work, they do wish to persuade teachers to regard their performance with approval. Considered in this light, a research paper is an **argument**, even though a teacher might have instructed you not to "take sides." Nevertheless, the paper itself is an argument that asks for a good grade.

Whatever ground your project covers, you will probably make an argument at some time during your investigation. We are aware that the term *argument* sometimes has negative overtones because people fear that it is disrespectful to disagree with someone's opinion, especially when that opinion concerns religion or politics. In this book, however, we use the term *argument* in a less evaluative way to refer to sets of statements that support or refute a position taken up by participants in a discussion. Recall that a position is any controversial belief or statement. By *controversial,* we mean any belief or statement with which someone might reasonably disagree. If we say, "This bus stops at the corner of College and University," we have not taken up a position because the accuracy of this statement can be checked against the bus schedule, or by asking a bus driver or by locating a bus stop on the corner in question. Any statement that can be verified with evidence of this kind is not controversial—that is, no sensible person disagrees with it—and hence it does not take up a position. We both know people who love to argue about statements like this, but anyone who argues about verifiable facts is wasting breath.

When someone expresses an attitude about something ("that was really scary"), she does express a position. Despite the popular view that there are only two sides to every issue, we have found that issues can produce many positions, and the complex issues that interest us most can yield a range of positions. Take the issue of war, for example; media pundits usually divide people who discuss war into two camps—pro- and antiwar. But there are many other positions available on the issue of war: depending on the circumstances, someone who is pro-war, for example, might favor positions ranging from all-out military conquest (or even nuclear annihilation) to limited war—isolated military strikes or a few covert military actions. Someone who is antiwar might take up any number of positions as well, ranging from absolute pacifism (all war is wrong) to favoring so-called "just wars" or limited wars of retribution. In addition, a person who is against a specific war may support a different conflict, because the positions that people take up are influenced by context, that is, by critical situations. It is more accurate to say, then, that there are many sides, or positions, available on every issue. Furthermore, the available positions on an issue can be of different kinds. Statements that claim to be true express positions, as do those that define or evaluate people, things, or events, and those that recommend policy. Though it now seems impossible that anyone could do so, American slaveholders once argued that the institution of slavery was grounded in compassion and Christian sympathy. Such people portrayed slaves and their masters as happy families, rather than acknowledging that slaves' biological families were actually torn apart by slavery. Abolitionists had to work hard to contest such claims before they could get people to listen to their proposals to abolish slavery. They did this by telling vivid stories about slave auctions, in which members of families were split apart and sold away from one another.

In the previous chapter we noted that when a position is put into words, we call it a **claim**. Arguments consist of claims and evidence supporting those claims. Some of the available positions on an issue are worked out as claims in an argument, and some remain unspoken or unwritten even though they are relevant. In other words, an issue consists of all the positions made available within a critical situation. Abortion, prayer in school, the price of gasoline, deforestation—all of these are issues. Issues are embedded in critical situations; to say this another way, life in a community creates issues. The character played by Tom Hanks in the film *Castaway* was shipwrecked and washed up alone on a desert island. Hanks's character was faced with a host of problems: how to get food and shelter, how to get rescued, how to remain sane. But these are problems, not issues; the only issues facing him were raised by his memories of his former life in a community—was his job being performed correctly? Did his fiancee grieve for him? But in the absence of other stakeholders, there could be no disagreement, no critical situation.

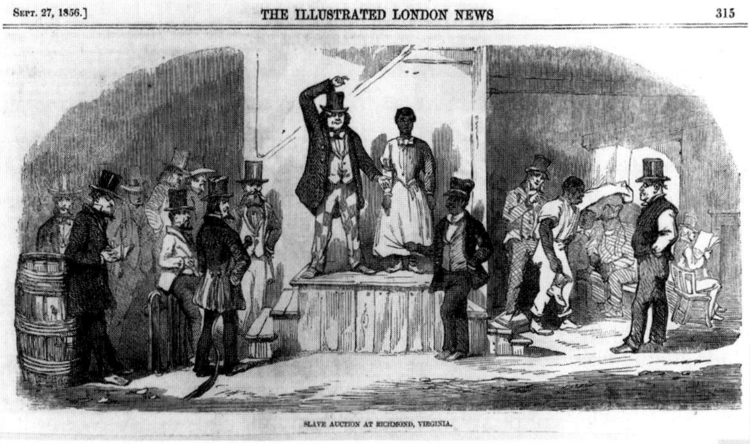

A Slave Auction
Abolitionists put vivid images of slave auctions before the public as a means of protest. Perhaps no other image held as much visual power as an indictment of the slave system.

FINDING THE POINT OF STASIS

Rhetoric is often thought about in a very narrow sense, to mean convincing someone that her position is wrong or that someone else's position is right. But critical situations harbor many available positions. If we disagree with you about the health benefits of vegetarianism, for example, we might take any of several available positions (vegetarianism is not healthy; vegetarianism does not protect against disease as well as a diet that contains meat, and so on). At the outset of an argument we are probably not aware of all of these (just as you are probably not aware of all the claims made available by your position). If we are to have an argument about this issue, and if we don't want the argument to degenerate into shouting or angry silence or worse, we must begin by agreeing with one another about what exactly is at issue in our disagreement. Ancient rhetoricians called this point of agreement ***stasis,*** which means "stand." Stasis marks the place where people who disagree come together, where they rest or stand in agreement on what the controversy is about. If such agreement does not occur, people can talk right past one another, sometimes for years, without even beginning to argue—let alone reaching agreement. Take, for example, the argument over abortion rights. In its current configuration this argument has been going on for over thirty years. People who oppose abortion ordinarily do so because they think that abortion is murder. People who want to keep abortion legal do so because they think that women should be able to control their reproductive practices. Neither side is arguing with the other; rather, they are having two separate arguments—one about when life begins, and another about the political rights of women. No wonder this argument can't be ended. If people who are arguing about abortion actually want to engage their opponents, they will have to find some stasis—that is, a position about which they can agree to disagree. In other words, finding the stasis allows argument to start.

We begin with a relatively simple example in order to illustrate the process of agreeing to disagree. Games are played with rules that are intended to define such things as winning and losing, and what is a fair play and what is foul. In football, for instance, in order to score a touchdown a player must carry or throw the football over the goal line. This seems simple enough. But as football fans know, disagreements can break out about actual performances of the act of moving a football over a chalk line. For example, what is *possession?* If the player carrying the ball runs with it over the line, did he have a firm hold on the ball or was it taken away from him before or as he ran or fell over the goal line? Was the player still "in play" when he carried the ball over the line? That is, had his knee touched the ground before or as he carried the ball over the line? If the score is achieved by passing, another set of questions arises: Was the ball or the player who caught it, or part of his body, inside the lines or planes that mark the limits of the goal area? Was he in this area when he gained possession? Perhaps he was inside when he caught the ball, but came to earth outside the line, for instance. If the ball is knocked out of his hands by an opposing player while both are jumping, who can be said to retain possession if the ball goes out of bounds? We have seen games in which these questions and others like them were raised about possible scores because it is not always easy to determine exactly what happens on a football play, even when cameras are filming it from several directions.

When people encounter issues that are important to them or to members of their communities, they generally take up a position or positions on that issue. A position "takes sides" on an issue. If, for example, a referee decides that our team moved illegally prior to the snap of the football, he takes up a position on that event. Furthermore, when he calls our team offside, he makes a claim about the event. As we said, there are many available positions on any issue, and many ways of stating claims that represent those positions. If we disagree with the referee, we can simply state that his claim isn't true: "Our team did not move!" Or we can take up another position: "Well they moved first, drawing us offside!" Or we can ignore the referee's claim altogether, instead expressing opinions about his eyesight, his sexual habits, or his ancestry. But if we want to enter into actual argument with the referee, this last approach will not work (it might, in fact, result in another foul being called). If we want to persuade the referee to change his position, then, we must agree to begin with his original point: that our team was offside. Coaches know that if they want referees to reconsider they must dispute this claim and no other.

WORKSHOP 3: Different Values and Respectful Conflict

Arguments are inherently matters of conflict. Rather than trying to avoid such conflict, we recommend approaching it as a powerful learning opportunity and an intellectual resource. This workshop provides the framework for sharing our own value-based positions in a productive and respectful manner.

The referee who must rule on such disagreements cannot count on players, coaches, or fans to make fair decisions in such cases, because their desire for one side or the other to win may, in fact, affect what they see. That is, fans, players, and coaches are stakeholders in the critical situation. Fortunately, football and other games are bound by explicit rules that are meant to help referees decide what to do in cases where disagreement might arise concerning a play. The important question in such a rule-bound situation is: did players' performance fulfill or break the relevant requirements? Because rules exist that carefully define what "fulfilling" and "breaking" mean in this situation, all parties can agree that this is the crucial point at issue. Either the team performed within the area allowed by the rules, or they did not. Disagreement about the referee's answer to questions of this kind may persist, but at least everyone can agree about the place where disagreement begins.

Determining the stasis is crucial to any argument. However, figuring out the stasis is more difficult than it may seem at first glance. Most people who are engaged in arguments want to advance their own position as quickly and forcefully as possible. And so they do not want to take the time to determine whether they are actually arguing the same point as other participants. This hasty approach can lead to stalemate (or shouting or even violence), however. If speakers and writers do not agree on what they disagree about, argument cannot begin. For example, one of our students researched, discussed, and wrote about capital punishment for a solid month before his actual position came into focus. Until that time, he could not decide whether he was most concerned about the actual procedures of death row, or moral justifications of capital punishment, or the question of victims' rights, or recommending a policy change (the abolition of the death penalty). Until he figured out with which of these practices he most disagreed with, he was not able to settle on a position. That is, until he decided on the point of disagreement, he could not begin his argument. Speakers and writers who are dealing with complex and controversial issues such as the death penalty often find themselves in this situation, and in the rest of this book we provide strategies that may help you to determine which of the many available positions on any given issue is the one you want to take up.

Doubtless there is no referee to whom you can appeal to make decisions in the critical situation that you are examining. So, let's try to determine what is at issue in a more complicated example where the stakes are quite high—September 11, 2001. The official account of the events of that day runs as follows: four aircraft were hijacked by 19 men associated with Al Qaeda, an organization led by Osama bin Ladin. Two of the planes were flown into the twin towers of the World Trade Center; another craft was flown into the Pentagon, and yet a fourth was forced to crash in Pennsylvania after its passengers mounted an attack on the hijackers. This account appears in the 9/11 Commission Report and in a report of the investigation undertaken by the United States Congress, as well. You may be surprised to learn that some people do not accept this account of events. Their alternative accounts are called "revisionist," or, less charitably, "conspiracy theories." One of the most startling revisionist accounts was put forward soon after 9/11 by French journalist Thierry Meyssan. In one of his books about September 11, Meyssan summarizes the evidence presented in official government and media accounts of the catastrophic incident at the Pentagon in terms that suggest his disbelief:

> To recap the official version: a hijacked Boeing eluded the F-16 fighters sent in its pursuit and foiled the anti-aircraft defense system in Washington. It landed vertically on the Pentagon parking lot while remaining in a horizontal position. It

> struck the facade at ground level. Its nose and fuselage are supposed to have penetrated into the building. One of its wings, perhaps both of them, burned outdoors, while the fuselage disintegrated inside. The fuel, stored in the wings, burned just long enough to start a fire in the building, and then was transformed into a puddle which moved itself to the spot where the plane's nose supposedly came to a halt. Not withstanding the respect owed to the high rank of the "eye witnesses"—including military officers and members of Congress—it is impossible to swallow such nonsense (*Big Lie,* 24).

As you can see, Meyssan thinks that the evidence assembled to support the official account is implausible. He claims, rather, that the Pentagon was struck not by a hijacked commercial airliner but by a missile: "all of this testimony and these observations could correspond with the firing of one of the latest generation of AGM-type missiles (28). He claims further that the missile was fired by United States military personnel: "only a missile of the United States armed forces transmitting a friendly code could enter the Pentagon's airspace without provoking a counter-missile barrage" (29). Meyssan implies, of course, that a government and/or military conspiracy orchestrated this event.

Perhaps your first response to Meyssan's argument was much like ours: "This is crazy! The United States military would never attack Americans!" Heartfelt and important as it is, this position does not quite achieve stasis with Meyssan's claim. Meyssan's position can be stated as follows:

> The United States military fired a missile on the Pentagon on September 11, 2001, killing and injuring many people and badly damaging the building.

If argument is to begin about this claim, anyone who opposes it must develop a counterclaim that denies the claim actually being made, not the claim of some other argument. Someone who opposes Meyssan's claim, then, and who accepts the accounts given by government officials and the news media, must take up a position that goes something like this:

> American Airlines flight 77, hijacked by terrorists, crashed into the Pentagon on September 11, 2001, killing all aboard and many inside while badly damaging the building as well.

What is in dispute here is not that something crashed into the Pentagon on 9/11. What is at issue is what, exactly, hit the building (aircraft or missile) and its source (terrorists or the United States military). If participants in this argument cannot agree that these are the precise points of disagreement, they are likely to argue right past one another, hence failing to convince anyone to abandon a position. If, for example, we were to confront Meyssan with our original response ("That's crazy! The United States military would never attack Americans!") we would be shifting the point at issue to another issue altogether: the possibility that the United States military would open fire on its own people. Arguing (and settling) this more general issue might help to get at the question of who launched the attack on this particular day, but it is far more likely to delay the beginning of that argument. Moreover, arguing this question about the military's motives and actions gives Meyssan a distinct advantage, because he has already assembled arguments and evidence to support his position.

TALK READ WRITE

Here are some issues that were pressing in American conversation when we were writing this book: abortion, gay marriage, prayer in school, the war on terrorism, sex education, censorship of radio and television, the war in Iraq. Generate a few claims about each of these or other issues you may choose. Try to generate at least a few positions with which you disagree. Now, try to generate claims that are in stasis with the positions you have already discovered.

INVESTIGATING YOUR SITUATION WITH STASIS

In the preceding chapter we asked you to map the communities within which your strongest commitments are held. Once you have identified a community and have chosen an issue raised there, you can begin to map the available positions on that issue. Perhaps you want to speak or write about vegetarianism, for example, and you are pretty sure that you oppose the practice. You may do so because someone in your family is a vegan, and this makes meal planning more difficult. But you may not be aware of all the reasons that can be developed to defend your position, and you may discover as you research your project that there are reasons for opposing vegetarianism that affect people other than your family. By doing a little reading you may discover, for example, that vegetarianism negatively impacts ranchers, and that some doctors think that a vegetarian diet is not entirely healthy.

Issues are often complex, and many positions may be taken on any given issue. We recommend, then, that you begin thinking about any issue that you want to examine by trying to answer the questions listed below. These questions represent a systematic way of mapping the possible arguments and positions made available by your project. They are powerful means of invention. Hence, they should be used before you do any research, because they help you to articulate what you already know and believe about the issue in which you are interested. In fact, they can be used again and again during the course of a project, whenever you feel that you have run out of things to say. So, you should consider all the statements you generate as you work through them to be potential positions that you could take up or reject in any argument that is made in the context of your critical situation.

If you work systematically and thoroughly, you should produce a full and useful analysis of the issue. Doing all of this intellectual work has several advantages. First and most important, it establishes the stasis—the place where an author and her audience disagree. Furthermore, writers and speakers who take the time to find the available positions on an issue can be assured that their claims are defensible because they are aware of the available positions that can (and assuredly will) be taken by others who are interested in the issue. Such an investigation also reveals what sort of evidence is necessary to support any claim that can be taken up on any issue. In short, speakers and writers who work through the questions in systematic fashion also find that the process clarifies their thinking about the point in dispute; it also forces them to think about the assumptions and values shared by members of their targeted audience; and it establishes areas in which more research needs to be done. In short, working through the questions starts you on the road toward expertise in your critical situation.

All issues entail a variety of positions. Ancient teachers of rhetoric divided the kinds of available positions into four kinds or categories. The kinds or categories are called **conjecture**, **definition**, **value**, and **policy.** The categories deal in turn with depictions or assessments of events or actions (conjecture); definitions of important terms; values raised by or inherent in an issue, such as loyalty or goodness; and considerations of what should be done or not done in a given situation (policy). Here are examples of the kinds, stated in their most general form:

Conjecture: Does something exist? Did an event happen? If so, how can the thing or event be characterized or described?

Definition: How can the thing or event be defined? What kind of thing or event is it?

Value: How should the thing or event be valued? What is its quality? Was it right or wrong? Bad or good? Happy or sad? Just or unjust?

Policy: What should we do? Should this thing or event be submitted to some formal procedure?

You can reformulate the questions if you like. But be sure to ask each one about any position that interests you as you think about your project. If asking these basic questions raises more questions, try to answer those as well. When you use any system of invention, you are not answering questions on a test. Rather, you are trying to generate ideas. So, follow whatever line of thought emerges as you work.

There is one rule: if the first category or kind of question does not seem to apply to the context that interests you, move to the next. If someone is accused of theft, for example, the first question that must be raised is conjecture: "Did she do it or not?" If all parties agree that she took the property in question, the stasis moves to a question of definition: "Was it theft?" (She might have borrowed it.) And if everyone agrees that the act can be defined as theft, the stasis becomes: "Was it right or wrong?" (The theft might be justified on any number of grounds—she took liquor from the house of a friend who is an alcoholic, for instance.) Last, if the question of value is agreed upon, the question then becomes: "Should she be tried for the offense?" This is the question of procedure or policy. In conjecture, the writer or speaker determines whether or not he and his audience agree about the existence of some thing or the commission of some act. If they do, this category is no longer relevant or useful, having been agreed to—waived—by all parties. In definition, the author determines whether or not she and her audience agree about the classification of the thing or the act; if they do agree about definitions of important terms in the argument, the category of definition may be passed by. Third, she determines whether she and her audience agree about the value of the thing or the seriousness of the act. That is, what is its relevance to the community as a whole? And last, she asks whether anything needs to be done to alleviate a problem inherent in the situation.

Let's apply the categories to Meyssan's claim. His argument is a rich source for invention because there is controversy about each category of available positions. You may recall that we stated his claim as follows:

> The United States military fired a missile on the Pentagon on September 11, 2001, killing and injuring many people and badly damaging the building.

No one denies that a catastrophic event occurred at the Pentagon on September 11, 2001. However, Meyssan conjectures the nature of that event very differently from the depiction given in news reports, which generally reported that a hijacked Boeing 757 was flown into the building. Conjectures are guesses or inferences. A conjecture does not establish the truth or fact of the matter under discussion; rather, it represents an educated guess about what might be the case or what might have occurred in a given situation. And because reality may be perceived very differently by people who occupy different social and political situations, people may paint very different pictures of that reality. For example, a man who tells a dirty joke to his colleagues at work may think that he is only being friendly, while a woman colleague who hears the joke may feel that it belittles women. Or, in another example of conjecture, a recipient of Temporary Assistance for Needy Families might describe a welfare check as the only means she has of feeding her children. A politician who is opposed to welfare, however, might characterize that very same check as a handout to freeloaders. These people have all offered conjectures about the way the world is or how people behave. In the examples given here, each party has some stake or interest in picturing the joke or the welfare check in the way that they do. Their disagreement about these facts shows that conjectures are rhetorical; that is, they are inventions that characterize a thing or an event in some way favorable to the inventor. Each disagreement creates a critical situation—a sexual harassment lawsuit, perhaps, or a debate about welfare reform.

Let's move to the second category: definition. Government officials and media reports defined the attack on the Pentagon as a terrorist act. Meyssan defines it, rather, as an act of aggression by the American military (or its government) against its own people and institutions. Definitions are a means of classification: they discriminate classes or kinds of things and events ("terrorist act," "government aggression") and place specific things and events in these classes. Considered in this way, definitions are inventions: creating a class and placing an event in it can generate a position or positions. The work of our students provides more examples of definitional claims.

The third category—value—is ordinarily a very rich source of claims because values are embedded in our beliefs and behavior. Most Americans, for example, probably accept values forwarded in the country's founding documents: freedom, equality, and justice for all. People who accept a set of religious or moral beliefs ordinarily oppose practices that run counter to those belief systems. We assume that most Americans, given their love for their country, would reject Meyssan's claim on the grounds that it is ridiculous, traitorous, or perhaps even dangerous because it might erode trust in government. To say that a position is "ridiculous" or "traitorous" or "dangerous" is to make a value judgment. Those who accept Meyssan's claim might counter, on the other hand, that those of us who accept the official account of this event are ignorant or deluded, hence making different value judgements.

The fourth kind of stasis question—policy—asks us to think about whether anything should be done if we accept or reject a given position. Anyone who is moved by Meyssan's claim either to accept or oppose it might want to find out more about him and his qualifications for writing such a book, to investigate reports of the event more thoroughly, and to compare the available accounts of this event and weigh the evidence for each. Such a person may take further action, such as starting a letter-writing campaign, setting up a Web site, organizing protests, and so on. In these venues she could advocate policy: that Meyssan's work be disbelieved or censored (or that, on the other hand, it should be more widely circulated).

WORKSHOP 9: Gathering Information through Interviews

Use the stasis questions as a basis for interview questions you can pose to stake holders who may have detailed information about pressing community matters. This workshop helps you prepare interviews to access that information.

TALK READ WRITE

Working with one other member of the class, ask the questions of conjecture, definition, value, and policy to the issue raised by your project and the position you have taken on it. Reflect and write: did you learn anything about your issue or your position by asking these preliminary questions?

Invention Journal: Finding Stasis in Your Critical Situation

1. Look at any of the issues that you have generated in your Invention Journal. Try to formulate a position on one or two of these. What position could an opponent take that would be in stasis with your position? Expect to find several positions available both to you and to an opponent.
2. Select one of the issues you worked with in Chapter 2, and examine it using the questions. The first time you try this, you may wish to use our

examples as models. But because every issue is different (because every rhetorical situation is different) you will soon discover that our models don't raise all the relevant positions on your issue, and they may raise some questions that are not relevant.

3. Once you have chosen an issue for your project, you can use the questions of conjecture, definition, quality, and policy to formulate the relevant positions it harbors. You may also be able to determine what supporting arguments and evidence you will need to develop your position further by using the four questions. So, here are some further questions to ask once you have composed a list of possible positions: Do any positions you found tell you what research you need to do? Do any tell you something about positions or related issues that might be raised by a member of an audience, or by someone who disagrees with you? Do any help you to begin to develop an argument, that is, a list of claims that support your position? Do any suggest what sort of evidence is required to support your claim? (See Chapter 9 for our discussion of evidence).

A FIRST EXAMPLE FROM ABOLITION: FREDERICK DOUGLASS ON THE FOURTH OF JULY

On the day after the Fourth of July in 1852, Frederick Douglass was asked to speak to the Rochester Ladies' Anti-Slavery Society in Rochester, New York. Douglass, the most prominent American abolitionist and arguably one of the most important political figures in American history, delivered an address titled "What to the Slave Is the Fourth of July." Two days later he wrote to his friend and fellow abolitionist Gerrit Smith that he "spent a great deal of time preparing this speech." We think Douglass's efforts are evident at every turn in this address. In July of 1853, few could predict the future of the abolitionist movement. Even as more and more people joined the cause, the Southern slave-holding states continued to make national political gains. Opponents of slavery were still reeling from the affects of the Fugitive Slave Law of 1850, which gave slave owners the legal right to pursue and capture people escaped from slavery even within the borders of free states. The slave trade within the United States was more profitable than ever. Despite the acclaim Douglass had already won as an orator and the author of the 1845 *Narrative of the Life of Frederick Douglass,* he was, nonetheless, an African American claiming a public political voice, a situation that cut against the racial common sense of the time. Add to this that Douglass sought to address the meaning of national independence from the perspective of the enslaved, and we can begin to understand the volatility and difficulty of the critical situation he faced on this occasion and others like it. How could a man on the political margins make a scathing critique of a political system (conjecture) and still hold that system up as a model to other nations (policy)? How could Douglass claim the authority of national democratic values while questioning the legacy of those values in the United States (value)?

Douglass began his speech by reviewing the history of America, which was only about 70 years old in 1852. In this history he took pains to demonstrate that America was founded because its citizens had embraced liberty for all, rejecting what they saw as British tyranny. Then, he said this:

1. [Conjecture:] Fellow citizens, pardon me, allow me to ask, why am I called upon to speak here to-day? What have I, or those I represent, to do with your national independence? Are the great principles of political freedom and of natural justice, embodied in that Declaration of Independence, extended to us? and am I, therefore, called upon to bring our humble offering to the national altar, and to confess the benefits and express devout gratitude for the blessings resulting from your independence to us?
2. Would to God, both for your sakes and ours, that an affirmative answer could be truthfully returned to these questions! Then would my task be light, and my burden easy and delightful. For who is there so cold, that a nation's sympathy could not warm him? Who so obdurate and dead to the claims of gratitude, that would not thankfully acknowledge such priceless benefits? Who so stolid and selfish, that would not give his voice to swell the hallelujahs of a nation's jubilee, when the chains of servitude had been tom from his limbs? . . .
3. But, such is not the state of the case. I say it with a sad sense of the disparity between us. I am not included within the pale of this glorious anniversary! Your high independence only reveals the immeasurable distance between us. The blessings in which you, this day, rejoice, are not enjoyed in common. The rich inheritance of justice, liberty, prosperity and independence, bequeathed by your fathers, is shared by you, not by me. The sunlight that brought life and healing to you, has brought stripes and death to me. This Fourth [of] July is yours, not mine.
4. You may rejoice, I must mourn. To drag a man in fetters into the grand illuminated temple of liberty, and call upon him to join you in joyous anthems, were inhuman mockery and sacrilegious irony. Do you mean, citizens, to mock me, by asking me to speak to-day? If so, there is a parallel to your conduct . . . .
5. Fellow-citizens; above your national, tumultous joy, I hear the mournful wail of millions! whose chains, heavy and grievous yesterday, are, to-day, rendered more intolerable by the jubilee shouts that reach them . . . . I shall see, this day, and its popular characteristics, from the slave's point of view. Standing, there, identified with the American bondman, making his wrongs mine, I do not hesitate to declare, with all my soul, that the character and conduct of this nation never looked blacker to me than on this 4th of July! . . .
6. What point in the anti-slavery creed would you have me argue? On what branch of the subject do the people of this country need light? Must I undertake to prove that the slave is a man? That point is conceded already. Nobody doubts it.
7. The slaveholders themselves acknowledge it in the enactment of laws for their government. They acknowledge it when they punish disobedience on the part of the slave. There are seventy-two crimes in the State of Virginia, which, if committed by a black man, (no matter how ignorant he be),

subject him to the punishment of death; while only two of the same crimes will subject a white man to the like punishment.

8. What is this but the acknowledgment that the slave is a moral, intellectual and responsible being? The manhood of the slave is conceded. It is admitted in the fact that Southern statute books are covered with enactments forbidding, under severe fines and penalties, the teaching of the slave to read or to write.
9. When you can point to any such laws, in reference to the beasts of the field, then I may consent to argue the manhood of the slave. When the dogs in your streets, when the fowls of the air, when the cattle on your hills, when the fish of the sea, and the reptiles that crawl, shall be unable to distinguish the slave from a brute, then will I argue with you that the slave is a man!
10. [Definition:] For the present, it is enough to affirm the equal manhood of the negro race. Is it not astonishing that, while we are ploughing, planting and reaping, using all kinds of mechanical tools, erecting houses, constructing bridges, building ships, working in metals of brass, iron, copper, silver and gold; that, while we are reading, writing and cyphering, acting as clerks, merchants and secretaries, having among us lawyers, doctors, ministers, poets, authors, editors, orators and teachers; that, while we are engaged in all manner of enterprises common to other men, digging gold in California, capturing the whale in the Pacific, feeding sheep and cattle on the hill-side, living, moving, acting, thinking, planning, living in families as husbands, wives and children, and, above all, confessing and worshipping the Christian's God, and looking hopefully for life and immortality beyond the grave, we are called upon to prove that we are men! . . .
11. [Value:] What, am I to argue that it is wrong to make men brutes, to rob them of their liberty, to work them without wages, to keep them ignorant of their relations to their fellow men, to beat them with sticks, to flay their flesh with the lash, to load their limbs with irons, to hunt them with dogs, to sell them at auction, to sunder their families, to knock out their teeth, to bum their flesh, to starve them into obedience and submission to their masters? Must I argue that a system thus marked with blood, and stained with pollution, is wrong? No! I will not. I have better employments for my time and strength, than such arguments would imply.
12. What, then, remains to be argued? Is it that slavery is not divine; that God did not establish it; that our doctors of divinity are mistaken? There is blasphemy in the thought. That which is inhuman, cannot be divine! Who can reason on such a proposition? They that can, may; I cannot. The time for such argument is past.
13. [Policy:] At a time like this, scorching irony, not convincing argument, is needed. O! had I the ability, and could I reach the nation's ear, I would, to-day, pour out a fiery stream of biting ridicule, blasting reproach, withering sarcasm, and stern rebuke. For it is not light that is needed, but fire; it is not the gentle shower, but thunder. We need the storm, the whirlwind, and the earthquake. The feeling of the nation must be quickened; the conscience of the nation must be roused; the propriety of the nation must be startled; the hypocrisy of the nation must be exposed; and its crimes against God and man must be proclaimed and denounced.

From "What to the Slave Is the Fourth of July?" (1852)

Analysis of Douglass's Use of the Four Questions

In this portion of his address Douglass used the four questions in the order we have listed them. The section on conjecture is the longest. First, he conjectured the Fourth of July holiday as a celebration of America's "political freedom" and "natural justice, embodied in that Declaration of Independence." This conjecture does considerable persuasive work when it is contrasted against another—that the nation devoted to freedom and justice had denied these rights to slaves. He then conjectured that the situation of slaves is made yet more miserable by celebrations of independence because the comparison highlighted and reinforced the differences between the conditions of slavery and citizenship. Then, employing a nice turn of phrase, he conjectured that it is white America whose soul is "black" because of practices associated with slavery: as proof he recited a myriad of laws and punishments that applied only to black people, including a proscription against their becoming literate.

Some who argued against abolition of slavery made the ugly argument that slaves were not human beings. In the next two paragraphs of his speech, then, Douglass employed definition to argue that slaves are indeed men. One simple way to create definitions is to establish a class, such as "men," and then to place whatever term you are interested in defining into that class. Then, you can add details that show the term's kinship with all other members of the class. This is called *species-genus* definition. Douglass used it here to establish that slaves undertake all the activities that free people do: they dig for gold, capture whales, feed sheep and cattle, have families, and practice Christianity. Another way to employ species-genus definition is to establish a class such as "animals" and show how the term you are interested in defining differs from all other members of that class. Douglass employs this strategy when he argues that laws made to deny slaves equality are not made or enforced against "the fowls of the air," "the cattle on your hills," "the fish of the sea," or "reptiles that crawl." The force of the two strategies of definition, taken together, establishes that according to America's own code of law, slaves cannot be animals. Therefore, they must be men.

WORKSHOP 13: Readers Responding

This workshop offers powerful strategies for approaching reading as serious writers do, with a critical eye for the most important arguments and ideas. Following the strategies presented in this workshop, you will gain skills as an engaged reader and become more able to put what you read to work in your own writing.

WORKSHOP 16: Summarizing Arguments, Ideas, and Texts

Writers regularly present the work of others as building blocks for their own work. This workshop offers strategies for writing strong summaries to incorporate into your own writing.

WORKSHOP 8: Following Pathways: A Metaphor for Critical Reading and Research

Reading and research are like travel. They take us into the territory of new ideas and arguments. The exercises in this workshop will help you identify unfamiliar ideas and references and to approach them as opportunities for learning, or in other words, "pathways" to knowledge.

Douglass then turned to the question of value, arguing vehemently that slavery is wrong. Douglass's evaluation of slavery as immoral rested on two claims. First, slavery was against Christian doctrine, and second, slavery deprived the enslaved of the chance for self-determination. Douglass skillfully exploited the power and prevalence of the precepts of Christianity and self-reliance in the United States in making this argument from values. Last, he turns to policy, urging himself (and his audience?) on to ever greater heights of oratory, in order that the injustice and cruelty of slavery be made so clear that the "conscience of the nation" will be aroused.

Invention Journal: Working Through the Questions

1. Use the stasis questions to focus your interest in the critical situation at hand and to identify as many perspectives and arguments as possible. Begin by writing a brief summary of your chosen critical situation. Now pose the first question, *conjecture*. Does the disagreement rest here (X exists; X is a problem)? Is the reality or existence of the situation in question? Look back at your summary; will others acknowledge the reality of what you've written? Is the existence of specific elements of the situation in question? Consulting appropriate sources, some of which may emerge during this analysis, write out all of the conjectures about your critical situation that you can imagine.
2. Now move on to the second question, *definition*. Is the major disagreement here X is a particular kind of thing or event)? Will others define the situation as you have, or are there alternate definitions? Look at the key terms of your situation summary; will they be disputed by those who have a different perspective?
3. Move on to the third question, *quality*. Is this the point of disagreement (X is a good or a bad thing)? What is the range of arguments made about the fairness, cruelty, stupidity, compassion, greediness, generosity, etc. at play in a given situation?
4. Finally, pose the final of the fOUf questions, *policy*. Is this where the disagreement lies (we should take X course of action)? What are all the available arguments about what should be done in response to the critical situation at hand?

AN EXAMPLE FROM THE CONTEXT OF 9/11: FLIGHT 77

If your project requires you to examine your situation in more depth, you can elaborate each of the four categories into several more specific questions. In the following list, we have applied more specific questions from each category to the event which occurred at the Pentagon on September 11, 2001. We used the system of stasis here to examine arguments that have already been made, rather than as means of invention. Nonetheless, our use of the questions turned up a few arguments that challenge those already made, thus demonstrating that invention can be stimulated by analysis of arguments advanced by others. There are avenues we did not pursue, nor did we thoroughly investigate the arguments raised by our use of the elaborated and more specific questions. Accordingly, our example should not be followed mechanically. Every context is different, and each issue provokes more interesting answers from one or two of the sets of questions than from the others.

There are at least four ways of making and investigating conjectures. One can ask: Is the thing, event, or position I am examining true? Does/did the thing or event exist? What is/was its origin? What caused it? What changes may occur in it or because of it?

Elaborated Questions of Conjecture

Does it exist? Is it true?

Where did it come from? How did it begin?

What is its cause?

Can it be changed? What changed because of it?

Speculation abounds on the Internet about events that occurred on September 11, 2001. Conjecture has proven to be an especially rich source of invention for people who do not accept official accounts of events that occurred on that day. Government sources and the mainline media assert that American Airlines Flight 77, a Boeing 757, was hijacked and crashed into the Pentagon, killing all on board—including the hijackers—and killing and injuring many people who worked inside the building. Those who do not accept this account conjecture that the Pentagon was hit by some other craft or by a missile. As we noted earlier, Meyssan conjectures that a missile—a much smaller object than a Boeing 757—caused the hole in the building. Other writers think the object may have been a smaller aircraft—perhaps an F-16, commonly used in the American military, or a small commercial jetliner. A truly wild conjecture holds that the craft that hit the building was indeed Flight 77, but that the passengers were no longer on board.

The official account gives a very clear answer to the question "where did it come from?": the plot was concocted and financed by Osama bin Laden. We still do not know the answers to other conjectural questions, though, such as how the plot began. Nor do we know exactly what caused bin Laden to risk so much in order to harm the United States, although here, too, speculation is rife. When we ask these questions with regard to the revisionist narrative, our answers are equally speculative. If the object that penetrated the Pentagon was a military plane or a missile, a huge military or government conspiracy has to be constructed to explain how this could have happened. Other causal possibilities exist, of course—the firing of a missile or the crash of an F-16 into the Pentagon could have been a horrible accident, occurring coincidently on the same day as the massive assault on the World Trade Center. Another causal possibility is that the missile or small plane was controlled by the government of another nation.

Many answers have been given to the question "what changed?" because of 9/11. Clearly, after that day Americans realized that our relative geographical isolation is no protection from terrorist acts. And, as Norman Mailer speculated in a work quoted earlier in this book, Americans also began to rethink their reputation in the world. Many were stunned when they realized that people in other parts of the world could hate Americans so much as to mount an attack of this magnitude. And for those who accept Meyssan's countering narrative about events at the Pentagon, the answer to the question "what changed?" is: our faith in our government and our military, whose traditional function is to protect us from assaults of this kind.

Sometimes use of the questions of conjecture establishes that there is no conjectural point at issue—although this is certainly not the case regarding the incident at the Pentagon. Sometimes use of these questions can also show that a writer or speaker wishes to take up a different position on an issue, or that she wants to examine another issue altogether. Because invention often produces surprises you must be prepared for the possibility that you will change your mind while doing this work. Considered as a way of mapping a critical situation, the questions reveal previously unexamined territory. When using this or any means of invention, then, you should always allow time for changes in your position to occur and mature.

Try to discover as many depictions of the state of affairs, their possible origins or causes, and their possible changes over time as you can. Once you have done that, you can move on to the category of definition. Here is an elaboration of that category:

Elaborated Questions of Definition

What kind of thing or event is it?

To what larger class of things does it belong?

What are its parts? How are they related?

As we suggested earlier, the official account of the event at the Pentagon classifies it as a terrorist attack. Thierry Meyssan and other sources classify the event, rather, as a military or government conspiracy. To ask "what are its parts" and "how are they related" discloses some other interesting arguments available in this critical situation. The necessary "parts" of a terrorist attack are by now familiar to most Americans: a clandestine organization named Al Qaeda whose leader hates America and who espouses terrorism as a way to get what he wants; a well-thought-out plan of attack that took several years to implement; 19 hijackers who were trained by Al Qaeda to carry out such attacks; careful planning; lax airport security; slow response to the hijackings by the FAA and NORAD, and so on. When we ask "how are these parts related," several answers suggest themselves—the 9/11 Commission concluded, for example, that government agencies manifested a certain level of incompetence when they permitted four planes to fly off course without being intercepted and shot down. On the other hand, when conspiracy theorists list or map these "parts" of the attack, they sometimes draw the conclusion that Al Qaeda simply cannot be responsible. They argue that hijacking four aircraft and flying them into buildings requires a level of planning, funding, and technological expertise well beyond the resources of a small band of terrorists. Moreover, conspiracy theorists say, classifying this event as a terrorist attack does not explain why America's defense systems did not protect Washington, D.C., and New York City as they should have done.

Elaborated Questions of Value

Questions of value may be asked in two ways: simply or by comparison. Simple questions attempt to determine the worth of a thing, idea, or event—its justice or rightness or honor—or how much the community desires it. Comparative questions put things, ideas, or events in the context of other values, comparing in order to determine priorities among the community's values.

There are three kinds of simple questions of quality: what to seek and what to avoid, what is right and what wrong, and what is honorable and what is base.

Elaborated Simple Questions of Quality

Is it a good or a bad thing?

Should it be sought or avoided?

Is it right or wrong?

Is it honorable or dishonorable?

Presumably, most Americans believe that the events of September 11 were a bad thing; moreover, most believe that those responsible for these events acted wrongly and behaved dishonorably. In order to avoid the possibility that such events happen again, Congress established the Department of Homeland Security and passed the controversial Patriot Act. Those held responsible by the official account, of course, must value things quite differently. Reportedly, the hijackers desired to become martyrs, and those who agree with them celebrate their honor and assert the rightness of their cause. And if we subject the position of Meyssan and other conspiracy theorists to the simple questions of value, other arguments appear. For a government to harm its own citizens is a very bad and dishonorable thing indeed, and, like most Americans, revisionists very much want those who are responsible to be brought to justice.

In this case the questions of value can also be turned on the competing accounts themselves in order to determine their relative quality. For example, under the second question the following claim can emerge: theories about the cause of 9/11 ought to be avoided unless they can be proven, because making claims of this importance without proof may be irresponsible. There are other interesting ways to ask the second simple question of value in this case. Of course terrorist or government plots against the people should always be avoided. But we could also ask if theories about such government conspiracies against the people should be sought or avoided. Answers to this question could be found by asking whether such theories are good or bad things. Do such conspiracy theories undermine faith in our institutions? Or are they merely pastimes that harm no one? Is it right or wrong, honorable or dishonorable, to fashion and disseminate such theories? Which of these accounts raises questions about loyalty? About justice? About courage? You will surely find that people make arguments based on these values when you examine your own critical situation.

Elaborated Comparative Questions of Quality

Is it better or worse than something else?

Is it more desirable than any alternatives?

Is it less desirable than any alternatives?

Is it more or less right than something else?

Is it more or less wrong than something else?

Is it more honorable than something else?

Is it less honorable than something else?

Is it more base than something else?

Is it less base than something else?

The controversy over events at the Pentagon on September 11 can perhaps be better understood if we compare the official account with the conspiracy account, always keeping our eyes on which is more or less valuable as a means of explaining what happened that day. Which account is better or worse? If we define "better" and "worse" as scientists do, the terms refer to the explanatory power of each version of the event. In scientific terms, the "better" account explains more of the evidence while making fewer unsupported assumptions. While neither account is entirely satisfactory in this regard, the official version better explains some of the evidence, such as the loss of Flight 77 and reports from eyewitnesses who were close to the Pentagon, as well as those who claim to have seen a large commercial aircraft flying very low up the Potomac River toward the Pentagon on the morning in question. However, the conspiracy account supplies better explanations of other bits of evidence. For example, revisionists point to photographs taken shortly after the crash, but before the facade collapse, that show a single small hole in the building. In these photographs bits and pieces of metal and wiring lie on the lawn of the Pentagon, but there are no larger pieces of debris such as one might expect from the crash of a Boeing 757 (of course any and all photographs taken after the event could have been doctored or "photoshopped"). Furthermore, some eyewitnesses say they saw a small craft fly into the building.

If, however, we think of "better" and "worse" as nonscientific terms that represent value judgments, we can unearth some very serious questions and arguments. Which explanation—terrorism or conspiracy—is better for the future of America? Which is worse? Which explanation is more honorable? It is much more comfortable to believe that enemies of America perpetrated this awful act, and hence behaved dishonorably (from our point of view), than to accept that our government behaved basely by lying to us and by arranging the murder of 3,000 people? Other questions of comparative value are available here as well: for example, which account is more terrifying? More unpleasant or disgusting?

As this example makes clear, the questions of quality are ordinarily very productive. Often, working through them systematically offers an opportunity to articulate and compare arguments that we take for granted but which may be controversial to others.

In questions of policy, the writer or speaker proposes that some action be taken or that some action be regulated (or not) by means of a policy or law. Questions of policy are usually twofold: someone who wishes to put forward a question or issue of policy must first deliberate about the need for it and then argue for its implementation.

Questions of Policy

Need Questions:

Should some action be taken?

Given the situation, what actions are possible? Desirable?

How will proposed actions change the current state of affairs? Or should the current state of affairs remain unchanged?

How will the proposed changes make things better? Worse? How? In what ways? For whom?

Implementation Questions:

Should some state of affairs be regulated (or not) by some formalized policy?

Which policies can be implemented? Which cannot?

What are the merits of competing proposals? What are their defects?

How is my proposal better than others? Worse?

Following on the events of September 11, the Bush administration proposed that military force be used in Afghanistan, and later in Iraq, to oppose the "war on terror." However, other courses of action were available to a government that accepted the official account of those events, and anyone who is interested in this issue should list those policy possibilities. Some of them are: doing nothing; using diplomacy to ferret out terrorists in other countries; mounting covert operations in this and other countries to find suspected terrorists and curtail their activities; asking the United Nations and/or NATO to pursue suspected terrorists and/or to intervene on our behalf with countries suspected of harboring terrorists, and so on. As we first drafted this chapter in 2003, furious debate was taking place about the second need question—which of these actions was most desirable. Proponents of war said that the U.S. military is the only policy instrument that is sufficiently well trained and equipped to find and stop terrorists and terrorism. Opponents of this policy argued that war is an undesirable response in part because it does not meet the basic need—discouraging and eliminating terrorism; rather it encourages the spread of terrorist ideology. A fierce debate also raged over the fourth need question: some commentators thought that a so-called "stable Iraq" would make the world safer, while others argued that preemptive armed intervention into the affairs of a sovereign country would make the world a far more dangerous place. As we revise this chapter prior to printing, more than four years later, the available positions on this issue are no less controversial than they were in 2003.

The implementation questions depend on decisions about values that are made during earlier explorations. If you decide that a policy should be implemented, you need to consider whether or not it will be acceptable to those concerned. When President Bush suggested going to war against terrorists, Congress and many Americans concurred. However, members of the United Nations and other countries balked at intervention into the affairs of Iraq. Some who did so raised a question of definition once again: can the Iraqi people and their leader be classified as terrorists? You can expect that policy recommendations will require the other questions to be revisited, as they were in this case.

The questions are useful for beating a path through the thicket of positions which often surround a controversy. There are many more positions and arguments available within the situations faced by abolitionists and 9/11 theorists than those we found by using the questions. However, even our preliminary use of this heuristic discloses its rich argumentative possibilities. Again, our examples should not be followed slavishly, as though they model all possible uses of the questions. The critical situations that gave rise to controversies are very different from one another. Because issues arise within specific situations, the questions can never be applied mechanically. The positions they turn up will differ from situation to situation, so anyone who uses them must be alert to all the possibilities they raise in any case. Writers and speakers should always be ready to follow any tangent thrown up by their consideration of the questions.

The more time and energy you allot to invention, the more arguments you will discover. We have only scratched the surface of the available arguments generated by application of the questions of stasis to the events of 9/11. While we were doing this exercise, we discovered that were we to map the issue to the fullest extent made possible by the questions of stasis, we would end up writing another book. This is, of course, another advantage of this means of invention—while engaging in it, you discover the scope or size or complexity of the issue you have chosen to study. Once you know this, you can decide whether you possess the available time and energy to address the issue at length, or whether it's necessary to confine your project to a small part of your potential area of investigation.

WORKSHOP 2: Arranging Your Composition

As you discover arguments through invention, consider how they will fit together when you sit down to write. This workshop is devoted to "arrangement," the skillful structuring of arguments.

WORKSHOP 15: Revising for Clarity

This workshop offers revising strategies for increasing the clarity of writing. Increasing the clarity of your ideas will help you connect with your intended audience.

WORKSHOP 12: Putting Together a Portfolio of Your Invention Work

Gathering your invention work together in a portfolio creates a record of your thought, research, and analysis. This workshop offers a simple framework for constructing a portfolio and writing a critical self-reflection on the progress of your project.

Invention Journal: Composing a Proposal

If you wish to recommend that a policy or procedure be implemented, here are some suggestions for composing it. Find out how similar policies are enacted in similar situations, and base your own proposal on that policy if it is a good model for your critical situation. Compose a plan for implementing the policy that you suggest. You should also determine how the policy that you recommend can be enforced. If you are recommending, on the other hand, that some public practice be implemented or changed, you must first compose your recommendation. Then, find out who can make the changes you suggest, and find out what procedures must be followed in order to make the recommended change. You should also try to find out how your recommended change can be implemented and enforced, and offer suggestions for achieving this.

LIST OF WORKS CITED

Bamford, James. *Body of Secrets: Anatomy of the Ultra-Secret National Security Agency.* New York: Random House, 2002.

Douglass, Frederick. *The Frederick Douglass Papers: Speeches, Debates, and Interviews.* Ed. John W. Blassingame. 5 vols. New Haven: Yale UP, 1979.

Meyssan, Thierry. *9/11 The Big Lie.* London: Carnot, 2002.

4

NAVIGATING RHETORICAL TIME

One of our students, Heather Johnson, wrote the following letter for the *New York Times* in late October of 2004:

> To the Editor:
>
> With Election Day quickly approaching, I have been campaigned ad nauseam especially in regard to the war on terror. Whether "W stands for "Women" or "W stands for Wrong on Women," I have yet to see substantial comment about the terror women face in regard to domestic violence. The U.S. Dept. of Health and Human Services estimates that 4 million women are affected by domestic violence each year, whether or not they are immigrants or minorities (Women Likelier to Be Slain by a Partner Than a Stranger, Oct 22). While this may be a small percentage of the 118 million who are estimated to turn out to vote next Tuesday, it seems substantial in comparison to the 537 Florida votes that may have determined the 2000 election. We should be concerned about international terrorists, but equal attention should be given to those living within our borders who terrorize women and children every day. It is hard to worry about Osama bin Laden when your partner is an imminent threat. If either candidate really wants the support of women, they should give more focus to women's issues. Or are they worried about losing the votes of the abusers?

This letter is a model of good timing. Johnson gives her readers a strong sense of the occasion of her commentary on domestic abuse by linking it to the upcoming election. In fact, every sentence of her letter to the editor draws its persuasive force from the proximity of the "quickly approaching" election. Presenting domestic violence as a conspicuous absence in the platform of both presidential candidates, Johnson capitalizes on the likelihood that other citizens are weary of the "ad nauseam" campaigning that was building to a fever pitch at the time of her writing. The disturbing statistics Johnson offers make a good introductory case for the need for immediate action to address a critical social issue and might well make voters wonder why the candidates had seen fit to ignore domestic violence as a campaign issue. Johnson also taps into the concerns of those who believe that the political focus on the "war on terror" takes financial resources and attention away from other pressing daily issues that citizens face. Finally, Johnson's letter catches the momentum of

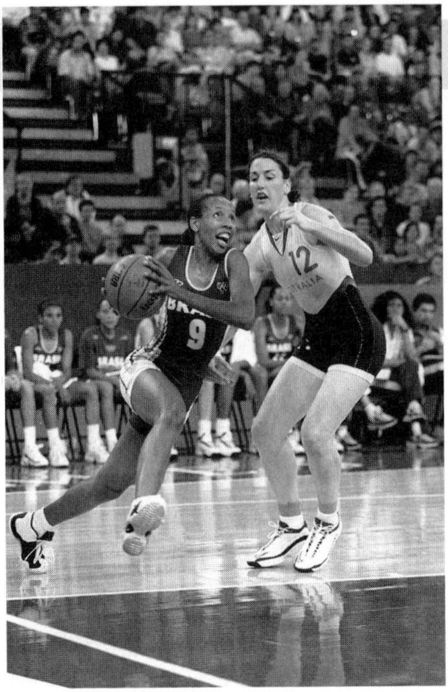

Point Guard Janeth Arcain
It's quite common to describe athletes such as WNBA star Janeth Arcain as "poetry in motion." We think that the graceful mind-body integration of Arcain's performance captures perfectly the notion of rhetorical timeliness.

widespread commentary during "Domestic Violence Awareness Month," widely publicized by the Family Violence Protection Fund throughout October.

If Johnson's letter is a good example of timing in a political discussion, a point guard handling the ball in a basketball game is a good example of timing in action. Driving to the basket she is aware not just of the placement of defenders and teammates to whom she might pass. She also maintains an awareness of the relative abilities of each of these players. Is the challenging defender too quick to beat off the dribble? Should she pull up and take a shot? If so, are any teammates in a position to get the rebound? Has the forward sprinting up the right side of the court sufficiently recovered from her ankle sprain to reach a leading pass? Can the center out-muscle her defender for a lob pass? Is the angle right for a behind-the-back pass to the other forward trailing up the opposite side of the court? Should she challenge the defender to her left who is already in foul trouble, perhaps drawing contact and thus causing her to "foul out" of the game? Is there time on the shot clock to slow down the pace of the game and run a set offensive play? A good point guard must weigh all such options in order to be master of the moment.

Examples of rhetorical timeliness abound in public life. A celebrity entertainer awaiting trial might take an opportunity to make a public appearance in the name of a philanthropic cause. A commentator refers to the anniversary of *Brown v. Board of Education,* a landmark legal case that challenged either to extol the democratic virtues of American schools in the twenty-first century or to make a cause for greater attention to issues of access and equity for underrepresented student groups. A policy announcement that government officials expect to be unpopular might be made late Friday afternoon in order to avoid more extensive public notice. Politicians from one party wait for new wrinkles in foreign and domestic policy to make the case that a president should be replaced in the next election. Reports of new jobs and economic upturn bolster the administration's economic policy. The first day of summer in Phoenix provides the occasion for informal environmental policy debate regarding forest fires and water conservation. A concerned citizen takes the opportunity afforded by a captive audience to preach a sermon to a bus full of people. There is no single measure of good timing, but all of these examples have in common some strategy of finding opportunities (as with scheduled or regularly occurring occasions for speech and writing) and creating opportunities (by persuading an audience about the "essence of the moment").

Often, performers and athletes embody a mastery of the moment to an impressive degree. It is a comedic truism that "timing is everything." A talented stand-up comedian responding to hecklers is able to turn the threat of embarrassment and professional failure into humor, likely at the expense of the heckler. Hip-hop artistry provides another example. A lyrical "battle" between two hip-hop MCs can be a showcase of quick thinking and elaborate references to contemporary politics and culture. Hip-hop artists commonly exhort us to wise up and understand "what time it is." A politically charged group like Public Enemy, whose Flavor Flav inevitably wears a clock around his neck, tells us that "knowing what time it is" means understanding the occasion, understanding, for example, that social revolution is what the moment demands. To "know what time it is" rhetorically is to understand and navigate the dynamics of a situation as it plays out.

Public Enemy in Performance

Public Enemy is among the groups of the first generation of what is often called "conscious rap," that is, artists committed to the politics of social change. A Public Enemy show often has the feel of a rally, not just a concert.

ANCIENT THINKING ABOUT RHETORICAL TIME

Our thinking about rhetorical time is strongly influenced by the ancient Greek notion of ***kairos,*** for which there is no completely satisfactory English translation; even among those who study and teach rhetoric, kairos remains an elusive concept. James L. Kinneavy's translation of kairos as "situational context" Can serve as a provisional definition. ("Kairos" 80). The phrase suggests how contexts shift in time, and we would do well to take our cue here, paying attention to the complexity and changeability of the critical situations in which we work. Kairos draws attention to the **qualitative** as well as **quantitative time.** Historians of rhetoric often juxtapose kairos with the Greek *chronos* (the root from which we get our English word "chronology"). We suggest that within the sequence of time as we measure it with clocks and calendars there are openings, moments which through some combination of circumstance, writerly or speakerly skill, and disposition of audience, amount to an opportunity for successful communication. Think of it this way: history deals us cards as it unfolds, but we can have some say in how we play those cards. Taking a "kairotic" stance as a writer or speaker means being prepared to make the best of a difficult circumstance and to make the most of an opportunity when it emerges. Heather Johnson's letter skill fully navigates a kairotic moment amidst chronology. Her letter gains evidence from Domestic Violence Awareness Month and the election year. She combined these elements to make a strong case for the critical need for action and change *now.* Johnson's intention was to influence her audience's sense of the meaning of the moment.

Johnson's letter raises important questions for serious writers and speakers seeking to understand how rhetorical time works within a critical situation. How can we make the most of opportunities as writers and speakers? How do we become aware of the most advantageous moments to present our work to an audience, to "go public" in other words? How do we make the most of unexpected developments that make our message timely or that give our arguments real punch? How can we anticipate audience reactions to our words given how dynamic and unpredictable any audience might actually be? How can we make our audiences understand the urgency of a critical situation as we understand it? There are no easy answers to these questions but connecting with audiences, winning support and changing minds will have a lot to do with timing. Forums and deadlines and other clock- and calendar-specific circumstances must be dealt with in order to reach an appropriate audience, of course. Opportunity for speakers and writers working on community-based projects might happen on schedule—at a city council meeting for instance. Or, it might occur randomly, as when new evidence comes to light and gives you greater confidence in the argument you want to make to a book club for mothers regarding genetically modified baby food.

To persuade audiences a speaker or writer must first *be heard,* which is in part a matter of picking the right time to go public. Some audiences are simply not ready to hear some arguments at some times. In the months after 9/11, for example, almost 90 percent of Americans supported America's going to war in Iraq; as we finish revising this chapter, however, more than half of Americans surveyed by a CNN poll

(55 percent) think the war was a mistake (May 1, 2006). In other words, arguments in support of the war got a much more supportive hearing in 2002 and 2003 than they received in 2006. How will the positions you are taking in your critical situation likely be heard in this moments?

INVENTION AND RHETORICAL TIME

It is crucial that serious writers and speakers also think about time along different lines as something that they can have a hand in inventing. In many cases, a speaker or writer can influence the way audiences perceive the moment at hand. If we view time a rhetoricians, we can begin to think of time as inseparable from the situations that move us to write and speak to audiences. Connecting with audiences—persuading, inspiring, informing, provoking, enraging, or calming them—is a matter of convincing them about the current state of events, or reality. Speakers and writers can actually *invent convincing moments* by persuading an audience that it is time to do something about domestic violence, or that it is time to go to war, that it is time to start recycling, to invest more money in public education, or to reconsider a law that no longer serves the public interest.

Physicists tell us that time is relative, and writers and speakers do well to take this as a principle. Rhetorical time is relative to the perspectives brought to bear on any situation; a situation is "current" only because there is difference and disagreement. Ancient rhetoricians understood that truths are contingent or uncertain when considered across a range of social experience by different people. The "reality" of the moment simply isn't agreed upon; we don't perceive events in the same way. This divergence of belief and perception, the inevitable complexity of thinking about the perceived truths of a current situation, renders kairos a matter of importance for any serious speaker or writer. Researching the rhetorical time frame begins with a mapping of different positions on "the now." For instance, after the attacks of September 11, 2001, people understood the moment in quite different ways. Across the country and around the world, there were different senses of a new historical moment. Some thought that a new age of terror had begun; others claimed that it was time for the United States to go on the offensive, to respond with force. Yet others said that the age of American political innocence was over, that it was time for United States citizens to come together courageously as one people, or that the long-delayed day of retribution for United States foreign policy had finally come. Clearly, one's place in the world would influence one's sense of the truth of any of these conjuctures. These multiple perspectives suggest the complexity of the writer or speaker's job in gauging the currents of thought and belief.

From the stands at a basketball game, the point guard's graceful pass, smooth shot, or quick move may look like instinct, but any athlete will tell you that the instincts must be trained, that being "in the zone" is as much habit than gift. Just as athletes must practice, you must invent, extensively researching and analyzing the dynamics of your critical situation to develop the most effective approach. Conceiving of a rhetorical time frame in which your project will be composed and will reach its audience helps you to understand opportunities and resources that might otherwise remain hidden or overlooked. The invention exercises in this chapter offer strategies for finding the greatest potential "in the moment" of the critical situation you are addressing. Thinking in terms of timing offers many advantages to writers and speakers. First, it helps us to connect with all the major stakeholders in a critical situation, thus informing us about what makes the situation urgent from a variety of perspectives. Second, rhetorical timing also helps us to identify the maximally effective range of times and places in which we can make our work public. Third, a sense of rhetorical timing can help writers and speakers to develop strategies for connecting with audiences in such a way that their work will be persuasive.

Fourth, writers and speakers who are sensitive to timeliness are also able to define the importance of the moment by linking critical situations to other events and situations, thus expanding the sense of importance or urgency for an audience. Last, a sense of appropriate rhetorical timing allows writers and speakers to locate the critical situation within a broader historical context, comparing it to important precedents. This allows us, in turn, to make strong arguments about causality and to emphasize the social stakes involved in our work.

The second half of this chapter is devoted to helping you develop rhetorical timing by using these strategies in the context of your own critical situations. Before we get to that, however, we want to introduce a landmark example of kairos in action.

WORKSHOP 3: Different Values and Respectful Conflict

If you get through several weeks of the project workshop, let alone an entire semester or quarter, without some disagreements, this would be unusual. This workshop requires that class members share their positions on social issues. It's unlikely all will always agree. This workshop offers some well-tested guidelines for fostering respectful and productive collaborative work.

CASE STUDY: PHILADELPHIA'S "LATE AWFUL CALAMITY" IN 1793

We turn again to the history of abolitionism for an example of powerful language use amid a challenging critical situation. In 1793, Philadelphia suffered a yellow fever epidemic in which thousands of people died. African American citizens were called upon to tend the sick and to bury the dead. A pamphlet written by Matthew Carey, a successful white printer, accused Philadelphia's African American inhabitants of charging unreasonable prices for carrying out these dangerous chores. Carey also charged that African American caretakers had looted the homes of sick and dying white people. Understandably there was concern in the African American community over the impact of Carey's pamphlet; the white population of the day was all too ready to rally around pronouncements about black criminality. Unsupported charges of African American offenses were often used to excuse real crimes against African Americans.

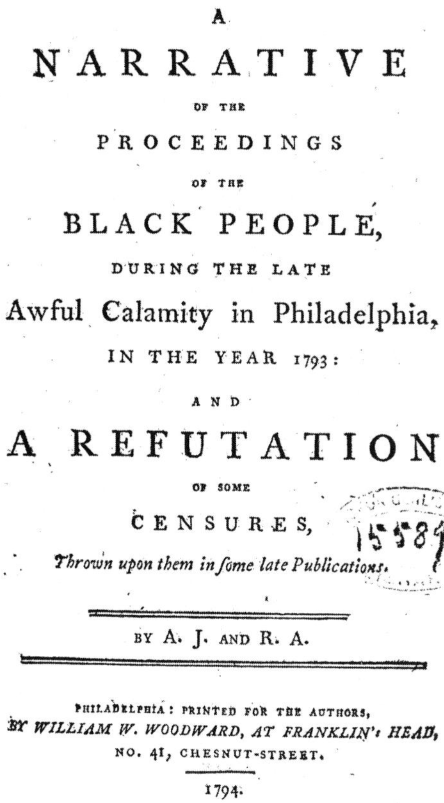
A
NARRATIVE
OF THE
PROCEEDINGS
OF THE
BLACK PEOPLE,
DURING THE LATE
Awful Calamity in Philadelphia,
IN THE YEAR 1793:
AND
A REFUTATION
OF SOME
CENSURES,
Thrown upon them in ſome late Publications.

BY A. J. AND R. A.

PHILADELPHIA: PRINTED FOR THE AUTHORS,
BY WILLIAM W. WOODWARD, AT FRANKLIN's HEAD,
NO. 41, CHESNUT-STREET.
1794.

The Pamphlets of Matthew Carey, Absalom Jones, and Richard Allen
Printer Matthew Carey's pamphlet recounting the yellow fever epidemic in Philadelphia in 1793 accused African American Philadelphians of taking advantage of the tragedy for personal gain. The response written by African American ministers Absalom Jones and Richard Allen not only disputed these charges, but also used the occasion to defend African American humanity generally and to speak out strongly against racial oppression in the young republic.

Richard Allen and Absalom Jones, prominent African American ministers and civic leaders, spoke for the community in their reply to Carey. "A Narrative of the Proceedings of the Black People During the Late Awful Calamity in Philadelphia" was printed and circulated in defense of the African-American community. However, the arguments put forth in the pamphlet are anything but defensive. Unfavorable circumstances may have pushed Jones and Allen to write, but rhetorical skill helped to turn those circumstances into the occasion of opportunity:

> It is unpleasant for us to make these remarks, but justice to our colour, demands it . . . . We conceive, and experience proves it, that an ill name is easier given than

> taken away. We have many unprovoked enemies, who begrudge us the liberty we enjoy, and are glad to hear of any complaint against our colour, be it just or unjust; in consequence of which we are more earnestly endeavouring all in our power, to arm, rebuke, and exhort our African friends to keep a conscience void of offence towards God and man; and, at the same time, would not be backward to interfere, when stigmas or oppression appear pointed at, or, attempted against them, unjustly; and, we are confident, we shall stand justified in the sight of the candid and judicious, for such conduct. (qtd. in Newman et al. 38)

This passage is a frank acknowledgment of the importance of rhetorical timing. Jones and Allen argue that to let the moment go by without making some defense of their community would be tantamount to accepting the unfair charges, the "ill name . . . given." By framing their remarks as a discussion among "candid and judicious" people, Jones and Allen refute the powerful contemporary assumption that black people are irrational, a commonplace that was in wide circulation within the white supremacist culture of the day.

Because Jones and Allen's pamphlet is one of the first patented texts written by African Americans, its publication marked a historically important moment. In this historical moment, as now, it was an article of faith that the ability to speak eloquently on ones own behalf was a mark of virtue. Jones and Allen addressed their audience in the manner of dutiful citizens, speaking out of necessity, maintaining the measured tone and qualified claims expected of the public discourse of the day in spite of the powerful emotions inspired by social crisis. This was a crucial matter of rhetorical timing because in the wake of the "calamity," the conduct of African American citizens is exactly what was in question. This moment demanded the utmost attention to proper decorum from these writers, who were entering public discourse. Above all, their formal response to Carey exemplified the capacity and desire for self-determination that is still assumed to be the moral bedrock of our national character. Thus, the twin plagues of racial oppression and yellow fever actually created a kairotic occasion, one which allowed Jones and Allen to make a powerful assertion of social identity.

Jones and Allen also used the occasion of the pamphlet to provide a rallying point and a much needed voice of encouragement for African American Philadelphians. The authors understood the strong arguments they made as a rhetorical resource with which to "arm" their compatriots. They took the opportunity as well to "rebuke" and "exhort" African American Philadelphians so that as a people they might "keep a conscience void of offence towards God and man." To be sure, Jones and Allen understood that the dispute over "conduct" sparked by the yellow fever epidemic was a dramatic example of the pressures always at work in a white supremacist culture. Any offense, real or perceived, could be used to legitimate racial hierarchy and racial violence. Jones and Allen, as ministers, took the opportunity to counsel against "offense towards God and man" and to note that, for African Americans, this call for moral perfection was a matter of survival.

The authors' sense of rhetorical timing also allowed them to tap into the emotional dynamics of the moment. Recollections like the one below of an "affecting instance" provide evidence not only that African descended people are eloquent, rational, and self-determining, but that they maintained strong emotional connections to others and were making a heartfelt response to tragedy, a response that should be shared between people whatever their race:

> An affecting instance—A woman died, we were sent for to bury her, on our going into the house and taking the coffin in, a dear little innocent accosted us, with, mamma is asleep, don't wake her; but when she saw us put her in the coffin, the distress of the child was so great, that it almost overcame us; when she demanded why we put her mamma in the box? We did not know how to answer her, but committed her to the care of a neighbour, and left her with heavy hearts. In other places where we have been to take the corpse of a parent, and have found a group of little ones alone, some of them in a measure capable of knowing their situation, their cries and the innocent confusion of the little ones, seemed almost too much for human nature to bear. (40)

Imagine how these lines must have resonated within a community in which so many had lost loved ones. Although it may seem incredible now, in the eighteenth century it was widely believed that people of African descent were not capable of strong familial connection, and other forms of what was called "right feeling." It would be more difficult for white readers to deny the humanity of African Americans after reading this pamphlet, whose authors display model civic behavior and offer evidence that they hold crucial civic virtues—intelligence, compassion, bravery, cooperation, usefulness in the community. This "affecting instance" offers a portrait of African American Philadelphians who, despite the most extreme circumstances, would be faithful stewards of the public good.

We should note also the greater commitments that influenced the way Jones and Allen navigated rhetorical time in this historic moment. The epidemic and ensuing controversy can offer a useful rhetorical lens on the larger situation of race relations in the new republic. The American Revolution had only very recently been fought. Jones, Allen, and the rest of Philadelphia's African American community were not slaves, and yet they retained a deep commitment to "enslaved brothers and sisters," as did most members of the black abolitionist movement that Jones and Allen's pamphlet helped to initiate. The authors spoke on behalf of a population that had virtually no public voice at all. Thus, Jones and Allen transformed the occasion of rhetorical self-defense for African American Philadelphians into a more ambitious act of social advocacy. The pamphlet ends with an "Address to Those Who Keep Slaves and Uphold the Practice." Following the account of African American's exemplary conduct during the epidemic, the "Address" urged readers to acknowledge that enslaved African Americans possess the same social capacity and innate humanity as free blacks in the North as well as the white population. This claim to a common humanity is made through biblical authority; Jones and Allen appeal to the overwhelmingly common Christian faith of their audience:

> We do not wish to make you angry, but to excite your attention to consider, how hateful slavery is in the sight of that God, who hath destroyed kings

> and princes for their oppressions of the poor slaves . . . Men must be willingly blind and extremely partial, that cannot see the contrary effects of liberty and slavery upon the mind of man. (42)

The authors knew their audience well enough to know that readers would likely be familiar with the book of *Exodus* and the story of god's wrath on Pharaoh, the most famous slave master of all time. *Exodus* tells the story of Moses leading the Hebrews out of Egypt after the Pharaoh refused to release them from slavery. In order to convince Pharaoh to release the people, Moses brought plagues upon Egypt and destroyed Pharaoh's army. If Jones and Allen could convince their audience to understand the present historical moment in light of the *Exodus* story, they could hope that their readers might begin to see that slaveholding is sinful, no matter when or by whom it is practiced.

WORKSHOP 8: Following Pathways: A Metaphor for Critical Reading and Research

Reading and research are like travel. They take us into the territory of new ideas and arguments. The exercises in this workshop will help you identify unfamiliar ideas and references and to approach them as opportunities for learning, or in other words, "pathways" to knowledge.

WORKSHOP 13: Readers Responding

This workshop offers powerful strategies for approaching reading as serious writers do, with a critical eye for the most important arguments and ideas. Following the strategies presented in this workshop, you will gain skills as an engaged reader and become more able to put what you read to work in your own writing.

WORKSHOP 16: Summarizing Arguments, Ideas, and Texts

Writers regularly present the work of others as building blocks for their own work. This workshop offers strategies for writing strong summaries to incorporate into your own writing.

While asking the audience to understand the moment in light of the *Exodus* story, Jones and Allen also drew on political history as a way to invent rhetorical time. Consider how resonant the word "liberty" must have been for Philadelphians less than ten years after the Revolutionary War had been fought. Though we take it for granted now, the excitement of political independence from British colonization was still in the air for Philadelphians living through the plague, and thus the juxtaposition of "liberty and slavery" created a very pointed irony ripe for the revolutionary moment. It was in Philadelphia, after all, where the Continental Congress had convened to prosecute the war, where the Declaration of Independence was written, where the Constitution had been written only ten years earlier.

In the course of defending the reputation of the African American community, Jones and Allen took the opportunity to establish the moral and intellectual worth of African Americans, to provide the black community with an ethical rallying point, to educate a white public about their African American fellow Philadelphians, and to deliver an antislavery sermon.

TALK READ WRITE

1. Have you ever waited for just the right time to ask your boss for a raise, to give a friend bad news, to ask a favor of someone? Did your sense of timing help secure the desired outcome? Discuss situations in which you practiced (or at least attempted) rhetorical timeliness.
2. Share your thoughts about rhetorical time with your classmates. Discuss the differences between quantitative and qualitative time. What does it mean to "invent the moment"? What questions or comments do you have?
3. As a group, name some issues or situations that are so important that they must be dealt with right now. What makes each one so timely? How might you convince an audience that a certain set of events has reached a must-act moment?
4. Look back at contemporary examples of kairos we mention at the beginning of this chapter. What can you infer about the political moment in which this textbook was written?
5. How might you begin to think about your critical situation as a moment in rhetorical time? How might that influence your project?
6. Read the full text of Jones and Allen's pamphlet. What further can you learn about the power of timely language that might help you be successful with your own project?
7. Compare Jones and Allen's full text with the other abolitionist works you have read so far. In what common ways do these authors and orators explain the moment of abolitionist struggle? Do you find common arguments about the historical meaning of slavery and abolitionism? How do these writers connect slavery to other issues to change their audience's sense of the pressing urgency of abolitionist struggle? How do these writers explain their own sense of the occasion that prompted their writing?

FINDING THE RIGHT WORDS AT THE RIGHT TIME

Rhetorical timing is the skillful interpretation and weaving together of elements to create a persuasive voice that audiences will receive as the wisdom of the moment. What you write and what you say, as it reaches readers and listeners, can actually influence how the critical situation is perceived. In other words, strong writing and speaking can invent the moment persuasively. What that means depends on the shape of your project. Is the post-9/11 world an age of freedom or fear? Does the long drought in the Western states constitute a moment of crisis? Is former President Bill Clinton's infamous infidelity in the past still relevant as a precedent for discussing the character of other political candidates? Similar questions have been asked about the extensive eulogizing of former President Ronald Reagan on the occasion of his death: what is the point of discussing the politics and policy of someone who was elected president over 25 years ago? These interesting questions suggest the importance of timing to the relevance of community-based issues.

STAKEHOLDER ARGUMENTS: MAPPING THE RHETORICAL MOMENT

Because we so often begin investigating critical situations out of personal, family, or local-community commitment, the perspectives of less familiar stakeholders are not always foremost in our minds. This is particularly true of stakeholders we distrust or with whom we disagree. However, successful speakers and writers must take into account all of the existing positions within a situation in order to grasp all of the arguments available to us at a given moment. Consider again the example of the point guard at the beginning of this chapter. To move gracefully through the time and space of a basketball court or through the rhetorical landscape of a critical situation, knowledge about the other players is necessary. Whether or not you agree with all of the available perspectives in a situation, studying each one carefully can help you invent arguments of your own. For one thing, stakeholders have already compiled research, invented arguments in favor of their positions, and sparked the public debate you are entering. They are your audiences whether they are opponents or allies, those for whom you will advocate or those against whose agenda you have aligned yourself. Taken together, the research and arguments assembled by the sum of stakeholder groups represent the moment in which you must intervene.

We recommend beginning your invention work by mapping the prevailing arguments that make up the critical situation in which you are interested. As you begin to do this, remember to avoid falling into yes-no, right-wrong, pro-con, black-white dichotomies. These simple notions limit your effectiveness as an investigator. Even if the issue seems clearly two-sided—a vote on a

WORKSHOP 9: Gathering Information through Interviews

Because you are a member of the communities in which you are planning a writing project, it is likely that you know personally people with detailed information about pressing community matters. This workshop helps you prepare interviews to access that information.

WORKSHOP 7: Finding Access: Publishing Your Work

What are the most meaningful publics for your work? What audiences, if persuaded by your work, can become agents of change in your critical situation? Once you identify the right audience, how do you reach them? To discover routes of access to your audience, work through the series of questions in this workshop.

proposition for instance—there are likely many possible arguments supporting each side. Arguments will also be made that are critical of both positions or that propose some other action altogether. The most important thing is to sort out which of these arguments have the most power in the current moment, whether you agree with them or not. Which arguments have the most authority with the audiences you hope to reach?

Invention Journal: Mapping Stakeholder Positions

1. Write out all of the stakeholder groups you can think of in the critical situation at hand. You should try to make your list of arguments as current as possible. Using search engines such as EBSCO Host or Lexis-Nexis, or an Internet research engine such as Google or Dogpile, find the most current statements from high-profile members of each of the stakeholder groups. For example, if you were interested in the ongoing debate about gay marriage, you would look for press releases and other public statements from groups such as Queer Nation and ACT UP, as well as from antigay preachers such as Fred Phelps. List and summarize all of the available positions. How does each explain the importance of the moment? What strategies does each use to convince readers and listeners that the stakes are high in the debate about gay rights or same-sex marriage? About protecting the integrity of marriage?
2. What is currently the dominant stakeholder position in this critical situation? In other words, which stakeholder group seems most likely to influence other people about the meaning of the moment in a given critical situation? Gather statements from the most well-known or influential spokespeople for this position. Getting a sense of the currently dominant perspectives on this critical situation will allow you to identify some of the most influential and widely held positions with which you will have to contend in your project work. Has the dominant group taken advantage of rhetorical timing in any way?

OPPORTUNITIES FOR ENGAGEMENT

Everyone has to deal with deadlines, and working against the clock can be stressful. If your project happens to be connected to a political campaign—perhaps you are supporting a particular candidate or a particular ballot measure—the rhetorical time of your critical situation will be clearly marked: you have until Election Day to reach your audience. Families of prisoners on death row have deadlines to meet to make a case for a retrial, to support or oppose legislation, or to make a last-minute appeal. If you are developing a workplace proposal, it is possible that you have to complete your work by the time of a semiannual meeting, or before the next budget is set, the end of the fiscal year. To be successful writers and speakers, we need to know not only when these deadlines arrive, but also what the moment requires and what possibilities it offers. Matters of opportunity and timing were certainly not lost on Jones and Allen:

> Mr. Carey's first, second, and third editions, are gone forth into the world, and in all probability, have been read by thousands that will never read his fourth—consequently, any alteration he may hereafter make, in the paragraph alluded to, cannot have the desired effect, or atone for the past; therefore we apprehend it necessary to publish our thoughts on the occasion. (38)

The authors understood that writing to Carey to ask for any retraction or restatement would have no effect on those who had already read one of the first three editions of his racist's creed. Therefore, a direct response to the reading public was the most fitting response.

Think as well of Frederick Douglass's "What to the Slave is the Fourth of July" discussed in the previous chapter, and the brilliant use Douglass makes of criticizing national politics on the occasion of our most honored national holiday. Consider also Heather Johnson's use of the Presidential election as means of generating occasion. These examples share a strong sense of the opportunity for and necessity of rhetorical action following some emerging schedule.

Invention Journal: Keeping a Rhetorical Calendar

1. Make a time line of all the important dates related to your project. Note important community meetings, professional conferences, and pending decisions. Don't forget to note course deadlines and due dates as well.
2. Write down all pending decisions that might impact your project work. Is there a vote coming up at the local or national level? Will a corporate merger influence your workplace project? Is a political group scheduling a press release to announce a major initiative? Is your local newspaper going to endorse a local position or take an editorial stance on a situation that concerns you?
3. Are there upcoming events that will bring your situation into the public eye? What are they? Think of the way Heather Johnson timed her letter to coincide with Domestic Violence Awareness Month.
4. Are there any holidays or other pending occasions that offer an occasion for commentary on your critical situation? What are they, and how can they help you as a speaker or writer? Charitable organizations increase their public presence during the holiday season, when people are opening their wallets for other purposes.

Speaker's Corner–London's Hyde Park
Finding a forum for argument can be among the most daunting tasks that face writers and speakers. Even if we can literally step up on the soapbox, as is possible at Speaker's Corner in London's Hyde Park, how much control do we have over who hears our words and how they will be received?

RHETORICAL TIME AS A GUIDE TO THINKING ABOUT AUDIENCES

Occasion often dictates audience. If your project is to be successful, you need to discover the right audience for it. We have already seen how timing and intention influenced Jones and Allen's decision about audience. Thinking through rhetorical time can not only help you pinpoint specific audiences, it can also refine your thinking about how to address an audience. Unless you have given thought to your audience's sense of the meaning of the moment—their current stake in the issue and their familiarity with the most authoritative arguments currently circulating—you will have a difficult time making a persuasive appeal.

To choose an appropriate audience, consult the current state of affairs in the moment. Is there a political issue you want to address? If there is a vote coming up in a city election, or if a school board or some other governing body is about to meet, clearly the voting members of these bodies are the people you want to address. If on the other hand the key vote has just passed, and your side lost, then it may be time to write or speak to members of your own political community about the next chance to vote your convictions. If the position you support is so out of the mainstream that few people even recognize it as valid—the assertion perhaps that mothers should be paid a wage for the labor of child bearing and child raising—you are likely better off writing to feminists with socialist leanings in order to be heard and to increase support for your stance. If the position you support is gaining political momentum—legalizing physician-assisted suicide, for instance—it may be time to write to your local representative. The current status of budgets and funding can determine audience as well. Writing a grant proposal to an organization that is in dire financial straits might not be worth your time. On the other hand, writing your proposal for a grant-making organization that has recently received a multimillion-dollar endowment is indeed timely.

Thinking through rhetorical time as a way to size up audience disposition is also important, and in this area, our students' work continues to impress us. At a time when revelations about sexual abuse and subsequent cover-ups rocked the Catholic community, Kellen Chavez's rich meditation on faith and human frailty, submitted to the *Catholic Sun*, finds unexpectedly strong ground on which to address his "family in faith":

> St. Francis of Assisi once said, "Above all the grace and the gifts that Christ gives to his beloved is that of overcoming self." My family in faith, it is essential that we are able to understand that the beauty of our gift to question, to think, lies not within our abilities to find enough faults in someone else to give us enough reason to doubt. The beauty lies in the fact that the intelligence that God has given to each one of us, gives us the opportunity to reflect on such a crisis as the sexual abuse that has crippled our Church, and use such reflection to overcome and make us better members of faith. We can comprehend the heinous nature of these crimes. We can understand the crippling image our Church receives when it pays out settlements to victims. We can look at all that has hurt our Church, which we love enough to be emotionally pained by these occurrences, and use it to strengthen our faith not only in the hope of a healing Church, but to strengthen our relationship with our God.

Through a keen understanding of the rhetorical moment, Chavez was able to craft an eloquent affirmation amid a crisis of trust and confidence within his community of faith. In the wake of a scandal that caused pain, uncertainty, and embarrassment for many Catholics, Chavez reminds his readers that faith bids them to understand a difficult time as an opportunity—to forgive, to recommit to core values and to be thankful for the gift of the human ability "to question."

WORKSHOP 10: Inventing Persuasive Voice

No matter how carefully audiences judge the reasoning and evidence of an argument, we still respond to *voice* in what we read. We still make judgments about how arguments "speak" to us. In this workshop, you will find resources for skillful control of the voice in your writing.

Invention Journal: The Right Audience at the Right Time

1. Go back to the last entry in your Invention Journal. If you have already chosen a time and a place for writing or speaking, can you pinpoint actual audience members? Can you find their names, or the names of the groups to which they belong? Which stakeholder arguments represent their position?

2. Once you have chosen an audience, consider the concerns and commitments of the people who comprise that audience as stakeholders. At this moment, what is at stake in this situation for your audience members? After you write out answers to this question, consider how these stakeholder commitments will influence your invention process.
3. Do the audiences you have identified consider the situation in question to be urgent, or do you need to establish the importance of the moment? How can you establish importance in the eyes of this particular audience?
4. Now, take the time to write to your audience. Address the critical situation at hand and write 250–500 words in which you make your case for the importance of the moment in your critical situation. Perhaps you will be able to cut and paste this writing directly into your final composition.

FRAMING WITH RELATED ISSUES

WORKSHOP 2: Arranging Your Composition

As you discover arguments through invention, consider how they will fit together when you sit down to write. This workshop is devoted to "arrangement," the skillful structuring of arguments.

WORKSHOP 15: Revising for Clarity

This workshop offers revising strategies for increasing the clarity of writing. Increasing the clarity of your ideas will help you connect with your intended audience.

Working effectively with rhetorical time may require that you create a context in which your audience can alter their sense of the critical situation at hand. Perhaps you can invent the moment by connecting your critical situation with other events in your community and beyond. In 2005, big jumps in gas prices were taken up by both supporters and critics of the war with Iraq as evidence to support their positions on the war. Supporters of the war argued that an American military presence in Iraq insured friendly control of that country's oil fields and production. Critics of the war connected it to American imperialism, and their position is summarized in the slogan "No blood for oil." They argued further that American military occupation is responsible for the insurgency that has created chaos in that country, chaos that has resulted in much diminished oil production.

Jones and Allen's account of the "late awful calamity" nicely demonstrates the strategy of making relevant connections to change perceptions of the moment. Consider the implication of this carefully worded passage:

> If you love your children, if you love your country, if you love the God of love, clear your hands from slaves, burden not your children or country with

> them. Our hearts have been sorrowful for the late bloodshed of the oppressors, as well as the oppressed, both appear guilty of each others blood, in the sight of him who said, he that sheddeth man's blood, by man shall is blood be shed. (42)

To what "late bloodshed" do the authors refer? Perhaps the "dreadful insurrection" was some racial violence, a local slave revolt or even the Haitian Revolution, then currently in full swing, in which Haitian slaves deposed French, English, and Spanish colonizers to win freedom and nationhood. Whether we read the reference as a veiled threat or a restatement of the Sixth Commandment—Thou shalt not kill—we should understand how skillfully the authors encourage readers to expand their sense of what is relevant in a given situation, in this case, the situation of African American slavery.

Often our students find powerful arguments to make in the context of their critical situations by surveying the connections of relevance made by other stakeholders. Students are increasingly interested in investigating the impact of corporate control of the music industry and the tendency of label consolidation to reduce variety and experimentation among recording artists. Students concerned about such a trend might find powerful arguments by referencing parallel contexts of corporate consolidation and its impact on the public good. Making such connections, writers gain a broader understanding of the economic moment in which the music is enmeshed. Writers thus may access a more diverse set of arguments with which to persuade audiences that corporate power deprives citizens of the good life, be it musical appreciation or decent medical coverage.

Many of our students are currently interested in immigration policy, which is a controversial issue in Arizona. The issue of immigration from Mexico to the United States is often discussed in tandem with other issues. Many believe, for example, that immigration is an important matter of national security because terrorists might enter the country undetected through the deserts of Arizona and New Mexico. Thus the U.S.-Mexico border is construed as a "front" in the "war on terror." Others understand questions about immigration to be more closely related to questions of the U.S. economy. Even though many agree that border issues are in essence economic issues, commentators understand the economics of the Southern border in many different ways: Mexican migrants are a crucial workforce in our national economy and should be allowed to work here legally; Mexican immigrants "steal jobs" from U.S. citizens; Mexican immigrants arriving in increasing numbers indicate the detrimental effects of the North American Free Trade Agreement or the Central American Free Trade Agreement. Still others argue that the increased rate of deaths among Mexican immigrants making perilous desert crossings is part of the larger conversation about human rights abuses perpetrated by U.S. policy. Others point to the involvement of faith communities in advocating for Mexican migrants as a sign of renewed commitment to social justice among religious or spiritual communities in this country.

Invention Journal: Connecting to a Broader Sense of the Current Moment

1. Brainstorm a list of current events that are either directly or tangentially related to your critical situation. How many related issues connect with your critical situation? Begin investigating by plugging in search-engine keywords associated with your critical situation. For each related issue, summarize its connection and comment on its possible importance. What connections do you see? Follow links, and explore. Keep careful notes on the threads you follow in your research.
2. Return to your list of stakeholder groups. How does each understand the interconnectedness of the critical situation at hand? What links to other situations does each make? What analogies do they use? What causal connections do they assume? After you have generated a list, summarize the possible importance of each of these connected events for your audience and for your own project work.
3. Make a cluster, map, or chart to illustrate the way your critical situation is connected with other issues and situations.
4. Now, take the time to write to your audience. Make a case for your position by relating your critical situation to other events or situations currently playing out around the world or close to home. Perhaps you will be able to cut and paste this writing directly into your final composition.

PROVIDING YOUR AUDIENCE WITH A HISTORICAL FRAME OF REFERENCE

Michael Irei, a student writing against the groundswell of support for a Constitutional ban on gay marriage, made a strong appeal to his audience to think about the current political and ethical question in a broader historical context:

> Throughout the history of our country, we have been fighting for the rights of all of our citizens. Today, the fight for gay rights and same-sex marriage is similar to the civil rights battle regarding race, which we have been fighting since the United States was founded. It seems just as preposterous not to allow same-sex marriages as it was to ever consider a law banning inter-racial marriages in the United States. Looking back, most would find it hard to believe that there was recently a time in this country when basic civil rights were not granted to citizens. Jim Crow laws were enforced. These were laws that enforced the racial segregation amongst public commodities, laws that took away rights of a group of people in this country. A constitutional ban of same-sex marriage would be similar; taking away the rights of a select group of people in the United States. If this amendment is enacted, it is very possible that we may look back in the future with confusion and amazement at the ignorance of denying the right of any two human beings to marry.

If Irei could persuade his audience to make this historical connection, to think of the struggle for gay rights as a logical extension of the history of civil rights, those who oppose gay marriage might have to reevaluate that position lest they appear to oppose expansion of the American value of equal rights for all. We think this is a particularly strong example of rhetorical timeliness. Although arguments for gay rights are not easily heard in the present historical moment, they may become more palatable when people are reminded of the moral precedent set by the civil rights movement.

Acting as a historian may be an important part of rhetorical timing in your critical situation. Inventing a sense of historical occasion can help you establish causality or the chain of events in which your critical situation is taking place; provide precedents to help your audience make sense of the current moment and to find powerful value-based arguments that appeal to any sense of identity felt by your audience. By *identity,* we mean their sense of knowing themselves in relation to everyone else and all those who have preceded us in time. How can you help your audience assess the importance of the critical situation as a historical moment?

In the abolitionist context, we've already seen how Jones and Allen place the situation of American slavery in the history of social revolution and racial violence. Consider also their creation of sacred or religious historical context. Their reference to *Exodus,* with its story of Moses leading the Israelites out of slavery, was taken up by many authors of the abolitionist oratory and writing that would follow. Capitalizing on the Protestant argument that the United States could become God's "city on the hill," a promised land finally realized, abolitionists argued that the nation would fall short of this spiritual goal until it purified itself by abolishing slavery. In this way, audiences were asked to consider their own lives and political commitments as part of a still-unfolding biblical history.

Speakers and writers often use historical precedent to make sense of the current moment and to enhance the persuasiveness of their own proposals. On September 19, 2001, just a few days after 9/11, George W. Bush addressed a joint session of the Congress. In that speech he mentioned another historical occasion on which America's strength and resolve had been tested:

> On September the 11th, enemies of freedom committed an act of war against our country. Americans have known wars—but for the past 136 years, they have been wars on foreign soil, except for one Sunday in 1941. Americans have known the casualties of war—but not at the center of a great city on a peaceful morning. Americans have known surprise attacks—but never before on thousands of civilians. All of this was brought upon us in a single day—and night fell on a different world, a world where freedom itself is under attack.

WORKSHOP 12: Putting Together a Portfolio of Your Invention Work

Gathering your invention work together in a portfolio creates a record of your thought, research, and analysis. This workshop offers a simple framework for constructing a portfolio and writing a critical self-reflection on the progress of your project.

Americans responded to the attack on Pearl Harbor "one Sunday in 1941" by entering World War II, one of the most massive conflicts ever fought among nations. President Bush's comparison allowed him to suggest that the events of 9/11 were sufficiently important to require an equally massive war effort. Many other commentators who urged the country to go to war with Iraq made explicit reference to the results of European appeasement of Adolph Hitler at the outset of the Second World War. Other public figures argue that the Patriot Act, enacted while people were frightened about terrorist infiltration of the country, was a watershed moment in the history of civil liberties. Indeed, some commentators have spoken of the terrorist attacks as the initiation of a new epoch, a new era of threat and/or citizen responsibility.

Putting your critical situations in a historical context can also help you make strong value-based claims about the situation at hand. Jones and Allen ask readers to choose between the value systems of Moses and Pharaoh. In nearly every venue of public discourse, the ostensible values of our Founding Fathers—fairness, equality, courage—are held up as rallying points.

Invention Journal: Writing the History of a Critical Situation

1. Make a time line of events leading up to the critical situation your project addresses. How far back can you trace your issue?
2. Return to your list of current stakeholder commentary and highlight every historical reference that is made. How are these references being used to persuade or inform? Which of them are most useful for your purposes?
3. Write out all of the possible outcomes of the critical situation in which you are interested. Now, write out all of the possible long-term consequences of each one. Now, consider how each of these predictions can be used to persuade or inform audiences.
4. Make a list of historical parallels to your critical situation. For instance, if you are interested in the question of gay marriage, you might look to the history of the civil rights movement as a place to make powerful arguments about the history of democratic reform.
5. Review your work in this Invention Journal, and then take the time to make a historical argument for your audience. Demonstrating historical causality and presenting powerful historical precedents, write 250–500 words making your most persuasive case.

LIST OF WORKS CITED

Bush, George W. "Address to a Joint Session of Congress and the American People." <whitehouse.gov/news/releases/2001/09/20010920–8.html>. Accessed on December 6, 2006.

Jones, Absalom and Richard Allen. "A Narrative of the Proceedings of the Black People During the Late Awful Calamity in Philadelphia" (1974). *Pamphlets of Protest: An Anthology of Early African American Protest Literature.* Ed. Richard Newman, Patrick Rael, and Phillip Lapansky. New York: Routledge, 2001. 33–42.

Smith, John. E. "Time and Qualitative Time." *Rhetoric and Kairos: Essays in History, Theory, and Praxis.* Ed. Phillip Sipiora and James S. Baumlin. Albany: State University of New York Press, 2002. 46–57.

5

EXPLORING THE COMMON SENSE OF THE COMMUNITY

In January 2005 the president of Harvard University, Lawrence Summers, spoke to a group of scholars assembled for an academic conference. The scholars were discussing why so few women become successful scientists and engineers. In his talk about the issue, Summers speculated that there are innate differences between women and men, differences that keep women from excelling in some fields. Summers's remarks angered a number of women scientists who were present. Perhaps what was most shocking about the comments was their source; observers were surprised that the president of Harvard would come so close to advocating male supremacy. Summers later claimed that he was misunderstood.

Writing in *Vanity Fair* in response to this episode, James Wolcott discussed some longstanding cultural assumptions about gender that, according to him, long ago passed their expiration date. Addressing the status of the so-called "battle of the sexes," he noted the existence of

> a protracted buildup of exasperation over the persistent under-representation of women in positions of prominence and authority, and the mulish inability of powerful men to recognize the scope of the problem, or their tendency instead to rationalize it with voodoo genetics and Victorian-parlor sociology. Women are sick of hearing the same old sea chanteys. They've had their fill of men who insist on protecting their privileges and pretend it's the natural order of things. (June 2005: No. 538, 96)

Wolcott used the phrases "voodoo genetics" and "Victorian-parlor sociology" to describe a set of beliefs about gender. Wolcott's terms imply that "powerful men" rationalize their exclusion of women from positions of authority by appealing to beliefs that are both scientifically suspect ("voodoo genetics") and thoroughly outdated ("Victorian-parlor sociology"). Despite their flaws, these beliefs are widely held; that is, they are held in common by a lot of people. For many people, they appear to be, in Wolcott's phrase, "the natural order of things."

In this chapter, we use a number of terms to refer to beliefs and sets of beliefs that are in wide circulation. The terms are **common sense**, **commonplaces**, and

ideology. *Common sense* means something like "beliefs that most people hold." Ancient rhetoricians called such beliefs *commonplaces,* and we follow their example. We do not use these words to indicate self-evident facts or the clear right or wrong of a situation. Here, common sense refers to beliefs that are held by large numbers of people—regardless of whether the beliefs are true or false, right or wrong. Commonplace beliefs often connect to other beliefs, making up a network or system of truth claims. We will use the term *ideology* to refer to sets of commonly held beliefs which are so closely connected to one another that they always appear together. For example, the set of beliefs that Wolcott refers to, which concerns appropriate roles for men and women, is called *patriarchy.* Patriarchy is an ideology; that is, it is a system of beliefs that are closely woven together. Some of its commonplaces are "Women should be wives and mothers" and "Men are better at math and science than women are." Like all beliefs in any ideology they depend on and reinforce each other, and in this case both of these commonplace beliefs depend on a more general belief in the superiority of men to women in all fields of endeavor saving wifedom and motherhood.

Proverbs are obvious examples of common sense: "you get what you pay for"; "a stitch in time saves nine." Other commonplaces include these: "if you work hard, you will be rewarded"; "people have the right to say what they think"; "justice always triumphs." Commonplaces often go without saying because such beliefs are so widely held that ordinarily they do not require discussion. Nonetheless, they often guide our thoughts and actions, as Wolcott suggests. While we were writing this chapter, the United States Congress discussed proposed legislation that would impose a ban on flag-burning. This legislation sought to install a common-sense belief into the Constitution, the belief that an attack on the flag is an attack on the country. Of course, it is not always true that flags are burned as a symbol of hostility to America. Manufacturers of flags in fact recommend that old and tattered flags be disposed of by burning. Nonetheless, Americans are often offended when a flag is burned for other reasons than disposal.

Here are some more examples of commonplaces that circulate in American discourse: "anyone can become president of the United States," "all Americans have equal rights." Please note that even though these statements are widely accepted, they have not yet been realized in practice. And so we uncover a second feature of commonplaces: even though they are widely believed, they are not always (or even often) true. Because of this, commonplaces may be controversial outside of the communities that subscribe to them. Even the most revered bit of common-sense wisdom is contested or disputed in some circles.

This is not to say that commonplaces aren't useful to writers and speakers. In this chapter, we offer discussion and exercises meant to help you harness the rhetorical power of the common sense of the communities in which you write and speak. Handled carefully, appeal to commonplaces can be powerfully persuasive. Most arguments contain at least a few commonplaces, and they are useful because they help rhetors to establish connections with audiences. That is, a rhetor's use of a commonplace establishes that he or she is a member of the community, that he or she knows its language and its beliefs. But commonplaces must be used with care because they are often not true or only partially true. Forty years ago, people commonly thought that women could never become great athletes. But when Title IX made it possible for schools and colleges to fund women's athletic activities, girls and women took advantage of the opportunity offered to become, in the words of another commonplace, "all that they can be." Today, the examples of Mia Hamm, Jackie Joyner-Kersee, Lisa Leslie, and Venus and Serena Williams show just how misguided the commonplace was. Perhaps a similar sort of institutional and cultural change, a change that encourages more women to study math and science, will soon render obsolete the commonplace about their abilities in those fields.

Commonplaces are particularly powerful (and particularly volatile) because of their entanglement with community identity. Commonplaces not only give expression to how we think about the world, but also to how we think about who we are both individually and communally. They exist within community belief as a means of holding the community together, and because of this they may be offensive to groups who do not live within the community that employs them. As an example, we recall a student whose commonplace beliefs about animal rights ("meat is murder," for instance) confused, surprised, and offended many of her classmates who were not a part of the animal rights community. Later in the chapter, we discuss the common sense of what we might call the "American ideology," a powerful set of ideas that represents a national identity to which many people in this country subscribe. Religious or spiritual communities are also held together by commonplaces. The notion, for instance, that people ought to "turn the other cheek" as a demonstration of love and forgiveness is a commonplace among Christians. Racist commonplaces do the same sort of work, although in much less savory fashion, of offending and excluding, of showing or implying that a particular "we" is not like "them," that this "we" is better than "them."

No matter what common sense they express, it remains true that people use commonplaces as aids for thinking. They are the beliefs we don't question when we consider the situation at hand. Some beliefs have been in place for so long that the people who subscribe to them seldom actually articulate them. As a general rule, the need to articulate deeply held beliefs comes about only when some new belief or practice challenges an older one. Such is the case currently with vegetarianism and animal rights, which in the last few decades have challenged the centrality of meat-eating to American dietary beliefs and practices.

A commonplace is not a simple slogan, but an expression of a belief about the world and people in it, how things are and how they ought to be. Commonplaces hold us together in agreement and divide us, sometimes bitterly, into different communities. Learning to negotiate commonplaces in speech and writing gives us access to the big ideas that people turn to again and again to make sense of things.

WORKSHOP 4: Ethics in Writing and Speaking Inventory

This workshop helps generate thinking and conversation about ethical issues in public writing and speaking. Working through the inventory individually or as a group, you have a chance to work towards ethical practices of communication.

TALK READ WRITE

1. Take 10 minutes to write out as many commonplace sayings—proverbs, truisms, adages, maxims, axioms, etc.—as you can. Consult a dictionary of proverbs as a way of getting started. Discuss why each commonplace strikes you as true or false, right or wrong, wise or foolish, moral or immoral. Try to think of situations in which each commonplace holds true; now, think of situations where it is patently false.
2. Find a large parking lot and look at bumper stickers. Write them down. What commonplace beliefs are compressed into a sticker that reads "Sex Education Prevents Abortion" or "Fight Terrorism: Go Solar"? What might you deduce about the community life of the owner of the bumper sticker based on the words or images?
3. Return to Wolcott's passage at the beginning of the chapter. In your opinion, are the commonplaces of patriarchy or male supremacy still persuasive in our culture? Think of examples that suggest patriarchy is not still part of our common sense. Now, think of examples that suggest patriarchy still has a firm hold on our beliefs.

COMMONPLACES AND IDEOLOGY

Commonplaces are the phrases, statements, and sentiments that give voice, as it were, to ideological positions. Once again, an ideology is a coherent set of beliefs that people use to understand events and the behavior of other people. Ideologies influence human action; that is, they exist in language, but they are worked out in practice. For instance:

- Believing that English should be the "national language" of the United States, a man votes against a bilingual education bill.
- A family gives one-tenth of its income to the church believing that this is God's law.
- Jury members acquit the defendant in a rape trial believing that the alleged victim "wanted it."
- A woman joins a protest because she feels that the world needs to "give peace a chance."
- A soldier acts with great bravery, putting himself at great risk, because he holds the conviction that he is helping to secure freedom for his fellow citizens.
- A member of the Ku Klux Klan puts on a sheet and joins a march at city hall believing that this is "a white man's country."

- A woman arranges her schedule so that she is always home when her children come home from school because as she understands it "that's what good mothers do."
- An athlete trains past the point of exhaustion, telling herself "no pain, no gain."

These examples suggest that ideologies are sets of statements that tell us what to do and how to do it. Not only that, they tell us how to understand ourselves and others, how to understand nature and our relation to it, and how to value what we know—that is, they tell us what is thought to be true, or right, or good, or beautiful in a community.

Commonplaces and the ideologies they constitute are so basic to a mode of thought and behavior that people who subscribe to them may remain unaware of their allegiance to them. The person who says "no pain, no gain" may or may not remember the origin of this phrase within the sport of bodybuilding; the commonplace has become so widespread and so useful that we can now apply it to activities as diverse as studying for exams or giving up a favorite food for Lent. The commonplace can also be re-articulated as a statement ("achievement requires suffering") but this is far less memorable than the original formulation. However, our translation does show how commonplaces can function within arguments, serving rhetors as claims that need little or no proof because they are widely accepted.

Each of us is immersed in the ideologies that circulate in our communities once we begin to understand and use language, which perhaps is why we so often inherit our parents' ideological positions. Hence, ideologies actually produce "selves"; the picture each of us has of our selves has been formed by our experiences, to be sure, but it has also been constructed by the beliefs that circulate among our family, friends, the media, and other communities that we inhabit. We may think of ourselves as Christian or Jewish, or as a New Ager, or as an atheist. In each case, we adopt a set of beliefs about the way the world works from some relevant community (in the last case, we may have reacted against dominant ideologies). Even though identities are shaped by ideologies, they are never stable because ideological belief can be questioned and rejected. People do this all the time: they undergo religious conversion; liberals become conservative; skeptics decide that extraterrestrials have in fact visited earth; Americans stop eating meat and take up exercise because they have become convinced it is good for them.

Sometimes, people resent being reminded that ideology informs their way of thinking. We mean no disrespect when we say that religious beliefs and political leanings are ideological. Quite the contrary: human beings need ideologies in order to make sense of their experiences in the world. Powerful ideologies such as religions and political beliefs help people to understand who they are and what their relation is to the world and to other beings.

Some ideologies are more sweeping than others, some are highly respected in given cultures, and some are older or more powerful than others. In societies, the power of an ideology is measured by the degree to which it influences the beliefs and actions of relatively large groups of relatively powerful people. Ideologies that are subscribed to by large groups of people are called "dominant" or "hegemonic" (from Greek *hegemoon,* "prince" or "guide"). Ideologies subscribed to by small or marginalized groups are called "subordinate" or "minority." The relations between dominant and subordinate ideologies are complex and they change over time. The ideology of racial equality was a radically marginal position at the beginning of the nineteenth century but it gained greater influence in the next two centuries. And in another example, 40 years ago environmentalism influenced the discourse and practice of only a few people; that is, it was a subordinate or minority discourse in America. Today, however, environmentalism may be in contention for dominant status among American belief systems. Any proposed construction project must entail an environmental impact statement, and ordinary citizens recycle or otherwise find ways to conserve energy. In the process of gaining wider support, environmentalism has challenged the hegemony of other, far more powerful discourses—chiefly those of individualism and capitalism. Environmentalism has not yet become a dominant discourse precisely because it calls into question hegemonic discourses that are central to American thought. It could be argued that environmentalism has yet come of age as a belief system, for example, as is attested by the resistance Americans have shown to buying smaller, less-polluting vehicles and to cutting back on the amount of driving they do. However, when gas prices rise, Americans do become concerned about mileage, and sales of gas-guzzlers decline. This demonstrates that sound environmental practice may in some cases be driven by economic concerns.

To repeat: an ideology is a set of beliefs, doctrines, and familiar ways of thinking that are characteristic of a group or a culture. They can be economic, ethical, political, philosophical, or religious. When we call someone a capitalist or a socialist, we assume that she subscribes to a set of coherent beliefs about the best way to structure an economy. If we say that someone is a Christian, Muslim, or Jew, we imply that he holds a recognizable set of religious values. If we describe someone as a conservative or as a liberal, we imply that her political practices are guided by a distinct set of beliefs about human nature. If we refer to someone as a feminist or an environmentalist, we imply that his ethical, economic, social, and political practices are governed by a coherent philosophical position. Capitalism and socialism, Christianity, Islam and Judaism, conservatism and liberalism, feminism, and environmentalism are examples of ideologies.

Most people probably subscribe to commonplaces drawn from many and diverse ideologies at any given time. Because of this, and because our subscription to many of our beliefs is only partially conscious, our ideological beliefs may contradict one another. For instance, if John believes on religious grounds that abortion is murder, he may find that belief to be in conflict with his liberal politics, which teach that women have the right to determine whether or not they wish to carry a pregnancy to term. Thus, John's ideology potentially contains a contradiction. This is not unusual, because ideology is seldom consistent with itself. In fact, it may be full of contradictions, and it may (and often does) contradict empirical states of affairs as well. For example, the commonplace which affirms that "Anyone can become president of the United States" overlooks the reality that all presidents to date have been relatively wealthy white men. Some thinkers about ideology argue that its function is precisely to smooth over contradictions in our lives. How can Americans be persuaded to go to war, for example, where chances are good that the lives of loved ones will be put in danger? A skilled rhetor who urges our going to war can deploy commonplaces drawn from American patriotism to downplay fears of injury or death and to make people forget about the horrors of war.

An understanding of ideology is necessary for speakers and writers because it is often possible to predict how people may react to an argument when they hold firmly to a certain set of beliefs. Our predictions must be cautious, however, because ideologies are themselves contradictory, and because people espouse them with varying degrees of intensity. Caution is also necessary because ideologies are complex and various; for example, there are varieties of Judaism, Christianity, and Islam, just as there are different kinds of feminism and environmentalism. And people don't always behave according to the beliefs inherent within an ideology they espouse, as is the case when a labor rights activist stiffs the person serving his meal at a restaurant.

TALK READ WRITE

1. Re-examine our examples (p. 106) that show the connection between belief and action. Choose one, and work out the chain of beliefs that connects the action to the ideology. For example, how does the man who believes that "this is a white man's country" connect his attendance at a Klan rally to that belief? Does he imagine, for example, that the rally will persuade spectators to accept his belief? And if the rally does persuade others, how does the conversion of new believers to white supremacy support his ideology or otherwise assist his cause? Or, does he think that the rally will frighten nonwhite people into leaving the country?
2. This exercise should produce a list of statements that, taken together, make up an argument. The connections made between statements in the argument likely are not altogether coherent, as they are not in our example about the Klan member. This work can be difficult, because we are asking you to make explicit the connections that link beliefs to one another within an ideology—connections that are not often brought to consciousness or uttered in language.
3. One of the most prominent ideological clashes in this country is the one between liberal and conservative thinkers. List positions or beliefs that make up the common sense of liberal ideology. Now, do the same for conservative ideology. If you need help with this activity, visit some liberal and conservative Web sites. Those posted by members of state and federal legislators are a good place to start. Alternatively, searches for liberal or conservative blogs will turn up a wealth of sources that support one or the other of these ideologies.
4. Now try to think of positions and beliefs that cut across this ideological divide. What common ideological ground can you find between liberals and conservatives in the United States?
5. Besides liberalism and conservatism, list other major ideological clashes that you know of. In this chapter we mention patriarchy and feminism,

WORKSHOP 3: Different Values and Respectful Conflict

Arguments are inherently matters of conflict. Rather than trying to avoid such conflict, we recommend approaching it as a powerful learning opportunity and an intellectual resource. This workshop provides the framework for sharing our own value-based positions in a productive and respectful manner.

environmentalism, and capitalism, among other examples. How do these different ways of thinking influence events in the world?

6. Return to your communities map in chapter two. Based on your community involvement, how would you describe the ideologies or sets of beliefs that guide you in your own life?
7. Write out the commonplace assumptions you find in any textbook (including this one). Or, find and list the commonplace assumptions made in arguments appearing on the editorial page of your daily newspaper, the campus newspaper, or a cable TV channel.

CASE STUDY: IS THERE AN AMERICAN IDEOLOGY?

Groups often coalesce around ideologies such as environmentalism (Greenpeace, The Sierra Club) or fascism (the American Nazi Party). Groups also coalesce around specific issues: members of Operation Rescue were united by their opposition to abortion; members of NOW (The National Organization for Women) are united by

Children Saying the Pledge of Allegiance

Children around the world are taught to espouse national values. Across the United States, children daily recite the Pledge of Allegiance to the United States flag and "the republic for which it stands."

their desire to enact legislation that will secure equality for women. Members of each of these groups may or may not share the same ideologies, however. Some members of Operation Rescue, for example, opposed abortion on religious grounds, while other anti-abortion activists oppose it for moral or political or social reasons. Members of NOW may subscribe to a variety of feminisms—liberal, radical, cultural, materialist, third-wave, postmodern—and it is conceivable that a member of NOW may not be a feminist at all.

If commonplaces circulate among groups, is it possible that groups as large as the American citizenry accept similar commonplaces? Is it possible, in other words, that the identity we call "an American" is defined to some extent by beliefs that are shared by all Americans? Some writers have argued this point. E. D. Hirsch claims that there is a perceptible American ideology that centers on values embedded in the Declaration of Independence and the Constitution of the United States. Hirsch describes America's "civil religion," as he calls it, as follows:

> Our civil ethos treasures patriotism and loyalty as high, though perhaps not ultimate, ideals and fosters the belief that the conduct of the nation is guided by a vaguely defined God. Our tradition places importance on carrying out the rites and ceremonies of our civil ethos and religion through the national flag, the national holidays, and the national anthem (which means "national hymn"), and supports the morality of tolerance and benevolence, of the Golden Rule, and communal cooperation. We believe in altruism and self-help, in equality, freedom, truth telling, and respect for the national law. Besides these vague principles, American culture fosters such myths about itself as its practicality, ingenuity, inventiveness, and independent-mindedness, its connection with the frontier, and its beneficence in the world (even when its leaders do not always follow beneficent policies). (98–99)

We like the term "civil religion" because it suggests something important about ideological positions—we adhere to them with a belief and tenacity nearly equivalent to faith. Hirsch also underscores the code of individualism and self-reliance that permeates so much of our national culture. "Independence," as a political idea forged during our revolutionary history, is perhaps the cornerstone of what it means to be successful or even virtuous in the United States. Hirsch is also correct that many Americans feel that the nation has a special relationship to a divine creator. Notice also Hirsch's emphasis on ritual and the ceremonial times and places when our "civil religion" is reaffirmed.

Here is another discussion of American commonplaces, this one written by Howard Zinn. Unlike Hirsch, Zinn is a critic of American ideology:

> We grow up in a society where our choice of ideas is limited and where certain ideas dominate: We hear them from our parents, in the schools, in the churches, in the newspapers, and on radio and television. They have been in the air ever since we learned to walk and talk. They constitute an American *ideology*—that is, a dominant pattern of ideas. Most people accept them, and if we do, too, we are less likely to get into trouble.

> The dominance of these ideas is not the product of a conspiratorial group that has devilishly plotted to implant on society a particular point of view. Nor is it an accident, an innocent result of people thinking freely. There is a process of natural (or, rather *unnatural*) selection, in which certain orthodox ideas are encouraged, financed, and pushed forward by the most powerful mechanisms of our culture. These ideas are preferred because they are safe; they don't threaten established wealth or power.
>
> For instance:
>
> "Be realistic; this is the way things *are;* there's no point thinking about how things *should be.*"
>
> "People who teach or write or report the news should be *objective;* they should not try to advance their own opinions."
>
> "There are unjust wars, but also just wars."
>
> "If you disobey the law, even for a good cause, you should accept your punishment."
>
> "If you work hard enough, you'll make a good living. If you are poor, you have only yourself to blame."
>
> "Freedom of speech is desirable, but not when it threatens national security."
>
> "Racial equality is desirable, but we've gone far enough in that direction."
>
> "Our constitution is our greatest guarantee of liberty and justice."
>
> "The United States must intervene from time to time in various parts of the world with military power to stop communism and promote democracy."
>
> "If you want to get things changed, the only way is to go through the proper channels."
>
> "We need nuclear weapons to prevent war."
>
> "There is much injustice in the world but there is nothing that ordinary people, without wealth or power, can do about it."
>
> These ideas are not accepted by all Americans. But they are believed widely enough and strongly enough to dominate our thinking (3–4).

Zinn's list shows that commonplaces do change. For instance, the commonplace about the threat of communism is not now so powerful nor so widespread as it was prior to the collapse of Soviet Communism. Insert the word "terrorism" in place of "communism," however, and the commonplace immediately regains currency. All the commonplaces Zinn lists have enjoyed currency within American discourse, and many still harbor the power to stir people to action. What is interesting in Zinn's critical breakdown of American ideology is how firmly it is itself rooted in democratic ideals many of us hold to be uniquely American. Depending on their own ideological affiliations, Zinn's readers might simultaneously feel insulted by his irreverent take on Americanism and attracted by his desire to speak out against hypocrisy and abuses of

WORKSHOP 8: Following Pathways: A Metaphor for Critical Reading and Research

The exercises in this workshop will help you identify unfamiliar ideas and references in your reading and research and approach them as opportunities for learning, or in other words, "pathways" to knowledge.

power. Again, an ideology is not a formula. It holds different people differently, and the commonplaces of an ideology can be turned to new uses by writers and speakers.

Even though Hirsch and Zinn do not agree precisely about what beliefs constitute an American ideology, they do agree that it exists. Whether we can list its contents precisely or not, everyone who lives in America is affected by its ideology because its values are embedded in our public discourse. Our coinage reads "from many, one" and "in God we trust"; our elementary schoolbooks tell us that "all men are created equal"; our national anthem tells us that America is "the land of the free and the home of the brave." Whether we believe these commonplaces or not, they provide the terms within which American discourse works. Writers and speakers cannot escape the commonplaces of American public discourse, and they overlook them at their peril.

WORKSHOP 13: Readers Responding

This workshop offers powerful strategies for approaching reading as serious writers do, with a critical eye for the most important arguments and ideas. Following the strategies presented in this workshop, you will gain skills as an engaged reader and become more able to put what you read to work in your own writing.

WORKSHOP 16: Summarizing Arguments, Ideas, and Texts

Writers regularly present the work of others as building blocks for their own work. This workshop offers strategies for writing strong summaries to incorporate into your own writing.

TALK READ WRITE

1. Discuss Zinn's and Hirsch's analyses of American ideology. Do you agree that the commonplaces listed by each constitute accurate descriptions of American identity? Can you guess from perusing their lists of commonplaces whether Zinn and Hirsch are liberal or conservative? Which of them is more conservative than the other?
2. List five issues that are currently being discussed on national news. As we write, such issues include the war in Iraq, immigration policy, rising gas prices, health care, and the outsourcing of jobs to other countries. These may change (or not) by the time you read this. Now, try to figure out how some commonplaces of American ideology can and are used to make arguments for use in discussing these issues. Can you think of instances in which the commonplaces concerning these issues are used in contradictory ways?
3. To question American ideology may go against the grain of national pride, and so it may be that some people are offended by our discussion of "an American ideology." Discuss this with classmates. Is open discussion of American beliefs offensive? What in particular offends? Is such analysis politically dangerous or healthy?

CLAIMING CONTESTED COMMONPLACES

Supporters and opponents of "Operation Iraqi Freedom" have claimed patriotism as a basic premise in their argument, and this seeming contradiction is not a new phenomenon. During the Vietnam War, those who opposed the United States' participation in that war were widely castigated as unpatriotic. A popular slogan, "love it or leave it," suggested that anyone who did not support the war did not support America and hence was not wanted in the country. Those who opposed the war, however, thought of themselves precisely as patriots—as people who loved their country and showed as much by dissenting from its foreign policy (an act which is quintessentially American, according to Hirsch). Some opponents of the war actually went to prison in order to express their dissent. The boxer Muhammed Ali, who was then called Cassius Clay, is probably the most famous person who refused to serve in the war. But thousands of men were incarcerated for burning their draft cards or otherwise refusing to be inducted into military service.

While Americans may disagree about what counts as a patriotic act, the value of patriotism—love of country—circulates in American discourse with such power that it affects lives and actions. At present, there is much disagreement about the specific acts that can be classified as patriotic (Voting? Serving in the military? Supporting the military? Supporting war? Speaking ill of perceived enemies?). For instance, people who oppose the war in Iraq are often accused of unpatriotic behavior. In response, peace activists coined the phrase, "peace is patriotic."

TALK READ WRITE

What ideological pull does this image have for you? Does it affirm your sense of patriotic values? Does it strike you as a deviation from patriotism?

"Peace Is Patriotic"

Invention Journal: Judging the Common Sense of Your Audience

1. Locate your audience among the various stakeholder groups involved in your critical situation. Now ask these questions: What is my audience's ideological orientation? What commonplaces circulate in communities with which my audience identifies? List them if you can.
2. Find the public statements of prominent members of your audience. For instance, if you are trying to convince members of a church to accept gay members in the congregation, find sermons or other official statements made by clergy about gay sexuality. Based on the commonplace statements and assumptions that you find, summarize the ideological orientations that confront you as a writer and speaker. Bear in mind that the thoughts and words of one audience member, even one with great authority, is not necessarily representative of the group. When possible, interview those who you consider to be a part of your audience. What common sense do they express?

ARGUING THROUGH THE COMMONPLACES

Commonplaces offer a wealth of rhetorical resources. They can be used as major premises for arguments, and they can also be used to persuade others to join the community and to accept its commitments. For instance, the appeal to family values is a well-worn commonplace. Even though it was initially put into circulation by conservatives, it has since been adopted by people who subscribe to other political ideologies. A first principle of contemporary American conservatism is that morality is best transmitted across generations when people live in a nuclear family headed by two parents, where moral authority rests with the father. Hence, a conservative writer or speaker is likely to argue that Americans could solve problems as diverse as high rates of teenage pregnancy, drug abuse, or inadequate public schools if only we would return to traditional family values. The commonplace of "family values" is a shorthand way for conservatives to express their dismay that most Americans no longer live in nuclear families; its use also strengthens their sense of community. As we have suggested, an understanding of ideologies and the commonplaces that capture them, whether the common sense of a group or a whole culture, is important to us as writers and speakers because people do not respond to a rhetorical proposition out of context. Their responses and orientations to a particular critical situation are determined by the ideologies to which they subscribe.

As we have suggested, the phrase "family values" is largely associated with conservative political discourse. The image depicting two mothers with their children, however, lays claim to the politics of family values, challenging the

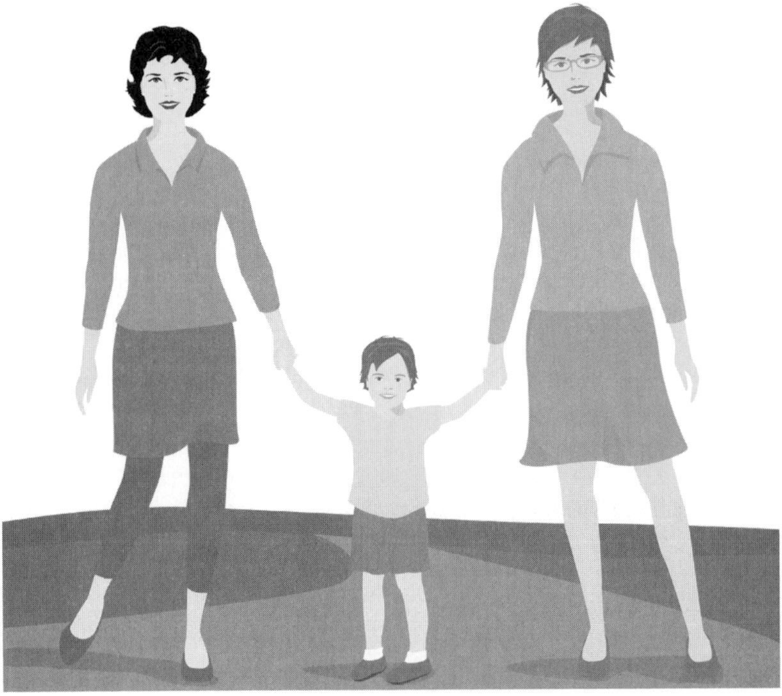

"True Family Values" Images

People from many different ideological positions claim to speak for "family values." This is just one example of the way ideological projects attempt to organize values and beliefs.

explicit exclusion of non-traditional values depicted in the man-and-woman-with child picture. Including same-sex parents under the banner of "family values" is clearly not a typical conservative gesture. Our reactions to these images, and to their juxtaposition, might tell us something about our own ideological orientations.

Like all commonplaces, the appeal to family values is very general—which explains why it has so easily been appropriated by liberals. Nor is it necessarily a good causal explanation for dilapidated schools or drug abuse, issues which may or may not be caused by a perceived decline in so-called "family values." Nevertheless, this commonplace was so pervasive for a while that it even appeared on a bumper sticker: "Hatred is not a family value." Commonplaces can be powerful, then, but their effects are not always under the writer's or speaker's control. This is particularly true when events contradict a commonplace. During the run-up to America's invasion of Iraq in 2003 and for a while afterward, for example, most Americans believed that Saddam Hussein—the dictator of Iraq—was somehow involved in the horrible events of 9/11. In fact, the connection between Iraq and 9/11 became a commonplace during that time. In 2005, however, the *National Journal* published an account that challenged the connection. Here is part of MSNBC's version of the story:

> After Sept. 11, the administration insisted that a connection existed between Iraq and al-Qaida. President Bush, in an October 2002 speech in Cincinnati, said the United States had "learned that Iraq has trained al-Qaida members in bomb-making and poisons and gas."
>
> And Vice President Cheney, in a September 2003 appearance on NBC's "Meet the Press," alleged there was "a relationship between Iraq and al-Qaida that stretched back through most of the decade of the '90s."
>
> But the National Journal report said that the few believable reports of contact between Iraq and al-Qaida "involved attempts by Saddam Hussein to monitor the terrorist group."
>
> Saddam considered al-Qaida "as well as other theocratic radical Islamist organizations as a potential threat to his secular regime," the Journal reported. "At one point, analysts believed, Saddam considered infiltrating the ranks" of al-Qaida with Iraqi intelligence operatives as a way to get more information about how the organization worked, the Journal said . . . .
>
> The Journal story asserts that little has changed to refute the initial absence of information linking Saddam and the al-Qaida network.
>
> "In the four years since Bush received the briefing, according to highly placed government officials, little evidence has come to light to contradict the CIA's original conclusion that no collaborative relationship existed" between Iraq and al-Qaida, the Journal reported.
>
> Reporter (Murray) Waas quotes one former administration official, whose assessment is a problematic contradiction of the administration's longstanding assertions:
>
> "What the President was told on September 21 was consistent with everything he has been told since—that the evidence was just not there."
>
> (MSNBC.com: http://msnbc.msn.com/id/10164478/)

Clearly, this information counters the commonplace that Saddam Hussein was behind 9/11. As this information became more widely known, the commonplace became less influential. Those who continued to hold onto it in the face of contrary evidence must have done so because it was closely connected to other beliefs in their ideology.

THE COMMON SENSE OF YOUR CRITICAL SITUATION

It's time now to wade into the ideological tides of your critical situation.

It is possible that one or more ideological differences that polarize opinion and draw up "battle lines" can be found at the heart of your critical situation. If this is the case, and if you want your argument to be successful, you must invent ways to navigate around and through beliefs that may compromise your success in persuading others to accept your argument. In what follows we provide a number of activities that should help you to understand the ideological stakes in your critical situation.

Invention Journal: Mapping Ideological Conflict

1. On paper or using a spreadsheet, create a column for each of the stakeholder positions in your critical situation. Now, find or review a range of comments by stakeholders in the issue. In each column, write out any expressions of common sense that you find.
2. Find public statements made by major stakeholders in your critical situation. Read carefully, underlining or highlighting familiar phrases that convey beliefs shared among members of this stakeholder group generally. Compare conflicting phrases and statements and summarize what you see to be the core difference in the ideologies that inform the various stakeholders.
3. Are any commonplaces shared by the different stakeholder groups involved in this critical situation? If so, how is the commonplace understood or used differently by the different groups? This can be an important exercise because it may help you find common ideological ground on which arguments can be made across community contexts.

COMMONPLACES, IDEOLOGY, AND AUDIENCE

The ideological orientation of your audience has everything to do with whether a commonplace phrase or statement will persuade or alienate. The persuasive power of rhetorical commonplaces depends upon the fact that they express assumptions held in common by people who subscribe to a given ideology. For example: a first principle of environmental philosophy is preservation of the earth's ecosystem. Within the environmentalist community, people have developed commonplaces that express this principle: "Earth first"; "Good planets are hard to find." These slogans represent the received wisdom of the environmental community in a shorthand that reminds its members of their shared beliefs. They can be deployed whenever the group needs to be energized or reminded of their ideological commitments, or when they wish to persuade others to adopt their ideology. For an audience of environmentalists, the expression of these principles is a rallying point.

The flip side of this, of course, is that commonplaces presented to the wrong audience, say those suspicious of environmentalism, can mean disaster for your argument, unless you intend to alienate your audience. When environmentalists argue for limits on industry, for instance, those who adhere to the ideology of *laissez faire* are often unwilling to entertain further discussion. (*Laissez faire* dictates that government not interfere in economic matters). Upon hearing ideologies different from their own, many audience members may shake their heads and say, "You just don't get it." Across an ideological divide, these commonplaces appear anything but commonsensical.

WORKSHOP 7: Finding Access: Publishing Your Work

What are the most meaningful publics for your work? What audiences, if persuaded by your work, can become agents of change in your critical situation? Once you identify the right audience, how do you reach them? To discover routes of access to your audience, work through the series of questions in this workshop.

WORKSHOP 9: Gathering Information through Interviews

Because you are a member of the communities in which you are planning a writing project, it is likely that you know personally people with detailed information about pressing community matters. This workshop helps you prepare interviews to access that information.

Invention Journal: Adapting Contested Commonplaces

1. Write out all of the commonplace phrases and statements that circulate among the stakeholder groups in your critical situation. Now, think of ways to negotiate these commonplaces. If they are harmful to your argument, can you challenge them in some way that will not offend members of your audience? Restate them? If this is not possible, can you simply admit that you disagree with a commonplace? To do so may enhance your *ethos* because your audience may perceive you as an honest speaker or writer (see Chapter 6 for a discussion of *ethos*).
2. Consult the list of commonplaces to which your audience adheres. Are there any on which you can agree? As we have suggested, one of the most powerful ways to persuade an audience is to speak from the authority of

their common sense. If you are able to agree with the audience on a given commonplace, this may also enhance your ethos.

3. Review the writing you did in the other Invention Journals of this chapter. Of all the commonplace statements you have mapped, which will be most effective in your argument? For instance, advocates for gay civil rights have often appealed to Christian principles ("we're all God's children") in making their case for specific policy changes. Advocates of gay rights can also cite passages from the Bible to make their case when speaking or writing to Christian audiences.
4. Now, compose an appeal in support of your position that takes one or more of your audience's commonplaces as major premises.

COMMONPLACES AND THE VOICE OF HISTORICAL AUTHORITY

People making arguments in the public sphere often make reference to the people who helped found our nation, relying upon them as sources of rhetorical authority. The words of George Washington, Thomas Jefferson, Benjamin Franklin, and others resonate so strongly because they express national common sense in the voice of historical authority. Abigail Adams's caution to her husband John to "remember the ladies" when writing the founding documents is also frequently cited today. Texts older than the United States Constitution and Declaration of Independence are sources of powerful commonplace arguments. Think of how often writers and speakers refer to the Bible, Koran, or Talmud, for instance. Think how powerful an argument might be, made to the right audience, drawing commonplaces from all these texts.

WORKSHOP 2: Arranging Your Composition
As you discover arguments through invention, consider how they will fit together when you sit down to write. This workshop is devoted to "arrangement," the skillful structuring of arguments.

WORKSHOP 10: Inventing Persuasive Voice
No matter how carefully audiences judge the reasoning and evidence of an argument, we still respond to *voice* in what we read. We still make judgments about how arguments "speak" to us. In this workshop, you will find resources for skillful control of the voice in your writing.

WORKSHOP 15: Revising for Clarity
This workshop offers revising strategies for increasing the clarity of writing. Increasing the clarity of your ideas will help you connect with your intended audience.

Invention Journal: Arguing Using Historical Commonplaces

1. From what major texts can you draw the wisdom of the ages? Are there holy books that might gain your audiences' confidence? Political documents? Works of literature? Famous speeches?
2. Think of major historical events that have influenced your critical situation. For instance, if you are writing about affirmative action, the history of slavery and emancipation and civil rights might provide you with commonplace statements and arguments that will enhance your argument. What were the commonplace assertions that writers and speakers made during these major events? How can they be adapted to your purposes as a writer or speaker?
3. Throughout history, there have been those whose words have seemed to capture something important about key issues or debates or about life in general. Benjamin Franklin, Emily Dickinson, Martin Luther King, and many others have left their share of commonplaces for the rest of us to use and admire. Used in moderation, well-placed quotations can have persuasive power. Consult a dictionary of quotations that is arranged by subject to see whether or not you can find quotations that support your argument by lending it power and authority.

THE POWER OF IMAGES IN COMMONPLACE ARGUMENTS

Images often have a visceral power when we encounter them; they hit us in the gut, persuading us before we can think why. People say that "seeing is believing," meaning that visual evidence is proof positive. But the converse is true: beliefs influence how and what we see. Images present us with a powerful way to argue through commonplaces. If the context of your project allows it, consider using images that will connect with your audience's common sense.

WORKSHOP 12: Putting Together a Portfolio of Your Invention Work

Gathering your invention work together in a portfolio creates a record of your thought, research, and analysis. This workshop offers a simple framework for constructing a portfolio and writing a critical self-reflection on the progress of your project.

Invention Journal: Seeing and Believing

1. As succinctly as possible, write out the major claims you think you will make in your project. For each claim, write out a list of values that support that claim. For example, if you are arguing that the United States-Mexico

border should be militarized to keep out Mexican migrants, you might ascribe to national pride as a value. The image of the United States flag, most obviously, is a visual shorthand for expressing national pride. What images work in the context of your project?

2. Return to your previous Invention Journals in this chapter, and find points of ideological connection between you and your audience. With one, two, or several other people, brainstorm a list of images that capture this point of common sense agreement.
3. Once you have chosen images that may appear in your project, decide what text will accompany the image. How will you *frame* the images so that your audience views them as you want them to be seen? For example, an image of an armed U.S. citizen standing in the desert near the Mexican border will be interpreted differently by different viewers. Will the person be viewed as a patriot protecting national integrity or a vigilante taking the law into his own hands? Take time now to write 100–200 words contextualizing the images you are using.

LIST OF WORKS CITED

Hirsch, E. D. *Cultural Literacy: What Every American Needs to Know*. Chicago: Chicago UP, 1987.

Wolcott, James. "Caution: Women Seething. Why Such Outrage over Harvard President Larry Summers's Hazy Musing that Women may be Innately Less Gifted at Science." *Vanity Fair* 538 (June 1, 2005).

Zinn, Howard. *Declarations of Independence*. New York: Harper Collins, 1990.

6

ESTABLISHING CHARACTER AND CREDIBILITY

A powerful source of support for any argument derives from the skilled presentation of a writer's or speaker's character. Ancient teachers of rhetoric called this tactic *ethos,* from the Greek word for "character." Arguments based on character can convince audiences that they, and their authors, are worthy of respect and belief. To demonstrate the power of ethos, we turn to one of the all-time great performances of character in argument. What follows is from Sojourner Truth's address to the Women's Rights Convention called in Akron, Ohio, in 1851. Truth was born a slave in New York in 1797, and over the course of her long life (she lived until 1883) she earned a reputation such that she is now recognized as an icon of American values such as freedom, determination, and of course, truth. The passage below is from an account of Truth's speech written in 1859 by Dana Gage, feminist, abolitionist, and president of the 1851 Convention. Gage's account is only one of several that were written and widely cited, which suggests how valuable Truth's reputation and powerful words remained for the reformers that followed after her. In her account, Gage describes the scene just before Truth took the stage. Many local clergy from different denominations (all of whom were white and men) were in attendance to criticize the very notion of women's rights. These men were shouting down the speakers, asserting the natural superiority of men and the commonplace notion that the Bible supported the idea of male superiority. Gage noted that the courage and resolve of the women conventioneers was beginning to fail; Gage, in fact, feared that the Convention might be broken up.

The women at the Convention were particularly nervous about the presence of Sojourner Truth. Gage reports that her fearful colleagues begged her, "'Don't let her speak, Mrs. G. It will ruin us. Every newspaper in the land will have our cause mixed with abolition and niggers, and we shall be utterly denounced." From Gage's account, we can begin to imagine the enormous odds against Truth: Even her *allies* were unwilling to acknowledge her, and her very presence at this public event brought objections and "hissing" from the crowd. Just at the moment when things seemed about to unravel, Truth took the stage to the general "disapprobation" of

THE SHADOW TO SUPPORT THE SUBSTANCE.
SOJOURNER TRUTH.

Sojourner Truth
Sojourner Truth's strength of character, legendary at the podium, was understood as a political asset by abolitionists and early feminists.

the audience. By Gage's account, however, one verified by other accounts, her very presence on stage silenced the crowd. Almost immediately, Truth singled out a man who apparently had argued that a woman's reputation was based on gentility and passivity:

> "Dat man ober dar say dat womin needs to be helped into carriages, and lifted ober ditches, and to hab de best place everywhar. Nobody eber helps me into carriages, or ober mud puddles, or gibs me any best place!" And raising herself to her full height, and her voice to a pitch like rolling thunder, she asked, "And a'n't I a woman? Look at me! Look at my arm! (and she bared her right arm to the shoulder, showing her tremendous muscular power). I have ploughed, and planted, and gathered into barns, and no man could head me! And a'n't I a woman? I could work as much and eat as much as a man—when I could get it—and bear de lash as well! And a'n't I a woman? I have borne thirteen chilern, and seen 'em mos' all sold off to slavery, and when I cried out with my mother's grief, none but Jesus heard me! And a'n't I a woman? (Painter 166–167)

Gage reports that the audience moved between rapt, silent attention and thunderous applause. Her summary of Truth's impact on the audience should make all public speakers envious: "I have never in my life seen anything like the magical influence that subdued the mobish spirit of the day," Gage recalled. Truth's speech "turned the jibes and sneers of an excited crowd into notes of respect and admiration" (168).

How was Truth able to command such respect and influence despite her status as an illiterate African American woman and a former slave? As you can imagine, Truth spoke a different English than that used by her audience, a dialect that might have drawn the ridicule of many white listeners (especially those predisposed to white supremacist values). Still, Truth's questioning refrain, "a'n't I a woman," delivered amid her testimony of the trials of labor and motherhood as a slave, was a brilliant ethical appeal. The repetition demanded that listeners question their own way of judging character. The account of her experiences demonstrates the capacity of women to be productive citizens and to endure hardships, attributes that were more likely more readily associated with traditional masculinity. At the same time, Truth's recollection of bearing 13 children and having them "mos' all sold off to slavery" evokes the great crimes of slavery against women and family that Truth had survived. Furthermore, when she explains how she "cried out with my mother's grief," and " none but Jesus heard," she claims credibility as an admirable woman, fiercely devoted to her children and strong in her Christian conviction. Truth's ethical argument, her ethos posed as a question—And a'n't I a woman?—thus not only gave her the authority and credibility to speak before the audience, but it also shook the foundations on which the characters of men and women were then judged. Truth's skillful defense of her own intrinsic human worth powerfully question hierarchies of gender and race, categories so often manipulated with oppressive intention.

According to Webster's dictionary, the English word *character* retains two of the important senses it carried for ancient teachers of rhetoric: (1) the pattern of behavior found in an individual or group; and (2) a good reputation. Our English term *personality* does not quite capture the meaning of *ethos* because the ancient Greeks believed that character was created by a person's habits and reputation rather than by her experiences. Following their example, we employ the

WORKSHOP 13: Readers Responding
This workshop offers powerful strategies for approaching reading as serious writers do, with a critical eye for the most important arguments and ideas. Following the strategies presented in this workshop, you will gain skills as an engaged reader and become more able to put what you read to work in your own writing.

WORKSHOP 16: Summarizing Arguments, Ideas, and Texts
Writers regularly present the work of others as building blocks for their own work. This workshop offers strategies for writing strong summaries to incorporate into your own writing.

WORKSHOP 8: Following Pathways: A Metaphor for Critical Reading and Research
Do you want to find out more about Sojourner Truth or the history of abolitionism? The exercises in this workshop will help you identify unfamiliar ideas and references in your reading and research and approach them as opportunities for learning—as "pathways" to knowledge.

terms *character* and *ethical proof* in this chapter to refer to proofs that draw their strength from community evaluations of a writer's or speaker's reputation. In short, a writer's or speaker's ethos is constructed by a community of readers and listeners.

You may feel uncomfortable with the notion that rhetorical character can be constructed, since Americans tend to think of character, or personality, as fairly stable. We generally assume, as well, that character is shaped by an individual's experiences and determined through the force of one's own will. Americans don't talk as much as they used to about persons having a good character, but apparently they still care about such things, and they are very much interested in the character and personal habits of public figures. The "character issue" is regularly raised in presidential elections, although in this case *character* ordinarily refers to a candidate's personal moral choices: Has he been faithful to his spouse? Has she used drugs? Ancient rhetoricians were not as interested in private moral choices such as these as they were in the virtues that counted in public affairs: courage, honesty, trustworthiness, modesty, intelligence, and fair-mindedness. The Greeks thought that character, to the extent it was under the control of an individual, was constructed by the moral practices in which a person habitually engaged. An ethos was not given by nature, but was developed by habit. Thus, it was important for parents and teachers not only to provide children with examples of good behavior, but to insist that young persons practice habits that imprinted their characters with virtues rather than vices. Because the Greeks thought that character was shaped by one's practices, they considered it to be much more malleable than we do.

SITUATED AND INVENTED ETHOS

People who know you well—friends and family—have already constructed some notion of who you are, of your character. That is, they will know whether you can be trusted to present your case honestly and thoroughly. In a classroom setting students are acquainted with one another and with the teacher, but members of this group do not know one another well, at least at the beginning of a semester's or quarter's work. But writers and speakers most often compose for people whom they do not know—city council members, state legislators, readers of magazines, newspapers' opinion pages, blogs, books, or textbooks (as we are doing here). Because writers and speakers face both kinds of audiences—those they know well and those they don't—we distinguish between two sorts of ethical proof: *situated* and *invented.* If a writer or speaker is fortunate enough to enjoy a good reputation among members of an audience, she can use this good reputation as an ethical proof. This is situated ethos. When Sojourner Truth spoke to groups who harbored racist or sexist beliefs, her situated ethos worked against her. But when she addressed abolitionists and women's groups, she could take advantage of her situated ethos as a woman and former slave because this status gave her authority and credibility among members of these audiences.

At the 1851 Women's Rights Convention, however, we see that Truth also invented an ethos, that of a powerful person who can survive the most horrible trials and yet remain strong and determined to achieve freedom for her people. An invented ethos is necessary and useful in two critical situations: when writers and speakers are not acquainted with members of an audience, and when the audience might be hostile either to them or to the position they forward. In either of these cases, writers and speakers can invent a character suitable to an occasion by means of careful word choice and other strategies we review later on in this chapter.

The ancient interest in character is still useful to writers and speakers because it highlights the role played by this important kind of proof in contemporary rhetorical exchanges. Ethical proofs are varied and subtle. No matter how entirely you think the quality of your project exists on the page or in the words that you speak, audiences still make judgments about your arguments based on their assessments of your character.

TALK READ WRITE

1. Is character an outmoded concept or not? In conversations with friends, families, coworkers, or other community members, do you discuss the character of those around you?
2. Read the entire account of Sojourner Truth's 1851 speech. What makes it a powerful rhetorical performance? Visit historical sites on the Internet that discuss Truth, her history, and her legacy. How is it that her ethos has remained strong two and a half centuries later?

Situated Ethos

Often, life itself assigns ethos. We are born into character expectations that others have of us. Because critical situations are embedded in social relations, the social standing of participants in such a situation can affect ethos. Social status confers power, as do certain situations. A differential power relation inheres within any rhetorical situation, for example, simply because writers or speakers have the floor, so to speak. As long as they are being read or listened to they have control of the situation. But audiences have power too, particularly in the case of written discourse, where readers are relatively free to quit whenever they please. Few authors enjoy absolute power over either hearers or readers. We all know how easy it is to mute television commercials or to skip to the end of a murder mystery to see how it turns out.

But differential power relations exist outside of rhetorical situations as well, and these affect the degree to which an invented ethos can be effective. An author's ethos may be either bolstered or compromised by his or her reputation or position in the community despite the soundness of his argument, the quality of his evidence, etc. Within classrooms, for example, teachers have more power than students, and usually teachers can silence students whenever they think it's necessary or proper to do so. The credibility of a student in a first-year course, no matter how brilliant and eloquent she is, may still be judged as lacking simply because of her place in an institutional hierarchy that assumes the superior knowledge of the professor. Conversely, well-known people, and especially those who are well-known because they hold some authoritative or prestigious position in the community, might be received as credible spokespeople even if they know relatively little about the situation at hand; think of how many times you have been persuaded by actors or musicians who speak out on social and political issues.

Authors and audiences may exist in unequal social relations to one another for a variety of reasons. Within the culture at large, in general, older people have more authority than do younger ones, and wealthy people have more power than do poorer ones, in part because they have better access to the channels of communication. We could argue that in some sectors of our culture, young men of color are often distrusted and assumed to be "criminal minded." Perhaps the most well-known statement about this problem of assessing ethos based on race was made by Dr. Martin Luther King Jr. in his landmark "I Have a Dream" speech: "I have a dream my four little children will one day live in a nation where they will not be judged by the color of their skin, but by the content of their character." King's hopeful statement is a commonplace of social justice, and it also points out vividly the social barriers of situated ethos.

WORKSHOP 3: Different Values and Respectful Conflict

Arguments are inherently matters of conflict. Rather than trying to avoid such conflict, we recommend approaching it as a powerful learning opportunity and an intellectual resource. This workshop provides the framework for sharing our own value-based positions in a productive and respectful manner.

Like all other rhetorical considerations, situated ethos depends on the context of the critical situation. For example, our own situated ethos in the classroom, as teachers, is relatively strong as long as we are discussing course materials. However, if the conversation turns to other topics, like how to fix an air conditioner, for instance, or what to think of the relative merits of the horror film *Saw* and its sequel, *Saw II,* our situated ethos is diminished. That is, the situational ethos lent us by our institutional authority does not extend to our qualifications as electricians or movie reviewers, at least with some audiences. Ministers also have powerful situated ethos in many social situations—even people who do not practice the same faith might well grant a certain respect to a priest, rabbi, or minister—but before an audience of young and rebellious teenagers, ministerial exhortations to resist sexual temptation might well fall utterly flat. Thus, the cultural authority lent by social status can actually become an ethical liability in some contexts.

In short, situated ethos might help or hinder your cause in writing and speaking, and so you have to decide how to negotiate the way your authority is positioned in the critical situation at hand. Consider the work of one of our students, Jared Miller, who argued for "smart growth" in opposition to what he sees as uncontrolled and ill-considered development of homes in desert areas at the boundaries of metropolitan Phoenix:

> As Arizonans, we are now faced with difficult choices carrying severe consequences. Our children will bear witness to the effects of these choices firsthand in their lifetimes. Previous generations didn't have to concern themselves with these issues. With the abundance of resources there was never a problem. Those days are gone and the luxury of their ignorance. It is a shame we boast about our growth rate

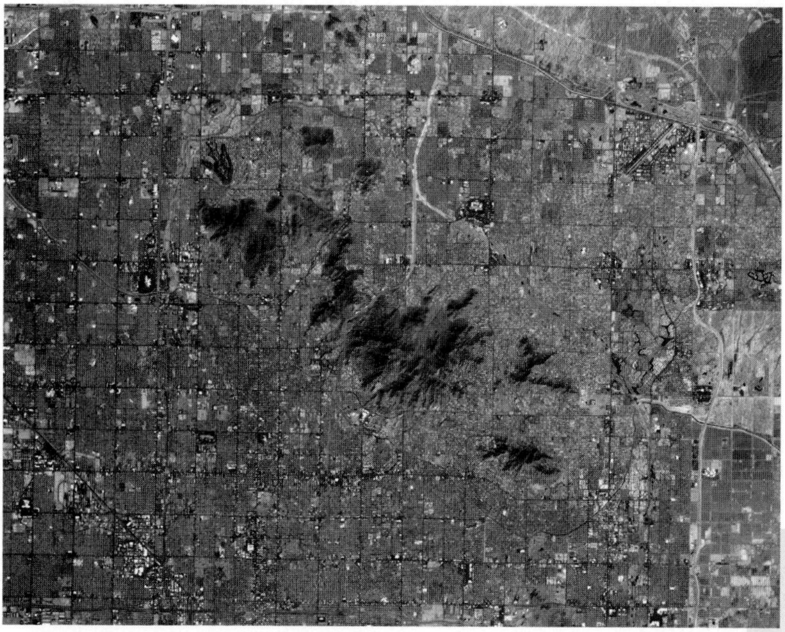

Map of Phoenix Urban Sprawl
Western cities like Phoenix have witnessed massive development and often bitter debates about the environmental cost of "urban sprawl." The map pictured here indicates the kind of growth that has made Phoenix one of the largest and most populous metropolitan centers in the country.

> while ignoring its adverse effects. We must take action to slow urban sprawl in order to preserve our lifestyles, our communities, and our environment.

Miller highlights his position as an Arizonan, a person who has experienced first-hand the changing landscape of Phoenix and who has an immediate stake in the situation of "urban sprawl."

TALK READ WRITE

To what extent does situated ethos determine perceptions of character and credibility? In other words, when we write or speak, to what extent do economic class, gender, race, age, body type, disability and other factors influence how we are perceived? At its core, this question asks us to think about the power of prejudice in our society. As a group or individually, brainstorm a list of situations in which the situated factors listed here are obstacles to be overcome for writers and speakers. Think of speaking and writing contexts in which they matter a great deal and/or are less influential.

Invention Journal: Starting Where You Are

1. Here are some questions to ask about the power relations inherent in your critical situation: how disparate are the power positions of the various participants? Will your project increase, maintain, or decrease the disparity? How rigid or flexible are the power relations, and does your project function to increase, maintain, or decrease the stability?
2. How is your ethos situated in the context of your critical situation? Does your status or experience grant you authority? Is it a problem to overcome? If you are situated as an authority, how can you best highlight situated ethos? Recall how Jared Miller drew on the ethos of a native Arizonan. If you are situated in a way that is damaging to your ethos, what can you do to mitigate the problem? Recall how Sojourner Truth took her race, gender, and "previous condition of servitude," all thought to be marks of poor character for public spokespeople, and transformed them in the presentation of an honorable self.

Invented Ethos

Writers or speakers who use invented ethos, you will recall, construct a character within their composition. Aristotle taught that an effective ethos had at least three features: in order to be persuasive a writer or speaker must seem to be intelligent, must seem to be of good moral character, and must possess good will toward their audiences. Writers and speakers can construct a character that seems intelligent by demonstrating that they are well-informed about issues they discuss. They project an appearance of good moral character by describing themselves or others as moral persons and by refraining from the use of misleading or fallacious arguments. They can project good will toward an audience by presenting the information and arguments that audiences require in order to understand the critical situation at hand.

Demonstrating Intelligence by Doing the Homework

Writers and speakers can create a character that seems intelligent by demonstrating that they are informed about the issues they discuss and by refraining from using arguments that are irrelevant or trivial. General audiences can be assumed to be relatively uninformed about difficult or technical issues, so in this case, speakers and writers must take special care to convince an audience that they are well informed without overwhelming the audience with details. On the other hand, it is equally important to seem well informed when members of the audience are themselves relatively well informed about the issue at hand. In this case, the writer or speaker must quickly ensure readers or listeners that he has studied the critical situation carefully. Jared Miller, for example, demonstrates that he is a knowledgeable commentator on development in Phoenix, Arizona, by highlighting the sources of his information at every step of his argument. Moving readers inductively to the conclusion that further growth must be controlled, Miller refers repeatedly to recent studies on environmental impact, population growth, and water conservation.

Writers and speakers may also assure readers of their trustworthiness by using language that suggests an insider status, by sharing an anecdote that indicates experience or knowledge in a particular area, or by describing his or her qualifications in the area. Kristin Breitweiser is one of five women who fought hard to establish an official investigation into the events of September 11, 2001. Breitweiser's husband was killed in the attack, and her status as the spouse of a victim lends her considerable situated ethos. But when she speaks she also relies on a persuasive invented ethos. Here is an excerpt from a speech she made while accepting an award for her work:

> I am honored to accept the Ridenhour Truth Award and I accept it on behalf of all men, women and children who have sought Truth in their lives, including the four women—Mindy Kleinberg, Lorie Van Auken, Patty Casazza, and Monica Gabrielle—who fought along with me to seek the truth about 9/11. I am humbled by the ceremony of this award, and I accept it also in honor of my late husband, Ron Breitweiser.
>
> In the past three years I have spent a lot of time talking about being a 9/11 widow and a victim's advocate for intelligence community reforms. I appeared frequently in the print and televised media discussing my transformation from a stay-at-home mom whose specialty it was to design children's gardens to a victim's rights advocate whose specialty has become national security. My transformation was urgent, drastic and *not chosen by me* . . . .
>
> How did I get here today? I got here by asking questions. I got here by being an American citizen. Not by choice, widowed at 30 and finding myself frightened and with no faith in my government, I decided to seek the truth as to why my husband died. I wanted to know that my daughter and I were safe living in this country. Along with four other widows, I played a role in our democratic process by simply asking who, what, where, how, and most importantly, why 9/11 happened.
>
> ("Are We Safer," *The Nation* April 21, 2005)

Breitweiser says she is humbled by her receipt of this award, and this strengthens her ethos because humility is not something we might expect from such a celebrated person. She reaffirms her humility when she dedicates the honor to the memory of her husband. She also readily admits that she had no special expertise in victim's rights or in matters of national security prior to 9/11, pointing out that her current expertise, for which she is receiving the award, was not something she achieved by choice. This poignant admission increases our sympathy for her position and that of other victims of those tragic events. Furthermore, she characterizes her experiences since 9/11 as those of any ordinary American citizen, perhaps out of modesty; but her account of the questions she asked may also stimulate others to become more active citizens.

A writer or speaker may also use specialized or technical language to demonstrate adeptness in a particular field. As an example, we reprint two of the opening paragraphs of an article about the collapse of the Twin Towers of the World Trade Center on September 11.

> To a structural engineer, a skyscraper is modeled as a large cantilever vertical column. Each tower was 64 m square, standing 411 m above street level and 21 m below grade. This produces a height-to-width ratio of 6.8. The total weight of

> the structure was roughly 500,000 t, but wind load, rather than the gravity load, dominated the design. The building is a huge sail that must resist a 225 km/h hurricane. It was designed to resist a wind load of 2 kPa—a total of lateral load of 5,000 t.
>
> In order to make each tower capable of withstanding this wind load, the architects selected a lightweight "perimeter tube" design consisting of 244 exterior columns of 36 cm square steel box section on 100 cm centers . . . . This permitted windows more than one-half meter wide. Inside this outer tube there was a 27 m 40 m core, which was designed to support the weight of the tower. It also housed the elevators, the stairwells, and the mechanical risers and utilities. Web joists 80 cm tall connected the core to the perimeter at each story. Concrete slabs were poured over these joists to form the floors. In essence, the building is an egg-crate construction that is about 95 percent air, explaining why the rubble after the collapse was only a few stories high.

This article was written by Thomas Eagar and Christopher Musso, and it was published in a professional engineering journal (JOM 53, 12: 2001, 8–11). JOM stands for *The Journal of the Society of Minerals, Metals, and Materials,* and a link at the top of the Web page where this article appears tells us that Eagar is affiliated with the Massachusetts Institute of Technology (MIT). But most readers do not require this information in order to discern that the authors of this piece are engineers; the technical terms and abbreviations, in addition to the mathematical references, make that clear. There is considerable controversy surrounding the collapse of the towers, and it is important for people who publish essays and books about this event to establish their credentials as engineers or as people who are otherwise knowledgeable about such things as stress and gravity load.

We remarked earlier that speakers or writers who wish to appear intelligent and well informed must demonstrate that they have done whatever research and contemplation is necessary to understand an issue, and they must avoid making irrelevant or trivial arguments. A rhetorical disaster may ensue when writers or speakers fail to establish themselves as well informed about the issues they discuss. Here is an example of failed ethos produced by a writer who did not do the necessary research on the issue at hand—why people go to college:

> Many students go to college to find a husband or wife. While there are some who attend for the purpose of getting themselves an education, these are few and far between. The majority of companion seekers are men because by the time they reach college most of them are ready to settle down after the wild life of high school. In most cases, men are tied to home, security, and have problems in adjusting to being completely on their own. In the opinion of this author, men are looking to fulfill their need of security by finding a wife in college.

There is no hint here that the author did any research on this subject, even to the extent of asking one or two college men whether or not his conclusions were true. Audiences whose experiences and aims do not match the generalizations made here will feel excluded by the assertive tone, while others may be offended by it. This tone is mitigated somewhat in the last sentence, where the writer tells us that these generalizations are only an opinion.

Here is a revision of the passage:

> Although I have some friends who are here to get themselves an education, I know many students who come to college to look for a husband or a wife. For instance, my roommate is having problems adjusting to being completely on his own, and I think he's still tied to home and security. In fact, he has admitted to me that he is looking to find a wife in college who will give him the security he misses. This need for security seems to be the case with many of my male friends.

While talking with the author, classmates discovered that the generalization about wife-seeking men was based on only one example—that of a roommate. They encouraged the author to limit his generalization to what he knew from experience. As a result, the second version manifests a character who does not make claims about that which he is uninformed.

Invention Journal: Doing the Homework

1. Have you done your homework? Is your research up to date? You must be honest with yourself at this point. Is the body of commentary and your analysis of the critical situation large enough to convince your audience that you are well informed?
2. What are your credentials within your critical situation? Do you have degrees, titles, or certificates that give you expert status? If you do have some official mark of expertise, how can you highlight this in your project? For example, when academics send out articles for publication, they are sure to include their title–Professor Big Brain, Ph.D., and the name of the university with which they are affiliated. If you don't have degrees, titles, or certificates that qualify you as an expert, don't be dismayed. You likely have experience that qualifies you as someone with an "insider" perspective. Write out a one-page history of your involvement in your critical situation. Can you use this history to establish your status as a knowledgeable person within the critical situation?

Establishing Good Character

There are probably as many ways to demonstrate good moral character as there are virtues—and vices. A Roman rhetor named Cicero encouraged rhetors to extol their "merits or worth or virtue of some kind, particularly generosity, sense of duty, justice and good faith" (*On the Parts,* viii 28). He also suggested that rhetors weaken charges or suspicions that had been cast upon their character, and to elaborate on misfortunes or difficulties that had befallen them in order to strengthen their audience's estimate of their ability to bear suffering (*On Invention,* I xvi 22). Certainly, the Sojourner Truth speech with which we began this chapter is a strong example of demonstrating good moral character (that of the hard worker, the devoted and caring mother, the devout Christian). "A Narrative of the Life and Labors of the

Rev. G. W. Offley" offers another example from the abolitionist context. Offley wrote this 1859 reflection of his life expressly to teach young people about the proper way to live life, which is to say, how to mold a good character through experience. Notice how he invents a moral character in this passage:

> During my boyhood father hired me to a slaveholder for a term of four years to pay his house rent. From the time I was nine years old I worked and supported myself until I was twenty-one years old, and never received one dollar of my wages. When I was ten years old I sat down and taking an old basket to pieces, learned myself to make baskets. After that I learned to make foot mats and horse collars, not of leather but of corn husks; also two kinds of brooms. These articles I used to make nights and sell to get money for myself. When I was sixteen years old I commenced taking contracts of wood-chopping, at fifty cents per cord, and hired slaves to chop for me nights, when the moon shone bright. In the fall and winter we would make our fire and chop until eleven or twelve at night. We used to catch oysters and fish nights, and hire other slaves to peddle them out on Sunday mornings. By this way I have helped some to get their freedom.

Offley's recollection of his industry and community-commitment is a strong proof of moral character. Despite the considerable constraint of slavery, Offley demonstrates his stature as a "self-made man," a character that has assumed nearly mythical status among American virtues. We can only admire the 10-year-old who disassembled a basket to teach himself the process of weaving with the goal of raising money for himself and others. Even contemporary readers might admire Offley's entrepreneurial spirit. Through determination and self-effort, Offley generated economic opportunities by means of which other slaves could earn the money to "get their freedom"; his hard work and generosity attest to the good moral character of this resourceful person.

Writers and speakers establish their trustworthy character by associating themselves and the positions they take with the values of the community and/or by rejecting vices that the community finds offensive. Let's return to Jared Miller's letter to Arizonans addressing the problem of urban sprawl: As a native Arizonan, something he rightly mentions in his text, Miller understands the desire of the millions who have moved to the state in the last 20 years to escape the problems of urban life, to catch the remnants of the "Go West!" experience, or to find a land of opportunity. He knows, as well, that many residents make the most of Arizona's low taxes. Through intelligent discussion and reference to his research (which demonstrates his knowledge), Miller aligns himself with community values:

> Arizonans are beginning to experience many of the same symptoms of congestion familiar to larger urban areas. Traffic, pollution, over-crowded schools, and lack of affordable housing are all problems that we see on a daily basis. Along with the complications arising from our massive size, soon Arizonans will be burdened with an even greater issue—a serious lack of infrastructure. Hospitals, emergency services, sanitation, sewage, and roads are already behind the growth curve. Catherine Reagor of *The Arizona Republic* writes that an estimated cost of $174 billion will be needed within the next twenty-five years to pay for these types of services.

Miller is likely to seem trustworthy to an audience of middle-class Arizonans because he shares their concerns about quality of life and financial well-being. He also distances himself from values that might be repugnant to his audience. Understanding the difficulty of making a conservationist argument to a non-conservationist audience, Miller carefully characterizes his own value-based commitments. "In the sixties and early seventies," he writes, "people who thought as I do were known as hippies or tree-huggers, ridiculed and scorned by 'normal people.' Today, they are called environmentalists and conservationists. Now they are regarded with respect and even admiration. Today, they are more mainstream and are spearheading programs to protect and preserve our resources." Here, Miller reminds his audience that environmentalism is no longer a fringe issue and that environmentalists like himself have everyone's best interest at heart.

Moral standards are often used as means of proof in contemporary rhetorical situations. Opponents of abortion characterize pro-choice advocates as "baby killers" and "murderers"; people who support the war in Iraq say that those who oppose or protest the war are unpatriotic; public officials are often charged with immoral behavior such as infidelity or harassment. In order to establish their good moral standing, writers and speakers may cite approval of their character from respected authorities. People establish their character in this way when they ask teachers or employers for letters of reference and when they list the names of teachers and former employers on their resumes. References are often asked about the same qualities of character in prospective employees that concerned ancient rhetoricians: intelligence, honesty, and trustworthiness. Writers and speakers can also shore up an audience's sense of their character simply by refraining from the use of unfair rhetorical tactics: faulty reasoning or non-representative evidence, threats, name-calling, or lies. Jared Miller, for instance, decided not to include the sharp criticisms of greedy developers that appeared in his research; he decided that such accusations could too easily be interpreted as a mark of disrespect. As such, they might damage his ethos as a careful and concerned community member.

A slightly different interpretation of good character seems to be very persuasive in modern discourse. This is the ethos that conveys a person as an authority, either by virtue of respectable credentials or long experience in some activity. The covers or inside pages of books often list "other works by the same author," in order to establish the writer's history as a published author (and to sell more copies of her books). Advertisements for movies often list actors' credits for other films, thus demonstrating that they have done good work previously or to associate the movie being advertised with better-known or more successful films. This usually happens when the producers think that the actors' name recognition isn't tied closely enough to their face recognition—two kinds of ethos that are very important in the movie industry.

Richard Clarke, who wrote a controversial book about the events of September 11, establishes his credentials as an insider on the jacket of his book:

> Richard Clarke was appointed by President Clinton as the first National Coordinator for Security, Infrastructure Protection, and Counterterrorism in May 1998 and continued in that position under George W. Bush. Until March 2003 he was a career member of the senior Executive Service, having begun his federal service in

> 1973 in the Office of the Secretary of Defense, as an analyst on nuclear weapons and European security issues. In the Reagan administration, Mr. Clarke was the Deputy Assistant Secretary of State of Intelligence. In the first Bush administration, he was the Assistant Secretary of State for Political-Military Affairs.

All of these titles and positions are listed in order to assure readers that Clarke has been working in high positions in the federal government for many years. His history of employment shows that various presidents and their administrations have had sufficient confidence in his work to keep him on. To a politically informed eye, this list of jobs also shows that presidents representing both major political parties appointed him to high-ranking positions, which suggests that he is not a partisan. This is important because Clarke expresses very strong opinions in his book about the failure of the Bush administration to prevent 9/11, and it is important that these opinions seem to stem from his expertise rather than a party bias.

Invention Journal: The Right Character

1. Return to your Invention Journal from Chapter 5, "Judging the Common Sense of your Audience." What are the commonplace assumptions and ideological commitments that influence how your audience perceives the critical situation at hand? What values do they espouse when talking or writing about the situation? Consider how carefully Jared Miller assessed his audience's adherence to the values associated with a comfortable life. Think of Cicero's triumvirate of values: duty, justice, and good faith. How can you lay claim to these important civic virtues? For example, Jared Miller framed his argument as an act of duty (as an Arizonan). He held to good faith, or the honest pursuit of truth and good conduct, in his evaluation of development practices that would most benefit the state's citizens. Sojourner Truth, on the other hand, associates the abolitionist cause with justice. Take the time now to write a page or two in which you explain your own position as one informed by duty, justice, and good faith.
2. You can also invent a good character by gauging the values of the community to which you will make your case. Make two columns and list the virtues and vices that your audience will associate with the critical situation at hand. Now, write a sentence or a small argument that appeals to two or three of these virtues and vices.

Achieving Good Will

Writers and speakers can demonstrate their good will toward an audience by carefully considering what readers or listeners need to know about the issue and the critical situation from which it is drawn. We all know how frustrating it is to begin watching a film or television show after the exposition has been given. The exposition, which gives viewers the background of the plot and any details they need to follow its development, usually appears early on, either spoken by a character or given in voice-over by a narrator. Readers and listeners require the same sort of information when they encounter an argument: what is the critical situation, what issues are raised by it, what is your position? In order to demonstrate your good will toward your audience, you should supply any necessary information that they might not already possess. At the same time, though, you should be careful not to repeat information that the audience already knows.

Book reviewers usually operate on the ethical principle of good will: they must assume that people will listen to or read their reviews in order to decide whether to buy or read a given book. Book reviewers are obligated to have good will toward their audiences because people put their trust (and their money) on the line when they take reviewers' advice. Reviewers demonstrate this good will by telling audiences just enough about the plot or the argument of the book to allow them to decide whether to read it, but they don't give away the ending or all of the details. They also demonstrate good will by providing audiences with their frank opinion about the work. Here, for example, is an excerpt from Bruce Crumley's review of Thierry Meyssan's *9/11: The Big Lie:*

> Move over Fox Mulder, here comes Thierry Meyssan. Like the unrelenting FBI hero of the popular *X Files* TV series, Meyssan is a player in the conspiracy business. But in contrast to the fictional Mulder's sympathetic crusades—one geek's quest to combat a farcical cabal of sociopathic humans and the world-conquering extraterrestrials they serve—Meyssan's campaign has attracted audiences with a singularly despicable suggestion: that the terrorist attacks of Sept. 11 were carried out by U.S. government officials as part of a murderous economic and military plot.
>
> Meyssan makes that astonishing proposition in the book *l'Effroyable Imposture* (*The Horrifying Fraud*), a controversial tome that topped France's best-seller list in six of the seven weeks since its release. Meyssan defiantly dismisses the universally accepted version of the 9/11 tragedy as "a loony fable" patched together by the White House and the Defense Department "as one lie called forth another." He maintains that neither American Airlines Flight 77 nor any other aircraft crashed into the Pentagon on 9/11—the explosion supposedly detonated on the ground. He similarly rejects notions that the planes that struck the World Trade Center towers were flown by al-Qaeda terrorists and argues they were in fact directed from the ground by remote control.
>
> So what does Meyssan think really happened? Although he stops just short of the categorical, the militant libertarian champions the theory (previously limited to Internet forums and sites, including his own) that the attacks—and the 3,000 victims they claimed—were the work of officials in the U.S. government and military, looking for an excuse to launch war on Afghanistan and Iraq. "If the energy lobby was the main beneficiary of the war in Afghanistan, the biggest victor of Sept. 11 was the military-industrial lobby," Meyssan writes. "Its wildest dreams have now been fulfilled."
>
> To support his theory, Meyssan plays up factual oddities or gray areas surrounding the attacks—a skeptical focus facilitated by secrecy rules imposed in the ongoing investigations. He notes that no film footage of the Pentagon explosion exists and regards eyewitness testimony of the crash as suspicious, contradictory or flatly incredible. He similarly argues that the photos offer no evidence of the debris

typical of an airplane crash (discounting expert explanations that the extreme violence of the impact and heat of the explosion caused virtual atomization of the jet), and says the area of destruction to the Pentagon is impossibly small given the size and span of the craft.

After setting the stage with a comparison to Fox Mulder of the *X Files*—who is the most famous conspiracy theorist in popular culture—Crumley quickly and efficiently informs his readers about Meyssan's argument, and he provides details from Meyssan's discussion of the evidence as well. He quotes Meyssan directly, which establishes that he has actually read the book. Although he goes on to dismiss Meyssan's work, he has nonetheless shown good will toward his audience by providing them with enough information to decide whether or not they want to read the book. You might find it helpful to compare the ethos invented by Crumley in this review to that constructed by James Robbins in his commentary on Meyssan's work:

> Well, it did not take long for the ridiculous to find its way into print. In what is billed as the "first independent inquiry" into the events of Sept. 11, French left-wing activist Thierry Meyssan comes to the shocking conclusion that the Pentagon was *not* hit by American Airlines Flight 77. His book, *L'Effroyable Imposture* (*The Frightening Fraud*) is apparently a hot seller in his native land, the first 20,000 copies having been whisked off the shelves with more to follow. Meyssan, who had published his views as early as October 8 on his website, the Voltaire Network, (the *philosophe* must be spinning in his grave having his name appropriated by this imbecile), proves, at least to his own satisfaction, that the damage to the Pentagon could not have been caused by a Boeing 757, but was in fact the result of a carefully planned truck bombing or missile strike . . . . Note that I haven't read the book—I'm waiting for the movie.

We think that Robbins destroys his credibility as a reviewer when he admits that he has not read the book in question, and so it is an open question whether he fulfills his obligation to show good will toward readers. Readers who already agree with Robbins will perhaps be amused by his essay, although they will not learn much about Meyssan's book from it. Those who do not know the work in question, and who have not already taken a position on the issue raised by Meyssan might be put off by Robbins's admission that he hasn't read the book (if not by his name-calling). Robbins takes readers' response for granted, which is perhaps appropriate given that the *National Review,* the magazine in which this piece was published, has a well-defined political position.

As another means of securing good will, speakers and writers can say why they think their presentation of an argument is important, and what benefits will accrue to those who read or listen to it. In other words, you should try to let your audience know what is at stake in what you have to say. Jared Miller explains the importance of his letter: "I am encouraging better planning and focused thought that will produce sensible and sustainable communities. I want others to consider what I have offered and rethink the decisions we are making concerning growth." We made an ethical appeal of this sort at the beginning of this book when we suggested that our approach to composition would help you to become a more successful author. Of course, this tactic works only if audiences do not suspect ulterior motives. Television advertisements for life insurance sometimes begin with scenarios depicting loved ones whose lives have been disrupted by the death of a provider who left no insurance. While the companies that sponsor these ads seem to have good will toward their audience insofar as they wish to protect people from harm, viewers know that these companies also want to sell insurance. In this case, they do it by frightening people—a tactic that is marginally ethical. Try, instead, to assure readers that you are writing or speaking in their best interests.

Invention Journal: Inventing Good Will

1. How can your project be framed as work for the community? What can you write or say that will convince your audience that your argument has been made in their best interests, and that there is a great deal at stake in what you have offered them? Go back to the stakeholder's list you composed in Chapter 2, or take time now to describe your audience and imagine their stake in the critical situation. What are their major commitments and concerns?
2. Now, take time to write some passages that explain the importance of your project for your audience. This writing might become introductory comments in your project, or perhaps they will elsewhere. In any case, it is important that you think through the investments that your audience might bring to your discussion of the issue.

WORKSHOP 10: Inventing Persuasive Voice

No matter how carefully audiences judge the reasoning and evidence of an argument, we still respond to *voice* in what we read. We still make judgments about how arguments "speak" to us. In this workshop, you will find resources for skillful control of the voice in your writing.

WORKSHOP 15: Revising for Clarity

This workshop offers revising strategies for increasing the clarity of writing. Increasing the clarity of your ideas will help you connect with your intended audience.

TALK READ WRITE

1. Find one, two, or even a half-dozen short pieces of professional writing—magazine or newspaper articles for instance, or selections from Web sites, books, newspapers, or magazines, fiction or nonfiction. Or read transcripts or watch videos of a half-dozen public addresses. Analyze each carefully. Describe the characters presented by the authors. Do you admire and respect each author's character as it is displayed in the text? Why or why not?
2. How does the author of each piece establish an ethos? Specifically, how does he or she convince you that he or she is intelligent and well-informed? What

tactics does the author use to establish his or her good character? His or her good will toward readers? Make a note of these tactics for future reference.

3. Do any of the pieces display an ethos that is not successful? If so, explain why ethos fails in each instance.

Voice and Rhetorical Distance

Ethos or character can be created in a composition by means of certain stylistic choices. Rhetoricians give the name "voice" to this self-dramatization in style. Of course, voice is a metaphor in that it suggests that all rhetorical situations, even those that use written or electronic media, mimic the relation of one person speaking to another. Written or electronic discourse that creates a lively and accessible voice makes reading more interesting. The available repertoire of possible voices is immense: there are cheerful voices, gloomy and hopeful ones, stuffy ones, hip ones, homey ones, funny ones, sincere ones, angry ones—the list is endless.

Voices affect the rhetorical distance that can seem to exist between rhetors and their audiences. Once again, *rhetorical distance* is a metaphor representing the degree of physical and social distance that exists between people speaking to one another. But writers can also narrow or widen the rhetorical distance between themselves and their audiences by means of stylistic choice. When creating a voice, writers or speakers should consider the situation for which they are composing: how much distance is appropriate given their relationship to an audience; how much distance is appropriate given their relationship to the issue. As a general rule, persuasion occurs more easily when audiences can identify with a speaker or writer. Identification increases as distance decreases.

Intimate Distance = Closer Identification, More Persuasive Potential

Formal Distance = Less Identification, Less Persuasive Potential

Authors who know an audience well, or whose audience is quite small, can use an intimate distance (unless some factor in the situation prevents this). The distance created in personal letters, for example, is ordinarily quite intimate, while that used in business correspondence is more formal because rhetors either do not know their correspondents personally or because convention dictates that such relationships be kept at arm's length, so to speak. Compare the distance created by Bruce Crumley and James Robbins in the excerpts from their work reprinted earlier in this chapter. Although both pieces are written in first person, Crumley's tone is more distant than Robbins's. He achieves this by giving information about the book rather than by asserting his opinion of the book and the character of its author.

Some of our own recent experience serves well as an example. One of us recently went to the chair of the department in which we teach to request departmental money to support a food drive competition sponsored by faculty across the campus. Our chair, bless him, was all too happy to help. Our request, made as we popped into his office unannounced, went something like this:

> Hi, (chair's first name). I wanted to ask about something. You know about the campus food drive, right? Okay, I hate to come again with hat in hand, but is there any spare

departmental cash that you could give us? We're trying to sweeten the pot a bit for folks giving food. I know that (the first names of several other departmental chairs on campus) are going to pony up. We don't want to look bad, right? Okay, great, thanks for stepping up yet again. How much can we afford? Fantastic. You're the man!

The relative lack of distance here worked well, in part, because it allowed us to highlight the friendly relations that exist among the faculty on campus. It also allowed a nonthreatening and humorous way to suggest that not giving would likely be perceived as bad community behavior. Our chair, after agreeing to give money, asked that we send a formal request via e-mail so that the expenditure could be properly recorded and justified in the departmental budget. Here is the text of the e-mail:

Dear Dr. (chair's last name),

I am writing to request departmental funds to support the Kids in the Colonias Food Drive. As you know, this annual event has become an important tradition on our campus demonstrating our commitment to the communities this university serves. We have already received donations from (names of other departments on campus), and I have been asked by the organizers to speak with you about the degree to which our department can participate monetarily this year.

Thank you for your help. Please know that your past generosity supporting events like this is recognized and appreciated. Please let me know if you have any questions.

Sincerely,
(first and last name and departmental affiliation)

Clearly, there is considerably more distance in this formal request than was established during conversation. Note that a shift in audience requires this; we are no longer just addressing our friendly chair, but also potentially higher university authorities or even an auditor. The use of official titles increases the distance and formality, as does the inclusion of a brief explanation of the event (what was unspoken common knowledge in the office-visit request). The lack of colloquial phrases such as "pony up" and "You're the man!" acknowledge the more formal requirements of the situation as well.

However, some critical situations can create exceptions to the distance-intimacy equation. Formal language is ordinarily appropriate in a courtroom, for example, even though an attorney, a defendant, and a judge constitute a very small group. In addition, the attorney may know both the judge and the defendant well. Nonetheless, she probably ought to use formal language in her conversations with both, given the official and serious nature of courtroom transactions. And sometimes very large groups are addressed in quite intimate language: performers at concerts and television evangelists, whose audiences number in the thousands or even millions, nonetheless address their audiences quite personally and intimately.

WORKSHOP 2: Arranging Your Composition

As you discover arguments through invention, consider how they will fit together when you sit down to write. This workshop is devoted to "arrangement," the skillful structuring of arguments.

Our attitude toward the issue also influences distance. Where writers or speakers remain as neutral as possible, expressing neither a supportive nor rejecting attitude, distance tends to be greater. On the other hand, a strong expression of an attitude—approval or disapproval, for example—closes distance.

More Attitude = Intimate Distance

Less Attitude = More Formal Distance

Some audiences and situations demand attitude. At a political rally, an enthusiastic and supportive audience will expect a speaker to express the attitude of the group, to fire up the crowd. Much less attitude is called for when you present a proposal to your employer; here, you hope that the details in the proposal speak for themselves. On the other hand, your employer might appreciate employees who display confidence. In this case, an enthusiastic and assertive attitude might be called for. The attitudinal dimension of rhetorical situations determines what predispositions exist among the participants in a rhetorical act that will influence their response to the situation.

TALK READ WRITE

1. Return to the pieces you collected earlier. Now, analyze them in terms of the rhetorical distance created by their authors' voices. Do the authors assume they know readers well, or do they establish a formal distance? How do they achieve this distance?
2. To practice creating an effective ethos, write a letter to someone who is very close to you—a spouse, parent, or friend. Now, write a letter that says the same thing to someone who is less close to you—a teacher, for example. Now, write the letter to a company or corporation. What happens to your voice in each case? What features of your writing are altered?

Invention Journal: Establishing an Ethical Relationship to Audience

1. As we have been saying, the rhetorical principle of distance examines how far apart, socially or situationally, participants are from one another in a critical situation. Here are some questions to ask about voice: Have I established the optimal distance for persuasion, or should it be closed or opened up? Take time to write a summary of your relationship to the audience. Is your relationship formal or more intimate? Is it appropriate to

speak as a peer, or is more deference in order? If you have a draft, read it out loud with friends or classmates in the room. Ask them about the appropriateness of rhetorical distance. If you are just now at the drafting stage, write a paragraph and experiment with rhetorical distance, always keeping in mind the overall context of your critical situation.

2. Does your critical situation require more or less attitude? Will your audience take neutrality as a virtue or a cop-out? Remember that even if you are trying to lead readers to strong conclusions, you could present your case with less attitude. One way to make a decision about attitude is to think about your audience's general disposition towards your claim. If they agree with your position, more attitude might work well. If they are a hostile audience, your attitude may only push them farther away. What is your audience's disposition: acceptance, indifference, or rejection? Consider carefully.

WORKSHOP 12: Putting Together a Portfolio of Your Invention Work

Gathering your invention work together in a portfolio creates a record of your thought, research, and analysis. This workshop offers a simple framework for constructing a portfolio and writing a critical self-reflection on the progress of your project.

WORKSHOP 7: Finding Access: Publishing Your Work

What are the most meaningful publics for your work? What audiences, if persuaded by your work, can become agents of change in your critical situation? Once you identify the right audience, how do you reach them? To discover routes of access to your audience, work through the series of questions in this workshop.

LIST OF WORKS CITED

Breitweiser, Kristen. "Are We Safer?" *Nation Online* 20 April 2005. http://thenation.com/blogs/outrage?pid=2336.

Clarke, Richard A. *Against All Enemies: Inside America's War on Terror*. New York: The Free Press, 2004.

Crumley, Bruce. "France's No. 1 Best Seller Claims the U.S. Orchestrated the Sept. 11 Attacks. Why Do People Read This Stuff?" *Time/Europe* 20 May 2002 (vol. 159, no. 20) http://time.com/time/Europe/magazine/article/0,13005,901020520–237165,00.html.

Eagar, Thomas and Christopher Musso. "Why Did the World Trade Center Collapse? Science, Engineering, and Speculation." *Journal of the Society of Minerals, Metals, and Materials* 53, 12 (2001): 8–11. tms.org/pub/journals/JOM/0112/Eagar/Eagar-o112.html.

King, Martin Luther. *A Call to Conscience: The Landmark Speeches of Dr. Martin Luther King Jr.* Eds. Clayborne Carson and Kris Shephard. New York: Warner Books, 2001.

Offley, G. W. "A Narrative of the Life and Labors of the Rev. G. W. Offley, a Colored Man, Local Preacher and Missionary; Who Lived Twenty-Seven Years at the South and Twenty-Three at the North; Who Never Went to School a Day in His Life, and Only Commenced to Learn His Letters When Nineteen Years and Eight Months Old; the Emancipation of His Mother and Her Three Children; How He Learned to Read While Living in a Slave State, and Supported Himself from the Time He Was Nine Years Old Until He Was Twenty-One." *Documenting the American South.* Chapel Hill, NC: University Library, The University of North Carolina at Chapel Hill, 2000. 19 April 2007 http://docsouth.unc.edu/neh/offley/offley.html.

Robbins, James. "9/11 Denial: The French Best-Seller and Its Company." *National Review Online* 9 April 2005 http://nationalreview.com/robbins/robbins040902.asp.

Painter, Nell Irving. *Sojourner Truth: A Life, A Symbol.* New York: W. W. Norton and Company, 1996.

7

REASONING WITH AUDIENCES: LOGIC ON THE GROUND OF A CRITICAL SITUATION

Have you ever been told to "be reasonable"? Or, perhaps you have asked someone else to "listen to reason." These statements assume that some other *un*reasonable person won't listen to or can't acknowledge some ostensibly logical and self-evident truth. Of course, those who urge us to listen to reason are not always the purveyors of truth they claim to be.

The Greek word *logos* gives us the English words *logic* and *logical.* In archaic Greek, *logos* meant "voice" or "speech." Later, it came to refer to "reason" as well, and it still sometimes carries this sense in English. However, the social situations in which arguments happen are so complex and unpredictable that no strictly logical formulae could ever cover all of the possibilities opened by argument. And so, when we use the word *logical* in this chapter to describe a kind of argument, we mean something like "arguments created by the careful sequencing of statements." Participants in a critical situation place statements one after another in order to persuade others to accept their claims. Ancient teachers called such statements **premises**, and we use this term as well. Inventing logical arguments is the process of creating paths of thought that your audience can follow, that will at once feel familiar to them and lead to a new realization, a realization that is closer to your position. We refer to these relational chains as **lines of reasoning**. Audiences may follow along such sequences agreeably. On the other hand, they may reject certain statements that make up the path down which your argument leads, or they may resist the relationships that you establish among premises—the stepping stones along that path. Consider this simple example of a pathway made of premises. Read the boxes from left to right:

Good schools keep class sizes small.	**Sunnyside School keeps class sizes small.**	**Sunnyside School is a good school.**

You can probably see that the first premise about class size and the quality of education will need some support, and we can easily find support in scholarship on education or simply by talking to experienced teachers. If you can convince your audience of this first premise, the second should be easy enough to demonstrate; call Sunnyside School and ask them about class size or "student-teacher ratios." With these first two premises in place, will your audience "move" to your conclusion in praise of Sunnyside School? Is class size alone enough to move an audience down a path toward enrolling their children at Sunnyside School? What other premises—stepping stones—would help an audience arrive at your conclusion?

Your goal in logical argumentation is to reason with an audience, to bring them to conclusions that you have decided are important. Like other types of proofs, logical arguments are embedded in situations. In other words, lines of reasoning are well-traveled patterns of thought by which people make sense of and communicate about the world around them. Think carefully about the lines of reasoning that already make up the rhetorical terrain you are attempting to travel. You seem reasonable to your audience only if you are able to make persuasive sense of the premises or major ideas that circulate in relation to the critical situation at hand.

Working through this chapter, you will add important terms and procedures to your working knowledge of rhetoric. Among those terms and procedures are:

- **Premise**—a statement or assertion necessary for the logic of an argument (the steps along the way of your lines of reasoning).
- **The enthymeme**—the sequence of premises by means of which you engage audiences; enthymemes appeal to both reason and to shared belief.
- **Conclusions**—the destination to which you hope to lead your audience.
- **Deductive and inductive reasoning**—two primary ways to move through lines of reasoning. *Deductive* reasoning brings audiences from general premises to more specific conclusions. *Inductive* reasoning takes leaders from particular premises to more general conclusions.
- **Analogy**—any persuasive comparison.
- **Rhetorical example**—specific instances that bring your audience into the movement of your argument.

The exercises that follow are meant to immerse you in the practice of tracing and organizing lines of reasoning. In the rest of this chapter, we return to each of these concepts in order to help you put them to work on the ground of your critical situation.

TALK READ WRITE

1. Return to the example of the Sunnyside School. What further premises would be needed to help audiences reach the stated conclusion?

2. Each person in your workshop group or class should write a statement that she believes to be acceptable to most reasonable people: global warming is accelerating; the 2008 Phoenix Suns will be the strongest team in the Western division; gender inequity in the workplace continues to plague our society; speed bumps work well to slow traffic in residential areas; people tend to act as they have in the past, and so on.
3. After you have compiled a list of such statements, discuss their plausibility with members of your group or class. Who will believe or accept each one without additional supporting statements? Obviously, a die-hard Suns fan might firmly believe that next year's team will be superior to all the others in its division without any supporting evidence at all; hence she might take this statement as a starting point from which to argue that the Suns stand a good chance of doing well in the championship playoffs. Fans of other teams, however, might require some supporting statements before they accept the central claim. A Spurs fan might want to know the Suns' win-loss record from the previous year, might want to hear that they have made off-season trades for talented players, and need to learn that their acknowledged star, Amare Stoudamire, will remain with the team through the next season.
4. Now chart some of the original statements along a horizontal line. Place the original statement in the center of the page, and on the left, list any statements that support a central statement. On the right, list statements that follow from the central statement. for example:

Statements that support		Central statement	Statements that can follow from	
The Phoenix Suns traded for star player Grant Hill during the summer of 2007.	Star player Amare Stoudamaire has recovered from his knee injury.	The 2007-2008 Phoenix Suns will be the strongest team in the Western division	The Phoenix Suns stand a good chance of doing well in the playoffs.	Media attention to the Phoenix Suns will continue to increase.

5. As a class talk about the lines or chains of statements you have charted out. What arguments could be derived from these sets of related statements? Would they be convincing? If so, to whom? Are there any gaps in the lines of reasoning? That is, have any important premises or connections been left out?
6. Now, individually or as a group try this same exercise with a published argument. Read an editorial in any newspaper, or study the transcript of a public address. Underline or copy as many statements as you can find that assert something is true or at least acceptable to reasonable people. Discuss the list of statements. Do they support one another? Contradict

one another? Do the statements work together to lead readers to a conclusion or conclusions? Narrow your list to one or two of the most important statements in the piece. Do these major statements follow from the rest? What is the ultimate conclusion to which the writing leads you? Once you figure out how the statements work together, chart them in the manner suggested above.

LOGIC ON THE GROUND CIRCA 1866

As an illustration of how social context informs logical arguments, consider the reasoning at work in the arguments of the African American abolitionist poet and orator Frances Ellen Watkins Harper. When Harper was asked to speak in New York at the National Women's Rights Convention in 1866, she found herself in a challenging and complicated critical situation. After the Civil War, many white suffragists were angry that politicians were working hard to attain voting rights for African American men, arguing that votes for white women should come first. Harper was dedicated to the cause of women's suffrage, but as an African American woman, she understood that the votes of African American men were important in the tough political struggle for universal suffrage that lay ahead. Also, the African American community needed voting rights in order to determine their own destiny and to work their way toward freedom and out of poverty. Thus, Harper found it necessary to negotiate her way between conflicting political agendas: she had to counter majority opposition to African American and women's rights on the one hand, and to quell internal dissension between black-suffrage advocates and women's suffrage advocates on the other. Harper found brilliant rhetorical means for drawing these audiences together and moving them towards conclusions based on premises that they could all accept. Here is part of what she said on that day:

> We are all bound up together in one great bundle of humanity, and society cannot trample on the weakest and feeblest of its members without receiving the curse in its own soul. You tried that in the case of the negro. You pressed down for two centuries; and in so doing you crippled the moral strength and paralyzed the spiritual energies of the white men of the country. When the hands of the black were fettered, white men were deprived of the liberty of speech and the freedom of the press. Society cannot afford to neglect the enlightenment of any class of its members. . . . This grand and glorious revolution which has commenced, will fail to reach its climax of success, until throughout the length and breadth of the American Republic, the nation shall be so color-blind, as to know no man by the color of his skin or the curl of his hair. It will then have no privileged class, trampling upon and outraging the unprivileged classes, but will be then one great privileged nation, whose privilege will be to produce the loftiest manhood and womanhood that humanity can attain.
>
> I do not believe that giving the woman the ballot is immediately going to cure all the ills of life. I do not believe that white women are dewdrops just exhaled from the skies. I think that like men they may be divided into three

classes, the good, the bad, and the indifferent. The good would vote according to their convictions and principles; the bad, as dictated by prejudice or malice; and the indifferent will vote on the strongest side of the question, with the winning party.

In this passage, Harper puts together a chain of premises as a way of reasoning with her audience in order to convince them that their opposition to African American suffrage is not logical. We should note that Harper didn't invent her arguments out of thin air; she worked from deeply held beliefs shared by members of her audience. For example, Harper's assertion that "we are all bound up together in one great bundle of humanity" was a commonplace that would have been very persuasive to those listening. In the predominantly Christian culture of her times, notions of Christian charity assumed an ideal of interconnectedness and mutual responsibility. Women's rights and anti-slavery activists had by that time both adopted this theological belief ("one great bundle of humanity") as a matter of democratic principle. Harper's reasoning is powerful because it is based on this important premise about human interconnectedness.

Harper's logical argumentation makes use of what ancient rhetorical theorists called **enthymemes**. When enthymemes are used skillfully by writers and speakers, the audience is persuaded because they participate in the process of reasoning, supplying premises and conclusions based on their own understanding of issues and of how the world works. This kind of community-based use of logic requires a careful study of the kinds of reasoning and shared beliefs that are ordinarily at play when particular audiences consider particular issues. This is what we mean when we say that people reason together.

Harper's enthymeme begins with a general **premise**: we are all human beings, whether black or white, male or female. We are, in Harper's phrase, "one great bundle of humanity." Harper's argument here is **deductive**, that is, it moves from a generalization to a conclusion. A deductive argument begins by establishing a class or group. The argument then identifies some smaller or more specific items that are shown to belong to the large group or class in some specific fashion. If we were to graph Harper's argument, it would look like this:

Major Premise: Women and African American men are human beings;

Minor Premise: In America, all adult human beings should be entitled to the right to vote;

Conclusion: Women and African American men are entitled to the right to vote.

If you have taken a logic class, you have seen arguments diagrammed like this. In rhetoric, however, things are neither so neat nor so formal. Harper assumed, and rightly, we think, that her audience would realize a further, implied, conclusion: "It is not logical to support votes for white women and yet to deny votes to African American men." This conclusion would carry force for the women assembled at the convention because as women's rights activists they continually battled the stereotypical view that women are emotional rather than logical.

Harper had at least one other option for arranging her logical argument, and that was to present an **inductive** argument, in other words, one that runs from particular to more general statements. Working inductively, she could have led her audience through the premises in this line of reasoning:

Particular Premise: Women have political insight that can enrich democracy.

Particular Premise: African American men also have political insight that will enrich democracy.

Conclusion: Universal suffrage (which would include women and men of all races) will enrich American democracy.

We can only speculate about why Harper chose deductive as opposed to inductive logic. It seems likely, however, that Harper made a shrewd judgment about which premises would be most compelling for her audience. The premise from which she built her deductive reasoning, the premise about a common humanity, was easy to accept for her largely Christian audience, making it an effective enthymeme.

Harper also uses other means of logical persuasion, among them, arguments from **example**. Her argument from example appears in the beginning of the speech when Harper recalled the death of her husband. Without full rights of property ownership, she was unable to hold onto her home and possessions after her husband's death. Later in her address, after a compelling account of becoming homeless with her "orphaned children," Harper asserted that "justice is not fulfilled so long as woman is unequal before the law" (217). She thus uses her own experience as an example of the social ill of gender inequality generally.

A biblical **analogy** helped Harper to make her case against racial and gender oppression. An analogy is a comparison, either simple or complex, meant to make a persuasive point. Speaking of her experiences as an African American woman dealing with both racial and gender prejudice in American cities such as Washington, D.C., and Philadelphia, Harper asserted that she felt "as if I were in the situation of Ishmael, my hand against every man, and every man's hand against me" (218). In the book of Genesis, Ishmael was the "illegitimate" son of Abraham and the slave Hagar. The analogy with the situation of Ishmael is particularly helpful to Harper's case. Like Harper, Ishmael was not legitimate in the eyes of powerful members of society, and yet he was chosen by God for a great destiny. The hard road prophesied for Ishmael, that he would be constantly attacked from different directions, was a fair comparison with Harper, whose white suffragette sisters distrusted her commitment to African American male suffrage. The fact that Ishmael was the descendant of slaves made the analogy all the more fitting. The logic or reasoning of the analogy runs like this:

- Ishmael's slave heritage made him a target for oppression.
- Harper, an African American with a slave heritage, was in a situation comparable to Ishmael.
- Harper's slave heritage made her a target of oppression.

This analogy is important to the overall argument because Harper wanted her audience to understand her own experience as exemplary of African American women in 1866.

Logic, when grounded in community beliefs, connects strongly with audience. Working through this chapter, you will discover the best way to bring your audience down paths of reason to the position that for you is critical.

ENTHYMEMES: REASONING WITH AN AUDIENCE

Using enthymemes helps us produce what we might think of as *living logic*, that is, logic that will ring true to audiences as they consider the situations of their daily lives. The word enthymeme comes from the Greek term *thymos*, "spirit," the capacity whereby people think and feel. Ancient Greeks located the *thymos* in the midsection of the body. Quite literally, then, an enthymematic proof is a visceral appeal, that is, one felt "in the gut." As we saw in the example of Frances Harper's address, enthymemes depend on premises that are grounded in community belief. The premises of enthymemes are often commonplaces, but they need not be. (For more on commonplaces, see Chapter 5.) Enthymemes are powerful because they are based in community beliefs, and they work best when listeners or readers participate in constructing the argument. Building on premises that audiences are likely to accept, enthymemes take an audience's existing knowledge as a foundation. In a sense, enthymemes offer audiences a way into your argument, starting them down the path of reasoning you present, moving them towards the conclusions you hope they will reach. A writer or speaker can then move from this acceptable premise to statements that an audience may find less acceptable or that they had not previously considered. If the audience readily accepts a major premise, some of the minor premises that move forward to the conclusion might not even have to be stated; the audience will provide them on their own. In fact, leaving premises or conclusions unstated allows audience members to invest in your argument by supplying some of the logical steps themselves and thus becoming co-creators of your logic.

Consider the following example. Here is an enthymeme we have used with student audiences on occasion:

Premise: Working steadily each day far in advance of deadlines gives writers the time to do their best work.

Premise: Working steadily each day far in advance of deadlines will help writers avoid all-night writing sessions.

Conclusion: Scheduling daily working time well in advance of deadlines is worth the effort.

Can you think of any additional, unstated premises? Here is one:

Uustated Premise: Staying up all night writing for a deadline is stressful and unpleasant. Audiences might also reach a further unstated conclusion: students doing their "best work" will received higher grades.

Some people put off writing tasks because they are busy or, let's face it, because writing is difficult. So, students often procrastinate when faced with a writing deadline. Thus, they are unlikely to set up an extended writing schedule far in advance. However, those who have experienced the unpleasantness of jamming towards a deadline might supply this unstated premise based on that experience and thus decide to devote some early writing time to their projects. Note that this line of reasoning is made persuasive by the enthymematic connection, the knowledge that the audience brings to the scene of the argument.

Writers and speakers should make decisions about what to leave unstated based on the specifics of their audience, their intentions, and the overall situation in which they are working. In the following example, both a premise and the conclusion are left unstated:

> There are few good roles for actresses in Hollywood because men have all the power to make script and casting decisions.

The unstated premise could be phrased this way: *Men aren't interested in scripts that feature good roles for women.* Clearly, this is not a premise with which everyone would agree, though many actresses over the years have criticized just such masculinist bias in the film industry. Audiences who do believe this unstated premise will likely arrive at one unstated conclusion with all the more conviction: *Masculine bias in the film industry must be eliminated.*

Analysis of the enthymemes you have constructed can assist you with invention. In the example about the film industry, the unstated premise must be stated in order to determine whether it is convincing; once it is stated, a writer or speaker who wants to be persuasive can determine whether or not the suppressed premise needs to be stated in the completed project, and whether it needs to be supported by evidence. Such an examination in this case shows that some evidence should be assembled in order to shore up both premises. That is, a writer or speaker using this enthymeme needs to assemble examples of good scripts for women having been turned down by male directors or producers. Statistics that show the relative numbers of good roles for male and female actors during a given time period would also be persuasive. Furthermore, the major premise itself may not be widely accepted among certain audiences, so it might be more successful with potentially hostile audiences if it can be supported with factual or statistical evidence as well. For instance, a writer or speaker making this argument

WORKSHOP 3: Different Values and Respectful Conflict

Arguments are inherently matters of conflict. Rather than trying to avoid such conflict, we recommend approaching it as a powerful learning opportunity and an intellectual resource. This workshop provides the framework for sharing our own value-based positions in a productive and respectful manner.

WORKSHOP 9: Gathering Information through Interviews

Because you are a member of the communities in which you are planning a writing project, it is likely that you know personally people with detailed information about pressing community matters. This workshop helps you prepare interviews to access that information.

might offer a discussion of the career of powerful male producers and directors, analyzing their films to demonstrate that shallow, stereotype-ridden roles of women dominate these pictures. On the other hand, an audience of actresses might be receptive an argument made by Reese Witherspoon in her acceptance speech at the 2006 Academy Awards, where she won the Oscar for best actress. Witherspoon thanked the writers of *Walk the Line* for creating a role that captured the complex humanity of a "real woman" (June Carter Cash). The audience of film professionals quite easily understood the premises that Witherspoon left unspoken—there aren't many such roles for actresses, and "I am grateful to have been given this one."

It is important for ethical reasons that responsible writers, speakers, and readers learn to see both the overt and implied connections made between and among enthymematic premises. We should examine arguments in which connections are not made overtly but are only implied, or in which connections are not made at all. Skilled manipulators of public opinion exploit the power of enthymemes every day, particularly through the use of images such as the display of a battered American flag over the ruins of the World Trade Center or the arrival of a flight-suited president on the deck of an aircraft carrier. The first image sets off a chain of reasoning that concludes with something like the claim "America can survive anything, even the loss of thousands of innocent lives and the destruction of our tallest buildings." This argument was used in the months following September 11 to mobilize a sense of nationalist unity among Americans that in turn aroused their support for pre-emptive military action in Afghanistan and Iraq. The second image suggests the military competence of the President, which implies in turn that he can make able foreign policy decisions. The weakness of such arguments is readily apparent when we carefully inspect the connections made between their premises. The fact that New York City survived one attack has little predictive value; a military uniform has no necessary connection to competence in foreign policy.

TALK READ WRITE

1. Review the following enthymemes. For each, write out any unstated premises that you detect. Then, explain what audiences would be most persuaded by the enthymeme. In other words, with which audiences will the unstated premise have persuasive pull?

   Premise: This neighborhood is bordered by busy streets on all sides.

   Unstated Premise: ____________________

   Conclusion: We should not buy a house in this neighborhood.

   Premise: Candidate X for state representative was seen stumbling out of a bar last month.

   Unstated Premise: ____________________

   Conclusion: We should not vote for Candidate X.

DEFENDING PREMISES

As you lead audiences along the path of a line of reasoning, they may stop dead in their tracks, unconvinced by the relations you have established between this or that premise. An audience will sense some leap in your logic or that they have been asked to stretch too far without some smaller steps in between. Frances Harper's reasoning was challenged in this way at the 1866 Woman's Rights Convention. The transcript from the Convention illuminates audience reactions to Harper's account of her bad experiences in Philadelphia, experiences she used as examples of a national problem of discrimination against African American women: "Let me go to-morrow morning and take my seat in one of your street cars—I do not know that they will do it in New York, but they will in Philadelphia—and the conductor will put up his hand and stop the car rather than let me ride." "They do not do that here," a woman from the crowd responded, presumably referring to New York. Harper replied:

> They do in Philadelphia. Going from Washington to Baltimore this Spring, they put me in the smoking car. (Loud voices—"Shame.") Aye, in the capital of the nation, where the black man consecrated himself to the nation's defense, faithful when the white man was faithless, they put me in the smoking car! They did it once; but the next time they tried it, they failed; for I would not go in. I felt the fight in me; but I don't want to have to fight all the time. Today I am puzzled where to make my home. I would like to make it in Philadelphia, near my own friends and relations. But if I want to ride in the streets of Philadelphia, they send me to ride on the platform with the driver. (Cries of "Shame.") Have women nothing to do with this?

Following this passage Harper gives another example of an African American woman who was left sitting all alone in a street car—when she boarded the street car, the conductor told all the other passengers to get off. Harper then asks: "Are there not wrongs to be righted?" When her audience balked at accepting her minor premise, Harper supplied vivid examples from her experience and that of another woman to shore up her implied generalization about the shabby treatment afforded to African American women in northern cities.

WORKSHOP 13: Readers Responding
This workshop offers powerful strategies for approaching reading as serious writers do, with a critical eye for the most important arguments and ideas. Follow the strategies presented in this workshop to gain skills as an engaged reader and become more able to put what you read to work in your own writing.

WORKSHOP 16: Summarizing Arguments, Ideas, and Texts
Writers regularly present the work of others as building blocks for their own work. This workshop offers strategies for writing strong summaries to incorporate into your own writing.

WORKSHOP 8: Following Pathways: A Metaphor for Critical Reading and Research
The exercises in this workshop will help you identify unfamiliar ideas and references in your reading and research and to approach them as opportunities for learning—as "pathways" to knowledge.

Whether you are speaking in public or writing for a broader audience, some of your conclusions, premises, analogies, and examples are likely to be questioned. In this case, you may need to provide further reasoning or more evidence. We offer this kind of defense in conversation quite regularly. Imagine you and friends are picnicking near a river. Someone suggests swimming across to the apple grove on the other side. You argue that the undertaking is too dangerous. Rather than agreeing with you, people start stripping off their clothes and heading for the water. Talking quickly, you provide premises you assumed the group would have thought of themselves. "The water is too cold." Your friends are unimpressed. "So what, it's a hot day," one says. "It will be refreshing." You counter by giving them the major premise they have missed: "Cold water can slow your muscle function and shorten your breathing." Another says, "It's not *that* cold." In order to give evidence to the contrary, you plead with the person, "Dip your foot in and see for yourself." Still unconvinced, the group moves to the bank. "Wait!" you say, providing a new line of reasoning, "The current is too fast." The group understands your unspoken premise: "It is unsafe to swim in fast water." However, they don't judge the current of *this* river to be dangerously fast. "Looks pretty mellow to me," says the would-be swimmer about to dive into the water. "Wait!!" you plead again, grabbing a handful of birch leaves from the ground and scattering them on the surface of the river. The group watches as the deceptively swift water carries the leaves quickly downstream. With this further evidence, the two lines of reasoning you have provided regarding water temperature and the speed of the current persuade the group to put their clothes back on and forget the quest for apples.

When inventing enthymematic arguments, you need to anticipate which premises will need to be defended, and you need to provide that defense in advance. Evaluating a key piece of immigration legislation circulating in the United States House of Representatives during the spring of 2006, our student Edwin Molina raised serious reservations about key provisions of House Bill 2037, a bill presented by its sponsors as a hard-nosed deterrent against so-called "illegal immigration." Molina's recommendation against HB 2037 provides a good example of defending premises. In support of the premise that outlawing undocumented labor was unenforceable, Molina reminds his audience of current controversies in this area, arguing that "if you take a look at Wal-Mart, hiring low wage illegal immigrants seems to be an irresistible practice." Molina might have provided much more evidence of the overwhelmingly common practice of hiring undocumented workers, but any more evidence was probably unnecessary. Audiences, especially in Molina's Southwest, needed only one gentle reminder of this common if controversial practice. We recommend charting out premises and conclusions as we've done with the samples above when you encounter arguments that you want to use as part of your project. The following exercises will give you some practice in this difficult art.

TALK READ WRITE

1. Read the full text of Harper's New York address and find all the enthymematic arguments she used. Map them as we do in the previous examples.

2. Find editorials in your campus newspaper, your local paper, or a national paper such as the *New York Times*, *Washington Post*, or *Wall Street Journal*. Working with a group, read the editorials carefully and graph the enthymemes you find there.
3. List as many commonly accepted premises as you can, premises such as "Children are our future," "Democracy is the best form of government," or "Hard work pays off." After you have your list, invent enthymemes based on these premises. To what conclusions could you lead readers? What unstated premises might be accepted by your audience? Which premises will be questioned and will need to be defended?

Invention Journal: Enthymematic Connections to Audience

1. Create an enthymeme to use in your project. Begin by writing out the conclusions you want your audience to reach: tuition should be capped; you and your coworkers deserve a pay raise; the sociology midterm was not a fair test; the city should provide a street light on a busy corner in your neighborhood. Try charting the premises that will lead audiences to your conclusions as we have throughout this chapter thus far. Remember that you may well have several enthymemes making up your argument and that your enthymemes might be complex; the conclusion of one enthymeme might provide the starting premise for another enthymeme.
2. If you did the exercises in the Invention Journals in Chapter 5, return to that work and find the commonplace statements or premises that you share with your audience. To what conclusions can you lead your audience from these points of ideological agreement?
3. Which of the premises in your lines of reasoning are most in need of defense? In other words, which ones will most likely be challenged by your audience? What evidence or further reasoning is needed to convince your audience of the premise you have set forth?

WORKSHOP 7: Finding Access: Publishing Your Work

What are the most meaningful publics for your work? What audiences, if persuaded by your work, can become agents of change in your critical situation? Once you identify the right audience, how do you reach them? To discover routes of access to your audience, work through the series of questions in this workshop.

DEDUCTION: REASONING FROM THE GENERAL TO THE PARTICULAR

Enthymematic lines of reasoning follow two basic directions, **deductive** and **inductive.** Aristotle defined **deduction** as "a discussion in which, certain things having been laid down, something other than these things necessarily results through them" (*Topics* I i). The word *deduction* comes to us from Latin, where it means "leading down." The ancients thought of this sort of argument as "leading down" because deduction always begins with a generalization, a premise that makes a claim about a fairly large class or group. The premises that follow are more specific. So, the movement of deduction is "downward," from very general to more specific. One example of this sort of reasoning goes as follows:

General Premise: All people are mortal.

Particular Premise: Socrates is a person.

Conclusion: Therefore, Socrates is mortal.

The first statement is a general premise accepted by everyone. This premise is general because it makes an observation about an entire class: all people. The second statement is a particular premise, also accepted by everyone. This premise is particular because it refers to only one person out of the class of people. The last statement is a conclusion, arrived at by comparing the premises: if Socrates fits in the class "people," he also fits in the class "mortal," and thus his death is inevitable.

This deductive argument meets the standards of categorical *logic* because it has all the necessary parts in all the right places, but parts and placement are not so important in rhetoric. What is important in rhetoric is that the beginning statement—the major premise—is usually a commonplace. That is, rhetorical deduction works best if it begins from a generalization that most members of an audience find unobjectionable. Take Harper's major premise, for example: African American males and white women are human beings. While many people in America in 1860 denied the humanity of both groups, no one in her audience at the Woman's Rights Convention would contest her premise. Had Harper been addressing an audience who found her major premise to be controversial (it asserted the common humanity of all people), she might have changed it. For example, she might have reasoned along these lines, as she did on other occasions:

General Premise: Oppressed peoples will eventually rebel against their oppressors.

Particular Premise: African Americans are oppressed.

Conclusion: African Americans will eventually rebel against their oppressors.

In the nineteenth century, even those who were unwilling to grant humanity to women and African Americans might be persuaded by this line of reasoning, especially given all the historical examples of slave rebellions that could be and often were offered to further illustrate the point.

TALK READ WRITE

1. Consider the following ancient premise, which is still powerful across cultures: *We should be kind to others.* Taking this as a

general premise, chart out particular premises that follow to conclusions. For example:

> ***General Premise***: We should be kind to others.
>
> ***Particular Premise***: Insults are unkind.
>
> ***Conclusion***: We shouldn't insult others.

2. Think of arguments following from the premise, "we should be kind to others" that are more specific to current public issues, such as school vouchers, the HPV vaccine, or campaign finance reform. Discuss ways in which the particular principles might need defense.
3. Find an article in a campus, local, national, or international newspaper that argues deductively from a major premise. Try to graph its deductive argument. The important thing in this part of the exercise is to identify the master premise—the generalization from which the argument begins—and the conclusion.
4. Now, map the minor premises that tie the major premise to the conclusion. Try to find all of them, and list them in an order that makes sense to you. When you see them laid out systematically like this, are you convinced by the original argument? Were you convinced when you first read the piece? If you respond differently to the original argument and to your graph of it, try to explain why.

Invention Journal: Crafting Deductive Lines of Reasoning

1. Can you find or generate a generalization from your critical situation that could serve as a major premise of a deductive argument? If so, write it down. Invent the conclusion you want to draw from it, and then compose minor premises that can form a chain or linkage of arguments from major premise to conclusion.
2. If there are statements that you are certain your audience will accept, you may be able to make powerful deductive arguments. (For example, addressing a church group, a member of the group can often rely on the rallying power of commandments, prophetic edicts, citations from sacred texts, and other statements of faith-based principle.) Write out any such statements of which you are aware. How may these serve as major premises that will lead to minor premises and conclusions? Chart them in the manner illustrated in this chapter. (If you are a churchgoer, you may hear a priest or minister using this technique to develop a sermon or a homily.)

INDUCTION: REASONING FROM PARTICULARS TO A GENERALIZATION

Ancient rhetoricians recognized another movement between premises. Aristotle defined this movement as "the progress from particulars to universals." Later logicians called this movement **induction** (from the Latin *inducere*, "to lead into"). Induction leads away from particulars and into a general conclusion. A particular is any individual item, person, or event that can be put into a class. Particulars are also called "instances" or "examples." Induction is used much more often these days than is deduction, perhaps because people who live in a global economy are less certain about the truth of large generalizations than were ancient thinkers.

Edwin Molina's essay, referenced above, demonstrates the capable use of inductive reasoning. In his critique, Molina raised serious reservations about House Bill 2037. In fact, each criticism he raised became a premise on the way to his conclusion that the Bill should be rejected. This bill had several key provisions. First, the bill invokes United States Code 8, which stipulates that it is illegal to employ unauthorized residents in this country. Second, the bill forbids undocumented immigrants to buy or rent property. Third, the bill charges that the very presence of any unauthorized migrant in this country is a Class 6 felony (it is currently a misdemeanor to be in the country illegally). As HB 2037 sponsors explained it, these measures, especially the prospect of jail time, would deter migrants from entering the country illegally. After carefully summarizing these key provisions, Molina moves on to a policy recommendation:

> The bill is not feasible. It requires that everyone involved be honest. In a perfect world, maybe every landlord would refuse to rent to undocumented immigrants, but this world is not perfect. There aren't very many landlords who would give up their money for the government's sake. . . . Again, this world is not perfect, and if you take a look at Wal-Mart, hiring low-wage immigrants seems to be an irresistible practice for companies in today's world, seeing that increasing profit is the number one priority of all companies; as a matter of fact, increasing profit is the number one goal of nearly all individuals! I would scrap this bill; it would never work. This bill also has no financial plan behind it; it contains no explanation of how it will finance jailing the estimated five-hundred thousand "illegal immigrants" who are detained each year. Nor does it explain how space could be found for immigrants in America's already overcrowded prisons and jails.

We can map Molina's inductive reasoning like this like this:

Minor Premise: HB 2037 lacks a clear implementation plan.

Minor Premise: HB 2037 doesn't explain how landlords will be held accountable for their renting practices.

Minor Premise: HB 2037 doesn't explain how employers will be held accountable for their hiring practices.

Minor Conclusion: HB 2037 doesn't explain how the state will afford all the imprisoned felons it would create by further criminalizing immigration.

Conclusion: HB 2037 should be rejected.

Readers of Molina's text will likely understand an important unstated premise in this argument: The United States economy increasingly depends on the labor of migrant workers.

Here is another example of an inductive argument made by the authors of the report compiled by the 9/11 Commission:

> In February 1998, the 40-year-old Saudi exile Usama Bin Ladin and a fugitive Egyptian physician, Ayman al Zawahiri, arranged from their Afghan headquarters for an Arabic newspaper in London to publish what they termed a fatwa issued in the name of a "world Islamic Front." . . . Claiming that America had declared war against God and his messenger, they called for the murder of any American, anywhere on earth, as the "individual duty for every Muslim who can do it in any country in which it is possible to do it." . . . Three months later, when interviewed in Afghanistan by ABC-TV, Bin Ladin enlarged on these themes. . . . Bin Ladin's 1998 declaration was only the latest in the long series of his public and private calls since 1992 that singled out the United States for attack. In August 1995, Bin Ladin had issued his own self-styled fatwa calling on Muslims to drive American soldiers out of Saudi Arabia. (47–48)

Although they mention only these statements by Bin Laden as direct evidence of his involvement in the events of September 11, 2001, the authors of the report assemble a good deal of additional evidence about his activities and those of his surrogates to support their claim that an organization headed by Bin Laden, Al Qaeda, was responsible for the attacks made on American cities on that day. This litany of Bin Laden's threats to attack Americans, along with examples of his connections to previous attacks on American assets, such as that on the *USS Cole*, is intended to lead readers to accept the report's conclusion: Bin Laden and Al Qaeda orchestrated the 9/11 attack.

TALK READ WRITE

As a group, brainstorm possible inductive lines of reasoning that could lead an audience to believe that *education in the United States is in crisis*. What particular premises could form persuasive pathways for your audience to follow to this conclusion?

Invention Journal: Crafting Inductive Lines of Reasoning

If you already know the conclusions you want your audience to reach, think of premises that support your claim or major premise. Do you have a sufficient number of particulars to convince your audience? As always, your audience's orientation to the situation you are addressing will determine the level of your challenge in persuading them.

ANALOGY–REASONING BY MEANS OF COMPARISON

In an **analogy**, a writer or speaker places one hypothetical example beside another for the purposes of comparison. An analogy can be a particularly powerful means of persuasion because it offers new light on the situation at hand, encouraging readers and listeners to look at the familiar from a different vantage point. Analogies can also be useful because they serve as a reference point for audiences who might be unfamiliar with the circumstances of a critical situation.

In a simple analogy two or more things are compared. President Lyndon Baines Johnson, in a commencement address delivered at Howard University in 1965, used the following simple analogy to underscore the need for affirmative action:

> You do not take a person who for years has been hobbled by chains and liberate him, bring him up to the starting line of a race and then say, "you're free to compete with all the others," and still justly believe that you have been completely fair. Thus it is not enough just to open the gates of opportunity. All our citizens must have the ability to walk through those gates. . . . We seek not . . . just equality as a right and a theory but equality as a fact and equality as a result.

Here, President Johnson compared those who could benefit from affirmative action to a runner who has been denied the opportunity to train at the level of her competitors. This analogy became so popular among advocates of affirmative action programs and policies that it assumed the status of a commonplace in that discourse.

In complex analogies, on the other hand, two examples exhibit a similar relation among their elements. The physician William Hervey, who is credited with discovering the circulation of the blood in human beings, used a complex analogy to do so. He reasoned that if sap circulates in vegetables and keeps them alive, it was reasonable to assume that blood circulates in animals and performs a similar function for them. Here the similarity lies in the relationship of circulation, rather than between the items mentioned—sap and blood, vegetables and animals. For another example of complex analogy, consider the analogy used by one of our students, Michael Irei, whose work we discussed in a previous chapter. In his argument against a constitutional ban on same-sex marriage, Irei offered this analogy:

> Throughout the history of our country, we have been fighting for the rights of all our citizens. Today, the fight for gay rights and same-sex marriage is similar to the civil rights battle regarding race, which we have been fighting since the United States was founded. It seems just as preposterous not to allow same-sex marriages as it was to ever consider a law banning inter-racial marriage in the United States. Looking back, most would find it hard to believe that there was recently a time in this country when basic civil rights were not granted to citizens based on race. However, Jim Crow laws that enforced racial segregation were in place until the mid-1960s. A constitutional ban of same-sex marriage would be similar, taking away the rights of a select group of people in the United States. If this amendment is enacted, it is very possible that we may look back in the future with confusion and amazement at the ignorance of denying any two human beings the right to marry.

Those who follow the reasoning of this analogy are given a powerful new lens on the question of same-sex marriage. Those who oppose same-sex marriage might argue, however, that the analogy does not hold up because discrimination on the basis of race is different from discrimination based on sexual orientation. To make this argument stick, those who defend it could try to claim that one's "race" is not a choice, while sexual orientation is. The latter claim is widely contested in some circles.

Invention Journal: Finding the Right Analogies

1. Can you think of a simple or complex analogy that might work in your project? That is, is the situation or issue outlined there similar to some other situation or issue? Is the comparison persuasive? If so, write out the analogy and write out an explanation of why you think the comparison is persuasive. You may or may not want to use the explanation in your text; often the force of an analogy is strongest when people in an audience make the connection on their own.
2. If you decide to use a simple analogy, be sure to examine it carefully in order to make sure that the comparison is apt in most of its features. As the commonplace warns, it is dangerous to compare apples and oranges. Much can be learned, however, from a comparison between Delicious apples and Macintosh apples. And if the analogy you want to use is complex, be sure that the relations between items in both examples are apt in most of their features. Dr. Hervey learned much from comparing the circulation of sap and blood; today, he might make a useful analogy between the circulation of information in digital environments and the circulation of blood in the body, reasoning that people are more familiar with the bodily concept than they are with the way technology works. Are there sufficient similarities between the ways in which these two systems work to render the comparison useful and persuasive?

RHETORICAL EXAMPLES: MAKE YOUR REASONING SPECIFIC

A rhetorical **example** is any particular that can be fitted under the heading of a class, and that represents the distinguishing features of that class. A rhetorical example names some thing, being, event, or action, whether historical or fictional, which may persuade an audience that the thing named belongs to the generalization we are defending. Rhetorical example is often effective; if you want to convince your neighbor that he should keep his dog inside the fence which surrounds his property, you can remind him of a past instance when another neighbor's dog, running free, spread garbage all over both front yards. The marauding dog serves as a rhetorical example in this argument. You might also remind him of another neighbor's dog that while off leash was killed by a car.

The argument from example is certainly a favorite of advertisers—think, for instance, of the ads for beer that show people drinking beer and having a good time.

Examples can cause audiences to recall similar circumstances in which they have participated, or in which they would like to participate. You can also hope that the vividness of any examples you use will cause an audience to draw conclusions at which you have only hinted. Ed Molina, whose essay is discussed above, offered a good example in support of the premise that landlords would have little incentive to deny undocumented migrants as renters. "Even Chuck Gray, a sponsor of 2037, and an employee of the United States government, when speaking of his experiences with tenants as a landlord, stated: 'I have been a landlord before and rented, they gave me the check and it was good and I let them live there.'" The fact that one sponsor of the bill found its provisions impractical is quite persuasive in the context of Molina's argument.

Rhetorical examples are persuasive because they are specific, and they call up vivid memories of something the audience has experienced. Here is an excerpt from Phil Scraton's remembrance of events on 9/11:

> In a Verona hotel room we watched the dramatic live transmissions from downtown Manhattan. Firefighters and rescuers raced into the disaster zone passing dust-covered, ghost-like workers coming from the opposite direction—running or staggering for their lives. Cameras homed in on others trapped in offices high above the flames, some throwing themselves from windows to avoid choking or burning to death. As the towers collapsed, clouds of grey toxic dust covered all and everything in their path. Then came the first reports of agonized telephone calls made from one of the planes and by those facing death trapped in their offices. (1)

Scraton's account is effective because it evokes sensory impressions from that day, mentioning sights and sounds that most of us saw and heard on television. A recital of sights, sounds, smells, tastes, and tactile sensations involves readers in the scene being created, and may make them more receptive to persuasion. Rhetorical examples also work well when they evoke memories of specific historical events that are fresh in the memories of members of the audience.

Historical and Fictional Examples

Successful examples may be drawn from history. For example, Presidents George H. W. Bush and Bill Clinton both used the example of Vietnam as a reason for their hesitation to intervene in a local war between ethnic groups in Bosnia. Later, people who opposed the war in Iraq used the historical example of the Vietnam War to argue that Americans should not become involved again in a war against people who had not attacked us directly. Or, if a speaker or writer wants to claim that politicians ought not to be trusted, she can briefly mention a number of examples taken from history—Nathan Hale, Benedict Arnold, or Richard Nixon, who, whether fairly or not, was called "Tricky Dick." The brief argument from example works because people respond to the specificity of examples. It works best when the examples selected (Hale, Arnold, Nixon) seem to squarely represent the class (politicians who should not be trusted).

Using a procedure called "extended example," a writer or speaker can mention only one of these figures and establish his untrustworthiness by naming and describing several instances of it. For example, to use Nixon as your extended example, you could say he lied to the American people on at least two occasions, he broke several laws, and he destroyed evidence which would implicate him in illegal acts. You can give as many vivid details as possible in order to evoke the audience's memory of the incident and thus to induce their sympathy with your argument.

Successful examples can also be found in fiction. Aristotle drew his fictional examples from Aesop:

> A horse was in sole occupation of a meadow. A stag having come and done much damage to the pasture, the horse, wishing to avenge himself on the stag, asked a man whether he could help him to punish the stag. That man consented, on condition that the horse submitted to the bit and allowed him to mount him javelins in hand. The horse agreed to the terms and the man mounted him, but instead of obtaining vengeance on the stag, the horse from that time became the man's slave. (*Rhetoric* II xx 1393b)

According to Aristotle, Aesop used this fictional example to warn people that they should not give power to a dictator simply because they wished to take revenge on an enemy.

Fictional examples include fables, images, and small stories. Such stories may be drawn from literature or film, or you can compose your own fables for illustrative purposes. Advertisers often use animals or fabulous human beings to sell their products. One has only to recall Joe Camel or the gecko who sells insurance for Geico to realize how effective these fabulous images can become. Arguably, the amiable and talkative lizard does not actually persuade people to buy insurance from the company it represents, but it certainly contributes to the company's name recognition.

Fabulous examples work best if the narratives from which they are drawn are well-known and liked by the audience. A writer or speaker who is interested in establishing the possibility that UFOs are piloted by friendly extraterrestrials, for example, might revive an audience's memory of the vivid scenes of such visitations portrayed in popular films such as *E.T.*; writers and speakers who want to portray aliens as hostile, on the other hand, can turn to the vivid depictions of this scenario in the *Alien* films or *Independence Day*.

Fables are most effective when morals, or generalizations, can be drawn from them. So, a writer or speaker who utilizes the movie fables mentioned above should point out exactly how these fictions reinforce the notions that the intentions of extraterrestrial visitors are friendly or hostile, and should also directly connect the lessons taught by the films with the point of the argument.

Invention Journal: Examples That Persuade

1. Find a historical example that supports your position. Find or invent a fictional example that supports your position. Make a list of the similarities and differences between your example and the case you want to compare it to. Are any of the differences so obvious that they might harm the effectiveness of your example?
2. Be sure that you understand the relation between your fictional/historical example and the situation outlined in your project. In order to be effective an example must be similar to the case at hand in most respects.

IMAGES AND REASONING

Images are an important source of persuasion. But images can be tricky when used to support lines of reasoning, because responses to images vary so widely from person to person. Hence, the way you frame or contextualize the image for your audience is particularly important. The now iconic image of the Twin Towers collapsing on September 11, 2001, presented without any commentary, leads listeners to different conclusions unless you carefully qualify the image's relation to your argument.

Upon viewing this image an observer might conclude that the United States should continue to prosecute the war on terror in order to ensure that nothing like this can happen ever again. A second person might conclude that it is only a matter of time before another catastrophic terrorist attack occurs, and yet a third might conclude that we should stop building skyscrapers. The number of conclusions that can be reached are as various as the situations and preoccupations of those viewing the image.

TALK READ WRITE

Consider this image of the so-called "Turner Rebellion," in which a Virginia slave led a group of fellow slaves in an attack resulting in the deaths of more than 50 white people. What conclusions might slave owners reach based on viewing such an image? What conclusions would occur to other enslaved African Americans? Abolitionists in the North?

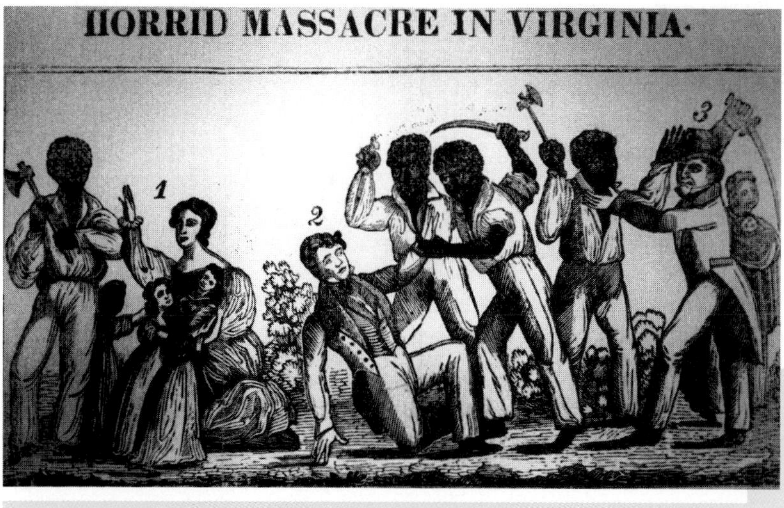

Turner's Rebellion

Invention Journal: Reasoning through Images

WORKSHOP 2: Arranging Your Composition

As you discover arguments through invention, consider how they will fit together when you sit down to write. This workshop is devoted to "arrangement," the skillful structuring of arguments.

WORKSHOP 15: Revising for Clarity

This workshop offers revising strategies for increasing the clarity of writing. Increasing the clarity of your ideas helps you connect with your intended audience.

WORKSHOP 12: Putting Together a Portfolio of Your Invention Work

Gathering your invention work together in a portfolio creates a record of your thought, research, and analysis. This workshop offers a simple framework for constructing a portfolio and writing a critical self-reflection on the progress of your project.

1. Find an image that supports one or more of the premises in your argument. How will audiences who are receptive to your position read this image and its connection to your claim? How will a hostile audience react? Is there any chance that the image might persuade an indifferent audience to become interested in your argument? If so, please explain how.
2. Images often work well as rhetorical examples. How might you use images as examples in an inductive line of reasoning? For example, if you were lobbying for a no-smoking law in your town, images of smoke-filled local establishments might serve to demonstrate the premise that second-hand smoke degrades the healthfulness of the local environment.
3. If you have found images that you want to use in your project, you need to frame them in such a way that your audience can understand their place in your argument. How will you contextualize any images you have chosen to use? Where will they appear in your enthymemes? In your text? For each image you are using, write a few sentences that will help your audience see the image as you intend it to be seen.

LIST OF WORKS CITED

The 9/11 Commission Report: Final Report of the National Commission on Terrorist Attacks Upon the United States. New York: Norton, 2004.

Aristotle. *On Rhetoric: A Theory of Civic Discourse*. Trans. George Kennedy. Oxford UP, 1991.

Aristotle. *Topics*. Trans. W. A. Pickard-Cambridge. *In The Works of Aristotle*. Ed. W. D. Ross. London: Oxford UP, 1966.

Harper, Frances Ellen Watkins. *A Brighter Coming Day: A Frances Ellen Watkins Reader*. Ed. Frances Smith Foster. New York: The Feminist Press, 1990.

Johnson, Lyndon Baines. "To Fulfill These Rights: Commencement Address at Howard University, June 4, 1965." http://lbjlib.utexas.edu/johnson/archives.hom/speeches.hom/650604.asp.

Scraton, Phil. Introduction. *Beyond September 11: An Anthology of Dissent. Ed. Phil Scraton.* London: Pluto Press, 2002. 1–10.

8

ARGUMENT AND EMOTION

In the fall of 2001, one of us taught an early morning class in advanced composition. On September 12—the day after the attacks on the World Trade Center and the Pentagon—it was immediately clear upon arrival to the classroom that the scheduled class plan would have to be scrapped. Students needed to talk about what had happened the previous day. As was the case all over the country, students in our class knew people who had been in or near the WTC when the attack occurred and who were still unaccounted for. Fear, confusion, anger, and sadness were palpable in the room, abetted by the newly felt sense that terrorists might strike anywhere. Even though this class operated under an agreed-upon set of guidelines about tolerance and respect for the opinions of others, the room was very tense. Many students wanted to know: why would anyone so viciously attack innocent civilians? Our fear was enhanced by our confusion. Names such as *Al Qaeda* and *Osama bin Laden* were unknown to most of the people in the room on that day. Loud and angry exchanges broke out several times, and it was difficult to stay focused on specific questions or claims that people raised. The intense emotions in the room, in other words, disrupted the sense of community achieved by members of the class prior to that morning.

And there were arguments, or at least heated disagreements. Even if we didn't find, or maintain, any agreed-upon ground for argument, several claims kept surfacing. Most prominent, perhaps, was the call for retaliation—"Let's go get them"—even before any target for retaliation was clear. These claims were met with loud approval by many of those who shared a sense of outrage and vulnerability. As proofs to support such claims, students recalled in detail the horrific and heartbreaking scenes that were still playing out on all media outlets around the clock. Others argued that the nation should wait and get more information before taking any action. One student expressed a position that was quite different from most others held by members of the class: he claimed that the United States had been targeted because its policies in the Middle East had antagonized many people. Borrowing a phrase from Malcolm X, this student said that the attack was an example of "American chickens coming home to roost." This assertion was met with vigorous personal attacks; some students claimed that such a position was treasonous. Others demanded a chance to respond. But while many people spoke loudly and assertively in class that day, others maintained a studied silence, listening intently but clearly unsure about what could be said safely. Many emotions were expressed in class that day: anxiety, fear, anger, and indignation among them. Perhaps students who remained silent were experiencing fear as well, or perhaps they were ashamed, or pitied students who were so visibly upset. Or perhaps they envied those who spoke out so easily.

Because humans are emotional creatures, writing and speaking are inescapably emotional processes. This is always true, although its truth is not often as evident as it was in class that morning. Nonetheless, recent research in neuroscience and psychology suggests that human perception depends on emotion. We relate emotionally with the environments in which we move, but most often we do not take notice of our emotional responses to our surroundings. When necessary, though, powerful emotional responses can draw our attention to elements of the environment that may affect us in some important way. If we encounter something dangerous, or especially pleasant, our emotional responses can serve as important cues for how to act. In such cases emotions arouse the portions of the nervous system that control thought and language.

One of the premises guiding us as we wrote *Critical Situations* was that its readers are committed writers and speakers. We assume that most important commitments are deeply felt, whether they are made to family, to a group of friends or an organization, to a profession or vocation, or to a political or religious affiliation. The depth and strength of such commitments are sometimes so strong that we generate powerful emotional responses when we encounter someone who does not share these commitments, who challenges our belief in communities or values that we hold dear. This happened in our classroom on September 12, 2001: the claim that the attacks were retaliations against American foreign policy challenged the belief that America can do no wrong (this belief is called *nationalism,* generally, or *American exceptionalism,* specifically).

Students who report that they don't like to argue cite the emotional intensity aroused by conflict as the primary reason they avoid arguments. But it is not possible to engage in argument without arousing emotion because it is not possible to engage in any human activity without engaging the emotions. Emotions influence the way we hear or read arguments, just as they influence the way we speak and write them. Emotional appeals can affect audiences immediately and dramatically in a given moment, so much so that argument can seem risky when emotions are intensely felt. However, there are ways to argue that do not stimulate disabling emotions such as rage or frustration. We hope that other chapters in this book demonstrate some of these tactics. The goal of this chapter is to provide strategies for writers and speakers who want to tap into the useful emotions aroused by a critical situation—emotions such as compassion, respect, and fellow-feeling—in such a way as to persuade audiences rather than repel them. Careful analysis of the emotional connections in your critical situation can become a powerful means of inventing persuasive arguments.

EMOTIONS ARE NOT IRRATIONAL

Modern western cultures have made a virtue of objectivity. To be objective means to keep emotional reactions in check. "Rational" discourse—used in the sciences, the law, in the public sphere—is to be kept free of the supposedly corrupting force of human feeling. In higher education, we often make sharp distinctions between thinking and feeling; scientific objectivity and analytical perspective are understood to be hallmarks of academic research and writing. People who value objectivity take "the facts" and "logical argument" to be the surest and most ethical ways to go about convincing people. Because of the modern reverence for objectivity and reason, emotional writing and speech are sometimes viewed with suspicion. Even though heartfelt talk or writing is sometimes viewed as an outpouring of truthful expression "from the heart," as it were, more often it is characterized as a sign of intellectual weakness. This perception is reinforced by popular media, where sensationalistic melodramas and exploitative reality shows abound. For example, talk show host Jerry Springer has for years capitalized daily on the spectacle of emotional verbal exchanges on *The Jerry Springer Show.*

People who appear on these shows come across as conniving, self-centered, dishonest, and manipulative, and hence such shows reinforce the idea that arguing is an irrational activity that ought to be avoided by civilized people.

The shouting matches and barely restrained physical assaults of *Springer* do not represent the habits of persuasion we hope to pass along in this book. We reject any suggestions that emotional arguments are inherently "irrational," "fallacious" or "inappropriate." "Gut reactions" are not a signal of an undisciplined intellect; rather, they signify engagement with the surroundings. As we argued in Chapter 4, the ability to find the right arguments for use at the right time (*kairos*) depends on such engagement.

Many scholars argue that writing and speaking are social acts, and certainly that is true insofar as these practices bring us into contact (desired or not) with others. The situations that bring us together to argue may also inspire strong feelings because all parties are invested in communities and values that render the outcome of an argument vitally important, not just to participants but to others with whose beliefs they identify.

Thinking through such connections helped Hillary Dinello pursue her goals as a writer. Dinello's fiancé was called up for active duty in the military, and her project—which included the composition of a letter addressed to spouses of deployed soldiers—offers a strong example of an appeal to emotion: "Since I have become part of the community and gone through a deployment," Dinello explained in retrospect, "I realized that it was not only important to think of the soldiers, but the families as well." In writing to members of other military families, she drew on her own emotional experience, including her concern over the financial ramification of deployment, her disappointment when her fiancé's return was delayed, the loneliness of separation, and her fear for a loved one in harm's way. "I won't tell you I know exactly how you feel or exactly what you are going through," Dinello wrote. "However, I am going to tell you that I have been through a similar

WORKSHOP 3: Different Values and Respectful Conflict

Arguments are inherently matters of conflict. Rather than trying to avoid such conflict, we recommend approaching it as a powerful learning opportunity and an intellectual resource. This workshop provides the framework for sharing our own value-based positions in a productive and respectful manner.

situation and tell you how I made it through my fiancé's deployment last year." Framing all of her suggestions as "help" and "support," Dinello made strong appeals to the emotions of spouses or loved ones who were quite likely feeling overwhelmed by loss and stress. Turning her attention to the challenges many military families face, Dinello offered a deceptively simple encouragement: "Being a single parent is not easy, especially for those who have never done it before. Being a single parent during a deployment is especially difficult, but it can be done." Dinello's powerfully empathetic identification with her audience was achieved by direct appeal to their emotional experience, experience that she understood because she had undergone it herself.

The power of emotional argument as a connection between writers and audiences dramatizes the communal quality of all argument. Emotional language in arguments signals the strongest commitments of speakers and writers and of audiences, and so, studied carefully, it offers us a key to thinking about audience and rhetorical strategy, helping us to make the right arguments at the right time. We tend to think of arguing as mark of division among people, but we forget that arguments also signal connections and common interests. It might be said, in fact, that participants in serious arguments have a very close relationship to one another. Recall our discussion in Chapter 7 of the *enthymeme,* Aristotle's term for the interactive process of reasoning among people engaged in argument. In his theory of argument, persuasion is initiated by speakers or writers whose words convince a listener or reader to accept some new or different way of thinking or believing. The ancient Greek root word for enthymeme is *thymos;* this word meant "spirit," which was understood as a person's ethical and intellectual sensibility. Spirit was thought to reside in the midsection, literally *in the gut.* Carefully invented arguments were persuasive, then, if they appealed to the emotions as well as to reason. All of which is to say that ancient rhetoricians did not separate thinking from feeling as sharply as modern philosophers have done.

We agree with Aristotle: the sharp distinction between reason and emotion is incorrect. If we are right about this, it follows that writers and speakers who hope to persuade won't be helped by overly simplistic divisions between emotions and the intellect. To the contrary: the emotional intensity with which people hold beliefs actually determines the relative ease with which beliefs can be changed. For example: someone who believes that extraterrestrial aliens regularly visit Earth may or may not be emotionally invested in that belief. His or her investment is likely to be intense only if some moving experience, such as a memory of having been abducted by aliens, stimulated it. On the other hand, someone who believes in extraterrestrial aliens because he or she is a fan of the *X-Files* will not be so deeply invested. A writer or speaker who does not believe in extraterrestrials stands a far better chance of persuading the second person to that position, because the *X-Files* fan cares less about the issue. When deeply held convictions are challenged, then, those who hold them are likely to respond with great intensity, as did students in our class on September 12, 2001. Students who invested emotional energy into maintaining a belief in American exceptionalism became angry when they heard the claim that the 9/11 attacks were undertaken in retaliation for misguided American foreign policy.

Consider the following familiar line of reasoning:

Major Premise: Terrorism is a heinous crime.

Minor Premise: Tighter control of national borders will reduce the risk of terrorism in the United States.

Conclusion: We should do all we can to limit or halt immigration across our national borders.

Clearly, not everyone will be moved by such reasoning. Our response to this argument depends on our assessment of the quality of its reasoning, of course, but it depends heavily on our emotional investments in the issue as well. People who are outraged that vigilante posses are patrolling the borders might reject this chain of premises by challenging both the second premise and the conclusion. On the other hand, those who fear terrorism might find this line of reasoning acceptable. But arguments about border control are motivated by other fears that are not so obviously in play—by fear of contamination of "Americans" by differently raced "others," for example.

To recap: emotions influence the way we understand the arguments we encounter. Emotions also influence stakeholders, determining the ways in which they perceive the social situations in which arguments arise. Often, emotion is a factor in moving a person past the point of accepting a premise (closing borders prevents terrorism) to belief or action (voting to build a fence on the border or joining up with vigilantes). Human behavior isn't dictated simply by logic or reason; we are emotional creatures.

Speaking or writing, listening or reading, all the processes of working through the logic of an argument, are inseparable from those feelings in the gut that signal the body making up its own mind, so to speak. The only arguments that can be conducted without appeals to the emotions are those that nobody cares about. Writers and speakers whose arguments are successful will engage in careful study of the way people *feel* their way through conflicts.

TALK READ WRITE

1. Think of a time when you were in an argument that was fueled by strong emotions. What was the argument about? What emotions were aroused? Why? What part did emotion play in determining how the argument played out in the end?

2. As a group, brainstorm a list of five to ten controversial social situations. Now consider why each of these is conversial. What emotions are aroused by their premises?
3. Here is an example of a social situation that stimulates intense emotional response: in 2006 the South Dakota legislature passed a ban on abortions within the state. In response, abortion rights activists attempted to place a provision on the ballot that would rescind the ban. The *New York Times* published an account of South Dakotans' emotional reactions to these events: "Ordinary people . . . said they had found themselves tangling unpleasantly with their closest friends over a question they had never really discussed much outside their homes. Some said they feared that as the fight over the ballot measure intensified, it would bring only more painful division" (April 16, 2006: A14). What emotions are aroused by these discussions? Discuss how the emotional connections of those involved have influenced the course of the debate. (South Dakotans voted against this ban in the November 2006 elections.)

CASE STUDY: IN DEFENSE OF ABOLITIONIST PASSIONS

Across the history of the antislavery movement of the nineteenth-century, abolitionists were often accused of letting their passions rule their arguments against slavery. Influential abolitionist Wendell Phillips defended the rhetorical practices of firebrand abolitionists in "The Philosophy of the Abolition Movement," an address given at the Massachusetts Anti-Slavery Society in Boston on January 27, 1853. Phillips begins by recounting the charges made by a recent critic:

> [Abolitionists] indulge in fierce denunciation, instead of appealing to their reason and common sense by plain statements and fair argument . . . that we might have won the sympathies and support of the nation, if we would have submitted to argue this question with a manly patience; but, instead of this, we have outraged the feelings of the community by attacks, unjust and unnecessarily severe, on its most valued institutions, and gratified our spleen by indiscriminate abuse of leading men, who were often honest in their intention, however mistaken in their views . . . that we have utterly neglected the ample means that lay around us to convert the nation, submitted to no discipline, formed no plan, been guided by no foresight, but hurried on in childish, reckless, blind and hot-headed zeal,—bigots in the narrowness of our views, and fanatics in our blind fury of invective and malignant judgment of other men's motives. (100)

Phillips professed to "reject with scorn" the assertion that the judgment of radical abolitionists was in any way impaired, emotionally excessive, or based on anything but "truth." To say otherwise revealed "gross ignorance" about "the cause and the whole course of its friends." Accusations of impropriety and inappropriate procedure,

EXPULSION OF NEGROES AND ABOLITIONISTS FROM TREMONT TEMPLE, BOSTON, MASSACHUSETTS, ON DECEMBER 3, 1860.—[SEE PAGE 767.]

Woodcut of Abolitionist Meeting
Abolitionist lectures were known to be emotionally tumultuous. The speakers were intense and feelings were strong on all sides. It's no surprise that the oration of abolitionist Frederick Douglass would cause the kind of uproar pictured in this woodcut.

Phillips reasoned, "have uniformly been brought against all reformers in all ages." With unrestrained contempt, Phillips turned the criticisms around, using them as a lens to examine the ethics and the intelligence of the critics themselves. Phillips found these calls for a less-confrontational and uncompromising approach to be ridiculous, because they either actively obstructed the ultimate goal of abolitionism—the emancipation of enslaved African Americans—or misjudged the best route to achieving emancipation. Throughout the lengthy address, Phillips defended the effectiveness of the uncompromising and often-inflammatory rhetorical approach of radical abolitionists.

Philips's address occurred at a timely moment within the history of abolitionism. His was not a fledgling cause but a growing political power, and he recognized that it was time to speak forcefully. By the time of Phillips's address in 1853, abolitionists had swayed public opinion, gained powerful political support in Washington, won many supporters, and made wealthy Southern planters anxious about the future of their empire, which was based on slave labor. Clearly, he believed that anyone who preferred the maintenance of good manners or proper decorum to a demonstrably successful rhetorical strategy did not understand the moral and political stakes of the argument. Phillips and many of the other abolitionists discussed in this book scandalized audiences by claiming that governments and churches were doing the work of the devil in making excuses for slavery. They shocked and disgusted audiences through vivid descriptions of the brutality of the slave system. And, as Phillips acknowledged, they made personal attacks on the character of well-respected public figures who were willing to compromise with the demands of slave owners. As provocative as these measures were, the abolitionist movement also became the occasion for the public speech of African American men and women, which itself outraged contemporary attitudes about the appropriate social order. Despite their refusal to observe the approved decorum of the time, the provocative strategies adopted by the Anti-Slavery Society and other organizations like it worked quite successfully.

Phillips's address offers a lesson in crafting emotional appeals that are appropriate for well-chosen audiences. He spoke during a period of a much-criticized political compromise with regard to the slavery question, and so the audience at the Anti-Slavery Society was likely impatient and angry with timid abolitionism. But Phillips had another, larger and less immediate audience in mind as well. He sought to anger the moderates and reactionaries who would read his speech and to draw his opponents into public exchange. Many abolitionists believed that they enjoyed a rhetorical advantage in an open debate. After all, a system as demonstrably horrific as slavery could only be defended if it were misrepresented, as it often was by its advocates. Those who supported slavery often deployed commonplaces, which asserted that slavery was good for the slaves and that slaves were happy in their condition. Advocates for slavery also used a pernicious double standard, claiming that all men are created equal—except for slaves. Abolitionists were able to use these positions to subject their opponents to refutation and ridicule. For example, in his 1853 address, Phillips successfully undermined the presumed rationality of his critics after pointing out the factual and logical inconsistencies in their complaints about zealous abolitionist tactics. At the end of this speech he defended the power and importance of emotional appeal in the fight to end slavery, even as his rhetoric enacted such appeals.

WORKSHOP 13: Readers Responding
This workshop offers powerful strategies for approaching reading as serious writers do, with a critical eye for the most important arguments and ideas. Follow the strategies presented in this workshop to gain skills as an engaged reader and become more able to put what you read to work in your own writing.

WORKSHOP 16: Summarizing Arguments, Ideas, and Texts
Writers regularly present the work of others as building blocks for their own work. This workshop offers strategies for writing strong summaries to incorporate into your own writing.

WORKSHOP 8: Following Pathways: A Metaphor for Critical Reading and Research
The exercises in this workshop will help you identify unfamiliar ideas and references in your reading and research and to approach them as opportunities for learning—as "pathways" to knowledge.

We invite you read the full text of Phillips's address and to use it as a good example as you analyze the emotional landscape of your own project. Read it to learn what you can about how to make the best arguments at the right time, when the stakes are high and when emotions are intensely felt.

TALK READ WRITE

1. Working as a group, choose a current social issue from the list you developed earlier. Write down your gut reactions to political or social controversies that have been in the headlines of major papers, magazines, television news, journals, and blogs. Try to name the emotions aroused by this issue: Calm? Anxiety? Fear? Benevolence? Shame? Pity? Indignation? Envy? Explain how these emotions influence the way people understand the issues in question and the arguments made about those issues.
2. Look at Phillips's summary of his critics' complaints against abolitionist rhetoric. Does he list any kinds of arguments that are said to be inappropriate today? Why are they now thought inappropriate? Answer this question by considering the standards of decorum, manners, or appropriate behavior that are often evoked as guidelines for the display of emotions.

DEVELOPING EMOTIONAL ARGUMENTS

The following invention strategies will help you map the emotional dynamics of your critical situation. As a way to begin understanding the lay of the emotional landscape, we suggest you begin by surveying the major emotional keywords to which stakeholders respond most strongly. Following this step, take stock of your own emotional connection to the subject of your research and the connections of all other stakeholder groups. In this way, you can develop the most effective strategies for connecting with audiences through emotional appeals. Suggestions follow that show you how to assess which emotions are at play in a critical situation and how to control the emotional tone of the arguments you construct.

Emotional Key Words

Consider how carefully we choose our words when raising a touchy or controversial question with a friend, coworker, or family member. We are aware that what we say will be scrutinized and we take pains to measure the possible effect of each word, even if that means keeping silent. Our decision whether to call a coworker's proposal "ambitious," "unrealistic," or "ridiculous" depends on our sense of our audience. Do we want to encourage or discourage further dialogue? Will strong words challenge our coworker thus

WORKSHOP 10: Inventing Persuavise Voice

No matter how carefully audiences judge the reasoning and evidence of an argument, we still respond to *voice* in what we read. We still make judgments about how arguments "speak" to us. In this workshop, you will find resources for skillful control of the voice in your writing.

inspiring her to compose a better proposal, or will they discourage her and thus cause her to quit working on the project? In public life, adherents to particular positions may listen and read with emotional intensity, and they may be extremely sensitive to emotional key words. Spoken in the right context, a single phrase or even a single word can have incredible emotional impact, calming audiences, affirming their dearly held commitments and beliefs, inspiring them to act, or provoking their fear or anger.

What those emotional key words are, of course, depends on the context. Consider the following passage from the home page of the Web site of one of our students, Kevin Marshall, which is devoted to speaking out against United States involvement in Iraq:

> At this stage of the current Iraq war, unemployment is up, gas prices are going through the roof, and there seems to be *no end in sight. Casualties are mounting* for military personnel as well as civilians. The actual dollar figure, while disputed, is in the billions of dollars and will continue to rise. Our armed services are under-equipped and under-supplied. Families have to buy protective gear for their *sons and daughters in Iraq.* With *no end to hostilities in sight* how much money will families have to spend to give their *loved ones* the protection they not only need, but deserve?

We have italicized the phrases we think carry the most emotional weight in this passage. The phrase "no end in sight" was and still is much used as a description of the Iraq war among its critics. Marshall's argument about the lack of planning and a clear exit strategy in Iraq are given emotional force through the suggestion of an indefinite state of war—"no end in sight." The stakes of this lack of planning are emphasized through reference to "sons and daughters," who could become part of the "casualties" that are "mounting." These emotional key words give force to the logic of Marshall's argument, guiding an audience to think about policy issues through the lens of their own feelings for loved ones.

In his 2005 State of the Union Address, President George W. Bush sought to emphasize the threat against which his administration had defined its foreign policies and thus to mobilize concern and perhaps fear in support of the war on terrorism:

> We have seen *our vulnerability*—and we have seen its deepest source. For as long as whole regions of the world *simmer in resentment and tyranny*—prone to ideologies that *feed hatred and excuse murder*—violence *will gather,* and *multiply in destructive power, and cross the most defended borders, and raise a mortal threat.*

The language we have italicized emphasizes the immediate danger posed to Americans by anti-American sentiment felt elsewhere in the world. In this passage, the president uses an appeal to fear to gain support for his policy of preemptive action abroad—the war in Iraq for instance—by raising the specter of a "mortal threat" intent on crossing "the most defended borders." This language conjures the specter of angry terrorists bent on doing violence to citizens of the United States. He evokes 9/11with a single word—*vulnerability*—that suggests that similar attacks could be equally devastating. The President's emotional appeal is also a response to critics of the war who argued that safety could best be achieved by directing resources to securing our borders and protecting likely targets in this country. By arousing fear of terrorists abroad, the president communicates the urgent necessity of international action in favor of a more thoroughgoing policy of homeland security.

Invention Journal: Words That Move Us

Find commentary from individuals and groups involved in your critical situation. Read them carefully with a pencil or highlighter in hand. Track all the key words and phrases that carry the potential for powerful emotional impact. Pay particular attention to words that repeat from one text to another. When you have a list of key words and phrases, analyze the language carefully. Write about each of the key words and phrases, trying to explain what gives the words emotional power in this context. Break down the logic of each word. For instance, the word *innocent* is a common word used to describe the victims of terrorism. It implies the following line of reasoning: "Terrorist violence is particularly reprehensible because it targets innocent noncombatants." The word *innocent* connotes childhood and the blamelessness we attribute to children. *Innocent*, as a description of terrorism's victims, establishes the context of justice in which the guilt of the terrorists can be convincingly established. Collaborate with your classmates and others, and discuss your analyses when you are through. What have you learned about the emotional terrain of your critical situation?

WORKSHOP 5: Ethics of Emotional Appeal

All argument involves emotion. Work through the exercises in this workshop to help you find the ethical line between strong emotional argumentation and manipulation, both in your own writing and in the arguments that you read.

Statement of Your Own Emotional Connections

We recognize that our next suggestion for invention could be misconstrued as an exercise more appropriate for a counselor's or therapist's office than for a textbook about writing and speaking. However, our interest is rhetorical rather than therapeutic, because we believe that emotions have public impact. Emotions are aroused and intensified by the arguments made about issues that interest communities. Reflecting on your own emotional experience of a critical situation is a powerful way to generate ideas for making strong arguments; in other words, it can be a powerful means of invention. One of our students, Tiffany Marshall, had an intense emotional reaction to what she saw as the lingering "broken home" stigma surrounding single-parent households. "Angered and surprised" by some condescending comments she encountered, she was motivated to develop a Web site dedicated to dispelling myths and stereotypes about single-parent homes. Reflection on her own situation helped Marshall to think carefully about the likely emotional connections of her intended audience: the parents and children of single-parent households. Marshall clearly kept in mind how hurtful such stereotypes can be.

Presenting extensive research on the experience of children raised in single-parent homes and the social stigma they encounter, Marshall wrote compassionately to people who are making the transition, for one reason or another, from dual- to single-parent homes:

> While it seems hard and your family may feel as though [your home] is broken, there are ways of coping with these feelings and getting to a place where you can accept your family as new and different, but not broken.

In the letter to readers on the homepage of her Web site, Marshall uses the second-person pronoun *you* to address the audience directly, acknowledging the degree to which many people have been hurt by assumptions about what makes up a traditional home. Marshall does not waste time or space on fierce denunciations of those who patronize single-parent homes; nor does she offer sentimental expressions of empathy for those who live in them. Rather, she addresses her audience directly:

> I am here to say that you are not at a disadvantage because one parent is raising you. And single parents, your children are not doomed because they are being raised by one parent. Despite what many psychologists and politicians say, being raised by a single parent can be just as healthy as being raised by two parents.

The phrase "I am here" assures readers of her commitment to young people sensitive about fitting in and to parents who worry or feel guilty that they have made a decision that might harm children. Marshall put considerable thought into the emotional experiences she shares with her audience, and she found methods to make strong connections with them.

Invention Journal: Your Own Emotional Connections

1. Write out your emotional reactions to your critical situation. Even if you aren't "passionately" involved in the situation right now, try to imagine how emotional you might become in a debate or argument with those who hold a different point of view.
2. Wait a few days and then write a commentary on the work you did in response to your own initial writing. Underline the emotional keywords you used. What stakeholder groups might use this same language? What stakeholders would describe their emotional connection differently? How do different stakes in a situation inspire differents emotions?
3. Imagine your audience perhaps writing a quick description of who they are. Now look over all the writing you have done in this invention journal. How does your audience's likely emotional positions compare with yours?

WORKSHOP 9: Gathering Information through Interviews

Because you are a member of the communities in which you are planning a writing project, it is likely that you know personally people with detailed information about pressing community matters. This workshop helps you prepare interviews to access that information.

Taking the Pulse of Stakeholders

Like any other means of persuasion, emotional appeals must be written with great attention to context. We have encouraged you to use the term *stakeholder* as a guide for research and analysis to encourage a more focused inquiry to the social dynamics of your critical situation. Careful study of the commitments made by stakeholders in an issue can, in other words, move you towards a more comprehensive knowledge of the situation in which you are working. Though it is far from an exact science, trying to understand how emotional connections vary from one stakeholder position to another helps you understand the power of your own words in a variety of contexts. The following strategies of invention will help you gain a working knowledge of what kinds of emotional argument are typically used in your critical situation. They also help you to understand and predict how your emotional appeal will be interpreted across a range of positions. We hope that our map metaphor may be helpful once again as you study this emotional terrain.

Invention Journal: Mapping the Emotional Landscape of Your Critical Situation

1. Return to your stakeholders' map (Chapter 2) or take the time now to list once again all the major stakeholders in your critical situation. Summarize what you take to be their emotional connection to the situation. Use a graph or a flow chart to make some broad strokes to get your thinking and analysis underway. For instance, if there has recently been a tuition increase at your college or university, you would probably list the following stakeholders: students and their families; faculty; administrators; the faculty and administrators of other local schools competing for the same students; state politicians who must justify and respond to complaints about the tuition hike; local business people who might be impacted by a decrease in enrollment or by student-customers with less money to spare. You might divide "students" more carefully: students on scholarship; in-state students; out-of-state students; students on financial aid and/or with limited funds. For each group, chart out the stake in the situation and the likely emotional response:

   Tuition Increase=> Students with limited funds=>

   Must fund or family must fund education=>

   Afraid that they won't be able to afford tuition=>

   Anger and frustration because higher education is so expensive.

WORKSHOP 7: Finding Access: Publishing Your Work
What are the most meaningful publics for your work? What audiences, if persuaded by your work, can become agents of change in your critical situation? Once you identify the right audience, how do you reach them? To discover routes of access to your audience, work through the series of questions in this workshop.

2. Write a description, complete with dialogue, of the following scenario: Members of each of the major stakeholder groups are having dinner together, and a conversation about a divisive social situation ensues. Try to describe the emotional reactions of each person at the dinner. Would their emotions influence how they heard other perspectives and how they expressed their own? If so, how? (This exercise is a good one to do collaboratively. Writing a script and acting it out in class can generate a lot of discussion about the emotional terrain of argument.)
3. Transcribe or cut and paste passages and paragraphs from the writing of prominent audience members. If you are interested in national immigration policy, for example, senators from border states such as Arizona, California, and Texas are important voices representing the position of many. The commentary of immigrants-rights and humanitarian groups likely represent a different viewpoint. Highlight emotional keywords. Analyze the writer or speaker's use of emotional language.
4. Remind yourself of the audience or audiences you will address in your project. What emotional connections does your audience hold in the context of your critical situation? Name the emotions likely to arise for them. How will you take these emotions into account as you write?

Emphasizing and De-Emphasizing Emotional Connections

Writers and speakers can create the emotional emphasis they desire through the use of detail. Discussing an injury or an illness with her doctor, a patient might describe her pain quite differently depending on how she hopes to influence treatment. The difference between reporting "a headache and some stomach upset" or "crippling headaches and nausea" might make all the difference, for instance, in obtaining a prescription for strong pain medication. "Be careful where you step," someone might say to a hiking partner while on a desert trail. "We see rattlesnakes here all the time." This enthymeme is persuasive if it stimulates the listener's fear of snakebite and so increases their caution. A parent who is trying to convince a child to take care on the trail might make the point in more detail: "You have to stay on the trail and watch out for snakes. If you are bitten, you can get very sick and even die." The risk here is that too much emphasis on the danger will discourage the child from hiking on this or any other day.

Details often evoke an intense emotional connection with audiences. For instance, in a June 27, 2005, briefing, George W. Bush's second press secretary, Scott McClellan, didn't try to hide or minimize increased U.S. casualties in Iraq. Rather, he sought to highlight one specific emotional meaning of deaths in Iraq: "We've all seen on the TV screens the images of bloodshed and violence," McClelland told the press corps. "They are disturbing. The President is disturbed by those images. The terrorists have inflicted great suffering. There have been tremendous sacrifices. But the cause for which we are in Iraq is an important one, and there is great progress being made on the ground." Strategies of emphasizing and de-emphasizing work together here. Introducing the effects of war as "images on the TV" is one step removed from a discussion of casualties on the ground; certainly we shouldn't be surprised that McClellan did not add emphasis by naming a number of dead or wounded.

Invention Journal: Questions of Emphasis

1. Think carefully about your audience in order to emphasize emotional connections as effectively as possible. Write down your audience or possible audiences—the state senate, voters in an upcoming election or referendum, cancer survivors, secondary school teachers, jazz aficionados, your coworkers, believers in the American way, whatever audience or audiences are appropriate. Once you have designated and described your audience, do some exploratory writing trying to decide whether your audience is:

    Accepting of your arguments

    Resistant to your arguments

    Neutral or indifferent to your arguments

2. Now, write out all your reasons for thinking that your audience is accepting, resistant, or neutral. You might find it helpful to read public statements made by members of your audience regarding the situation at hand.
3. Once you have gauged your audience's disposition towards the situation at hand and their strongest points of emotional connection, write out and support the major claims you will make in your project. Pay careful attention to the way your language emphasizes or de-emphasizes emotional impact.

Setting Emotional Tone

An ancient and still useful distinction worth considering is that between language that *honors* and language that *disparages.* Obviously, you can't be certain how audiences will respond to any language, but attention to word choice in context increases your chances of rhetorical success. Words of praise, called **honorific language**, include such terms as *brave, honest,* and *trustworthy.* Words of condemnation, here called **disparaging language**, include such terms as *two-faced, liar,* and *schemer.* The use of even a few words that stimulate strong emotional responses can create a powerful tone in any composition.

Here is James Wolcott, honoring the work of writer and critic Dwight Macdonald on the one-hundredth anniversary of Macdonald's birth:

> Sometimes the most important thing a critic leaves behind is a *singular, wised-up, cant-free voice* that is *pure intelligence at play,* and at its best Macdonald's voice *shoots off the page* as if he were broadcasting live and *cutting through the static* . . . . Macdonald's saving grace—what set him apart from the other *touchy high-strungs*—was his *ample accommodation for conflicting viewpoints* even when they rammed his hull, as long as they had wit and merit. He believed in *being open* to reversals of opinion, including his

> own. He dissected *The New Yorker* in the debut issue of *Partisan Review,* yet later *hopped a* board as a staff writer, *a professional* relationship that *blossomed into blushing romance*. . . . Right or wrong, his verdicts would mean nothing to us now if he hadn't invested them with *a humming force of personality and humor* that *opened up daylight* wherever his mind *gusted.* Every intellectual era needs its dedicated pirates, and Dwight Macdonald was one of postwar's finest. He wrote and spoke as if *fear and conformity were foreign to his nature and affronts to the spirit of liberty.* If he were alive, he'd scoff at what *wimps* we've become under the *threat* of terrorism. He'd scold us for letting ourselves down. (*The New York Times Book Review,* April 16, 2006: 27)

We have italicized the honorific passages that Wolcott uses to celebrate Macdonald's contributions. Wolcott is writing an essay of appreciation, and it is conventional to praise a subject in this genre. But Wolcott wittily balances his assessment of Macdonald's honorable achievements with those that are not so deserving of praise.

As an example of skillful disparagement, consider the following review of the film *300* written by Nicole Quezada. Quezada had major reservations about race, gender, and sexual stereotypes used in the film, which she skillfully compared to the classic of white supremacist propaganda, *Birth of a Nation.* Despite some grudging admiration of the spectacular cinematic effects of *300,* Quezada didn't hold back on her critique of the film's politics:

> For a movie that promises *only entertainment, 300* most certainly entertains. It's the *racist, xenophobic, jingoistic, masculinist vigilante spirit* that accompanies this entertainment that is *so disconcerting. 300* may only promise a good time (that is, if your idea of a good time is *bad dialogue* and *highly stylized violence*—at least Tarantino has the decency to work on his words as much as his gore) but it delivers messages of false honor and *"u(nited) s(tates) vs. them"* sentiments worthy of army recruitment pamphlets (or rather, DVDs, videogames and websites).With lines like "my son gave up his life for his country" and "freedom isn't free" there is little doubt the film's reference to current our current political moment.

We have italicized Quezada's disparaging language. The first instance, in which Quezada notes that *300* delivers *only entertainment,* lets readers know that the film doesn't merit much in the way or artistic appreciation. The litany of phrases that follow, *racist, xenophobic, jingoistic, masculinist vigilante spirit,* deliver the heart of Quezada's criticism, that the film makes a virtue of prejudiced character assassination. Her negative assessment continues with her assertion about the film's *bad dialogue* and *highly stylized violence,* which we should note, some filmgoers would take to be a complimentary comment. Finally, Quezada uses disparagement to suggest something further about the politics of *300.* As she interprets the film, *300* takes a partisan stance on the politics of our current era of war in the United States. Referring to the patriotic phrases the Athenians in the film utter, which she finds *jingoistic,* Quezada punningly renders the phrase "us vs. them" as *"(nited) (tates) vs. them,"* a disparaging strategy by which she furthers her claim that *300* is propagandistic.

We offer a word of caution about setting emotional tone and about emotional appeals generally. Be sure the intensity of your appeal is appropriate for the context. Quezada published her review in a venue of politically like-minded readers, so she could feel confident wih the strong language of her critique. Excessively honorific or disparaging language may strike even sympathetic audiences as misplaced and so reduce your credibility.

Invention Journal: Honorific and Disparaging Language

1. Make two columns on a sheet of paper. On one side, list all the ideas, people, initiatives, perspectives, and events that you want to honor in the context of your critical situation. On the other side, list all that you want to disparage. Decide which will be most important to include when you compose your project. For each of these, write a few lines that honor or disparage. For example, if you are writing in support of a policy measure, you may want to praise politicians who support the policy and disparage those politicians who oppose it. Or, if you are writing to recommend a colleague for an award, you should certainly be extensive in your praise. Conversely, a high-ranking official convicted of perjury might make a reasonable target for disparagement if you are arguing for a conviction. Again, we strongly encourage you not to be too extreme with your honorific and disparaging language. Measure the impact you want to make on readers. There is a big difference between indicting a politician's "monstrous misjudgment" and calling attention to the "serious flaws" in a policy. There are certainly good times for strong language, but name calling, verbal abuse, and also sugary sweet and fawning praise often come off as, respectively, mean-spirited and insincere.
2. Now, try writing about an honorable idea, a person, an initiative, a perspective, or an event in a disparaging way. Next, try writing about something you disparage in an honorific way. What happens? Has this exercise changed your original evaluations in any way?

WORKSHOP 2: Arranging Your Compostion

As you discover arguments through invention, consider how they will fit together when you sit down to write. This workshop is devoted to "arrangement," the skillful structuring of arguments.

WORKSHOP 15: Revising for Clarity

This workshop offers revising strategies for increasing the clarity of writing. Increasing the clarity of your ideas helps you connect with your intended audience.

WORKSHOP 12: Putting Together a Portfolio of Your Invention Work

Gathering your invention work together in a portfolio creates a record of your thought, research, and analysis. This workshop offers a simple framework for constructing a portfolio and writing a critical self-reflection on the progress of your project.

Visual Rhetoric and Emotional Appeal

There is an old commonplace that asserts "a picture is worth a thousand words." It is certainly true that images can have powerful emotional impact, particularly when they confront readers with unpleasant truths, depict moving human experience, provide evidence of immoral acts, or stop us in our tracks with sublime beauty. Visual eloquence, however, requires a certain amount of craft. Images must he delivered to the right audience at the right time, and they must be framed so that audiences see images as they are intended by writers and speakers. For example, how might the images from Hurricane Katrina in the following section be framed to deliver powerful emotional arguments?

Your project may well include visual images, and because we often have visceral reactions to images, you should consider this component of your work very carefully. Our student Kevin Marshall struggled with decisions about using images on his antiwar Web site. In the end, Marshall did run some disturbing photographs on his home page (though they appeared near the page bottom after a good deal of explanation of the intentions of the site) and then offered links for further images with a caution: "Warning: The Images linked to this site are graphic. Parental discretion is advised." We applaud Marshall's willingness to take so much care in considering the possible emotional impact of arguing with images.

Invention Journal: Cataloging Powerful Images

1. Use the "image" search function of Yahoo, Google, or other search engines to find images relevant to your critical situation. For example, if you are researching the influence of advertising on young women's body image, ads from fashion magazines depicting startlingly thin young models will be relevant. A proposal for a neighborhood cleanup day, for example, might include a photograph of an overgrown and litter-strewn common area. Such images, respectively, might inspire disgust and anger (over the violence of prevailing ideas about female beauty) and embarrassment (about a lack of pride in ownership). Remember that to use thse images in your project, you must cite them properly.
2. For each image you have gathered, write out predictions of the way your audience will respond emotionally upon viewing it. Be as specific as possible in explaining why the image will have an emotional impact. How does your audience's stake in the situation influence *how* they will see the image and what emotions they may have in response?

Once you have chosen images that may appear in your project, you will have to decide what text will accompany the image. How will you *frame* the images so that your audience views them as you want them to be seen? For example, an image of

Scenes like those pictured here of crowds of African Americans stranded amidst their own city after Hurricane Katrina shocked many.

For many, photographs like this of New Orleans residents waiting for rescue after Hurricane Katrina became emblematic of the lack of governmental commitment to poor people and African Americans in particular. The United States flag waved by one of the people on this rooftop could be read as a claim to the rights of citizenship in a desperate moment.

New Orleans citizens stranded on a rooftop after Hurricane Katrina could be framed as an appeal to an audience's concern about climate change, or it could be framed to rouse anger about the lack of government preparedness. Framed differently, the image could celebrate the strength of will that enables people to survive disaster.

LIST OF WORKS CITED

Bush, George W. "State of the Union Address," January 2005. http://www.whitehouse.gov/news/releases/2005/02/200502–11.html.

Davey, Monica. "Ripples from Law Banning Abortion Spread Through South Dakota." New York *Times,* 16 April 2006, A14.

McClellen, Scott. Press briefing, 27 June 2005.

Wendell Phillips. *Speeches, Lectures, and Letters.* Boston: Walker, Wise and Company, 1864.

Wolcott, James. "Dwight MacDonald at 100." *New York Times Book Review,* 16 April 2006: 27.

9

CRITICAL INFORMATION

Evidence is *not* self-evident. In other words, the information that we use to support the arguments we make will be persuasive only if we choose and present it skillfully. A mundane example illustrates the point well. Imagine a group of young men entering a liquor store. When they bring a case of beer to the counter, the cashier eyes them hesitantly and asks, "Can I see some ID, please?" The young man holding the beer says that he has forgotten his driver's license but assures the cashier, "I'm 23 years old." Unconvinced, the cashier says, "I need to see ID." One of the young man's friends says, "Really, he's 23. I've known this guy my whole life." The cashier shrugs, unimpressed. "Fine," says a third young man producing a driver's license from his wallet, "I'll buy it." The cashier takes the license and scrutinizes it, glancing from the ID photo to the young man's face and back again. She rubs the numbers listed under "Date of Birth" looking for ink smudges. Meanwhile, the beer is getting warm.

As an audience, the cashier has high standards for evidence because the stakes are high: she will be fired if she sells alcohol to those who are under the legal drinking age. As a consequence, she views personal assurances, the testimony of friends—even an actual driver's license with a photograph and date of birth indicating a 21-year-old individual—with some suspicion. Nor does the way in which the evidence was presented render any of this evidence persuasive: the man carrying the beer has no license, his friend has a defensive tone, and the date on the license shows a hint of smudge. In fact, the cashier construes all of these signs as persuasive evidence of an alternate claim: that the young men are too young to buy beer legally.

We define **evidence** as anything offered as proof of a claim. Today evidence is primarily thought of as the facts at hand—data or statistics. But this is a rather limited view. Aristotle distinguished between arguments that were produced by a speaker's or writer's craft and evidence produced by the situation itself (the material facts surrounding a crime for instance—fingerprints, DNA, pieces of clothing and so on). Writers and speakers can employ arguments of the first kind—reasoning, demonstrations of character or credibility (ethos), and emotional appeals—in support of their claims, and we have addressed these crafted sorts of arguments in previous chapters. Facts and statistics are in Aristotle's second category—they are produced by the critical situation itself. However, factual evidence must be worked with carefully if it is to be useful.

In this chapter, we address factual evidence, particularly personal experience, testimony, statistics, and images. We will also pay attention to the presentation or "framing" of evidence. Each of these varieties of evidence, chosen and organized carefully within your project, can be powerful on its own. Used in combination, they can move audiences to accept the claims you make regarding your critical situation.

Not all situations require all these kinds of evidence because not all audiences will be as skeptical as the cashier imagined above. In the end, the nature of your audience will determine the quality and kinds of evidence most appropriate for use in your argument. You can decide what sorts of evidence you need to support your claim by paying careful attention to context and to audience. Evidence that is persuasive in one situation might strike your audience as weak in another. And when you have brought the appropriate evidence to the table, you need to organize and present that evidence in the most effective manner.

CASE STUDY: EVIDENCE OF TERROR

Ida B. Wells, whose work we introduced in Chapter 2, was a master of argument supported by factual evidence. In the late nineteenth and early twentieth centuries Wells had an international reputation as a civil rights activist, journalist, and relentless opponent of the horrifically common murder of African Americans in the South. The following passages are taken from her 1895 expose titled *Red Record: Lynch Law in All Its Phases.* Wells's title announces to readers that the evidence to be presented recounts bloody deeds. This work displays a pageant of factual evidence skillfully used:

> Not all nor nearly all of the murders done by white men, during the past thirty years in the South, have come to light, but the statistics as gathered and preserved by white men, and which have not been questioned, show that during these years more than ten thousand Negroes have been killed in cold blood, without the formality of judicial trial and legal execution. And yet, as evidence of the absolute impunity with which the white man dares to kill a Negro, the same record shows that during all these years, and for all these murders only three white men have been tried, convicted, and executed. (75–76)

Wells is careful to preface the evidence she puts forward as "statistics as gathered and preserved by white men" (75). Clearly, Wells was aware that she might be charged with bias or with exaggerating or fabricating the truly shocking statistics contained in her book. In the late nineteenth century, the opinions of African American women were all too easy to dismiss because of the political power of racism and sexism in this era. Thus Wells had to make a careful case for the authority or trustworthiness of her statistics. "The data compiled by that journal and published to the world January 1, 1894, up to the present time has not been disputed," she asserted. "In order to be safe from the charge of exaggeration, the incidents hereinafter reported have been confined to those vouched for by the [Chicago] Tribune" (82). Wells knew that the testimony and statistics would be more authoritative if they were cited from a major paper. Wells carefully juxtaposed the "more than ten thousand Negroes . . . killed in cold blood" with the "three white men" who have been "tried, convicted and executed" (75, 76). Wells gave these statistics meaning through skillful arrangement; the overwhelming disparity between the two numbers indicates the enormity of the injustice.

And of course, Wells's statistical evidence was exhaustive. Long passages in her book list the names of victims of lynching and the crimes of which they were accused (none were ever tried in a court of law). These statistics go on for pages, and the cumulative effect is quite powerful. It isn't just that the number of victims is so shockingly large. There is rhetorical power in giving the names of the victims. The frequency of these horrendous murders, too horrible to be believed for many readers, takes on the full dimensions of tragedy humanized in this way:

> From the record published in the *Chicago Tribune* January 1, 1894, the following computation of lynching statistics is made referring only to the colored victims of Lynch Law during the year 1893:
>
> ARSON
>
> Sept. 15, Paul Hill, Carrollton, Ala.; Sept. 15, Paul Archer, Carrollton, Ala.; Sept. 15, William Archer, Carrollton, Ala.; Sept. 15, Emma Fair, Carrollton, Ala.
>
> SUSPECTED ROBBERY
>
> Dec. 23, unknown negro, Fannin, Miss.
>
> ASSAULT
>
> Dec. 25, Calvin Thomas, near Brainbridge, Ga.
>
> ATTEMPTED ASSAULT
>
> Dec. 28, Tillman Green, Columbia, La.
>
> INCENDIARISM
>
> Jan. 26, Patrick Wells, Quincy, Fla.; Feb. 9, Frank Harrell, Dickery, Miss.; Feb. 9, William Filder, Dickery, Miss.
>
> ATTEMPTED RAPE
>
> Feb. 21, Richard Mays, Springville, Mo.; Aug. 14, Dug Hazleton, Carrollton, Ga.; Sept. 1, Judge McNeil, Cadiz, Ky.; Sept. 11, Frank Smith, Newton, Miss.; Sept. 16, William Jackson, Nevada, Mo.; Sept. 19, Riley Gulley, Pine Apple, Ala.; Oct. 9, John Davis, Shorterville, Ala.; Nov. 8, Robert Kennedy, Spartansburg, S.C.
>
> BURGLARY
>
> Feb. 16, Richard Forman, Granada, Miss.
>
> WIFE BEATING
>
> Oct. 14, David Jackson, Covington, La. ... (82–83)

Charges of arson, robbery, assault, rape, burglary, and wife beating do not usually carry a death sentence. And yet, each supposed perpetrator was horribly executed, without trial. The names and dates in combination confront readers with a grisly calendar of murder carried out by lynch mobs who did not fear punishment. Imagine the power of such a list in an era where the crime of lynching was a silent conspiracy, denied and covered up in the South and all too easily ignored or written off as a Southern issue by the North.

Wells offered testimony about the murder of a man named Hamp Biscoe and his family. She drew the details from an account given in a major newspaper. The situation that confronted Hamp Biscoe and his family was all too common. White men claimed that Biscoe owed money for fees associated with the purchase of the land where his family built their home. As Wells and others pointed out, African Americans who owned property or had achieved some social success were often the targets of lynch mobs. Wells suggested that Biscoe's refusal to pay the bogus debt did not motivate the attack. Drawing on an article by one Mr. Carlee, who wrote for a major local paper, Wells offered the firsthand testimony of Hamp Biscoe's son, given as he himself lay dying of wounds inflicted during the assault on Biscoe's home:

> The subsequent proceedings were briefly told by Mr. Carlee in the columns of the *Arkansas Democrat* above mentioned, from whose account the following excerpt is taken . . . that night, about 8 o'clock, a party of perhaps twelve or fifteen men, a number of whom were known to the guards, came to the house and told the Negro guards they would take care of the prisoners now, and for them to leave; as they did not obey at once they were persuaded to leave with words that did not admit of delay.
>
> The woman began to cry and said, "You intend to kill us to get our money." They told her to hush (she was heavy with child and had a child at her breast) as they intended to give her a nice present. The guards heard no more, but hastened to a Negro church near by and urged the preacher to go up and stop the mob. A few minutes after, the shooting began, perhaps about forty shots being fired. The white men then left rapidly and the Negroes went to the house. Hamp Biscoe and his wife were killed, the baby had a slight wound across the upper lip; the boy was still alive and lived until after midnight, talking rationally and telling who did the shooting. (89–90)

The testimony of a dying boy, given at the scene of his family's murder, carries persuasive authority. Wells's re-framing of young Biscoe's testimony becomes powerful evidence for her claim that the horrific crimes perpetrated under "lynch law" must be stopped.

Decades later, in her autobiography, Wells would offer detailed reminiscence of her personal motivations for taking up anti-lynching work, including recollections of the murder of her friends and neighbors that went unpunished. But in *Red Record,* Wells understood the necessity of maintaining a stance of journalistic objectivity. She thus kept her personal observations and experiences to a minimum. She offered only the briefest comments, and those comments were depersonalized through the use of third-person self-reference: "the writer hereof" (157). Though brief, Wells's account of death threats and the burning of the

WORKSHOP 13: Readers Responding
This workshop offers powerful strategies for approaching reading as serious writers do, with a critical eye for the most important arguments and ideas. Follow the strategies presented in this workshop to gain skills as an engaged reader and become more able to put what you read to work in your own writing.

WORKSHOP 16: Summarizing Arguments, Ideas, and Texts
Writers regularly present the work of others as building blocks for their own work. This workshop offers strategies for writing strong summaries to incorporate into your own writing.

WORKSHOP 8: Following Pathways: A Metaphor for Critical Reading and Research
The exercises in this workshop will help you identify unfamiliar ideas and references in your reading and research and to approach them as opportunities for learning—as "pathways" to knowledge.

Free Speech, the newspaper she owned and operated, is persuasive evidence that the lynchers themselves could not defend their actions. This persecution, Wells pointed out, was perpetrated in response to her "assertion of...fact" and "defense of her race" (79). Although it is brief, this account of personal experience might well have convinced readers of Wells's courage in publishing that it was necessary to publish a document like *A Red Record* (thus, bolstering her ethos). Wells's brief account of her personal experience with racism also attests to the desperation with which white supremacist vigilantes were attempting to censor the truth about lynching.

TALK READ WRITE

Re-read the passage from Wells above, or read the entire text. Which kind of evidence used by Wells—personal observations and experience, first and second hand testimony, and statistics—was likely most effective? Think of contemporary or other historical situations in which each of these three kinds of evidence—personal experience and observations, testimony, and statistics—are used persuasively. What is it about each of those situations that calls for a particular kind of evidence?

CASE STUDY: WHO WERE THE HIJACKERS?

Evidence can be tricky because it is often persuasive, particularly when it is carefully assembled into a convincing list of factual statements. But it is often hard to know whether statements claiming to be factual really are so. Take, for example, the report of the 9/11 Commission, which is widely reckoned to be the definitive account of the events of September 11, 2001. This report has been roundly criticized by those who do not accept the evidence painstakingly reviewed by members of the 9/11 Commission and their staff. One such critic is David Ray Griffin, who has written several books about 9/11. In one of his books, Griffin attempts to establish gaps in the evidence assembled by the Commission, claiming that its members or staff regularly omitted or distorted evidence that would cast doubt on its version of events (19). This is a highly controversial claim, of course, because the stakes are very high in this argument, as we shall see. Griffin argues, for example, that six of the nineteen people identified by the Commission as the hijackers cannot have been among this group, because they are still alive:

> Waleed al-Shehri—said to have been on American Airlines Flight 11, which hit the North Tower of the World Trade Center—was interviewed after 9/11 by a London-based newspaper. He also, the Associated Press reported, spoke on September 22 to the US embassy in Morocco, explaining that he lives in Casablanca, working as a pilot for Royal Air Maroc.
>
> Likewise, Ahmed al-Nami and Saeed al-Ghamdi—both said to have been on United Airlines Flight 93, which crashed in Pennsylvania—were shocked, they told *Telegraph* reporter David Harrison, to hear that they had died in this crash. Al-Nami,

> who was working as an administrative supervisor with Saudi Arabian Airlines at the time, added: "I had never even heard of Pennsylvania." Al-Ghamdi said he had been in Tunis the previous ten months learning to fly an Airbus. According to the BBC, *Asharq Al Awsat,* a London-based Arabic newspaper, also reported having interviewed al-Ghamdi.
>
> The Saudi embassy in Washington reported that three other alleged hijackers—Mohand al-Shehri, Salem al-Hazmi, and Abdulaziz al-Omari, were all alive and living in Saudi Arabia. Salem al-Hazmi, who was accused of hijacking Flight 77, "had just returned to work at a petrochemical complex in the industrial eastern city of Yanbou after a holiday in Saudi Arabia when the hijackers struck," David Harrison reported. Al-Omari, supposedly the pilot of Flight 11 but in reality working as a pilot for Saudi Airlines, "visited the US consulate in Jeddah to demand an explanation" for the US claim that he was a hijacker, and a dead one at that.
>
> In spite of these revelations by mainstream news sources, however, *The 9/11 Commission Report* simply repeats, in the first few pages (1–5), the FBI's original list of nineteen names, then later gives their photographs (238–39).... How can we believe that the Commission's report was based on "exacting investigative work," as we were told by Kean and Hamilton in the Preface, if the staff did not even learn, from sources such as the Associated Press, the *Telegraph,* and the BBC, that six of the men originally identified as the hijackers were still alive? (19–20)

Griffin amply footnotes this passage so that skeptical readers can find and read the relevant issues of the newspapers he cites.

If the evidence assembled by his sources is accurate, Griffin's account casts suspicion on the care with which members of the Commission and their staff did their research. That is, if six of the alleged hijackers are indeed still alive, and if documentation of these facts was made available in major European and Arabic-language newspapers prior to the time the Commission began its research, members of the Commission and its staff either overlooked or ignored evidence that countered the version of events they forward. And while the ordinary person can look up the newspaper stories to check out the accuracy of Griffin's account, it is nonetheless difficult for most people to verify the factuality of either of these accounts. The men alleged by the FBI to be hijackers live far away, and they live in countries that keep close watch on American travelers. The decision about who to believe in this case, then, probably relies less on the persuasiveness of the evidence itself than on readers' assessment of the trustworthiness of the authors of the conflicting accounts. We suspect as well that many readers may dismiss Griffin's account out of hand, on the ground that the implications of his argument are simply too unsettling to accept.

TALK READ WRITE

1. Are you convinced by Griffin's evidence? Why or why not? Get hold of the 9/11 Commission report and read the passages cited by Griffin. Which account seems more trustworthy to you? Why?

2. What is at stake in this controversy over evidence? Identify the stakeholders in this argument. Then ask: what do the stakeholders stand to gain, or lose, if either version of the events of 9/11 is accepted by most readers?

PERSONAL OBSERVATION AND EXPERIENCE

Even though a good deal of psychological research suggests that the senses of sight, sound, smell, hearing, and touch can be misled (or be misleading), we live in a culture that takes physical perceptions as factual. In the right context, communicated skillfully, personal observations and experiences can be among the most persuasive forms of evidence. We often trust this kind of testimony because it seems so direct. "I saw it with my own eyes" we might say, relating something improbable to a friend. We tend to trust sensory perception. If you are an acknowledged expert on the situation you are addressing, based on your experience or your training, or if you share common experiences that will resonate with your audiences, then evidence based on personal observations may be persuasive.

For instance, our student Ameerah Al-Islam likely struck a chord with her audience recounting her own experience of the life-changing onset of her grandmother's Alzheimer's disease:

> It was a hot day, and I sat in my mother's car unwilling to step out of the air-conditioned car. While my mother was busy taking my little sister from her child seat, I sat in my seat staring out the window at my Granny. She seemed slightly different as I watched her looking out across the street with a distant expression on her face. She was standing in the rocks on the side of the house holding a soda can in her hand, standing so still. She finally moved, taking one last sip from her soda before tossing it in some nearby bushes and began to walk towards our house. My mother had just turned around in time to comment on what she had just seen. I could tell in the tone of her voice that she had immediately become concerned by what she had witnessed. She said, "Momma, why did you just do that? You can't do that." My Granny replied "Oh please . . . whatever!" and visibly insulted, stomped the rest of the way into the house.

Al-Islam has done a good job here capturing the surprise and concern raised by, as she put it, "the first visible signs of Alzheimer's disease in my Granny who I so cherish." Anyone who has witnessed dramatic changes in behavior from loved ones would likely make an emotional connection reading such a recollection of experience. Al-Islam made a strategically good decision when she included her mother's reaction to her grandmother's erratic behavior in her account because this choice lends a multigenerational perspective to her argument. Alzheimer's disease, like any serious illness, disrupts entire families, and so this account of experience works well as evidence of the seriousness of the disease. This account also demonstrates that the impact of this disease can be widespread, and thus it supports the need to find a cure.

The Problem of Generalizing from Personal Experience

As in all evidence use, *framing* personal experience is very important. "Facts" without interpretation are not persuasive. In fact, they might not be recognized as facts at all if they present themselves simply as disconnected data. By framing, we mean giving your audience enough information so that they will receive the testimony in the light most favorable to your argument. The frame provides the boundaries against which the central focus will take on meaning, just as it does in a painting or a photograph. Consider Al-Islam's success in setting up an interpretive frame for her audience. Her own observations of her grandmother's deteriorating health are supported by her mother's. More importantly, the details about her emotional response to her grandmother's health and behavior frame Alzheimer's disease as a family tragedy, one that has lasting impact across generations.

Each kind of evidence use presents its own opportunities and challenges for framing. When using personal observation, one important means of framing is to *qualify* your observations. To qualify an observation or claim means to limit its force. For example, Al-Islam implicitly qualifies her observations by avoiding generalizations from her experience; she does not try to claim that her grandmother's experience is typical for all who struggle with the disease. She might also have qualified her observation with a line such as this: "Based solely on my own experience, Alzheimer's disease devastates families." Or feeling confident that others would share her perspective, she might also have qualified more assertively: "Other families struggling with Alzheimer's will likely understand my own grief at seeing a loved one change so drastically." Such qualifications, like other framing devices, allow you to take control of your argument more effectively and to more precisely craft a connection with your audience.

Do you know the Buddhist parable about the elephant and the blind men? In an effort to demonstrate to his students how limited preachers and scholars are by their own perspective, Buddha told the story of a teacher who called together a number of blind men and presented them with an elephant. Positioned around the elephant, one felt the elephant's head, one its trunk, one the tuft of its tail, one its ear, one its tusk, and one its legs. The teacher asked the blind men, "What kind of thing is an elephant?" The man who touched the tail argued that the elephant was like a brush, while the one touching the ear argued that an elephant was like a blanket. The man touching the trunk said the elephant was like a plough, but the man touching the foot said the elephant was like a pillar. A bitter argument ensued, ending with thrown punches as each man answered based on his own relation to the whole and his sense of touch alone. The teacher in the Buddha's story was pleased with the outcome of this lesson, as the quarreling men illustrated how confidently—and mistakenly—we argue from the perspective of our own limited experiences.

WORKSHOP 3: Different Values and Respectful Conflict

Arguments are inherently matters of conflict. Rather than trying to avoid such conflict, we recommend approaching it as a powerful learning opportunity and an intellectual resource. This workshop provides the framework for sharing our own value-based positions in a productive and respectful manner.

The point, of course, is not to impugn the capacity of the blind but to suggest that we all, even those with the 20–20 vision, bring a partial perspective to important questions. As psychologists who do research on eyewitness accounts have proven, the senses can't be trusted nearly as much as we would often like to think. Moreover, we tend to argue our truths based on situated knowledge, that is, on knowledge influenced by our experience and place in the world. It is all too easy to generalize from our own experience. Assuming that everyone shares our perspective is much easier than doing the hard work of careful research and analysis that can help us understand where our own experience converges or diverges with that of our audience.

WORKSHOP 9: Gathering Information through Interviews

Because you are a member of the communities in which you are planning a writing project, it is likely that you know personally people with detailed information about pressing community matters. This workshop helps you prepare interviews to access that information.

Invention Journal: When Is Your Own Perspective Persuasive?

When you are trying to decide whether to use your own personal experience and observation as evidence, you should ask yourself the following questions: Am I an authority on the situation in question? Does my education or professional experience give me a kind of credibility that others don't have? Do I have enough direct experience of this critical situation that I can speak with authority to others who care about it? Will my audience recognize me as an authority? Do I share experiences with my audience that if discussed skillfully will allow me to make a connection with them? Can my personal experience or observations add something important to my argument?

If the answer to any of these questions is "yes," your perspective may well have the persuasive force of evidence. And even if the answer to these questions is "no," it may be that offering your own perspective will nevertheless be necessary to establish credibility. Many audiences expect firsthand knowledge of the events of the critical situation in question—they won't trust a writer or speaker who professes no personal knowledge of the matter under discussion. Unless the writing or speaking context is a rigidly formal academic or professional situation, putting yourself in the argument may well bolster your credibility.

If you have decided to use personal experience and observation as evidence, you now must decide how to use them. Many nonfiction books and essays begin with such accounts. Find one or two of these if you want to look at the ways in which authors use their personal experience as evidence.

To begin making decisions about how to put evidence to work, answer the following questions: What aspects of my experience are most relevant to my argument? What aspects of my experience might distract attention from my argument? Which aspects connect most directly with my audience's perspective on the situation at hand? What is the appropriate tone for writing or speaking about my experience? Should it be journalistic, de-emphasizing emotional connections as Wells does, or should it be unabashedly "personal," such as Al-Islam's memory of her grandmother?

Look back at your answers to the previous questions, and then write out your personal experience and observations in a manner that you believe will be most persuasive to your audience. Remember to keep the goals of your argument and the perspective of your audience in mind.

AUTHORITATIVE TESTIMONY

Testimony, as we use the term, refers to an account about a situation, events, or an issue. You may be most familiar with the term in a legal context. In a trial, lawyers attempt to orchestrate testimony to persuade juries to convict or to acquit. Whether they are questioning their own witnesses or cross-examining witnesses called by the opposing side, lawyers attempt to contextualize testimony in a light most favorable for their case. As you work on your own project, you need to find authoritative voices and use the testimony of individuals and groups that will strike readers and listeners as most relevant. Clearly, not any testimony will do. Several factors give authority to testimony in any given critical situation. These include community involvement, a significant stake in the situation, expert status, and eyewitness perspective.

Community Involvement

Whether we agree with them or not, people in positions of power and influence can offer persuasive testimony. People actively shaping the events of a critical situation will likely be acknowledged by audiences as authorities. Spokespeople for all major positions have a claim to authority, and so their testimony is important to consider in making and responding to arguments. Ida B. Wells commanded authority because she put her life on the line in the effort to stop lynching. The testimony of high-ranking military officers in the field bears the authority of people who understand military operations and who are actually "in country," as well. A student body president or faculty senator might make authoritative testimony on the allocation of tuition dollars.

A Significant Stake in the Situation

People without prominent public voices in a critical situation can still offer persuasive testimony. When people's lives are implicated in the events of a critical situation, their perspective may well command some authority. Audiences can be persuaded by the words of those who have the most to lose or gain. Any student who is impacted by a tuition raise, for instance, might be consulted as a source of testimony that could well move for an audience. People whose homes are destroyed by a hurricane offer compelling testimony to the storm's force. Workers who have lost their jobs as a result of outsourcing have a perspective on free-trade policies that could be persuasive.

Expert Status

Even when people are not directly involved in a critical situation they can speak with authority based on training or other kinds of experience. Academic work relies heavily on this kind of testimony. Professors go through years of training as undergraduate and graduate students to gain expert status so that they can speak with authority within their discipline. For instance, a historian offers an interpretation of ancient events, despite the enormous distances of time and space, based on exhaustive research and analysis. In public life, commentators on current events and policy make statements that command authority based not on direct involvement but on their experience carefully analyzing the political scene.

Eyewitness Perspective

Without expert status or direct involvement or any real stake in the situation at hand, fate might still lend authority to the testimony of an eyewitness. In court, juries might be persuaded by the bystander who witnessed a crime. Analysts reconstructing the events of 9/11 have relied heavily on eyewitness accounts.

Often, the strongest sources of testimony have each of these kinds of authority. Ida B. Wells, for instance, spoke from the authority of an expert (she had devoted a great deal of time to her research on lynch law, and she had been personally affected by the violence of white supremacist vigilantism). The persuasiveness of testimony depends, as always, on your audience. Eyewitness perspectives, for instance, are important if your intention is to give your audience a sense of "being there." Feature stories in newspapers often depend on the perspectives of people who have a significant stake in an issue and who have encountered events first hand. Evidence from certified experts is persuasive only to audiences who accept an expert's credentials or the worth of his or her training, however. During the trial of O. J. Simpson for the murder of his wife, for example, members of the jury were not impressed by the testimony of police officers who had searched Simpson's property without securing a warrant to do so. Jurors were aware of the reputation of the LAPD as a racist organization, and because of this they were reluctant to accept testimony from police officers who they identified as racists.

TALK READ WRITE

Think of a critical situation that has recently generated controversy either locally or nationally. Write out the major positions being argued in this controversy. Now, brainstorm ideas for testimony that might be brought to the argument by spokespeople for each position being argued. Next, do some preliminary research and find examples of each kind of testimony as it is actually used in this controversy. Discuss the persuasive merits of the testimony.

FRAMING TESTIMONY FOR THE RIGHT OCCASION

Which kind of testimony you use in your argument depends on the situation, your intentions, and your audience. Choosing and framing testimony that is appropriate for your critical situation should always be done while you are thinking in this broader context. Often, framing testimony effectively happens in a sentence or less. For instance, if we wanted to use Ameerah Al-Islam's testimony in an argument for stem cell research, we might frame her work this way: "Ameerah Al-Islam, who has studied Alzheimer's as a science student and who has witnessed her own grandmother's struggle with the disease, is a strong advocate of stem cell research." This way of framing the testimony is assurance for your audience that Al-Islam has a significant stake in the issue and that she has at least some claim to expert status.

Invention Journal: Orchestrating Persuasive Voices

1. Read important arguments being made by participants in your critical situation. What kinds of testimonial evidence are these people using? Which of these authorities might work well in your argument?
2. Make four columns on a sheet of paper, one each for the kinds of testimony introduced in this chapter (community involvement; significant stake; expert status; eyewitness perspective). List the testimonies you have assembled that fit under each head.
3. Once you have found persuasive testimony, try to frame it for your audience. For each piece of testimony you plan on using, ask yourself the these questions:

   What does your audience need to know about the person or persons giving the testimony to trust that it is trustworthy? What is their claim to expert status? What is their experience? What is their stake in the situation? What aspects of the testimony need to be explained or contextualized? If an expert testimonial uses specialized terms, for example, will those need to be clarified for a non-expert reader? Do you need to explain why the person being cited is an expert on the issue at hand?

   Now, write a few sentences or a paragraph for each piece of testimony that you might use in your project. Ideally, some of these may become passages that you can cut and paste directly into your final work.

WORKSHOP 6: Ethics and the Use of Evidence

Working through the exercises in this workshop will help you gain strategies for considering whether the evidence you encounter in arguments is being used in good faith or manipulatively. As important, you will have the chance to think through the ethics of your own use of evidence.

USING STATISTICS

The case that you are making may or may not lend itself to statistical argument. Even if flow charts and bar graphs aren't your cup of tea, we recommend that you at least consider the possibility that statistics and figures can help you to create a persuasive connection with your audience. As is true of testimony, statistics must be carefully framed in order to be persuasive because audiences distrust numbers presented without context. Perhaps an old joke is worth repeating in this regard: an announcer says, "Here are tonight's scores: 30–3, 6–4, and 2–1."

Whether they shock, inspire, or amaze, statistics can serve as powerful evidence for a claim. Think, for example, of the comparative statistics that are posted after half-time of football games: for each team the yardage gained by running or passing, the number of passes completed or intercepted, the number of sacks, and so on are posted. Sometimes these statistics reflect the score; sometimes they do not. They do serve as evidence on which spectators can base their opinion of a team's performance, however. Or, think of the statistics reported every weekend concerning the amount of money taken in by feature films. We can be sure that a film which does not meet expectations in this regard will not be shown in theaters for very long. Never mind that the popularity of a film has little to do with its quality and everything to do with the persuasiveness of its advertising; excellent films can have very short runs if they do not draw audiences, while truly bad films can remain in theatres for many weeks if they appeal to an audience willing to pay to see them.

No type of evidence is as often equated with "the facts" as is statistical evidence. In the minds of many people, numbers offer a strict representation of material reality. As we write, the temperature is 115 degrees Fahrenheit in Phoenix, where we live. This statistic will no doubt be used as evidence in arguments all over the greater Phoenix area. Workers will suggest to bosses that it is simply too hot to work outside. Children will ask their parents to take them to the public pool to cool off, and parents might counter that it is dangerous to play outside on such a hot day, even in a swimming pool. Someone might argue with a roommate or partner about turning the temperature of the air conditioning up or down. In support of any of these arguments, these hypothetical people might exclaim, "It's 115 out there!" On the other hand, during winter, these same people might be making quite different arguments based on the temperature: "I was late to work because my car wouldn't start"; "turn up the heat, please!"

Our point is that statistics don't mean much outside of the contexts given them in writing or speech. The joke about scores ("30–3," "6–4," "2–1") is funny because the announcer gives no context—teams, games being played—for understanding their meaning. Context plays a crucial role in shaping statistics in more serious debates as well. The political contexts that surround wars, for example, generate debate about the exact number of casualties that occur in war. It is, of course, difficult to count the number of casualties that occur as a result of any war, particularly when civilians are among those killed. During the Vietnam War, officials of the United States took advantage of this fact, regularly inflating the number of casualties that had been inflicted on the Viet Cong. Clearly, they did so to impress upon civilians the efficiency of the military, and, by extension, the success of the war effort. During the Iraq war, critics of the war often cited the estimated number of civilian dead, including women, children, and other noncombatants, when they wished to heighten awareness of the destructiveness of war. They cited the number of U.S. troops killed when they wished to generate sorrow and outrage. On the other hand, General Tommy Franks, the commanding U.S. officer during the invasion of Iraq, responded to persistent questioning about casualties by saying that "We don't do body counts." Perhaps General Franks's reluctance to reveal the number of soldiers killed in combat was caused by his awareness of American history. There is disagreement about death tolls because the political stakes associated with these estimates are very high: Americans demanded an end to the Vietnam War when the number of fatalities among soldiers became too high to bear.

How and why casualty statistics are derived deserves our attention if we are to think carefully about the rhetorical work that statistics can do. Tallying war deaths is done with different emphasis towards different ends. For instance, the number of deaths among coalition forces (the U.S., British, and other armies present in Iraq) has been used as evidence against the war for audiences most concerned about its impact on our own nation. Presented in another context, this number can be used as evidence of the commitment of coalition troops to the mission in Iraq, evidence, in other words, of sacrifice. Iraqi military deaths, or the deaths of those deemed to be insurgents, are used as evidence of military success. For other audiences, the deaths of Iraqi civilians is used for evidence that the war has created a humanitarian crisis.

TALK READ WRITE

1. Find an argument that is supported by statistics. List the statistics and the claim they support. Discuss whether the statistics are valid or worthy of belief and whether they actually support the claim forwarded in the argument.
2. The Web site of Iraq Body Count (iraqbodycount.net) offers an argument against the war built almost entirely on statistical evidence. Visit this site and discuss whether the presentation of statistical data is organized to have such a persuasive effect.
3. Discuss the strategies of framing statistics used on this site or in other arguments. Discuss how arrangement and presentation influence how we read these statistics.

Invention Journal: Do the Numbers

Finding the right statistics for your critical situation can be difficult. Not only must the statistics be directly relevant to your main claims, but also they must come from a trustworthy source. Here is an exercise that may help you to find relevant statistics.

1. What organizations involved in your critical situation gather statistics relevant to that situation? Amnesty International, for instance, compiles statistics relevant to many human rights and social justice issues around the world. Several agencies within the United States government keep statistics that will be viewed as authoritative on any number of issues. In her critique of corporate management in Philadelphia's public school districts, our student Laura Bivona found numbers about the low-income background of students, the debt of the school system, and the projected increase of the debt in school board documents. Consult your stakeholder map to find organizations and institutions that might be a source of important statistical information.
2. Newspapers such as the New York *Times*, the Chicago *Tribune*, the Washington *Post*, and the *Wall Street Journal* report on major national and international situations and may be sources of useful statistics. Articles in national or local newspapers and magazines also print important statistics.
3. Once you locate appropriate statistics, you need to frame them, putting them into the right context for your audience. To begin doing this, consider the following:

   Have you adequately explained the source of the statistics so that your audience will have confidence that the evidence is legitimate? Will the audience be satisfied if you simply name the source of the statistics or is further information necessary? For instance, it may not be enough to say that statistics about human-rights abuses are taken from Amnesty International. Will your audience be familiar with this organization or must you explain the group's status as an internationally known organization that advocates human rights? Will your audience accept data collected by this group? (Some people believe that Amnesty International massages statistics in order to further their goals.)

   Have you sufficiently shown the relative value of the statistics you are using? Numbers presented out of context lack persuasive meaning. For instance, if you hope to persuade your readers of the necessity of conserving energy by noting current gas prices, you need to demonstrate the seriousness of the situation by showing the spike in prices over the last year. Do other sources report different statistics? How can you persuasively claim that your numbers are more accurate? Should percentages be converted to totals or vice versa?

   Have you presented statistics in a convincing manner? To say that 20 students in a class object to a policy is less persuasive than saying that 90 percent of the students in a class object to a policy.

WORKSHOP 15: Revising for Clarity

This workshop offers revising strategies for increasing the clarity of writing. Increasing the clarity of your ideas helps you connect with your intended audience.

Now, write a few sentences or a paragraph for each piece of statistical information that you will use in your project. Ideally, these will become passages that you can cut and paste into your final project.

IMAGES AS EVIDENCE

Today images are used everywhere as means of persuasion. Attractive models are shown using or wearing a multitude of products; beautiful photographs of cars or wristwatches persuade us that these objects are works of art that we must possess. But advertisers are not the only people who rely on images to sell their arguments. When the United States government was building its case about the production of weapons of mass destruction in Saddam Hussein's Iraq, the U.S. secretary of state displayed aerial photographs of mobile chemical weapons laboratories to members of the United Nations as evidence of Hussein's refusal to comply with sanctions against weapons manufacturing. These images were carefully scrutinized, and their accuracy was questioned by people who opposed further political or military intervention in Iraq's affairs. For a time, however, the secretary's presentation persuaded Americans, if not members of the United Nations, that Hussein was a threat to our welfare. Subsequently, reporters and soldiers discovered that these so-called "weapons labs" were nothing of the sort (washingtonpost.com/wpdyn/content/article/2006/04/11/AR2006041101888_pf.html).

In a culture that values the evidence of the senses, particularly the evidence provided by our eyes, skillfully used images can powerfully support arguments. However, images must be chosen and framed carefully if they are to be persuasive.

A SLAVE AUCTION.

Slave Auction

Here is an image that was persuasive within the moment of its use. The image of a woman and child displayed for purchase at a slave auction was intended to inspire moral outrage against the slave system. This image is powerful in part because of its gender dynamics. A mother and daughter alone and defenseless on the auction block, arm clasped by the auctioneer, and surrounded by leering buyers, was likely to offend the sensibilities of nineteenth-century viewers. This image is still disturbing for these same reasons.

9–11 Research is a Web site devoted to disproving the official account of the attack on the Pentagon on September 11, 2001. Throughout the site, images are used as evidence. For example, the site prominently displays a mocked-up photograph intended to show that the impact of a Boeing 767 flown into the building at high speed would make a much larger hole in the wall of the Pentagon than that which in fact appeared after the smoke cleared. Go to the "9–11 Research" site to think more about images as evidence: http://911research.wtc7.net.

Invention Journal: Choosing Images

1. Brainstorm images that you think would offer strong support of your claim among members of your audience. Use the "Image" function at Google or another Internet search engine to find visual evidence.
2. Once you locate powerful images, you need to frame them, putting them into the right context for your audience. Have you made the source of the image clear, so that your audience will trust that it is not being used out of context? Not everyone will see an image in the same way. Are there details in the image that must be explained so that your audience views them from a perspective most favorable to your argument?
3. Write a few sentences or a paragraph to describe and frame each image you will use in your project. Ideally, these will become passages that you will be able to cut and paste directly into your project.

SITUATING EVIDENCE

If you have worked through the Invention Journals of this chapter, you have likely compiled a significant body of evidence to present to your chosen audiences. As we stated at the outset, however, your success in persuading these audiences with evidence depends on what you do with that evidence. Framing is one way to situate evidence. What follows are further invention exercises to help you put evidence to work.

Using a Variety of Evidence

Evidence is most effective when its different types are used in combination. An account of personal experience is much more persuasive when it echoes other facts and testimony. Statistics have more persuasive force when they are humanized through testimony or the recollection of personal experience than they do when standing alone. Consider Tom LeGault's letter to his university newspaper attempting to inspire student reaction to a tuition increase:

> My name is Tom LeGault and I am a full time student here at ASU West struggling to pay for the cost of living, let alone the new inflated tuition rates. This is my first year attending a university, but it didn't take me long to realize the pain and debt upperclassmen incurred when tuition increased 39.1% from spring of 2003 to fall of 2003. The benefits these students saw as a result of the tuition increase were almost nonexistent. Scholarship funding only increased 13% that year while instructor funding, which pays for professor salaries, only increased 2.5%.

LeGault skillfully combined personal observation and statistical data to make a case for the unfairness of the tuition increase at his university. Contextualizing the amount of tuition money and faculty pay as important factors in access and quality of education enhanced the authority of LeGault's statistics.

Invention Journal: Diversifying Your Body of Evidence

WORKSHOP 2: Arranging Your Composition

As you discover arguments through invention, consider how they will fit together when you sit down to write. This workshop is devoted to "arrangement," the skillful structuring of arguments.

1. Make a list of all the different pieces of evidence you have compiled so far. After you have written them all down, decide whether your argument depends too heavily on a particular piece or kind of evidence. Ask classmates, friends, and family to help you judge the persuasiveness of the body of evidence you have put together.
2. Using LeGault's or Ida B. Wells's work as a model, practice using different kinds of evidence in combination. Introduce statistics with personal experience or expert testimony to add context. Drive home the force of testimony with a figure or chart. Decide what combinations of evidence work best for you.

The Quality of Evidence

How good is the evidence you are using? How good is the evidence used by an opponent? Writers and speakers need to decide on the quality of evidence before making their work public. Evidence should be evaluated carefully. The following exercises will help you evaluate the evidence at play in a critical situation.

Invention Journal: Evaluating Evidence

1. Is the source of evidence respected and relevant to the critical situation in question? Do others making arguments about this situation cite this source? Have others questioned it? On what grounds? The credibility of

Internet sources can be especially difficult to trace. Undocumented information used online should be viewed with suspicion.

2. Is the source of your evidence trustworthy? What is the source's reputation? Is she an acknowledged expert? A trusted spokesperson? A rabid ideologue?
3. Does testimony, a personal account, or a statistic suggest a clear bias? We don't mean to suggest that people with an agenda are not trustworthy, but you should at least be aware of the ideologies that motivate sources that you intend to use as evidence.
4. Is there evidence that directly contradicts that which you plan to include in your work? How can you be sure that the evidence you have chosen to use is more trustworthy or authoritative than that which you have chosen not to use?

WORKSHOP 7: Finding Access: Publishing Your Work

What are the most meaningful publics for your work? What audiences, if persuaded by your work, can become agents of change in your critical situation? Once you identify the right audience, how do you reach them? To discover routes of access to your audience, work through the series of questions in this workshop.

WORKSHOP 12: Putting Together a Portfolio of Your Invention Work

Gathering your invention work together in a portfolio creates a record of your thought, research, and analysis. This workshop offers a simple framework for constructing a portfolio and writing a critical self-reflection on the progress of your project.

LIST OF WORKS CITED

The 9/11 Commission Report: Final Report of the National Commission on Terrorist Attacks Upon the United States. New York: Norton, 2004.

Epstein, Edward. "How Many Iraqis Died? We May Never Know." *San Francisco Chronicle,* 3 May 2003 http://sfgate.com/cgi-bin/article.cgi?file=/c/a/2003/05/03/MN98747.DTL.

Griffin, David Ray. *The 9/11 Commission Report: Omissions and Distortions.* Northampton, MA: Olive Branch Press, 2005.

Warrick, Joby. "Warnings on WMD 'Fabricator' Were Ignored, Ex-CIA Aide Says." *Washington Post,* 25 June 2006, A01.

Wells, Ida B. "A Red Record." *In Southern Horrors and Other Writings: The Anti-Lynching Campaign of Ida B. Wells, 1892–1900.* Ed. Jacqueline Jones Royster. New York: Bedford/St. Martin's, 1997. 73–157.

PART III

WORKSHOPS

WORKSHOP 1 AGREEING ON WORKSHOP GUIDELINES

The creative genius—a lone writer toiling away in solitude, waiting for inspiration—is a myth. We don't know any serious writers or speakers who work in isolation. We agree with the many scholars and other professional writers who argue that serious writing and speaking are inherently collaborative activities. Working alone, we can never get critical distance on our own arguments, on the style we use, on the kinds of evidence that we hope will be persuasive. Hearing what others have to say about the situations we are addressing is often an invaluable lesson in audience awareness. Collaborators help us hear and see things that will remain invisible to us if we compose in isolation.

We suggest that the class or working groups within it develop guidelines for use during workshops. Such guidelines should be a matter of consensus whenever possible. Your teacher may require certain procedures, policies, and assignments, but assuming that your class is organized around workshops, you will have some collaborative decision making to do. How will you work as a group? Who will make decisions?

Here is a list of roles that individuals can play within a workshop group:

The Careful Listener: There will be plenty of time to make comments and offer your own opinions, so you can often be most helpful by listening to the ideas your group members put forward. Ask questions for clarification. When helping as a careful listener, remember that your job in this role is to assist someone else. The person speaking has the floor, and the group's focus is on that person's project ideas. Careful listening gives the person a chance to talk through issues, hopefully clarifying matters along the way.

The Careful Reader: Working through the Invention Journals and through a drafting process, you will generate a lot of written material. As a group member, you must be a dedicated reader. Reading material produced by members of group requires a significant time commitment. Being a careful reader involves understanding how the writer's ideas are taking shape and what you can do to help clarify key points. Careful readers often help writers articulate more clearly what they are trying to say.

Commentator: As a commentator on the work of other members of a group, you take a more active role in the composing process of others. Offering commentary on group member's work entails much more than saying, "That's good," which doesn't give much useful information to a writer or speaker. Try to make your commentary useful. Sometimes this might mean paraphrasing in your own words what the writer is saying. Sometimes you will need to ask questions for clarification. Other times, to challenge an argument is the most useful thing you can do, forcing a group member to respond to a different viewpoint. Careful reading skills are crucial for making useful commentary. Comments on the work of others should be made in writing as often as possible.

Research Assistant: Based on your own experience as a researcher, you may be able to offer useful suggestions about where a group member can find information, how he might assess the quality of information, and how the information might be incorporated into the project. In addition, as a research assistant, you may be able to help a writer determine where in the text sources are needed or would be most useful.

Motivator: You need not cheerlead, but you should help motivate your group members by keeping them focused and on task. Remind them of their project goals. Encourage them to keep writing.

RECOMMENDED PRINCIPLES AND PROCEDURES

Principles are the ground rules for working together, and procedures are the day-to-day activities that structure the workshop. Here are the core workshop principles and procedures that we recommend you follow. Discuss these, and decide whether to accept this list or adapt them, depending on the particularities of your class structure or the collective will of the group.

Workshop Principles

- We accept responsibility for assisting with the success of one another's project work.
- We agree to support each other as careful listeners, readers, and commentators, to offer research assistance and to help keep one another focused and motivated.
- We agree to treat all work respectfully.
- We agree to be honest, open, and available to our group members.

Workshop Procedures

- Exchange reliable contact information.
- Make a schedule. Read through your syllabus and/or explain your own timeline for publication. Plan extra workshop time around deadlines so that you will be able to read drafts and do last-minute trouble shooting.
- Set priorities and goals at the beginning of the current work session. Your teacher may set these out clearly, or you may have to decide for yourselves.

- Agree on the method of discussion. Whether you meet face-to-face or through an electronic medium, set guidelines for discussion including a time-frame before you begin.
- Ensure that all group members have an opportunity to contribute equally.
- In the event of absences from the workshop, the member who missed is responsible for finding out what happened during the workshop and what is needed to fulfill his or her duties to the group.
- Plan to discuss the success of the group regularly.
- Modify workshop principles and procedures when necessary.

WORKSHOP EXERCISE: WRITING A GROUP CHARTER

You may decide that it's worth the effort to formalize the working arrangements of the writing workshop. If so, write a charter for your workgroup or your class as a whole. A charter is a document written and ratified by a group that states the rights, privileges, and responsibilities of its members. A charter lays out the organization of the group and the procedures it will follow to achieve its mission or stated purpose. Whether you write and adopt a charter as a small group or as an entire class, we hope you will refer back to this document while you complete your projects as a way to keep the workshop productive and to make sure the workload is shared equitably.

Composing the Workshop Guidelines

Reread the lists of principles and procedures you have developed. Now, write the sentences about the principles that begin: "We believe" or "We agree" or "We commit" or simply "We will." Once you have this litany or list, read it together and see if some ideas need clarification or a bit of further explanation.

Have you addressed the project goals of every individual in your group? Can you agree on any common hopes or expectations about your work? About making it public? In other words, what common reasons do you share for caring about this work?

Writing a Preamble

Although it may seem counterintuitive to write the preamble last, such documents are most often a kind of culmination or summary of the mission and intentions of the charter group. If you haven't already done so, complete this workshop, agreeing on lists of principles and procedures to which the workshop group will adhere. Then write a preamble for your group charter. You are likely familiar with the preamble to the Declaration of Independence, the announcement of those "self-evident" truths. Setting down your first principles in ceremonial fashion can be fun, and the process of writing may help you think more carefully about principles and procedures. You might also compose a document that can be shared with other groups in the class or taken with you as a concise statement about the theory and practice of collaboration.

Read several preambles as a guide to crafting your own. For starters you may read Preamble to the Declaration of Independence or the following preamble of the Full Earth Charter, a document widely endorsed as an authoritative statement on sound or "sustainable" environmental policies and practices. Or, find another preamble. The preambles of many groups are available on the Internet. Pick your search engine and look around. What interests you and/or might interest your workshop group members?

Here is the preamble to the Full Earth Charter:

> We stand at a critical moment in Earth's history, a time when humanity must choose its future. As the world becomes increasingly interdependent and fragile, the future at once holds great peril and great promise. To move forward we must recognize that in the midst of a magnificent diversity of cultures and life forms we are one human family and one Earth community with a common destiny. We must join together to bring forth a sustainable global society founded on respect for nature, universal human rights, economic justice, and a culture of peace. Towards this end, it is imperative that we, the peoples of Earth, declare our responsibility to one another, to the greater community of life, and to future generations. (Read the full charter at http://www.earthcharterchicago.org/index.html.)

WORKSHOP 2 ARRANGING YOUR COMPOSITION

Many factors can influence the arrangement of a composition. With hard work and maybe some help and luck, by now you have plenty of material to work with—arguments and evidence uncovered during invention. How to arrange the pieces depends on the disposition of your audience toward the situation in question—and perhaps toward—the situation in which you are composing, and the number and relative strength of the arguments available to you at the moment. Finding the best way to put together a composition is crucial; the strongest arguments might fail to persuade if they are not skillfully presented.

AUDIENCE AND ARRANGEMENT

Generally, above all other factors, strategies for arrangement should be chosen with reference to your audience and their beliefs and commitments in relation to the critical situation at hand. Throughout the Invention Journals in this book, you are guided to think carefully about the most appropriate audiences for your composition, and you should extend that thinking as you begin to organize your invention work. What follows are suggestions for arranging your composition and for arranging each part of the composition as a means of connecting with an audience. Our breakdown of arranging strategies draws on ancient thinking, which carefully charted very specific portions of argument arrangement. Not every composing situation requires each of the divisions of arrangement recommended in ancient systems. The suggestions that follow are a guide, not a formula. It is likely that you will omit some traditional elements of composition arrangement, combine others, and spend the greatest time developing specific sections. The challenge, as always, is making decisions that are appropriate for the context of your project work.

WHERE TO BEGIN? CRAFTING INTRODUCTIONS

Should you address the audience directly? Introduce yourself and your credentials? Offer background to the issue at hand? Get straight to your major conclusion? Tell a joke? As always, it depends. What are your audience's commitments within the context of the critical situation at hand? What do they believe to be true, and how are they likely to feel about what you have to say? Answering such questions allows us to judge what first words will gain us a hearing and do the most to put an audience in a state of mind for a favorable reception. Depending on the receptivity of our audience—ranging from friendly agreement to suspicion and hostility—you might begin in one of several ways:

1. **State up front your main conclusion and the premises that support it.** "Starting strong" can be an effective strategy, especially if your audience is predisposed to agree with your position.
2. **Offer brief background highlighting the importance of the situation, the stakes for the audience and perhaps all of society.** Are you addressing an issue about which people have become complacent? Is the situation in which you're intervening complex enough that most people remain uniformed? Do the major media perpetually ignore the situation in which you are intervening? If you judge that your audience could be favorably influenced by a "wake up call," beginning by highlighting the stakes of the situation at hand may be the way to go.
3. **Address your audience directly, highlighting your common stake in the issue.** Consider beginning with a strong effort to establish a connection with your audience. This might be called for if you are extremely close to an audience, a member of the stakeholder group you are addressing, or quite distant, addressing people who would benefit from a reminder that you and they have at least some common interest in reasoning together through the situation at hand.

ORIENTING YOUR AUDIENCE

Your audience will need more or less background information. But how much background or context is necessary? Often, the portion of your composition orienting your audience, providing background information, considering the different important aspects of the critical situation at hand, defining key terms and concepts, etc., can be effectively placed just after your introduction (though sometimes beginning with context can be effective). As you craft contextual material, consider the following possibilities:

1. **Provide a brief context.** If you write or speak to an audience you judge to be well informed, less context needs to be provided.
2. **Spend more time orienting your audience.** Audiences with less knowledge or a radically biased perspective (in your estimation) need more background, more context for thinking through the situation at hand in a manner fitting with your argument. If there are key terms and concepts with which your audience will be unfamiliar, this is the time to clarify those things.
3. **Break down the situation into its parts.** Often, a critical situation has more than one component part. An argument about student achievement, for example, might address student background, school funding issues and teaching methods. If the situation at hand is actually constituted by several separate situations, it may be worth your time to clearly delineate this for your audience.

4. **How much is too much?** As you attempt to orient your audience by providing context, take care not to overwhelm your readers or listeners with a deluge of detail or long historical narratives. Choose contextual details carefully. Be economical. Don't press the patience of an audience or confuse them with unnecessary digressions.

MAKING THE CASE

Writing teachers and students often refer to "the body" of a composition, a phrase meant to indicate the major section. Compositional bodies, like human bodies, come in all shapes and sizes. The bulk of your composition should be reserved for a presentation of lines of reasoning, ethical and emotional arguments, commonplace appeals, and the bulk of the evidence gathered. How to organize this persuasive material can be a complex matter, and there is no formula. With audience in mind, however, your can consider the following:

1. **Which arguments will be most persuasive for your audience?** As you know by now if you have worked through the Invention Journals in this book, some premises and appeals have more or less persuasive force depending on the audience. The premise that tugs at your belief system may leave others cold. How can the most audience-appropriate arguments be highlighted in your composition?
2. **Are there combinations of arguments that will be particularly persuasive for your audience?** Sequence can be important. Sometimes emotional appeals can be effectively combined with evidence-based arguments as a way to indicate the human dimension of statistical information. Also, consider how one line of reasoning might prepare the way for another. In the example of an argument about student performance, an argument about students' socioeconomic background will likely be strongly connected to questions of available funds in a particular school district. Teaching methods are strongly connected to the question of student learning styles.Try to imagine combinations that are mutually complimentary in this way.
3. **Are some arguments and evidence well suited for the introduction or conclusion of your composition?** If you have chosen to begin or end with your conclusion, a major premise or strong appeal, you should be careful to choose wisely. First and last impressions can have real impact, positive or negative.
4. **Are there arguments you must refute?** In the course of your invention work, you most likely came across arguments contrary to your major conclusions. Some of these alternate viewpoints can perhaps be ignored, but others, because they are influential, must be addressed. Be sure to make room for refutation when necessary.
5. **Which arguments should be *left out* of your composition?** Not every line of reasoning, appeal, or piece of evidence you discovered in invention is necessarily appropriate for your audience and situation. Be selective.

ENOUGH ALREADY? HOW AND WHEN TO CONCLUDE

For centuries, writing and speech teachers have agreed that keeping conclusions reasonably brief can keep you in your audience's good graces. Even this time-honored practice, however, should be judged in context with audience in mind. We hope you will find an effective course of action among these general approaches:

1. **Restate your final conclusion and major premises.** Offering a summary of your argument is a time-honored manner of concluding. If your argument is particularly complex, ending with a restatement can ground an audience in your key points, thus reinforcing your intentions as a last word.
2. **Address the audience directly, urging serious consideration of your major conclusion.** A final, impassioned plea can work well when you judge your audience to be passive, on the fence, or downright apathetic. Be careful, however, not to overstate the case. Apathetic audiences might be turned off by righteous conviction. As always, try to anticipate audience reaction and consider the possibility that less can be more.
3. **Conclude with an anecdote, further testimony, or another final piece of evidence.** Another reasonable piece of stock advice is to end by giving your audience something new, some further provocative thought or assertion.
4. **Conclude with a final line of reasoning or emotional or commonplace appeal.** Any argument worth having involves an element of risk. After all, you are likely attempting to bring an audience around to a new way of thinking about the critical situation at hand. If your argument is particularly controversial or divisive, ending with a bit of common-sense knowledge upon which most people can agree can help your case. (For that matter, beginning with a commonplace might be helpful in such a situation.)
5. **Thank your audience for their consideration.** Sometimes simple manners can be winning. When speaking in public or writing to a strongly community-oriented group, thanking the audience for their time and attention is well worth your while.

WHEN OPTIONS FOR ARRANGEMENT ARE LIMITED

Often, the arrangement of a composition is predetermined. Many of your decisions about arrangement might have been made for you by the dictates of the rhetorical situation. For example, if you are writing a workplace proposal, your employer might have very strict guidelines for how to present your proposal. If you are writing for a college course, your professor or instructor may give you very specific instructions for presenting your work. When asked to give a PowerPoint presentation, some organizational control is taken away from you simply by the conventions of the prescribed format. Public speaking opportunities might be radically constrained by time limits. For better of worse, we often must fit our best arguments into a genre or format or mode of delivery that we have not chosen.

If you are constrained by a predetermined genre or format, you have not lost all decision making power. Careful craft can allow you to make your case in any format. We have all seen how thoughtful presenters can use constraining conventions to powerful end. Find examples of the genre or format in which you are compelled to work. Study them to see how others have used genre constraints to their advantage.

WORKSHOP EXERCISE

1. As a group or individually, find an argument in a newspaper, magazine, Web site, or elsewhere. Examine its arrangement. Outline what seem to be its major divisions. Review each of the suggested divisions suggested above. How did the writer or speaker negotiate these divisions?
2. As you sit down to arrange your invention work and write a draft of your composition, return to the lists of questions and considerations provided above. Though many writers and speakers don't usually do so, we suggest making an outline, even if it is very general. As an example, consider the following outline of a hypothetical writing project arguing against standardized testing in public schools addressed to the parents of students.

   - Begin with a commonplace statement about the individualized nature of education: "Students learn best when their interests are involved and when they are challenged on an individual level."
   - Next, offer your major conclusion that "teaching to the test" results in an impoverished curriculum that ignores individual student interests and learning styles.
   - Next, provide a brief overview of how school curriculums are organized around high-stakes tests. Refer to the ethos of school accountability that has been prominent since the inception of No Child Left Behind.
   - Review several arguments by educators that conclude high-stakes tests limit student learning opportunities.
   - Conclude with an anecdote about a dynamic curriculum at an alternative school that has graduated dynamic and high-achieving students.

WORKSHOP 3 DIFFERENT VALUES AND RESPECTFUL CONFLICT

bell hooks, a well-known teacher and writer, argues that: "confronting one another across differences means that we must change ideas about how we learn; rather than fearing conflict, we have to find ways to use it as a catalyst for new thinking, for growth." In fact, conflict can become a powerful learning experience. We often avoid conflict because encountering new ideas, different perspectives, and unfamiliar ways of thinking can be a jarring experience. But avoidance of conflict is not a viable option in a serious workshop. Because we are planning work around situations that hold real meaning for us, each of us will bring core values and strong feelings to the workshop. If hooks is right when she claims that conflict is crucial to authentic learning, we shouldn't try to politely avoid difficult questions and disagreements. Instead, we should figure out how to make the most of conflict. To do so respectfully requires attention to how we communicate and how we share the *work* of the workshop.

Respect for others is an essential element of effective collaborative work. It is important to listen to others if only to learn how others think about the critical situations that capture our attention. For example, a former student, like most of his family and all his friends, was opposed to the U.S. military presence in Iraq. His commitments as a self-described "antiwar activist" were seriously tested when he ended up in a workshop that included a former Marine and the fiancé of a soldier then currently serving in Baghdad. In the end, all the members of this group learned something about positions they had previously misunderstood and distrusted. While no one changed his or her mind about the war, these students respected one another. And they produced good work: the antiwar activist put up a Web site; the retired Marine wrote a historical commentary arguing for long-term engagement in Iraq; and the affianced student wrote a pamphlet offering resources to the families of deployed personnel. As a result, each learned quite a bit about how to approach audiences whose positions differed from their own.

It is important that everyone in a group agrees to proceed with respect and tolerance before you attempt to complete the following exercises. Remember at all times that you get to decide how much you will or will not disclose in this and all workshop exercises. Workshop members don't need to be personal confidants. Remember as well that it is not your job to change your group members' minds, but rather to learn from one another. Helpful group members must be willing to commit to someone else's goals as a writer or speaker regardless of their own views on issues. You should expect your work to be the focus of the workshop on a regular basis, but you will also log many hours in a supportive role before the workshop disbands.

SUGGESTED GUIDELINES FOR RESPECTFUL CONFLICT

You may have already set up clear principles and procedures in accord with suggestions made in "Agreeing on Workshop Guidelines." If you have not already done so, list a set of workshop principles and procedures. We have put together the following list based on our own experience in the classroom and the experience of teachers we admire. Our general advice is to decide on ground rules in advance and to be clear about your expectations.

Share the work. Respect one another's time and energy. When reading each other's work, read in a timely fashion and with the intent to be helpful.

When the work of a group member is the focus of the workshop, try to understand his or her position. Try to figure out what you can do to help the author clarify and strengthen the writing. Be willing to take a supporting role, and do your best to see things through someone else's eyes.

Consult your institution's student and faculty code of conduct statements. Based on state and federal laws and the regulations and conventions of your institution, there may be very clear definitions of respect and disrespect that you should acknowledge and discuss. Your teacher may know how to locate these documents, or you may find them through a college or university Web site.

WORKSHOP EXERCISES

The following exercises are designed to help you share information about the beliefs and convictions that each of you hold. We strongly recommend that upon first sharing this information you listen or read without immediate response. At all costs, avoid responding by disagreeing. You must detach a bit and be ready to hear a range of beliefs, perspectives, and biases, as well as a range of expressive styles. Cut some slack whenever possible, and give your group members the benefit of the doubt. Remember, *do not contradict or criticize your group members' comments.* This is the time to share information and not to give feedback or to argue.

Exercise One

1. Where are you on the political spectrum? Would you identify yourself as conservative, moderate, liberal, leftist? Are you a Republican, a Democrat, a Green Party member, an independent, an anarchist, a nonvoter? Are you unsure of how to describe your political beliefs?
2. As a group, come up with a list of five "controversial issues." Make sure everyone contributes at least one issue. Now, choose two and take turns briefly explaining your attitudes, beliefs, and opinions on each issue.
3. Are there issues about which you are unwilling to compromise? What are those issues? Is it likely they will come up in the group? How will you deal with that situation if and when it occurs?

4. After working through the above questions, you should have a sense of where ideological or value-based differences exist within your group. Discuss these points of difference, and agree to discuss them openly and respectfully, and when necessary, to simply accept them and do your project work without discussing them.

Exercise Two

If one or all of your group members have chosen a situation to address in your final project, take 10–15 minutes to write out the position you have taken in your critical situation. Include what you take to be your most fundamental position or argument. Share these statements in the group. Readers should respond in writing, offering gut reactions to their group members' stated position. Without insulting one another, tell your group members how and why you agree or disagree with their way of thinking about the matter at hand. Hopefully, having "broken the ice" in this way will clear a path for further collaboration. Now that you have had the opportunity to voice your own perspective, you must be willing to put it on hold when one of your group member's work is the focus of the workshop.

If it is possible to do so respectfully, discussion of different positions within your workgroup can be an excellent way to learn about alternative views that you might need to address in your composition. In other words, your group members can serve as examples of the very people you hope to persuade or positions you will have to counterargue.

Exercise Three

Are there organizations or offices on your campus or locally that help groups who are struggling with issues of diversity? Many campuses have some version of a diversity office or a multicultural resource center. A representative from the student life office or the office of campus or residential life can offer many suggestions for how to maintain a respectful classroom environment. It may be worth your time to invite such people to speak to your class.

WORKSHOP 4 ETHICS IN WRITING AND SPEAKING INVENTORY

Ethics is the study or practice of principles and values that guide the actions of individuals or populations faced with questions of right and wrong. We can adopt this general definition in order to arrive at principles of right and wrong that can orient ethical practices of writing and speaking. It would be easy if there were strict ethical guidelines on which we could all agree. It could be argued instead that we must constantly reflect on our communicative practice and consult with others to gauge the ethics of our actions. The inventory that follows is intended to start conversations about the ethics of speaking and writing in critical situations.

WORKSHOP EXERCISES

Exercise One

Answer the following questions individually in order to start this conversation. You may or may not share the results of this exercise with anyone, but it is important that you ask these questions of yourself.

1. Do you have a set of ethical principles that you try to live by? If so, summarize those principles as briefly as possible. Keep in mind the definition of ethics provided above.
2. How are the above principles adaptable to writing and speaking? For example, if "honesty" is a principle by which you try to live your life, what amounts to honesty in writing and speaking practices? How might "compassion" come into play for writers and speakers? Diligence? Courage?
3. Even if we have a strong sense of the people to whom we plan to write or speak, we still have to imagine our audience insofar as we anticipate what relationship they have to the issues we are writing about. In a sense, we have to make up or imagine the audience as we engage in composing. How is this process of imagining audience connected to ethics in writing? For example, are you making assumptions about the attitudes or practices of those to whom you are writing or speaking?
4. Who has greater knowledge and experience in relationship to the critical situation you are addressing? Are you an expert or authority in the eyes of your audience? Are you a novice or an outsider? If there is a variable level of knowledge between you and your audience, how might this raise ethical issues?
5. Do you feel you share community commitments with your audience? What are they? Are you part of the same organizations, churches, professions, or other institutions? How do these connections set up certain expectations or responsibilities?

6. Do you address your audience across generational lines? Are there differences in economic situation? In race, ethnicity, or gender? Are there regional differences between you and your audience? How do these kinds of "distance" from your audience give rise to ethical questions?
7. What are some possible outcomes of your project when and if it is made public? Once you publish or make your work available for your audience, it may have some impact in the world. Do you feel any sense of responsibility for the fact that people may change their minds and their actions based on what you write or say? Explain.
8. Are there legal issues to take into consideration? Do you have permission to use all of the research material you have obtained, for example? Are you breaking copyright law? Are you a tagger breaking local ordinances about graffiti? Have you plagiarized work? Could your public speech be viewed as disorderly conduct? If you are engaging in writing and speaking practices that push the boundaries of such laws, are you are doing so with full knowledge? Are you prepared to deal with the consequences of such action? Is anyone else implicated legally that you should think about?
9. Based on your research and what you know thus far about your critical situation, can you offer examples of ethical and/or unethical writing and speaking practices in this situation? Can you note major players, for example, who give a radically partial account of the facts or who have fabricated "facts"?

Exercise Two

Once all the members of your class or your workshop group have finished working through this inventory, discuss your responses to the questions. You don't have to share your individual responses if you are not comfortable doing so, but you can still participate in a discussion of ethical practices in writing and speaking. As a group, write a list of ethical principles that you agree provide important guidelines for writers and speakers. Make sure everyone has a copy. If your class is electronically mediated, save a copy at a common site for convenience.

Exercise Three

With reference to the ethical principles list you developed as a group, write a paper or give a speech in which you explore the ethical landscape of your critical situation. Consider the following options:

1. Give a first-person account of your research process. Write about your interaction with ideas and perspectives that have challenged your ethical sense.
2. Write about the process of trying to persuade, and your own attempts to present an honest case.
3. Write about trying to negotiate "ends and means" questions that always emerge in ethical reflection.

4. Give a response to a piece of writing or speech you think is particularly ethical or unethical in the context of your critical situation. Summarize the text, and explain where the writers or speakers acted unethically in your estimation.
5. Find examples of spoken or written texts that you believe violate reasonable ethical standards. Choose from the abolitionist or post-9/11 case studies or find other texts elsewhere. Write an analysis of the ethical orientation of any of these texts.

WORKSHOP 5 ETHICS OF EMOTIONAL ARGUMENTS

Wendell Phillips's "The Philosophy of Abolitionism" is a defense of passionate argumentation. After reading the piece, are you persuaded by Phillips's argument about the necessity of aggressive emotional appeal? Try thinking through his argument about the necessity of extreme rhetorical measures in the fight to end slavery. Making inflammatory statements about politicians who looked the other way on the slavery question; recounting, often in graphic detail, the horrific crimes of the slave system; dire predictions about the collapse of any civilization based on slavery; warning against the wrath of god—pro-slavery critics routinely renounced these and other rhetorical strategies as manipulative and destructive in their own right. But can we question the ethics of the abolitionists? If their activities and arguments contributed even in part to the end of slavery, weren't they justified? Were they too emotionally manipulative?

Even if, like us, you are quick to say, "Yes, the abolitionists' emotional arguments were justified," try to imagine other positions as an exercise in understanding alternate perspectives. What negative outcomes might have resulted from the passionate appeals of Phillips, Frederick Douglass, Frances Harper, and the other abolitionists whose work has been discussed in this book? Might possibly valuable allies have been alienated by extreme passionate appeals? What kind of psychological impact might disparaging personal attacks have had for those targeted? Might aggressive abolitionist rhetoric have antagonized slaveholders so that they would have actually rallied together in the common cause of slavery? Discuss these questions as a class, or discuss your own work, using questions like these.

WORKSHOP EXERCISE

It is always easier in retrospect to answer the classic ethical question: Do the ends justify the means? Are questionable, possibly harmful actions justifiable if the overall goal is a good one? We strongly recommend that you check your ethical compass as you work through the composition process; certainly you must do so before making your work public. Go through the following steps, keeping the "ends and means" question in mind.

1. **As specifically as possible, identify your audience**. As we have emphasized, targeting an audience is not always easy. If you know specific readers, either individuals or groups who will be in your audience, write them down. If you define your audience as people holding a particular belief or position, indicate

these beliefs and positions. What stake does your audience hold in this situation? Write out as well what you take to be your audience's emotional connection to this situation. What emotions do the events of this critical situation inspire? Fear? Anger? Hopefulness? Worry? Happiness? Boredom? Amusement? If you have access to "actual audience members" (maybe a classmate with whom you disagree politically or philosophically), ask that person to read your draft and respond to this question.

2. **Looking at your project draft and/or your Invention Journals from Chapter 8, explain how you are attempting to appeal to your audience's emotional connection to the critical situation**. Be as specific as possible. We recommend exchanging drafts and Invention Journals with your workshop group members. While reading these, ask: What strategies does the writer use to make emotional appeals? Return to Chapter 8 to remind yourself of the available strategies for emotional argument, for instance: appealing to audiences' likely emotional connections; emphasizing or deemphasizing emotionally charged aspects of a situation; using disparaging or honorific language. Mark these passages in the draft with underlines or margin notations.
3. **Decide whether each instance of emotional argumentation that you have marked falls into any of the following categories of manipulation**. Be sure to remind yourself of the audience's emotional stake in the critical situation at hand. Honest response to the following questions can help you decide whether or not your text, or someone else's, is emotionally manipulative:

   - Are emotional appeals used to confuse or conceal elements of the situation at hand?
   - Is emotional argumentation used to exaggerate either risks or benefits relevant within the situation?
   - Does the emotional use of the writer or speaker's own experience crowd out other perspectives?
   - Is emotional argument used to appeal to bias or prejudice?
   - Are there overt efforts to frighten an audience in the argument? If so, do they exceed what is reasonable?
   - If visual images are used in the argument, are they likely to manipulate in any of the ways listed above?

If you find moments of unethical argumentation, discuss your options for revision. How might you "tone it down"? If you are underplaying the upsetting or disturbing aspects of the critical situation at hand, how might you more fully acknowledge the emotional stakes of your audience?

Remember, an ethical approach to emotional argumentation doesn't mean that you don't take steps to take control over the presentation of material, of emphasis, or that you don't plan your argument to have the strongest possible persuasive influence on your audience.

WORKSHOP 6 ETHICS AND THE USE OF EVIDENCE

In Chapter 9, we offered advice for "framing" evidence in order to make it persuasive within the context of your project work. We argue there that evidence is most persuasive when put in the proper context for audiences. Contextualizing evidence helps readers evaluate it within the flow of your composition as a whole. In this workshop, we ask you once again to check your ethical compass as you consider your manner of presenting evidence. Do you ever cross the line from skillful framing to manipulation?

WORKSHOP EXERCISE

Go through your draft or the draft of another workshop member. Identify every instance where evidence is used. Find personal observations, the use of testimony, statistical evidence, images, and any evidential strategy you can. Mark them with a pen or highlighter and then test each one against the following set of questions.

Have you presented evidence out of context?

It is not uncommon for writers and speakers to use evidence out of context, sources that are credible in their original context but only appear relevant when used elsewhere. For example, sources written decades ago may not be relevant to the current context of the critical situation you are addressing. Or, if you are building an argument about crime deterrence using evidence from legal experts knowledgeable about criminal statues and not deterrence per se, it may be you're using evidence out of context. Or, if you select a fragment of statistical evidence from a larger whole because it suits your needs, you may have ranged into dishonesty. Framing evidence is important, but consider the possibility that you have fundamentally changed the meaning of the evidence if you have used it out of context.

Have you used testimony or evidence that creates false authority?

It's relatively easy to find the voices of so-called experts to support claims, and it is also relatively easy to find statistical information to do the same. If the most authoritative sources don't help us reach our conclusions, it can be tempting to use less-credible sources. Advertisers often use celebrities to sell products even when the celebrity has no actual expertise to recommend hair products, or car insurance, shoes, etc. Rather than drawing on medical research presented in the *New England Journal of Medicine*, we might opportunistically opt for a Web site titled "Medical Advice from Mom." Without impugning the ethics of anyone's mother, we suggest that when you make a choice to use less-than-authoritative sources, you risk misinformation, miss an opportunity to provide your audience with the most reliable information available, and undercut your own authority. Look at all the evidence used in your draft. Discuss the question with your group members. Is the source written or compiled by people with verifiable expertise or experience relevant to the situation at hand?

Has evidence been omitted?

Obviously, you can't include all relevant evidence, and it is not your job to make arguments that run contrary to your commitments and intentions. However, you might be accused of "stacking the deck" if you present only evidence that supports your position. For example, if you are presenting statistical information that is contradicted by authoritative statistical data, your argument could be operating on shaky ethical ground. Or, if you are using the one testimony that supports your position while ignoring hundreds of others that contradict it, you might want to acknowledge these voices and attempt counterargument rather than pretending they don't exist.

Have you cited or acknowledged your sources?

Go through the draft and make sure you have acknowledged the original source of all the evidence presented. Writers include bibliographies or works cited pages not simply to abide by copyright law but to provide readers with resources and to allow them to go to the original sources and decide on their credibility. Following from the example above, if you have chosen to take testimony and statistical evidence from "Medical Advice from Mom," and not the Centers for Disease Control and Prevention, the National Institute of Science, or the *New England Journal of Medicine*, have you at least let your audience know where the information was located? If you haven't, you might well be plagiarizing. Also, you deny your audience the opportunity to go to the original source to judge its credibility.

Have you been fair in your use of your own experience and observations as evidence?

When we write about our own lives and from our own perspectives, the possibility that we slant things in a misleading way is considerable. Even if we don't mean to mislead, we are sometimes bound by our own way of seeing the world; all we can offer sometimes is a very limited perspective. It's particularly helpful to have other readers check our use of personal observation.

WORKSHOP 7 FINDING ACCESS: PUBLISHING YOUR WORK

Critical Situations was written based on the premise that students using it have real work to do. Assumed in this notion of real work is that students are serious writers and speakers who need to get their language out in the world. Unless you own a newspaper or radio or television station, reaching important audiences can be difficult. How do you plan to gain **access** to your audience? How will you get your text before their eyes? How will your words reach their ears? Some manner of **publication** is necessary, publication in the most general sense of making text available for a broader and/or more specific public readership.

Here is a list of possible forums for publishing your work:

Editorial page of a newspaper

Letter to a politician or public official

Poster or flier

A PowerPoint presentation

A public speech

A Web site

A blog

An office memo

It is often the case that the critical situation provides a venue or means of access. As always, stay atuned to kairos, looking to make the most of the moment as it presents itself.

WORKSHOP EXERCISE

The following prompts and questions are designed to help you identify and make the most of opportunities for access. Respond to each in writing. In sum, these responses should give you some good leads for discovering important points of access for publication. Take the time now to write a brief "plan to publish" or "route to access" statement that will guide you in your efforts to effect change in your critical situation. Discuss these statements as a workshop group or as a class, taking notes as you go. After going through all the activities, you should have identified the most promising opportunities for reaching broader audiences.

1. Return to your intention and goals for your writing project to identify publishing opportunities. It may be that when and where you need to publish is reasonably obvious. If you want to protest the firing of a teacher or principal,

the next meeting of the Parent-Teacher Association meeting may be the specific forum that offers you your occasion. If you are writing a formal request to your employer requesting a raise for you and your coworkers, the next company meeting might provide you with access to audience and a firm deadline.

2. Make a list of important dates and deadlines that offer opportunities. If you worked through the Invention Journals in Chapter 4 on "rhetorical timing," you may already have discovered important opportunities for access and publication. Is there a city council meeting at which you might speak? Is there a rally where you can hoist a sign?
3. Ask this important question: Who and where is your audience? Where do they live, work, recreate, and more importantly, where and what do they read? If you conceive of your audience more generally as people holding a particular set of positions or beliefs, this question may be harder to answer. If you are targeting local audiences, you may be able to make a more accurate assessment here. In answering the question about audience, you should think both specifically and more generally about your readers or listeners. Consider contacting people who are informed about the routes of access in particular organizations—editors, organization heads, president of the school board or neighborhood organization, i.e., anyone who understands how routes of access work in the context of a given forum.
4. If you are able to decide on the occasion, the when and where of your interaction with your audience, you may already know what **format or genre** is most appropriate. For example, if you are angry about Iraq war coverage in the Washington *Post*, and you want to criticize that coverage for an audience of *Post* readers, then a letter to the editor is a clear choice. If you're not sure about format, consider what is expected or allowed in a particular forum. For example, consult submission guidelines for editorial pages or other stakeholders to find out if you can submit a written statement, make an appointment, or add your name to a list of speakers.
5. While you are thinking about format or genre, it may be helpful to look at samples of the kind of text you are going to produce. For example, read letters to the editor if that is the format you have chosen. Attend a city council meeting to see how the process works and how citizens present their positions in such public forums. Read proposals to understand how they are structured.
6. It is quite possible that you will need to compose more than one text for your project. Are you trying to reach more than one audience? For example, if the campus organization to which you belong is planning a campus-wide meeting for students, and you are in charge of promotions, you should pursue several routes to public access. Fliers will work for targeting student foot traffic. An e-mail to the entire campus has the benefit of "coverage," that is, reaching a broader audience. You might still take the opportunity to visit classrooms to announce the meeting if you can wrangle an invitation from faculty.

WORKSHOP 8 FOLLOWING PATHWAYS—A METAPHOR FOR CRITICAL READING AND RESEARCH

Critical reading and research, unlike other kinds of reading, is actually made up of multiple activities, which we break down below. In short, we define critical reading and research as the practice of *reading as invention.* Reading as invention means reading with an eye out for important facts, arguments, references, etc., that are relevant to your project work. Throughout this book, we have used metaphors of travel, of search, of movement with purpose to help explain practices of reading, research, and writing. Critical reading and research is a powerful way to move down such paths of thought and activity, often a point of beginning or redirection.

Like all successful writing and speech, successful reading and research is goal driven. Clear intentions motivate readers and researchers to take control of texts and ideas as the heart of the composition process. As you work on your project, we hope you will keep in mind your goals for writing and speech as a guide and as motivation to get good work done. Critical reading and research is more targeted, as critical readers and researchers know largely what they are *reading for*. Reading as a process of invention is focused reading sensitive to opportunities as they become available.

Consider first that **critical reading means reading at the computer keyboard or with pen in hand!** It builds on the kinds of reading strategies we highlight in the "Summarizing Ideas, Arguments, and Texts" workshop, where we argue that summarizing is not just a skill for writing but also a powerful strategy for reading comprehensively. Writing summaries requires very careful reading and keeping a record of what you have read. Without this level of attention to the details of the text, you will miss opportunities for critical reading and research.

Below is a list of "pathways" important to follow. Getting in the habit of identifying these kinds of opportunities will help you to read as a practice of invention:

Other works by the same writer or writers: Because writers often focus on a relatively small set of issues, it is likely that a writer addressing a critical situation has done so in some other venue. Check to find out.

Names of stakeholders and other experts on your critical situation: Often, people who are cited in a source have elsewhere written or spoken about the critical situation in question. Such sources may also identify communities implicated in and impacted by the situation. It's worth tracking down these other sources to see how other stakeholders are discussing the facts and events of a critical situation.

Names of institutions relevant to your critical situation: Has the writer named businesses, branches or agencies of government, citizens groups, schools, media outlets, etc.? If there are particular institutions that bear some relation to the critical situation in question—perhaps as a major stakeholder—you should pursue research in that direction.

Names of other articles, books, and other documents relevant to your critical situation: If the source you are reading has a bibliography, works referenced list, relevant links, etc., you may find many other valuable sources. Always check bibliographies carefully. Within the body of the source, you may find an article or a book upon which the writer has based her own work. All of these opportunities should be explored.

Descriptions of events relevant to your situation: Critical situations have a history. They are created by action in the world. Whenever a writer makes reference to an event that is a part of your critical situation, it is worth it to get further details about that event.

Relevant ideas and claims you should explore further: Make a list of the major claims or conclusions in the source (as we recommend in the "Reader's Responding" workshop). Which of these is most important to your own argument? How has this writer supported these claims? How can you find further sources to support or disprove these claims?

Responses to the text or to the main ideas or arguments therein: Books get reviewed. Articles in newspapers elicit letters to the editor, and more generally, the major ideas put forward by any writer are a matter of broader discussion or debate. If you take each conclusion reached by a writer as a place to begin further research, you stand to gain a rich understanding of the conceptual content of your critical situation.

Interesting topics for another time: One of the pleasures of research is learning about issues and ideas unexpectedly, ones perhaps that have almost nothing to do with the critical situation you hope to address. Wandering down these paths can be well worth doing, but sometimes time constraints don't allow this extracurricular research. We recommend making a list of interesting issues and ideas to pursue at some other time.

AN EXAMPLE OF READING FOR PATHWAYS

We offer the following scenario as an example of the reading-as-path-following process. Imagine that you research shifts in public opinion on the war in Iraq. Scanning through a periodicals database or through an Internet engine search, you find an article by Christian Appy in the news magazine *Mother Jones* titled, "Military Families May Once Again Lead Us Out of War." Even this excerpt suggests several further pathways for research and reading.

> Sam Fulwood, another Plain Dealer columnist, responded to these losses by recalling Bush's 2003 "bring 'em on" taunting of the Iraqi insurgents. "Two years ago, tucked in the comfort and safety of the White House's Roosevelt Room," wrote Fulwood, "the president challenged 'anybody who wants to harm American troops.' John Wayne couldn't have said it with more cowboy swagger. 'Bring them on.'" As Fulwood concludes with a stridency rarely seen in Midwestern newspapers until recently, "The chicken hawk got his wish."
>
> Now, for the first time, not just in Ohio but all over the country, media outlets are beginning to raise a previously forbidden question: Should we withdraw? As the Cincinnati Enquirer framed it on Aug. 7, in response to the local casualties, "Do we seek revenge? Do we continue as usual? Or do we leave?" The last question, once asked only in a whisper if at all, is suddenly being voiced loudly and urgently. And when it was raised by an antiwar Iraq War Marine veteran named Paul Hackett, running as a Democrat in a special election for Congress, he came within two percentage points of winning in a district east of Cincinnati that had given George Bush a whopping 64% of its votes in November 2004, and has elected a Republican to the House of Representatives almost automatically for the past 30 years.
>
> In presidential elections, Ohio is often spoken of as a "bellwether state." It may turn out to play the same role when it comes to America's wars. What we are witnessing in Ohio and elsewhere is a real sea change in public opinion being led by people with the closest personal connections of all to the President's war. Disillusionment has soared not only because of mounting casualties and the obvious lack of progress in quelling the Iraqi insurgency, but also because the military is strained to the limits keeping 130,000 troops in Iraq. Many thousands of Americans are in their second tours of duty with third tours looming on the horizon.
>
> During the Vietnam era, Lyndon Johnson decided to rely almost exclusively on the draft and the active-duty military to fight the war, hoping to keep casualties (and so their impact) largely restricted to young, mostly unmarried, and powerless individuals. The Reserve forces, he understood, tended to be older, married, and more rooted in their communities. Now, the Reserves and the National Guard make up half of U.S. combat forces in Iraq, a figure that has doubled since early 2004. This increasing reliance on the Reserves only serves to accelerate antiwar resistance among military families.

As a researcher interested in war and public opinion, you have many important paths to consider after reading Appy's article. Appy, as it turns out, is a historian who has written extensively about public opinion surrounding war, so going no further than an author-search at your library will yield new directions for reading and research. At the beginning of the excerpt, a newspaper columnist, Sam Fulwood, is named as someone writing about the war. It may be worth checking to see whether he has addressed the issue of public opinion directly in any of his columns. In the article as a whole, a number of newspaper articles are referenced, and each would be worth reading. Also, President Bush has certainly spoken about the public perception of the Iraq war. Have you yet made a list of his comments? Have you gathered comments from other politicians, whether for or against the war, who claim to have taken the pulse of "the American people"? Though it may seem obvious, don't overlook the possibility that the institutions including the Army Reserve or National Guard have addressed the concerns of families and public response to the increased activities of their service people. Relevant events are also referenced throughout Appy's article. In this excerpt alone, we are told about some ostensibly inflammatory remarks made by President Bush and, perhaps unexpectedly, the relevance of the Vietnam War as a precedent. Thinking, reading, and researching down this pathway could uncover interesting historical arguments to be made about public opinion in wartime.

If you make a list of major claims or conclusions in Appy's article, several will stand out. The final claim in this excerpt, that increased Reservist and National Guard duty has "accelerated antiwar resistance" is worth checking out. While other commentators may have a similar view, members of the Reserves, National Guard, and their families may tell quite a different story. The central claim of Appy's article, that antiwar sentiment among military people and their families is changing national public opinion overall, is well worth researching in greater detail. If there is merit to Appy's conclusion, it will likely work prominently in your own composition. If not, your own search for factors influencing public opinion will go on.

WORKSHOP EXERCISES

Gather some of the sources you've found while researching your critical situation. Read them through carefully once, perhaps writing a thorough summary of each. Then, read each one again, annotating the text or at least making notes on a separate page. Find pathways for further reading and research by identifying these "openings" in the source text:

- Other works by the same writer or writers
- Names of stakeholders and other experts on your critical situation
- Names of institutions relevant to your critical situation
- Names of other articles, books, and other documents relevant to your critical situation
- Descriptions of events relevant to your situation
- Relevant ideas and claims you should explore further
- Responses to the text or to the main ideas or arguments therein
- Interesting topics for another time

We hope that after reading with these pathways in mind, you will have mapped out rich areas for further inquiry.

IDENTIFYING KEYWORDS AND PHRASES FOR FURTHER SEARCHING

Whether you are searching through Internet engines such as Yahoo, Google, Dogpile, etc., or through databases at a library, finding the right keywords and phrases to search with is crucial. They will, to follow our metaphor, illuminate the paths you hope to tread. Databases and other search tools often have different systems of doing effective keyword searches, and you should familiarize yourself with these recommended strategies. Often, you have a choice of "basic" or "advanced" search, and as is the case with Google, "advanced" is hardly more complicated than the "basic." Use the resources available to you. Enlist the help of librarians and teachers whenever possible. Here we offer a few strategies for searching:

1. **Begin with the most obvious terms.** Sticking with the above example, if we are researching public opinion during wartime, search using "*war*" and "*public opinion.*" Pair the phrases *"military families"* and *"public opinion."* Putting phrases in quotation marks is a common convention for many search devices.
2. **Experiment!** If you're using the wrong terms, success will be minimal. Shift your terms and try again. Shifting from the phrase *"public opinion about the war"* to *"opinion about the war"* or *"public opinion about the Iraq war"* can make all the difference. Or, perhaps it should be *"opinion about the war in Iraq."* Small changes can make a big difference.
3. **Try synonyms and related terms.** Search with *"casualties"* instead of *"deaths."* Using *"attitudes"* instead of *"opinion"* might yield more useful hits. Trying to find information about the changing opinion of service people and their families, *"morale"* might work as well or better than *"opinion."*
4. **Learn as you go**. As you begin to find a few relevant sources, pay close attention to the terms they use to discuss the critical situation. For example, moving from Appy's article to other sources, we might find that the phrase *"antiwar sentiment"* pops up with some frequency. We might also find that writers refer to *"protest"* as well as antiwar sentiment. Follow up in further searches using both of these terms.
5. **Check your spelling**. One wrong keystroke can throw a monkey wrench into your search. If you get no results when searching, double-check your typing.

WORKSHOP 9 GATHERING INFORMATION THROUGH INTERVIEWS

When you have the opportunity, make the most of ancient research technology—talk to people. Interviews are a valuable method of gathering statistics, finding compelling firsthand testimony, and figuring out the learned perspectives of experts. Your audience may be persuaded by evidence obtained through interviews. The directness of interview responses, arranged skillfully, presents evidence by allowing people who are close to a situation make claims that are current and supported by experience.

The following steps are an introduction to the interviewing process. Go through the steps as a class or in small groups. Work on the interviews in the classroom, or do so on your own time bringing them to class to share.

CHOOSING INTERVIEW SUBJECTS

A good interview contact has important information that you need. The people you interview can provide persuasive evidence because they have experience, expertise, and access to information that you haven't found yet. Here are some ways to locate important interview subjects:

Review your stakeholders list (see Chapter 2). Who are the major players? Are they local? How can you get their street or e-mail addresses, or their phone numbers?

Read newspaper accounts of your critical situation. Highlight the names of everyone associated with the situation. How can you get their contact information?

Identify local experts. Are there faculty members at your school or people in the local community who have important perspectives on your critical situation? To find them, make a list of the organizations, offices, community, and other groups that are associated with the situation.

CONTACTING INTERVIEW SUBJECTS

Preparation is necessary before you contact someone to arrange for an interview. People are more likely to agree to talk to you if you explain clearly why you want to talk with them. This also gives the interview subject a chance to prepare, and this will in turn increase the likelihood that he or she will be able to offer useful responses to your questions. Also, introducing the topic of the interview and your interest in it up front may elicit a few comments right off the bat. If the interview subject likes to talk, the interview may begin on the spot! Be prepared to make the most of the moment.

Before you begin an interview, make sure you know the interview subject's name and title and that you have a sense of his or her place within the context of the critical situation you are addressing.

Know the information you expect to get from the interview subject. Before the interview you may wish to prepare a list of questions to ask. But don't feel you have to stick to this list rigidly during the interview because the focus of your interview may change once it begins. Nonetheless, you should have some sense from the beginning how the interview subject's perspective can help your project. In fact, she or he might ask, "Why me?" You should have prepared an answer to this question beforehand.

Explain your interest. If you are an avid supporter of mandatory steroid testing in high schools, tell this to the coach or principal you hope to interview. This gives the interview subject a chance to tell you how he or she feels about the issue, which will help you understand your subject's stake in the situation.

Explain why you want to hear their perspective. Acknowledge the authority of the interview subject. Explain to the senator that her insight as a member of the Foreign Affairs Committee will be very helpful to your project. Tell the local chef that his bouillabaisse is legendary and you want to hear the story of its invention. Tell the professor of history that you need a historical perspective on issues of race relations in this country so that you can better understand the racial tensions emerging after Hurricane Katrina.

Explain what you plan to do with the information. The subject of the interview has the right to know how his or her words will be used. The subject may ask questions: Will the interview appear in some public forum? What kind of piece are you writing? Who do you want to read it? Make sure the subject understands your plans.

FOCUSING YOUR QUESTIONS

What do you need to know? We've broken down interview questions into four broad categories:

Is there very specific information that you seek? The names of people involved in an incident? Dates? Locations? Other details? Do you need verification of a statistic? Do you need an official position on an issue from the interview subject?

Are you looking for suggestions for further direction in research? At some point in the interview, ask a question along these lines: "Is there anyone else you would recommend I contact, or can you recommend other sources for me to consult?"

Do you value the overall perspective of this person? Might this interview subject be giving you what will be a valuable testimony or point of view for your project? Based on his or her experience or training, is this person's perspective so authoritative that you plan to highlight her or his words in your project?

Does this interview provide you an opportunity to test your ideas and/or to ask about the direction of your research? If you are talking to a knowledgeable person willing to engage your ideas, it is worth your time to explain your position, to make your best argument about the situation at hand. The interview subject might be able to point out a contradiction in your argument, offer suggestions for ways to make the case stronger, and give you references to other people who have made similar arguments.

CONDUCTING THE INTERVIEW: A FEW RULES OF THUMB

Once you have contacted the right people to interview, you will know if the interviews will be conducted by phone, e-mail, or in person (though they are often quick and easy to schedule, phone interviews are probably the least desirable of the three). Here are some general guidelines to follow during an interview.

Be on time. Be prepared. Do everything you can to be courteous to the interview subject. Without this person/people, there is no interview.

Begin the interview with introductions if they are necessary. Also, thank the person in advance for taking the time to talk to you.

Begin with a few words to orient the interview subject. For example, remind the person of your interest in the situation at hand.

Be on the lookout for important follow-up questions. Hopefully, you have arrived at the interview with a list of questions. However, in answering these questions, the interview subject may tell you things you don't understand. If that is the case, you should ask for further explanation if this seems appropriate. A second kind of follow-up question focuses on interesting new directions. You may never have considered connections made by the interview subject between the events of your critical situation and some other set of events. If you think it might be important to your project, ask for a few more details or perhaps a reference. "Very interesting," you might comment, and ask "Can you recommend a source or another person with whom I might speak to get more information?"

Stay focused on your goals. You want a free exchange of ideas in an interview, but your first goal is to gather information and ideas for your project. Don't let digressions go on for too long or ask too many follow-up questions on related issues that you can explore at some other time.

Record the interview if possible. Be sure to ask before the interview if you are going to make sound and/or video recordings of a face-to-face interview. Check your equipment in advance to minimize problems and as a courtesy to your generous and patient interview subject. E-mail interviews produce a complete transcript of the interview that you and your group members can look at as you begin to work the interview material into a draft. Taking notes can be difficult in the moment of the interview, especially if the subject of the interview talks a great deal and/or quickly. Try not to interrupt, but ask the interview subject to repeat important points you want to record.

Thank your interview subject at the conclusion of the interview. Ask if you may contact him or her for clarifications and further questions.

WORKING WITH INTERVIEW MATERIAL

How will you use interview material in your project? If you were focused going into the interview, you may know clearly what useful information you gained in the interviews—a specific statistic, eyewitness verification of facts, riveting testimony, memorable descriptions of events, a great turn of phrase you would like to use as a provocative introduction, or a wise conclusion. Perhaps you even secured material that is supportive or critical of your own stance in the matters at hand. To decide how to use interview material, ask yourself these questions:

Does the interview material give you persuasive arguments to include in your own work?

Does the interview material help you to counter other opinions?

Does it help you to support major claims?

Does it help you fill in details in things you are trying to explain?

Does it help you add a human element to make complicated issues seem less abstract?

Does it provide you with authoritative testimony?

Does it teach you anything about the critical situation?

Answers to these questions may differ as your project takes shape. Or, this information may actually help to shape the argument.

FOLLOWING UP ON THE INTERVIEW

The quality of your work and your good standing with the interview subject require that you follow up on the interview. You will need to talk again with the interview subject if you need to:

Get further information

Check facts

Verify quotations

Thank the person for granting the interview

As you continue work on your project, you will likely think of questions you wish you had asked during the interview. If you have established a good rapport with the interview subject, you can expect that he or she will be receptive to follow-up questions. This may be necessary because some of the facts of your critical situation may be controversial. For example, the newspaper and television news may report that 500 people attended a rally or demonstration, while many who participated put the number at closer to 1,000. If you have been interviewing a police officer present at the event or perhaps the rally organizer, you may find either confirming or contradictory calculations of that same number.

Another reason for following up on an interview is to assure that you have an accurate record of what was said. If a tape recorded response is garbled, or if your own notes are unclear, you should follow the practice of good reporters—call and verify a quotation. Misquoting people damages your credibility and might well offend the interview subject.

Sending a quick thank you note is always necessary, even if you require no further information. If the interview subject asks to see a final copy of your project, we recommend you oblige him or her.

WORKSHOP EXERCISE: TALKING AND WRITING ABOUT THE PROCESS

We recommend that you complete one or both of the following exercises in order to insure your success as an interviewer.

In order to learn from what went well (and not so well) in the interviewing process, meet as a group and share your experiences. Collaborate on putting together a list of "dos and don'ts." What further rules of thumb have you learned for future interviews? Review your interview questions and talk about how you might have changed the phrasing to yield more useful results.

Conduct interviews with instructors at the school you attend. Whatever situation you are researching, it is very likely that somewhere on campus, there are a number of instructors, graduate students, and advanced undergraduates who have studied the situation from a scholarly perspective. For instance, if you are interested in racial profiling as a social problem, a psychologist or advanced student of psychology might offer interesting perspectives and suggestions for further reading on the psychology of profiling. A justice studies professor could recommend places to find authoritative statistics about the incidence of racial profiling. Go through a university or college catalogue, or go to the institution's Web site. Make a list of academic departments or majors. Which scholars in which fields of study might have information important for your project? Once you have identified likely candidates, go through the steps of interviewing recommended in the body of this workshop. Set up practice interviews in your group before the actual interviews occur. One of your group members can volunteer to be the interview subject, and other group members can observe and comment.

WORKSHOP 10 INVENTING PERSUASIVE VOICE

"Voice" is one of the most common and helpful metaphors used to discuss writing. Obviously there is no one actually speaking in written prose; written language has no vocal chords. But readers *hear* voice in writing. We pick up tone and discern character or personality in what we read; this very often adds to or detracts from the connection we make through our writing. Consider the following list of voice descriptors that readers might attribute to the voice in your work:

Professional

Enthusiastic

Angry

Mortified

Serious

Condescending

Candid

Silly

Elated

Sarcastic

Try describing the voice of the following possibly familiar statements from familiar people:

Dr. Martin Luther King Jr.: "Let no man pull you low enough to hate him."

Oprah Winfrey: "I believe that one of life's greatest risks is never daring to risk."

Hillary Clinton: "It takes a village to raise a child." (African proverb)

Homer Simpson: "Mmm...Donuts."

Former Vice President Al Gore: "Political will is a renewable resource."

Dr. Phil: "Get real, will you!"

If you know something about these individuals, you may be able to make more general comment on the voice of each. With the exception of the fictional Homer Simpson, the list includes names of some very persuasive individuals. What is it that makes their voices so compelling? Perhaps with no further context, it is difficult to assess the voice of these phrases. How has each developed a voice appropriately crafted for the contexts in which they speak and write? Effective writers and speakers consider questions such as these.

Beyond those listed above, what other attributes of voice might we name? If audiences hear such attributes in what they read, how might that affect their way of reading what you've written? What opportunities for creating voice effects might you find as you write and revise your project text?

Maybe you've heard writers talk about "finding their voice," as if voice was present but just hiding or lost all along. We focus instead on voice as a matter of rhetorical and compositional craft. It can be invented, altered, and modulated to meet the needs of audiences and the intentions of writers. In this workshop, we offer strategies for working **voice cues** into your writing, cues that will activate **voice effects** for your readers.

Chapter 6 is devoted to "ethos," that is, the credibility of character readers will grant to writers and speakers. Therein, we introduced the idea of "rhetorical distance" in writing. Rhetorical distance is a metaphor for thinking about the kinds of audience-writer relationships implied and asserted in any kind of writing or speaking situation. The voice that readers discern in your writing will impact a reader's sense of distance in your writing. Along with rhetorical distance, we want you to think about the kind of **persona** voice cues can conjure for audiences. Readers attribute character or personality traits based a variety of factors, often reacting with emotion or judgment, as well as attributing feeling and motive to how they "hear" your writing.

Each of the following sections of this workshop introduces a different kind of voice cue. The sections are:

Developing the Right Voice for the Occasion

Grammatical Person (Pronouns and Voice)

Active and Passive Voice

Word Usage (Vocabulary)

Sentence Structure and Voice

Asserting Voice with Metaphoric Language

Punctuation

Shifts in Voice

Each is an invitation to begin experimenting and is not meant as a definitive statement; we hope if nothing else that this workshop will make you more conscious of voice in your own writing and in what you read. The exercises at the end of this workshop give you a chance to put voice to work, so to speak. They are designed for those just beginning the drafting process or those in the process of revising a draft. Read and discuss each of the sections, and then work through the exercises in a group or individually.

DEVELOPING THE RIGHT VOICE FOR THE OCCASION

Although many voices are possible in writing, not all options are appropriate for a given context. It may be that we all tend habitually towards particular strategies of voice in writing—maybe you're an exclamation-mark enthusiast, or maybe you refuse to use first-person pronouns. Levity isn't appropriate for addressing tragic circumstances (at least not usually). Colloquial informality probably isn't right for many ceremonial speeches. Your best professional voice will be lost on the guests at your child's fifth birthday party. What examples of mismatched voice and occasion can you imagine?

A sense of timing is as important in developing voice as it is in any other communicative practice. Before you are through drafting and revising, check to see if the voice in your writing "sounds" how you'd like it to. Also, learn to be a careful reader/listener of the voices of other stakeholders in your critical situation. Have the particulars of a critical situation made some voices more appealing than others in the current rhetorical moment? You might try to get a sense of the political and emotional "tenor" of the overall conversation you are entering *before* raising your own voice.

GRAMMATICAL PERSON (PRONOUNS AND VOICE)

"Grammatical person" refers to the pronoun form in use. Pronoun usage is important because it sets up the manner in which writers and speakers *address* readers and listeners and refer to ourselves as *I, you, he, we, they, us, she, he, it, them*, etc. In English, we most typically refer to **first, second,** and **third person** pronoun usage. Each of these types of grammatical person can be singular or plural. The choice of grammatical person in writing has major implications for the creation of voice. Here is a list of options for grammatical person:

I *am* (first-person singular)

You *are* (second-person singular)

He, she, one, or it *is* (third-person singular)

We *are* (first-person plural)

You *are* (second-person plural)

They *are* (third-person plural)

Consider the following comments on the voice cues and effect involved in pronoun usage. Think about your own pronoun habits as you read and discuss.

Generally, **first** and **second person** recalls the conversational context of people talking together, and creates a more intimate voice; used in combination, they strongly suggest the impression of presence, of a direct address from writers to readers. This intimacy, of course, might take many forms. A second person address can utter the statement: "You can go to hell!" as surely as it can give thanks: "Thank you for lending me the vacuum cleaner." From the classroom to the bowling alley, many informal exchanges among small groups operate primarily in first person and second person. As well, first person and second person are typical in matters of deliberation and commerce. "The jury finds you guilty" or "Thank you for using our product."

Over-reliance on first and second person can actually push readers away if writers assume too much intimacy. We should be careful of too-familiar and presumptuous first person collective "we" usages, such as, "We all look forward to the holidays." If readers disagree, they are likely to have a strong negative reaction to what you implicitly say about them. Also, an over-reliance on first person can create a TMI effect (too much information). Some readers will find too much self-positioning in writing unappealing:

> My extensive research, conducted during five of the most personally satisfying years of my life, will convince you of my insight on this matter.

Consider how overuse of first-person pronouns and excessive self-references creates a pompous voice, or an attitude of self-congratulations, or the air of a braggart.

Third person address often assumes the posture of greatest rhetorical distance. Much scholarly writing uses third person address. Students are often asked by teachers to write in third person, avoiding first and second person to create greater formality in the work. For example:

> The articles I read convinced me that a light rail is a good idea for all of us in our city.

Consider now a more academic third-person rendering.

> Many critics agree that a light rail system will benefit Phoenix.

The second example puts emphasis on the people, critics and their agreement about a light rail system instead of the student's work researching and writing. Third person address can also be helpful when you need to generalize. You might want to make a general statement that you will later follow up on with more detailed examples. Maybe you have a writing deadline but don't know all the particulars left to describe. For example:

> Several city officials reportedly met with Senator Bauderly after the press conference in what is being called an impromptu summit on local issues.

Third person here doesn't give us details about which *city officials* met with the senator who originally reported it, and who actually called the meeting *an impromptu summit.* Maybe the writer of this press release hadn't done his homework. Maybe it was the only information available.

For all its distancing potential, third person can help create a kind of intensity of voice. By placing greater emphasis on ideas and statements and less on the writer and readers, third person can help underscore the importance of an idea or principle.

> Acknowledgement of global warming and the need for more dramatic reduction of greenhouse gases have finally gotten the attention of the public.

This sentence keeps the focus on global warming itself and a growing public will to address the problem by placing it in the subject position of the sentence. Avoiding first or second person here and choosing the third-person collective, *the public,* conjures the grammatical effect of democratic political will—consistent with "the voice of the people"—that transcends any individual or segment of the national population. Using this particular third person term is a voice cue that invites audiences to participate in the discourse of citizens.

ACTIVE AND PASSIVE VOICE

Voice in writing is often classed as either **active** or **passive**, but we encourage you not to think in dichotomous terms about voice in either/or terms. Instead, think of active and passive voice as two points on a continuum across which you can gauge voice as both a reader and a writer.

As the terms themselves suggest, one common distinction that is made between active and passive voice regards the relative "action" playing out in the writing. Active-voice writing features people doing things. Passive writing by contrast de-emphasizes action. In passive voice writing, the subject of the sentence receives the action of the verb rather than carrying it out. Here is a simple example of the difference:

> Eric ate the olives. (Active)
>
> The olives were eaten by Eric. (Passive)

The first example lets Eric, the subject of the sentence, actually eat the olives while in the second example, the person doing the action, eating, is distanced from the verb. *Olives* and not *Eric* is the subject of the sentence. Eric is bracketed off in the *by Eric* phrase. Consider the difference in these longer sentences.

> Loss of jobs and property resulting from the 1863 New York City draft riots prompted relief efforts from African American aid associations.

Notice how the agents in the situation are missing or distanced from their action. African American aid associations are not as positioned actively as the source of the relief efforts. The rioters are acknowledged only by reference to the results of their actions. Finally, the people who lost lives, jobs, and property are more or less unaccounted for, at least grammatically, in this sentence. A sentence like this would add activity:

> African American aid associations helped those who lost family members, property, and jobs in the wake of the destruction wrought by New York City's "draft rioters" in 1863.

Which of these two sentences is preferable? We prefer the latter because the relative activeness functions to remind us that historical events, distant though they might seem, were experienced—perpetrated and survived in this example—by people.

Generally active voice is more engaging because it closes the distance between you and your audience by making assertions more direct. Consider the differences in these examples:

> Democracy requires cooperation as much as it does the assertion of rights (Passive Voice)
>
> Citizens of a democracy must cooperate as well as assert their rights. (Active)

Moving into a first-person address here would further increase the action and close the rhetorical distance.

> As citizens of a democracy, we must cooperate as well as assert our rights. (More Active)

How do these examples work in creating different voice effects? What voice cues can you identify as a reader?

Skillfully done, passive voice, dropping most or all explicit self-reference or direct reference to potential audience, adds gravity to statements by granting an abstract quality characteristic of many professional and legal writing contexts. It can also produce a gravity of voice consistent for strong political or ethical pronouncements:

> It is justice that must be sought, not revenge or the satisfaction of angry impulses.

Leaving the "actors" out of this sentence (those seeking justice and resisting *angry impulse*) has the virtue of highlighting "justice" as the subject of the sentence, juxtaposed with *revenge*. This passive voice also allows the writer to avoid making direct accusations or criticisms such as, "Your angry impulses imperil the process of finding justice."

WORD USAGE (VOCABULARY)

A single word can do much to create or detract from the voice you are trying to create in writing. The difference between describing an injury as "significant" and "dangerous," for example, will have different impact on the injured person and those who care about her. Audience perception of voice will change according to habits of word choice. If a doctor or nurse describes a wound as "dangerous," evaluates the bleeding as "a gusher," and sums up the situation as "life or death," the dire or pessimistic voice created will do little to reassure the wounded person. One of the reasons doctors so often use clinical terms (like "significant") is exactly because they reduce patient anxiety and produce the voice of trusted professionalism that reassures patients.

Word sizes are voice cues that readers will pick up on. Confronted with many big and maybe unfamiliar words in sentence after sentence can try some audience's patience. Other audiences will find writing jarring when it sticks to a one-two-three syllable range in word size. The impact of word size on voice depends on context. Many students (and faculty!) struggle with unfamiliar and polysyllabic terms. Think carefully about the conventions of word choice that circulate in the context of your critical situation?

Consider the difference between these two, roughly equivalent statements:

> The contingencies of their financial predicament bedeviled the intrepid entrepreneurs.
>
> Or,
>
> The ambitious small investors worried about factors they couldn't control.

The second example, choosing a more active construction and using less elevated vocabulary (words like *contingencies*, *predicament*, *bedeviled*, and *intrepid*) presents the investors' anxiety with more immediacy.

Of course efforts to "elevate" vocabulary to create a voice of scholarly sophistication or political wisdom can fail dramatically with missteps of word usage. Satirists and comedians love nothing better than the person who tries to fake ethos, that is, the person who pretends to be credible, and is found out.

SENTENCE STRUCTURE AND VOICE

There is life in a sentence, that unit of language that suggests the duration of human breath, adding emotional emphasis and capturing the cadences of spoken language. As a grammatical structure that organizes meaning at the level of individual statements, the sentence offers opportunity for delivering the very premises of your argument with *attitude* or *tone*.

College writing teachers often worry about "simplicity" of and repetitiveness of students' sentence structure. Often, less experienced writers have a tendency to stick to one kind of sentence:

> I don't like my writing class. The teacher never shuts up. The assignments are hard. I wish I could drop it. I can't because the course is a requirement.

The sentence structure here varies only a little. All the sentences are simple with the exception of the brief compound sentence at the end. Overuse of simple sentences, using fewer phrases and varying less in style across your writing, risks a plodding rhythm that can be monotonous for readers. Readers often want more voice cues. In the pattern of those rhythms, meaning gets punctuated and accentuated. Remember that simple statements can be delivered in compound and complex sentence structures. Of course many contexts demand brief and direct statements, and there is a terseness that captures something of the frustration of a student trapped in an unwanted requirement. As always, no absolute rules hold for how to use sentence structure because so much depends on the situation of the writing.

Complex and **compound sentences**, akin to what ancient rhetoricians called **periodic sentences**, combine more phrases than simple sentences and more carefully control meaning as it is distributed across the sentence. The different patterns of emphasis and subordination of phrases can allow for addressing more complicated or nuanced points. Compound sentences contain at least two dependent clauses, that is, two statements that on their own stand grammatically as full sentences. Complex sentences are those that add phrases to the basic, subject-noun structures often referred to as simple sentences. Look at this example of a **compound-complex sentence**:

> Frances Ellen Watkins Harper, who wrote poetry, journalism, novels, short stories, and other harder to classify texts, was in some ways very consistent across this remarkable range of genres, and these consistencies, which are both artistic and political, invite a discussion of how Harper innovated as a genre writer.

This sentence conveys a lot of information. The balancing of independent and dependent clauses organizes that information with relative clarity. However, this information could be offered to readers in simple sentences:

> Frances Ellen Watkins Harper wrote in many genres including the poem, novel, short story, and news article. She was politically and artistically consistent across this remarkable range of writing. These consistencies invite a discussion of Harper's innovations as a genre writer.

What voice effects do you pick up on in these examples, either of which would likely work well in a college course? How does sentence structure help to create these effects?

ASSERTING VOICE WITH METAPHORIC LANGUAGE

Even language that seems very straightforward uses metaphors. To say that "night fell" is metaphoric because, of course, nothing actually falls with the onset of night. When we "hit the books," we don't really hit them, usually. If I claim "my mind wandered," I metaphorically figure my mind as ambulatory and off course.

Readers will find different kinds of emotional or associated resonance that will help you write persuasively, or, cause you to hit a sour note you could have avoided. Calling the United States a "city upon a hill" will inspire quite different associations than calling the United States a "rogue state." Assertive use of more attention-getting metaphorical language that highlights its figural presence will probably get readers' attention, and their reaction may influence how they hear voice in your writing.

For example, referring to an unpleasant situation, say an 80-hour work week, as a "nightmare," is common enough that the metaphor (work weeks aren't literally nightmares, after all) conveys feeling without much effort. Calling the same 80-hour work week a "shit storm" will, for better or worse, make readers or listeners sit up and pay attention. The colloquial and profane quality of this voice-effect will either resonate with readers or offend their sensibilities. As a writer you will want to pay attention to how even individual words can do a lot of work conveying voice cues for readers.

Consider a final example:

> The closing of the auto plant slowly choked the life out of the city.

> The closing of the auto plant had a strong negative effect on the economy and culture of the city.

The more assertive metaphorical language of the first example sounds like the voice of a pessimistic resident of the city in question. The second example, more distanced and stripped of metaphoric cues for readers, sounds like the voice of a sociologist or maybe a journalist.

PUNCTUATION

Punctuation can be an effective means of controlling voice. Certainly the twenty-first century world of online writing and the proliferation of "emoticons" has increased the voice-potential of punctuation. Even standard punctuation marks, however, can make a big difference. For example, what if we were to suggest you:

> Experiment with punctuation!

Be careful when using punctuation for voice effect. Likely, this exclamation point does not work well because it conveys an enthusiasm far greater than most readers will accept. Parenthetical comments embedded in sentences create a more intimate voice. If not overdone, this strategy can create an energetic or enthusiastic voice. Mishandled, it can create the effect of a scatter-brained writer trying to get his or her thoughts sorted out. Underlining and putting words ALL IN CAPITALS is very assertive graphically, and unless you are writing in the context of various online forums, use of the vast array of emotive cues, acronyms, and other graphic symbols should be carefully evaluated during revision.

SHIFTS IN VOICE

Any shifts in the voice of a composition should be made for specific rhetorical effect. For example, in a piece addressing the need for more severe laws for drunk drivers, a writer turning to the example of a young person whose life was cut short by the recklessness of a drunk driver might want to shift from a legalistic to a more intimate voice. The writer might choose more emotive words than in the previous pages. She might also use third person plural to suggest the social cost "we" all incur as a result of drunkenness on the road. The writer might shift back to a more formal voice as she moves towards a reiteration of her policy recommendations. Unexpected metaphors, variations in grammatical person, changes in word choice or sentence structure trigger the effect of shifting voice. Whatever shifts occur, writers and speakers should avoid making them too abrupt or too frequent. Otherwise readers may be distracted.

WORKSHOP EXERCISE

It is important to begin your draft or begin revising an existing draft with a clear sense of the voice you intend and knowing that such a voice is appropriate for the context. **Read your draft or draft-in-process out loud to workshop members whenever possible. Many writers use this strategy for gauging voice.** You may choose to circulate copies of the draft so that listeners may read along. Readers/listeners should follow the steps listed below.

1. **Warm up.** Before turning to your drafts, or beginning to write your draft, practice as a group (we think that's easier) or individually. Read something out

loud and then discuss or jot notes about the voice you hear. Read a variety of texts for instructive contrasts. If time allows, practice imitating these voices and adapting some of the voice-creating effects you find for your own project writing.

2. Whether you are drafting or revising, write out your intention and audience. What is the main message or argument of your text? What is the lasting impression with which you want to leave your audience? Don't write more than several sentences; this should be a point of reference that you and your readers can easily keep in mind while you are drafting or evaluating drafts. Do your strategies of voice support your intentions as a writer?
3. Take time to read and "listen" to other voices sounding in the context of your critical situation. What sorts of "rhetorical distance" do other stakeholders establish in their writing? What sorts of vocabulary, diction, figurative language, grammatical person, passive and active structure do people tend to use? If this analysis proves difficult, first go through the rest of these exercises, and once more familiar with various voice-creating elements, go back and read/listen again. What range of voices is appropriate for your critical situation? Does the situation call for formality and greater distance? Is it more intimate or informal? What character or persona do you want to create?
4. Look at your draft and mark all of your pronoun usage. Overall, does use of grammatical person give you the voice effects you're looking for? Do you detect any unwarranted intimacy or overly formal distancing usages?
5. What is the range of active and passive voice in your writing? Review the example in the section above and mark places in your text that are particularly passive or active, or, where you have a combination of active and passive phrasing. Do these different kinds of phrasing help you invent the voice you intend?
6. Mark places in the draft where word choice, sentence structure and length, reference, figurative language, and punctuation create voice. Offer feedback on the success of the voice-creating strategy. As you draft, pay attention to your own strategies of voice invention. Experiment a bit—you can always delete or revise later.
7. If you're revising an existing draft, do you detect any shifts in the voice of this draft? Might the shifts detract from or increase the voice the writer intends to invent? Mark places in the draft where you "hear" the voice shifting. Perhaps pronoun usage changes, the diction becomes much more elevated, or sentence structures start to elongate. Make notes such as, "You seem to get much more informal in your diction in this next paragraph," or, "Do you want to sound so angry in the underlined sentences?" Or, "Your voice is too distant in this paragraph. You sound like you don't care." If you are just beginning a draft, and you have an outline or at least a sense of how you will arrange your text, consider where shifts in voice would work well to accentuate meaning and where consistency is preferable.

WORKSHOP 11 ORGANIZING A CLASSROOM DEBATE

We believe that arguments are the best way to arrive at solutions to problems and to discover useful community knowledge. In the exchange of ideas and careful examination of reasoning that only argument can provide, people can think together. Of course, this is a best-case scenario, and much of the argument we witness in the public sphere has little or nothing to do with arriving at solutions. Protecting power (and egos) is more often the point, it seems, of public exchange. Formal debating can reproduce the best and worst practices of public sphere argumentation. Debating can be a matter of showing off and "scoring points," or it can be carried on in the best sense of civil discourse as a process of collective deliberation, of thinking together towards mutually beneficial ends. In other words, we propose debating as a process of *invention*, a means of discovering powerful and conflicting ideas and elements of the critical situations in which we are involved.

WORKSHOP EXERCISES

General Guidelines

1. **Be good citizens.** Respect, tolerance, open-mindedness, and good humor are essential for productive debates. When the arguments start coming out onto the table, remember that you are not defending your honor or your ego. Debating as we recommend it is communal thinking, and mutual respect makes this possible.
2. **Present arguments and refutations.** Debate requires exchange, not just a sequence of position papers. However you schedule your debate, be sure to make time for refutations. A refutation, also called a counterargument, brings initial arguments into question, and points out hidden assumptions and faulty premises. In formal debates, refutations are as important as the initial arguments themselves. This process of give and takes makes reasoning together possible.
3. **Ensure equal time and equal resources.** One benefit of classroom debate that discourse in broader public spheres can't ensure is equal opportunity for access and resources for preparing arguments. Each group or individual debating should get the floor for the same amount of time and should have equal time to respond to opposing views.
4. **When possible, exchange written versions of opening and closing statements, major arguments, and refutations.** If you have time, presenting materials in advance will allow more detailed interaction (as each position has more time to prepare responses) and make the most of class time (if, for example, opening statements can be read in advance). This "written record" of the debate

can serve as the basis for a collaborative project when combined with written reflection on the process.

5. **Schedule time for follow-up and reflection.** If debating is to be a productive process of reasoning together, synthesis is necessary. As a group or individually, your class can discuss or write a reflection on the process. Which position was most persuasive? What was learned in the process of debating? In what ways did your debate represent the best aspects of public sphere discourse? In what ways did it represent the worst? What questions for further thought, research or debate came up along the way?

DEBATE FORMATS

Basic Structure

The following basic debate structure is relatively simple and can be adapted to meet the needs of your class format and time schedule.

First Position Presents Opening Statement

Second Position Presents Opening Statement

Third Position Presents Opening Statement

Etc.

First Position Presents Arguments

Second Position Presents Arguments

Third Position Presents Arguments

Etc.

First Position Gives Refutations

Second Position Gives Refutations

Third Position Gives Refutations

Etc.

First Position Gives Closing Statements

Second Position Gives Closing Statements

Third Position Gives Closing Statements

Etc.

Opening and closing statements are not necessary if debating time is limited. Your group may also prefer to hear refutations after each position group gives its arguments. The guidelines are flexible and should be altered according to specifics of your class.

Impromptu Debate

An impromptu debate is an excellent way to address thorny disagreements that arise in class. Impromptu debates can be organized quickly when interesting disagreements emerge in the course of discussion. If you engage in such a debate, follow these steps:

1. Decide on and write out the question you are debating.
2. As quickly as possible, divide the class into position groups.
3. Spend a brief period in your position groups preparing your arguments.
4. Each position group gives its arguments and hears the refutations of the other groups.
5. Wrap up discussion of the relative success of each position group.

Extended Debates

Scheduling debates in advance, allowing time for group and/or individual preparation, and reserving an entire class period (or several) allows a more rigorous research process and thus a potentially richer learning experience. Each position group could have its own day in class to present arguments and hear rebuttals. Major arguments could be circulated in advance, and class time could be reserved entirely for refutations. If computer resources are plentiful, the entire debate could be organized online, and class time could be reserved for reflective writing and discussion

WORKSHOP 12 PUTTING TOGETHER A PORTFOLIO OF YOUR INVENTION WORK

Even if you never finish a draft of a composition, your Invention Journals record your research, analysis, and writing thus far. We recommend compiling a portfolio of this work. People in many lines of work compile portfolios to demonstrate their skill and experience. Photographers, artists, advertising professionals, and many others put together portfolios that represent their very best. Job seekers often use portfolios to show prospective employers examples of their work projects. One possible difference in the portfolio process we recommend is that you may or may not be including what you consider to be your "best work."

A portfolio can show you and others what you have learned about your critical situation over the course of a serious invention process. As students of composition, a record of your own thought process should interest you for a number of reasons. Putting together a portfolio can also be an act of critical reflection, a chance, in other words, to slow down and think carefully about what the process of specific compositions can teach us about writing or speaking generally. Research in education indicates that this kind of reflective practice allows students to take control of the learning process and to more effectively integrate new knowledge with existing knowledge. Portfolios are also a useful way to review your research and analysis and allow you to plan further work.

In addition to your projects, or even as the main assignment of the course, your instructor may ask you to put together a portfolio of your invention work. As a class, you may decide on any number of formats for your portfolio, and we encourage you to experiment. The following organization is meant to encourage portfolio writing as a reflective practice, or, in other words, as a review of the learning process. Think of this as a kind of critical memoir, a first person account of your thinking and composition process.

WORKSHOP EXERCISE

Structuring Your Portfolio

1. Overview Return to your project goals. As a way of introducing your work, in as much personal detail as you like, discuss the community commitments that led you to this writing or speech. Explain how the situation came to be important to you. Your overview can be written as a narrative or a story of your own interests. Also include commentary on how much experience you had prior to this project as a composer of arguments. Were the challenges of this course brand new, or have you had other courses or experiences as a writer or speaker that prepared you for them? You might write this as a letter addressed to your classmates and instructor, or other groups with interest in your chosen critical situation.

Whatever format you choose, you should make clear your portfolio focus. Your self-analysis should:

- Address what you have learned about composition and argumentation and how you learned it.
- Address what you have learned about your critical situation and how you learned it.
- Address areas of writing, speaking, and argumentation where you can make improvements.
- Address future writing and research that may be necessary to meet your project goals.
- Address some or all of the above.

Whichever focus you choose, think of this focus as the major conclusion or thesis of the portfolio overview. The remainder of your overview should relate back to the self-analytical claim or claims you lay out in your overview. Even if your overview takes the form of storytelling—recounting the story of your invention work and how it unfolded—your readers should have a strong sense of what your portfolio sets out to demonstrate. Some straightforward claims about this will be helpful for your readers. For example: "Through the process of this research and writing, I learned about crafting arguments." Or, "As I worked on this project, I learned crucial lessons about the critical situation I chose to address." Or, "Reviewing my portfolio I see that the most important project work remaining to be done is." Providing specific examples will help to demonstrate how your learning has taken shape over the course of the project or the semester.

To support these claims and focus your portfolio, discuss the invention work you have included. For example, if the intention of your portfolio is to demonstrate what you've learned about your critical situation, discuss those portions of your Invention Journals through which you gained important background knowledge, uncovered previously unfamiliar arguments about the situation, or learned about the importance of the situation for a range of stakeholder groups. You might also explain how this new understanding has influenced your perspective on the critical situation and whether or not you've arrived at a position differing from the one you held going into the invention process. If you intend to demonstrate what you've learned about argumentation, make reference to those Invention Journals in which you undertook careful analysis of stakeholder arguments, developed refutations for arguments, assessed the quality of evidence, and where you began drafting your own persuasive response to the situation at hand. If you intend to explain what work remains to be done in preparing a final project, make reference to Invention Journals where you found yourself "stumped." Where did you find arguments for which you had no response? What kinds of evidence do you need that you can't find? What further means of appealing to a difficult audience are necessary? What plans do you have for moving forward and completing the project?

The best portfolios are those that demonstrate skill and experience in the most detail. The best way to do this is to include specific passages of your invention work in your overview essay. Drawing directly from your Invention Journals assures vivid demonstration of your work and allows you to support your general claims about your invention process. Use signal phrases just as you would to cite the work of others. Cite the portions of your Invention Journal that most clearly illustrate the claims of your overview.

2. Selections from Your Invention Journals Decide with your instructor and your classmates how much invention work to include in the portfolio. You might set a page limit or agree to include responses to Invention Journal prompts from each chapter you've worked through. We recommend you be selective, choosing only the pieces that demonstrate the main assertions you make in your portfolio overview.

3. Include a Bibliography of Sources You Found in Research Many of the Invention Journals require you to find and analyze source material relevant to the critical situation at hand. Including a bibliography or works cited page provides further evidence of the depth of your work. It is also a valuable document to have if you intend to move forward in addressing your critical situation.

WORKSHOP 13 READERS RESPONDING

Often, writing is the best way to approach a reading task. Writing about what we read requires careful engagement with the text and increases the chance that we will retain key ideas and information for future writing and thinking. To write a response to a text, we need to dwell on its details, to move past casual impressions to more defined positions on what we've read. Putting pen to paper (or fingers to keyboard) helps us to identify gaps in our current knowledge and to materialize thinking that might otherwise remain fuzzy. Also, returning to a written record of our response to reading material allows us to gauge the direction of our thinking. After further reading and research, do we find we no longer agree with our initial response? Has further study confirmed the statements we made in our response? A reader's response, then, is like a snapshot of the thinking process.

This workshop offers suggestions for reading-as-writing. Think of your reader's response as an extension of reading notes made in the margins of an article or book.

WORKSHOP EXERCISE

Read the following questions before you read the text with which you're working. When you have finished reading, look these questions over again. Then, write in response to each question.

1. What are the most important claims of this text? Which statements or assertions does the writer spend the most time explaining or defending? Which claims are repeated? Is there a central conclusion or thesis to which the writer points readers? Write down all major claims or summarize them noting the page numbers for future reference.
2. For each of these major claims, offer your "gut reaction." Do the claims seem to express what you consider to be common sense? Do they offend your sensibilities? Let yourself be biased here! Don't edit yourself. The whole point of this exercise is to record your first reactions, which will necessarily be shaped by your own way of thinking about the world and by your current knowledge about the content of the text you are reading. Any sound bytes, clichés or platitudes that leap to mind should be recorded.
3. Now, explain how each major claim is supported or illustrated in the text. Are there examples from public life? References to scholarship? Survey or questionnaire results? Emotional appeals? Photographs? As you write, you may want to note which of the claims in the text are well-supported and which claims are forwarded without support.
4. Write out all the unfamiliar concepts, events referenced, names, and words that you run across in your reading. Mark them in the margin. Use dictionaries,

encyclopedias, Internet search engines, and other sources to familiarize yourself with this new information. This kind of written follow-up on reading is an excellent way to build vocabulary as well as general knowledge of the world around you.

5. What do you take to be the primary or intended audience for this text? For whom does the writing and the argument or approach seem to be tailored? Note or copy passages of audience-specific language from the text.
6. The target audience may not be the only group for whom the text is relevant or important. Whether or not the writer or writers provide explicit comment on this point, explain for whom you think this text matters most. What community or communities need to have this information, hear this argument (even if it is to refute it)?
7. What is the single most important insight or impression you take away from your reading of this text? Provide some passages that hold the greatest meaning and relevance from your perspective. Briefly explain the importance of the passage(s) you've identified.
8. Describe the style or voice of the text. Is it formal or informal? Is it full of specialized terms, or does it seem to be written for a more general audience? Is the writing humorous? Sarcastic? Does it appeal to the emotions? However you describe them, copy passages that exemplify that voice or style.

WORKSHOP 14 REFLECTING ON YOUR COMMITMENTS

As you work toward publication of your composition, you may want to slow down and step out of "production" mode for a while. Our first commitment to students using this book is to help them get compositional work done in the context of critical situations; this book is then in a sense a manual or action-oriented guide. We do, however, see value in pursuing writing that will allow you to explore in greater detail your experience of the critical situation in question and the commitments, familial, political, professional, and emotional, that put that situation "on the map" for you. This act of reflection, thinking back on commitment and experience, might also afford you the opportunity to write a story from your life. Even if to us the "main event" is your public crafting of language to address critical situations, we don't want to discount the importance of understanding and representing the events and circumstances that led to writing or speech in the first place.

Narrative, that is, storytelling, is a fundamental human activity. Telling stories allows us to share and record experiences, impressions, and important events. As well, you may also find that reflective writing is a way to make powerful arguments. Writing narrative can bring you to important arguments as a means of invention, or serve as persuasive writing in its own right.

WORKSHOP EXERCISE

The following suggested exercises are not a step-by-step process for writing memoirs or "personal essays." Neither of us can claim any expertise in this area. Rather, we hope these prompts will help you to generate narrative material in the same way the prompts in the Invention Journals help you to invent arguments. We recommend writing in response to all or to selected prompts and then, if you want to shape the text for an audience other than yourself, to work on shaping your reflective writing into narrative form. For each of the prompts below, *write in as much detail as possible.* Each prompt, in fact, asks for specific kinds of detail.

1. Write your earliest memories of your critical situation. If you are developing a resource page for alternative cancer treatments, for example, write about your first encounters with cancer and cancer treatment, whether they are your own experience, or those of family members, friends, or neighbors. What were the circumstances? What were your reflections at the time?
2. Try to set up a timeline of events that represent your interaction in the circumstances of the critical situation. Move from your earliest memories towards the present. For example, returning to the example above, if your first memory of cancer is your uncle's struggle with lung cancer, you could follow with the course of his treatment, visits to his house or to the hospital, the family party thrown to

celebrate the remission of his cancer, a conversation in which your uncle confided his continuing anxiety about recurrence, your own decision to quit smoking cigarettes, and so on. The goal here is to create a sense of chronology and to generate as many instances as possible. Think of them as scenes in a film.

3. Write a sketch of all the key people involved explaining their relationship within the critical situation. Primary "characters" in our example would be the uncle, his wife, their children, other family members, doctors and nurses who help treat the uncle along the way, the manager who was kind in allowing a great deal of extra leave time from work, etc. If possible, try to capture what was most important or interesting about each person's involvement in the critical situation (or at least your perspective on it). You might write a sketch for each person in which you narrate their interaction in your uncle's struggle. As you write, let yourself comment on the attitudes, character, personal history, and quirks of each person.
4. Many narratives include dialogue, which helps readers understand the people in the story and their thoughts and emotions surrounding key events. Thinking back over your timeline and your interaction with each key person you've written about, make a list of important conversations that you remember. When did you and your uncle discuss his health? Did you talk to your aunt about her perspective on his recovery? Were there times when you spoke to his doctors or other caregivers? Did you have a conversation with anyone who expressed disdain over the use of alternative treatment methods? Did you ever talk with friends about your worry for your uncle and your fears that you would lose him? If you can't remember exact words, summarize the conversations in as much detail as possible.
5. Sometimes physical details in stories compel us most. Look back over the writing you've done thus far. Work on revising it to enhance descriptions of sensory detail. Sensory detail refers to the perception of the senses. Do you remember the particular medicinal smell of the hospital room where you visited your uncle? Do you remember the sight of his hair as it began to fall out during radiation therapy? Do you remember the feel of your aunt's sweater when you gave her a hug of encouragement? Write out as much sensory description as you can.
6. Look back over your writing, and think back on your experience. Is there a central insight or impression you would like to record? What did you learn from your experience about courage? The importance of family? The wonder or shortcomings of modern medicine? Perhaps something about your uncle—his sustaining sense of humor or his ability to be a good father, husband, and friend despite his illness? Maybe the effectiveness of alternative methods of treatment? Though it isn't necessary to make a single "main point" in a story, you may wish to.

SHAPING AND REVISING THE NARRATIVE

With any luck, you now have at least several pages of raw reflection—memories, vignettes, descriptions, conversations, rants, second thoughts, a whole host of written response to the compositional activity of "returning to the scene," so to speak.

What to do with this rich "mess"? Maybe you don't want to do anything further with this reflective writing; the act of recording memories and experiences can be worthwhile all on its own. However, if you want to move further into a narrative mode and perhaps write for other readers, you should think further about how to give your reflection narrative structure and emphasis.

1. A chronological narrative, that is, one moving sequentially through time, is the most traditional way of relaying events. In the second prompt above, you set up a timeline of events, and this timeline might well serve as a general frame for your story. Return to that timeline as a structure for telling your story. You may not want to take on the entire timeline (unless you have a book-length narration in mind). Select key moments to serve as the backbone of your story. Chronological structure allows a writer to follow a sequence of events and to trace her own experiences and reactions and those of others along the way. A chronological approach is appropriate especially when the events themselves are most important to your intention in narrating. For example, if the writer wants to describe the physical impact of radiation and chemotherapy treatments, a strict chronology of bodily and emotional reactions to a prescribed course of treatment may be the best option.
2. Another common storytelling structure is to narrate *in medias res*, a Latin phrase for "in the middle of things." In this approach, the writer begins narrating in the midst of the central events. This structure can be especially useful for reflective writing in which writers grapple with the meaning of events. This option allows writers to find important patterns of meaning when telling the story from point A, to point B, to point C, and so on may not capture the most important elements of the event or events in question. For example, the story of the uncle's struggle with cancer might begin with the crushing disappointment of the cancer's reappearance. From here, the writer's reflection could take readers back to the first appearance of the cancer, which, in retrospect was not as devastating as the reappearance. To illustrate this point, the writer could take readers to the point of the cancer's remission after a first course of treatment, taking time to illustrate the joy and relief of the uncle and his family. Perhaps from here, the writer returns to the challenges of the moment and looks forward hopefully, detailing the uncle's emergence from his sense of defeat as he once again, somehow, summoned energy to fight for his life.
3. Sometimes, a narrower focus actually reveals and expresses more. It may be that what is most important about your involvement and interest in a critical situation can be captured by a tighter narrative focused on a single event. For example, in the narrative about an uncle's struggle with cancer, our hypothetical writer might decide that her uncle's entire experience of struggle and survival could be expressed by telling the story of a determined trip to the farmer's market. Perhaps the uncle's custom was to head to the market every Saturday morning, and he had done so each Saturday for years without fail. What might be conveyed by a detailed story about his overcoming pain, fatigue, and lethargy to

get to the market just after the reappearance of the cancer? Think how sensory descriptions of his deteriorated physical state and perhaps the beautiful fall morning—even the gorgeous fresh produce—could teach readers something about the commitments that help people survive serious illness.

4. Remember that stories take many forms; keep the broadest possible definition of what counts as a narrative. Sometimes the most disjunctive or nonlinear accounts of human experience convey or teach the most.

WORKSHOP 15 REVISING FOR CLARITY

If you have been reading carefully, you know by now that we reject "one-size-fits-all" approaches to composition. The particularities of your situation will dictate what is and is not successful writing. Your audience will ultimately make this judgment, not textbook authors, not even you yourself in the end.

Readers often praise or complain about the clarity of what they read. We would like to offer some useful rules of thumb for achieving clarity in your writing. To say that writing or speech is "clear" is metaphorical. The prospect of "clear" writing bids us to imagine readers or listeners who can visualize our meaning. When someone tells us that our speech or writing is not clear, the suggestion is that language has gotten in the way of our message, muddied the waters, obscured the visibility of what is most important. How do we avoid confusions of language that will detract from the possibility that we and our audiences might "see" things in the same "light"?

CLARITY OF OVERALL STRUCTURE

When revising, stepping back and assessing the overall arrangement of your composition will help you cue audiences to the path you have charted for them in your writing. How you arrange the ideas, claims, evidence, and other elements of your composition is of crucial importance. If you imagine that you are taking your audience somewhere, then that route must be the best one available. Whatever detours you take (digressions and considerations of other topics) should enhance the audiences' appreciation of the destination (the major conclusions to which you hope to lead them).

CLARITY OF PARAGRAPHS

Paragraphs are a convenience for readers. Although we don't think in paragraphs, they help us organize and punctuate meaning. Each paragraph should serve a specific function, and there is virtually no end to the ways you might use a paragraph. Paragraphs deliver a major or minor premise, conclude, introduce a concept, provide background information, offer readers comic relief, and on. Taking your rhetorical strategizing down to the paragraph level, you increase your opportunities for effective communication. As you revise, look for opportunities to shift paragraphs around in order to more skillfully frame meaning in your writing.

DEFINITIONS, EXAMPLES, AND REFERENCES

What often makes writing difficult to understand are key terms that are not defined, examples that are not explained well or don't seem relevant, and references that are unfamiliar to your audience. Audience members who are unfamiliar with the situation about which you are writing will struggle to get through definitions, examples, and references that are new. Definitions, references, and examples should be clearly explained unless you have a very good reason for not doing so.

BEGINNING AND ENDING

Writers struggle with beginnings and endings, and rightly so. How you lead your audience into your composition, and the ideas they encounter as they finish reading are influential. Beginnings set the tone and pose key questions and claims, and endings offer writers a final chance to make an appeal, pass on information, underscore key points, point to the importance of the composition for the reader as she goes forward, etc. Though, as always in composition, absolute rules are rare. Below we offer general suggestions for strategies of introducing and concluding that can enhance clarity.

WORKSHOP EXERCISE

For yourself and readers of your draft, write out your intention and audience: What is the main message or argument of your text? What is the lasting impression with which you want to leave your audience? Don't write more than several sentences; this should be a point of reference that you and your readers can easily keep in mind while evaluating your draft. A draft that is "clear" forwards the intention of the writer or speaker. Clarity means that the audience is not distracted, confused, or sent on a tangent (at least not without purpose and intention). Depending on the work you are trying to get done in your composition and the audience you are addressing, strategies for clarity will vary quite a bit.

Once you have a statement of intention, readers should make an assessment of clarity based upon it. Review the intention statement before reading the draft; perhaps attach it to the draft or write it at the top of the first page. Now, assess the draft at several different levels. We recommend that readers go through your draft several times (no, we are not joking). Respond to the following criteria for clarity.

Clarity of Overall Structure

Readers make an outline of the draft. With a pen, mark off the major divisions of the draft. Note a section break when a new idea is introduced, a new argument is made. If outlining texts is challenging for you, and if you haven't already done so, read through the outlining strategies suggested in "Summarizing Ideas, Arguments, and Texts." The writer might also make an outline. Wait to show it to your readers until after they have made their outlines. Compare your senses of the overall structure and its clarity.

Clarity of Paragraphs

1. On a separate piece of paper or in the margin of the draft, write out the function of each paragraph. How does it work in the context of the draft as a whole? Does it introduce an idea? State a premise? Offer background information? You should also offer feedback on how to increase the success of paragraph function. What is missing? What is unnecessary?

Definitions and Examples

1. Read through the draft once for specialized or uncommon words that need to be defined. It is especially helpful to have multiple readers for this exercise. If two, three, or four readers are unfamiliar with a word or concept, it is likely that your audience will benefit from some clarification. Definitions don't need to be taken word for word from a dictionary or other reference source. In fact, it is probably better to offer a paraphrased definition or explanation, a brief one that doesn't impede the progress of your composition.
2. Whenever you encounter an example in the draft, an illustration of a premise perhaps or a case study meant to explain a concept or event, be sure it serves the purpose of clarity and doesn't distract. Is the example well introduced? Does it adequately illuminate as intended? Have you commented on it in such a way to demonstrate its relevance to your argument?

Beginning and Ending

1. Does the beginning of the composition engage and focus readers? Does it delay too long before getting to the point of the composition? Conversely, does it state the case too abruptly or in such a stiff and formulaic manner that readers' attention wanders?
2. Now, review the conclusion of the composition. Does the conclusion re-emphasize the intended meaning and its importance, or does it leave readers flat?

Write up Your Response

Whether you are reading your own draft or one of your classmates', write a response to each of the questions above. Also, mark up drafts with underlining and margin comments, etc, that will help the writer to revise most efficiently.

WORKSHOP 16 SUMMARIZING ARGUMENTS, IDEAS, AND TEXTS

Our compositions are built on the work of other writers and speakers. Learning how to identify arguments, ideas, and texts is an important skill. A student or parent writing to the school board to criticize a district-wide policy must be able to demonstrate a solid understanding of that policy; in this instance, it would be wise to summarize the policy early on in the letter. A letter to the editor responding to a newspaper article must offer a summary, or readers who missed the original article will not appreciate the letter writer's position. When reviewing a book or movie, whether positively or negatively, a reasonably detailed summary will give readers a point of reference for understanding the reviewer's evaluation. Scholars are careful to summarize key arguments, ideas, and texts of experts in a given academic field of study, so that their own work may be presented as an important extension of "the existing literature." There are countless situations in which writers and speakers must summarize. Writing summaries is also an important strategy of *careful reading*. Once we have written a careful summary of a text, we have made it our own, in a sense. With a summary on file, we have a written record of our interaction with a text, one which may be useful in the future when we want to recall what we've read and our own initial response.

This workshop offers strategies for writing strong summaries. As always, we encourage you to work through multiple drafts and to share your work with members of your workshop group.

HOW LENGTHY SHOULD A SUMMARY BE?

The challenge of effective summary writing is always balancing concision and thoroughness. How do we convey enough information to make our point while keeping the summary brief enough so that our audience won't be sidetracked? The length and detail of your summary depends on many factors. How long will your composition be? If you are constrained by time (when speaking) or page length (when writing), make brief summaries that touch on key points. If time and space constraints are not as great, or if your own composition is based heavily on the arguments or ideas of others, a more thorough and detailed summary is likely to be appropriate. When reviewing or analyzing another text, a detailed summary will help an audience understand the evaluation or analysis. As in all compositional matters, context dictates what practices are most appropriate or effective.

SUMMARY WRITING REQUIRES CAREFUL READING

Without a firm grasp of an argument, idea, or text in question, summarizing well will be difficult if not impossible; it is crucial that you read with great care. Few people can read a text of any complexity just once and have a firm grasp of its central ideas and strategies. We strongly encourage you to read texts *at least twice*. Furthermore, as a practice of active reading, be sure to engage the text *with a pencil or pen in hand.* Marking the texts to be summarized gives you a map to follow as you plan your summary.

Making Reading Notes

Along with multiple readings, making reading notes helps guide us as we write about what we've read. You may already have a system of annotation that works for you. If not, we recommend the following simple strategies:

- **Underline or highlight major claims and key phrases and topic sentences.** Any good summary captures the main claims of a text; these marks save you from having to skim through the text looking for them. Most texts are structured around key terms and phrases that reappear and are central to the overall meaning of the text, and these should be marked as well. As well, the central sentence, idea, or purpose of each paragraph should be marked. These annotations are especially helpful because they are in a sense a summary of the paragraph. Marking the important claims in each paragraph gives you the framework of the text or argument and the bones of your summary.
- **Write out the definitions of key terms.** Margin notes giving the definitions of key terms also help in summary writing. Do your dictionary work *before* you sit down to write your summary.
- **Annotate paragraph function.** In the margins, note the function of each paragraph within the overall structure of the draft. Is a major concept or event described or explained in a paragraph? Do paragraphs mark off major premises or conclusions? Is evidence introduced? Are particularly challenging comments made? Make your annotations as brief as possible, one or two sentences if possible.
- **Put a star, asterisk, or checkmark next to key passages** (perhaps next to major claims you've underlined). This strategy allows recall of core content with a quick scan of the margins.

Note: When working with library books or other borrowed material, consider making photocopies to annotate or recording your reading notes on a separate sheet of paper.

Writing an Outline

When you need to summarize an entire article, essay, book, or other text (or a large portion of one), writing an outline is very helpful. Outlining helps us to break down a text into pieces and provides the structure of your summary. Use a traditional Roman numeral outline or any other system. The important thing is breaking down the component parts of the text, so that you can see the parts of your summary. If you know how much space you have for your summary, you can then decide how much you will write in summary of each part.

The text that follows is the inaugural editorial of the abolitionist newspaper, *The Liberator*, written by editor William Lloyd Garrison. Read the text and the summary that follows. As you read, try your hand at marking major claims, key terms and phrases, and topic sentences:

January 1, 1831

To the Public

In the month of August, I issued proposals for publishing *The Liberator* in Washington city; but the enterprise, though hailed in different sections of the country, was palsied by public indifference. Since that time, the removal of the Genius of Universal Emancipation to the Seat of Government has rendered less imperious the establishment of a similar periodical in that quarter.

During my recent tour for the purpose of exciting the minds of the people by a series of discourses on the subject of slavery, every place that I visited gave fresh evidence of the fact, that a greater revolution in public sentiment was to be effected in the free states—*and particularly in New-England*—than at the south. I found contempt more bitter, opposition more active, detraction more relentless, prejudice more stubborn, and apathy more frozen, than among slave owners themselves. Of course, there were individual exceptions to the contrary. This state of things afflicted, but did not dishearten me. I determined, at every hazard, to lift up the standard of emancipation in the eyes of the nation, *within sight of Bunker Hill and in the birth place of liberty*. That standard is now unfurled; and long may it float, unhurt by the spoliations of time or the missiles of a desperate foe—yea, till every chain be broken, and every bondman set free! Let southern oppressors tremble—let their secret abettors tremble—let their northern apologists tremble—let all the enemies of the persecuted blacks tremble.

I deem the publication of my original Prospectus unnecessary, as it has obtained a wide circulation. The principles therein inculcated will be steadily pursued in this paper, excepting that I shall not array myself as the political partisan of any man. In defending the great cause of human rights, I wish to derive the assistance of all religions and of all parties.

Assenting to the "self-evident truth" maintained in the American Declaration of Independence, "that all men are created equal, and endowed by their Creator with certain inalienable rights—among which are life, liberty and the pursuit of happiness," I shall strenuously contend for the immediate enfranchisement of our slave population. In Park-street Church, on the Fourth of July, 1829, in an address on slavery, I unreflectingly assented to the popular but pernicious doctrine of gradual abolition. I seize this opportunity to make a full and unequivocal recantation, and thus publicly to ask pardon of my God, of my country, and of my brethren the poor slaves, for having uttered a sentiment so full of timidity, injustice and absurdity. A similar recantation, from my pen, was published in the Genius of Universal Emancipation at Baltimore, in September, 1829. My conscience in now satisfied.

I am aware, that many object to the severity of my language; but is there not cause for severity? I *will* be as harsh as truth, and as uncompromising as justice. On this subject, I do not wish to think, or speak, or write, with moderation. No! no! Tell a man whose house is on fire, to give a moderate alarm; tell him to moderately rescue his wife from the hand of the ravisher; tell the mother to gradually extricate her babe from the fire into which it has fallen;—but urge me not to use moderation in a cause like the present. I am in earnest—I will not equivocate—I will not excuse—I will not retreat a single inch—AND I WILL BE HEARD. The apathy of the people is enough to make every statue leap from its pedestal, and to hasten the resurrection of the dead.

It is pretended, that I am retarding the cause of emancipation by the coarseness of my invective, and the precipitancy of my measures. The *charge is not true*. On this question my influence,—humble as it is,—is felt at this moment to a considerable extent, and shall be felt in coming years—not perniciously, but beneficially—not as a curse, but as a blessing; and posterity will bear testimony that I was right. I desire to thank God, that he enables me to disregard "the fear of man which bringeth a snare," and to speak his truth in its simplicity and power.

Outline of Paragraph Function in Garrison's "To the Public"

PARA 1: Garrison notes the lukewarm reception of his plan to start an abolitionist newspaper. He notes that when the well-known abolitionist paper *The Universal Genius of Emancipation* moved to Washington, D.C., fewer people objected to the idea of a new paper.

PARA 2: Garrison claims that while touring New England to promote *The Liberator*, he found Northerners had greater racial prejudice than Southerners. This, he says, made him decide to publish the paper in Boston. He then audaciously writes that slaveholders and their sympathizers should all be afraid and "tremble."

PARA 3: Garrison deems the publication of his original prospectus for *The Liberator* unnecessary because it has already been widely circulated.

PARA 4: Holding up the Declaration of Independence as a guiding light, Garrison renounces his former belief in "gradual abolition" dedicating *The Liberator* to "immediate enfranchisement."

PARA 5: Garrison predicts that his uncompromising approach will be denounced as damaging to the cause of abolitionism, but he rejects that position. He then goes on in the strongest language to pledge his unending dedication to the cause, including the statement, "I WILL BE HEARD."

Citing Key Terms or Phrases in Your Summaries

Once you have decided how much time or space you have to summarize, and how much detail is actually needed, choose a few key terms or phrases to include. Picking key terms or phrases allows you to convey a stronger sense of the original text. Also, including some key citations allows you to introduce terms that you want to build into your own argument. For instance, if you are writing about the history of abolitionism, you might well want to include Garrison's important distinction between "immediate enfranchisement" and "gradual abolition." Also, because it is a relatively famous phrase, or just because it so clearly conveys Garrison's tone, you might want to include his challenging assertion made all in capital letters:

> Garrison promises an unrelenting attack on slavery and assures the public, "I WILL BE HEARD."

Summarizing Arguments or Ideas

When we are only interested in specific ideas or arguments of a writer or speaker, summarizing the entire text is unnecessary and would serve only to take the emphasis off your intended meaning. Take only what you need to keep the focus on *your* ideas and *your* argument. Imagine, for example, you are writing a public letter that criticizes local politicians for failing to speak on a key issue. You might refer to Garrison in this way:

> As William Lloyd Garrison noted in the case of slavery more than 170 years ago, compromising in order to avoid conflict might be a "popular" thing to do, but avoiding tough ethical issues is "pernicious."

You don't need everything Garrison said; the summary of this main idea works well on its own. Summarizing key arguments or ideas is much easier when you have good reading notes that identify important portions of the text.

Writing Your Summary Sentence

A first sentence introducing your summary provides a transition from what came before and cues readers that they are about to encounter material imported from elsewhere. Think of this sentence as the summary of the summary, or, the most condensed statement of the content you are introducing. Often, a summary sentence introduces the title of a piece being summarized or the cores of the argument or idea being summarized. For example, a summary of Garrison's "To the Public" might begin with the following sentence:

> William Lloyd Garrison's 1831 inaugural editorial "To the Public" announced *The Liberator* as a radical new voice against slavery.

A sentence like this has the virtue of giving readers key information (title, author, and year of publication), and it forecasts the content of the summary to come—a breakdown of Garrison's iconoclastic vision for the abolitionist movement.

Giving a Summary Emphasis

Though we want to be true to the original, emphasizing a particular element of the text you are summarizing can help you work it into the overall meaning of your own writing. You might signal emphasis in an opening summary sentence. For example, Garrison's "To the Public" could be introduced as "the raising of a new voice against slavery," or "a trenchant critique of weak-willed anti-slavery reformers," or "an announcement of Garrison's break with Benjamin Lund [the editor of *The Universal Genius of Emancipation*]." The details you choose depend on the focus of *your* composition. Emphasis might also be given to your summary anywhere else along the way. After finishing a summary of Garrison's "To the Public," for example, a closing line might leave a lasting impression: "Garrison's confrontational first editorial set the tone for the radical work *The Liberator* would do over the next 35 years."

Don't Plagiarize

It is easy to accidentally plagiarize when working with research material. Be sure you know what conventions of documentation are required of you in your writing or speaking context. Remember that even if you are summarizing without including any direct citations, you still must indicate the source of the ideas with which you are working.

WORKSHOP EXERCISES

For Your Project

As part of your process of drafting, go through your research material and mark texts or key ideas and arguments from texts that you think you will summarize in your own writing. Work through the strategies presented in this workshop as you go.

For Practice

1. Have each member of a workshop group or of the entire class write a summary of a short text you have all read. Compare summaries, and discuss which is most successful. Which summary strikes the best balance between concision and thoroughness?
2. Individually, in your workshop groups, or as a class, write a 20-word summary, a 50-word summary, and a 100-word summary of a text you have all read. Be sure to cite key phrases or passages in each version of your summary. Discuss the decisions that were made while tailoring the summaries to a particular length.

WORKSHOP 17 WHAT ARE YOUR COLLABORATIVE HABITS?

Which of the following statements seems more accurate to you?

Two heads are better than one.

or,

Too many cooks spoil the broth.

In our experience, people have very different perspectives on what is often called "group work." Depending on your learning style and your temperament, you might prefer completing tasks on your own. Well-meaning help from others may strike you as a distraction or even as an imposition. Or, because of experiences in school, you may have developed the attitude that group work amounts to "busy work," that is, pointless activities to kill time.

We prefer the word *collaboration* to the term *group work* because collaboration suggests that people work together toward a goal upon which they agree. Many students thrive in a collaborative atmosphere, finding great value in feedback and in the opportunity to bounce ideas off other people. When done well, collaboration is an essential element of the composing process. For this reason, most professional writers and speakers collaborate when they compose, consulting with colleagues or spouses or friends.

PREDICTING THE GROUP DYNAMIC AND PLANNING FOR SUCCESSFUL COLLABORATION

Take a few minutes right now to talk with your class or workshop members about your attitudes toward collaboration. Try to answer these questions: How well do you work with other people? When have you found working with others to be helpful or to be a hindrance? Describe these occasions to other class members, and take note of the practices that were helpful or hindering.

The following set of questions and the the subsequent exercise that follows are intended to help you identify your collaborative habits. Comparing your responses with your group members will help you predict strengths and possible pitfalls for the group. You should also be able to agree on some ground rules that will help your group become productive.

- Describe a positive experience you have had working with others. Include as many details about the situation and people involved as you can.

- Describe a negative experience you have had working with others. Include as many details about the situation and people involved as you can.
- Describe a positive experience you have had working alone. Include as much detail about the situation as you can.
- Describe a negative experience you have had working alone. Include as much detail about the situation as you can.

Now, discuss your responses with group members. List all of the common elements of positive collaborative situations that you and others have identified. Now, list all of the negative elements. Once you have generated these two lists, discuss how you might avoid falling into the common pitfalls of collaborative work. Discuss also how you can help to create the conditions for success that you have experienced when collaborating. While you are working through these exercises, be sure to think about the scheduling in your course. Consult the syllabus. Look to see when major work is due and when workshops are scheduled to meet. Try to get a realistic sense of how often the group will be working together.

We also recommend that you formalize some principles of collaborative work that the group agrees to follow. If you have already written a group or class charter (see "Agreeing on Workshop Guidelines"), you should now add new, collaboration-focused principles to it.

WORKSHOP EXERCISE: REFLECTION ON COLLABORATION

After several weeks of working together, write an account of the experience. Detail struggles and successes. Explain the place of each collaborator in creating the group dynamic. Group members may write these reflections on collaboration individually, sharing them or not, or they may compose collaboratively.

WORKSHOP 18 WHAT DO YOU WANT TO LEARN ABOUT COMPOSITION?

This workshop offers you an opportunity to set goals for yourself as a serious student of composition. It is likely that whatever course you are taking, your teacher and/or the department or program that offers the course will have a list of "learning objectives" or "course outcomes" towards which students are expected to work. As a supplement to those learning outcomes, we suggest you take the time to make some of your own decisions about what you want to learn about writing. Look at this as a chance to take further control of your education and to chart a careful learning path as you go about the work of serious composition.

This workshop is a good way to set goals at the beginning of a class, or you may wait until at least a month into the course before running this workshop; you may need to do some writing, reading, and research so your challenges and goals for composition are fresh in mind. We recommend returning to these goals throughout the semester to check your progress and perhaps set further goals. In fact, this workshop makes a useful precursor to the process of putting together a portfolio of your work (see the "Putting Together a Portfolio" workshop).

WORKSHOP EXERCISE

As a way of setting goals for yourself, we offer the following two-step process. **Step one** is the Writer's Inventory. The questions on the inventory are meant to help you generate a portrait of yourself as a writer, so that you can more clearly understand your interests, strengths, and weaknesses as a communicator. Respond in as much detail as possible to the following questions and prompts.

Step two of this workshop asks you to be a careful reader of your own answers to the Writer's Inventory. Look for common themes, collect incidents, pull out what you think are most strongly indicative of your strengths, weaknesses, and interests as a writer. From this, you should be able to make a list of **at least three learning goals** you would like to set for yourself as a writer. For each goal, explain briefly why you consider this goal to be important.

Writer's Inventory

Respond to the following prompts:

1. Describe your relationship to writing.
2. What do you currently understand to be "good writing"?
3. Discuss some specific piece of writing for which you have respect. Give as much detail as possible about what made the writing worthy of that respect.

4. Where do you need experience and practice as a writer?
5. Where do you need experience and practice as a reader?
6. Where do you need experience and practice as a researcher?
7. What aspects of writing are most interesting and enjoyable for you? Most challenging?
8. What role does writing play in your life now?
9. What do you project for your future as a writer? What kinds of writings will your profession or future course of study demand?
10. What situations and questions do you want to address as a writer? How can this class best function to help you meet those goals?

There is no standard length for responding to the questions of the Writer's Inventory. It is likely that some of the questions will capture your imagination more than others. Try to write a paragraph in response to each question or prompt. Be as detailed as possible.

Once you have your goals, attach them to the Writer's Inventory, and write a letter to your class and/or your teacher. Discuss things that you plan to do to meet the goals you have set for yourself. As a class, you can discuss your goals. It is likely that many of you share goals and that you could help one other be successful in meeting them. You might even talk about how the structure and procedures of the course could be altered (if circumstances allow) to better help you meet your goals.

GLOSSARY OF TERMS

analogy A line of reasoning that compares similar relationships

argument A statement or set of statements that support or refute a position taken up by participants in a discussion

character Community evaluations of a writer's or speaker's reputation; ancient teachers called these proofs from character *ethos*

claim A statement that expresses its author's position on some issue

commitment Dedication to a set of outcomes, ideas, or people who reside in communities affected by a **critical situation**

commonplace A statement that is in wide circulation and believed by many people

common sense Beliefs that most people hold; beliefs that are held by large numbers of people—regardless of whether the beliefs are true or false, right or wrong

community Any group of people who are interested in a discussion because they have a stake in its outcome

conjecture The first category of stasis; conjecture depicts or assesses events and actions

context Diverse beliefs and arguments that circulate around any **position;** also, cultural practices that give rise to beliefs and arguments

critical situation Any situation that contains or produces differences of opinion, conflicting perspectives, or disparate experiences among people for whom the situation is important

deduction Any line of reasoning that proceeds from a generally accepted statement to one that is less well accepted; usually the generally accepted statement is a generalization

definition The second category of stasis; definition states the meaning of important terms or draws limits around the area covered by an issue

enthymeme A rhetorical argument that works by deduction

ethos The created character or situated reputation of a writer or speaker

evidence Anything offered as proof of a claim

example A specific instance; can be drawn either from history or fiction

generalization Any statement about a group or class of items

ideology A set or sets of commonly held beliefs that are so closely connected to one another that they always appear together

induction Any line of reasoning that proceeds by listing examples or specifics and then drawing a general conclusion

invention The process of searching for available arguments in the discourse of communities

issue An issue is any thing, event, or idea about which members of a community may disagree

kairos An opening and opportunity in time and place of which a writer or speaker may take advantage; also, preparation or preparedness for such an opening

line of reasoning A chain of premises that leads an audience from accepted statements to a more controversial statement

policy The fourth category of stasis; policy considers what should be done or not done in a given situation

position The place where a person is located in relation to others; also, a person's relationship to an **issue**

premise A statement used in an argument, intended to persuade. Premises may be major, when they contain a generalization, and minor, when they indicate a specific item

qualitative time Time as experienced subjectively by individuals; here time can seem to speed up or slow down in relation to clocks and calendars; Greek *kairos*

quantitative time Time as measured by clocks, calendars, and seasons; ordinary time; Greek *chronos*

rhetoric The ability to find the arguments made available by a given **critical situation**

stakeholder Any person or group that has taken up a committed **position** within a **critical situation**

stasis A stasis marks the place where people who disagree about an issue can agree on what the controversy is about

testimony Any account about a situation, events, or an issue, given either by a witness or an expert

value The third category of stasis; value raises questions about what is important or unimportant, treasured or rejected by a community

PART IV

READING ROOM

A Selection of Works Referenced in *Critical Situations*

A NARRATIVE OF THE PROCEEDINGS OF THE BLACK PEOPLE DURING THE LATE AWFUL CALAMITY IN PHILADELPHIA

Richard Allen and Absalom Jones

Philadelphia's 1793 yellow fever epidemic amounted to a national crisis, all but halting commerce and political activity in the country's political capital and leading center of commerce. Absalom Jones and Richard Allen were leaders in Philadelphia's African American community, and when a well-known white printer accused the city's African Americans of looting and price gouging during the crisis, these men took it upon themselves to speak for the community. Their "Late Awful Calamity" pamphlet not only defended the character and conduct of African Philadelphians but also launched a scathing critique of slavery and racial oppression and made public arguments and ideas that would continue to animate abolitionist discourse until racial slavery was finally overthrown.

In consequence of a partial representation of the conduct of the people who were employed to nurse the sick, in the late calamitous state of the city of Philadelphia, we are solicited, by a number of those who feel themselves injured thereby, and by the advice of several respectable citizens, to step forward and declare facts as they really were; seeing that from our situation, on account of the charge we took upon us, we had it more fully and generally in our power, to know and observe the conduct and behavior of those that were also employed.

Early in September, a solicitation apperared in the Public papers, to the people of colour to come forward and assist the distressed, perishing, and neglected sick; with a kind of assurance, that people of our colour were not liable to take the infection. Upon which we and a few others met and consulted how to act on so truly alarming and melancholy an occasion. After some conversations, we found a freedom to go forth, confining in him who can preserve in the midst of a burning fiery furnace, sensible that it was our duty to do all the good we could to our suffering fellow mortals. We set out to see where we could be useful. The first we visited was a man in Emsley's alley, who was dying, and his wife lay dead at the time in the house, there were none to assist but two poor helpless children. We administered what relief we could, and applied to the overseers of the poor to have the woman buried. We visited upwards of twenty families that day—they were scenes of woe indeed! The Lord was pleased to strengthen, and remove all fear from us, and disposed our hearts to be as useful as possible.

In order the better to regulate our conduct, we called on the mayor next day, to consult with him how to proceed, so as to be most useful. The first object he recommended, was a strict attention to the sick, and the procuring of nurses. This was attended to by Absalom Jones and William Gray; and, in order that the distressed might know where to apply, the mayor advertised the public that upon application to them they would be supplied. Soon after, the mortality increasing, the difficulty of getting a corpse taken away, was such, that few were willing to do it, when offered great rewards. The black people were looked to. We then offered our services in the public papers, by advertising that we would remove the dead and procure nurses. Our services were the production of real sensibility;—we sought not fee nor reward, until the increase of the disorder rendered our labour so arduous that we were not adequate to the service we had assumed. The mortality increasing rapidly, obliged us to call in the assistance of five[1] hired men, in the awful discharge of interring the dead. They, with great reluctance, were prevailed upon to join us. It was very uncommon, at this time, to find any one that would go near, much more, handle, a sick or dead person.

Mr. Carey, in page 106 of his third-edition,[2] has observed, that, "for the honor of human nature, it ought to be recorded, that some of the convicts in the gaol, a part of the term of whose confinement had been remitted as a reward for their peaceable, orderly behavior, voluntarily offered themselves as nurses to attend the sick at Bush-hill; and have, in that capacity, conducted themselves with great fidelity, &c. Here it ought to be remarked, (although Mr. Carey hath not done it) that two thirds of the persons, who rendered these essential services, were people of colour, who, on the application of the elders of the African church, (who met to consider what they could do for the help of the sick) were liberated, on condition of their doing the duty of nurses at the hospital at Bushhill; which they as voluntarily accepted to do, as they did faithfully discharge, this severe and disagreeable duty—May the Lord reward them, both temporally and spiritually.

When the sickness became general, and several of the physicians died, and most of the survivors were exhausted by sickness or fatigue; that good man, Doctor Rush, called us more immediately to attend upon the Sick, knowing we could both bleed; he told us we could increase our utility, by attending to his instructions, and accordingly directed us where to procure medicine duly prepared with proper directions how to administer them, and at what stages of the disorder to bleed; and when we found ourselves incapable of judging what was proper to be done, to apply to him, and he would, if able, attend them himself, or end Edward Fisher, his pupil, which he often did; and Mr. Fisher manifested his humanity, by an affectionate attention for their relief.—This has been no small satisfaction to us; for, we think, that when the instruments, in the hand of God, for saving the lives of some hundreds of our suffering fellow mortals.

We feel ourselves sensibly aggrieved by the censorious epithets of many, who did not render the least assistance in the time of necessity, yet are liberal of their censure of us, for the prices paid for our services, when no one knew how to make a proposal

---

[1] Two of whom were Richard Allen's brothers.

[2] See: Mathew Carey. *A Short Account Of The Mignant Fever, Lately Prevalent In Philidelphia: With A Statement Of The Proceedings That Took Place On The Subject In Different United States.* Third Edition, Improved. (Philadelphia: Printed By The Author. November 30, 1793)

to any one they wanted to assist them. At first we made no charge, but let it to those we served in removing their dead, to give what they thought fit—we set no price, until the reward was fixed by those we had served. After paying the people we had to assist us, our compensation is much less than many will believe.

We do assure the public, that *all* the money we have received, for burying, and for coffins which we ourselves purchased and procured, has not defrayed the expense of wages which we had to pay to those whom we employed to assist us. The following statement is accurately made:

CASH RECEIVED.

The whole amount of cash we received for burying the dead, and for burying beds, is, ------- £233 10 4

CASH PAID.

For coffins, for which we have received nothing - £33 0 0

For the hire of five men, 3 of them 70 days each, and the other two, 63 days each, at 22/6 per day, -----378 0 0

411 0 0

Depts due us, for which we expect but little, - £110 0 0

From the statement, for the truth of which we solemly vouch, it is evident, and we sensibly feel the operation of the fact, that we are out of pocket, --------£177 9 8

Besides the cost of hearses, maintenance of our families for 70 days, (being the period of our labours) and the support of the five hired men, during the respective times of their being employed; which expences, together with sundry gifts we occasionally made to poor families, might reasonably and properly be introduced, to show our actual situation with regard to profit—but it is enough to exhibit to the public, from the above specified items, *of cash paid and cash received,* without taking into view the other expences, that, by the employment we were engaged in, we have lost £177 9 8. But, if the other expences, which we have actually paid, are added to that sum, how much then may we not say we have suffered! We leave the public to Judge.

It may possibly appear strange to some who know how constantly we were employed, that we should have received no more cash than £233 10 4. But repeat our assurance, that this is the fact, and we add another, which will serve the better to explain it: We have buried *several hundreds* of poor persons and strangers, for which service we have never received, nor never asked any compensation.

We feel ourselves hurt most by a partial, censorious paragraph, in Mr. Carey's second edition, of his account of the sickness, &c. in Philadelphia; pages 76 and 77, where he asperses the blacks alone, for having taken the advantage of the distressed situation of the people. That some extravagant prices were paid, we admit; but how came they to be demanded? the reason is plain. It was with difficulty persons could be had to supply the wants of the sick, as nurses;—applications became more and more numerous, the consequence was, when we procured them at six dollars per week, and called upon them to go where they were wanted, we found they were gone elsewhere; here was a disappointment; upon enquiring the cause, we found, they had been allured away by others who offered greater wages, until they got from two to four dollars per day. We had no restraint upon the people. It was natural for people in low circumstances to accept a voluntary, bounteous reward; especially under the loathsomness of many of the sick, when nature shuddered at the thoughts of the infection, and the talk assigned was aggravated by lunacy, and being left much alone with them. Had Mr. Carey been solicited to such an undertaking, for hire, *Query,* "What would he have demanded? but Mr. Carey, although chosen a member of that band of worthies who have so eminently distinguished themselves by their labours, for the relief of the sick and helpless—yet, quickly after his election, left them to struggle with their arduous and hazardous talk, by leaving the city. 'Tis true Mr. Carey was no hireling, and had a right to flee, and upon his return, to plead the cause of those who fled; yet, we think, he was wrong in giving so partial and injurious an account of the black nurses; if they have taken avantage of the public distress? Is it any more than he hath done of its desire for information. We beleive he has made more money by the sale of his "scraps" than a dozen of the greatest extortioners among the black nurses. The great prices paid did not escape the observation of that worthy and vigilant magistrate, Mathew Clarkson, mayor of the city, and requested we would use our influence, to lessen the wages of the nurses, but on informing him the cause, ie. that of the people over-bidding one another, it was concluded unnecessary to attempt any thing on that head; therefore it was left to the people concerned. That there were some few black people guilty of plundering the distressed, we acknowledge; but in that they only are pointed out, and made mention of, we esteem partial and injurious; we know as many whites who were guilty of it; but this is looked over, while the blacks are held up to censure.—Is it a greater crime for a black to pilfer, than for a white to privateer?

We wish not to offend, but when an unprovoked attempt is made, to make us blacker than we are, it becomes less necessary to be over cautious on that account; therefore we shall take the liberty to tell of the conduct of some of the whites.

We know, six pounds was demanded by, and paid, to a white woman, for putting a corpse into a coffin; and forty dollars was demanded, and paid, to four white men, for bringing it down the stairs.

Mr. and Mrs. Taylor both died in one night; a white woman had the care of them; after they were dead she called on Jacob Servoss, esq. for her pay, demanding six pounds for laying them out; upon seeing a bundle with her, he suspected she had pilfered; on searching her, Mr. Taylor's buckles were found in her pocket, with other things.

An elderly lady, Mrs. Malony, was given into the care of a white woman, she died, we were called to remove the corpse, when we came the women was laying so drunk that she did not know what we were doing, but we know she had one of Mrs. Malony's rings on her finger, and another in her pocket.

Mr. Carey tells us, Bush-hill exhibited as wretched a picture of human misery, as ever existed. A profligate abandoned set of nurses and attendants (hardly any of good character could at that time be procured,) rioted on the provisions and comforts, prepared for the sick, who (unless at the hours when the doctors attended) were left almost entirely destitute of every assistance. The dying and dead were indiscriminately mingled together. The ordure and other evacuations of the sick, were allowed to remain in the most offensive state imaginable. Not the smallest appearance of order or regularity existed. It was in fact a great human slaughter house, where numerous victims were immolated at the altar of intemperance.

It is unpleasant to point out the bad and unfeeling conduct of any colour, yet the defence we have undertaken obliges us to remark that although "hardly any of good character at that time could be procured" yet only two black women were, at this time in the hospital, and they were retained and the others discharged when it was reduced to order and good government.

The bad consequences many of our colour apprehend from a partial relation of our conduct are, that it will prejudice the minds of the people in general against us—because it is impossible that one individual, can have knowledge of all, therefore at some future day, when some of the most virtuous, that were upon most praise—worthy motives, induced to serve the sick, may fall into the service of a family that are strangers to him, or her, and it is discovered that it is one of those stigmatised wretches, what may we suppose will be the consequence? It is not reasonable to think the person will be abhored, despised, and perhaps dismissed from employment, to their great disadvantage, would not this be hard? and have we not therefore sufficient reason to seek for redress? We can with certainty assure the public that have seen more humanity, more real sensibility from the poor blacks, than from the poor whites. When many of the former, of their own accord rendered sevices where extreme necessity called for it, the general part of the poor white people were so dismayed, that instead of attempting to be useful, they in a manner hid themselves—a remarkable instance of this—A poor afflicted dying man, stood at his chamber window, praying and beseeching every one that passed by, to help him to a drink of water; a number of white people passed, and instead of being moved by the poor man's distress, they hurried as fast as they could out of the sound of his cries—until at length a gentleman, who seemed to be a foreigner came up, he could not pass by, but had not resolution enough to go into the house, he held eight dollars in his hand, and offered it to several as a reward for giving the poor man a drink of water, but was refused by every one, until a poor black man came up, the gentleman offered the eight dollars to him, if he would relieve the poor man with a little water, "Master" replied the good natured fellow, "I will supply the gentleman with water, but surely I will not take your money for it" nor could he be prevailed upon to accept his bounty: he went in, supplied, named Sampsom, went constantly from house to house where distress was, and no assistance without fee or reward; he was smote with the disorder, and died, after his death his family were neglected by those he had served.

Sarah Bass, a poor black widow, gave all the assistance she could, in several families, for which she did not receive any thing; and when any thing was offered her, she left it to the option of those she served.

A woman of our colour, nursed Richard Mason and son, when they died, Richard's widow considering the risk the poor woman had run, and from observing the fears that sometimes rested on her mind, expected she would have demanded something considerable, but upon asking what she demanded, her reply was half a dollar per day. Mrs. Mason, intimated it was not sufficient for her attendance, she replied it was enough for what she had done, and would take no more. Mrs. Mason's feelings were such, that she settled an annuity of six pounds a year, on her, for life. Her name is Mary Scott.

An elderly black woman nursed---------with great diligence and attention; when recovered he asked what he must give for her services---------she replied "a dinner master on a cold winter's day," and thus she went from place to place rendering every service in her power without an eye to reward.

A young black woman, was requested to attend one night upon a white man and his wife, who were very ill, no other person could be had—great wages were offered her—she replied, I will not go for money, if I go for money God will see it, and may be make me take the disorder and die, but if I go, and take no money, he may spare my life. She went about nine o'clock, and found them both on the floor; she could procure no candle or other light, but staid with them about two hours, and then left them. They both died that night. She was afterward very ill with the fever—her life was spared.

Caesar Cranchal, a black man, offered his services to attend the sick, and said, I will not take your money, I will not sell my life for money. It is said he died with the flux.

A black lad, at the Widow Gilpin's, was intrusted with his young Master's keys, on his leaving the city, and trasacted his business, with greatest honesty, and dispatch, having unloaded a vessel for him in the time, and loaded it again.

A woman, that nursed David Bacon, charged with exemplary moderation, and said she would not have any more.

It may be said, in vindication of the conduct of those, who discovered ignorance or incapacity in nursing, that it is, in itself, a considerable art, derived from experience, as well as the exercise of the finer feelings of humanity—this experience, nine tenths of those employed, it is probable were wholly strangers to.

We do not recollect such acts of humanity from the poor white people, in all the round we have been engaged in. We could mention many other instances of the like nature, but think it needless.

It is unpleasant for us to make these remarks, but justice to our colour, demands it. Mr. Carey pays William Gray and us a complient; he says, our services and others of their colour, have been very great &c. By naming us, he leaves these others, in the hazardous state of being classed with those who are called the "vilest." The few that were discovered to merit public censure, were brought to justice, which ought to have sufficed, without being canvassed over in his "Trifle" of a pamphlet—which causes us to be more particular, and endeavour to recall the esteem of the public for our friends, and the people of colour, as far as they may be found worthy; for we conceive, and experience proves it, that an ill name is easier given than taken away. We have many unprovoked enemies, who begrudge us the liberty we enjoy, and are glad to hear of any compliant against our colour, be it just or unjust; in consequence of which we are more earnestly endeavouring all in our power, to warn, rebuke, and exhort our African friends, to keep a conscience void of offence towards God and man; and, at the same time, would not be backward to interfere, when stigmas or oppression appear pointed at, or attempted against them, unjustly; and, we are confident, we shall stand justified in the fight of the candid and judicious, for such conduct.

Mr. Carey's first, second, and third editions, are gone forth into the world, and in all probability, have been read by thousands that will never read his fourth—consequently, any alteration he may hereafter make, in the paragraph alluded to, cannot have the desired effect, or atone for the past; therefore we apprehend it necessary to publish our thoughts on the occasion. Had Mr. Carey said, a number of white and black Wretches eagerly frized on the opportunity to extort from the distressed, and some few of both were detected in plundering the sick, it might extenuate, in a great degree, the having made mention of the blacks.

We can assure the public, there were as many white as black people, detected in pilfering, although the number of the latter, employed as nurses, was twenty times as great as the former, and that there is, in our option, as great a proportion of white, as of black, inclined to such practices. It is rather to be admired, that so few instances of pilfering and robbery happened, considering the great opportunities there were for such things: we do not know of more than five black people, suspected of any thing clandestine, out of the great number employed; the people were glad to get any person to assist them—a black was preferred, because it was supposed, they were not so likely to take the disorder, the most worthless were acceptable, so that it would have been no cause of wonder, if twenty causes of compliant occurred, for one that hath. It has been alledged, that many of the sick, were neglected by the nurses; we do not wonder at it, considering their situation, in many instances, up night and day, without any one to relieve them, worn down with fatigue, and want of sleep, they could not in many cases, render that assistance, which was needful: where we visited, the causes of compliant on this score, were not numerous. The case of the nurses, in many instances, were deserving of commiseration, the patient raging and frightful to behold; it has frequently required two persons, to hold them from runing way, other have made attempts to jump out of a window, in many chambers they were nailed down, and the door was kept locked, to prevent them from running away, or breaking their necks, others lay vomiting blood, and screaming enough to chill them with horror. Thus were many of the nurses circumstanced, alone, until the patient died, then called away to another scene of distress, and thus have been for a week or ten days left to do the best they could without any sufficient rest, many of them having some of their dearest connections sick at the time, and suffering for want, while their husband, wife, father, mother, &c. have been engaged in the service of the white people. We mention this to shew the difference between this and nursing the common cases, we have suffered equally with the whites, our distress hath been very great, but much unknown to the white people. Few have been the whites the paid attention to us while the black were engaged in the other's service. We can assure the public we have taken four and five black people in a day to be buried. In several instances when they have been seized with the sickness while nursing, they have been turned out of the house, and wandering and destitute until taking shelter wherever they could (as many of them would not be admitted to their former homes) they have languished alone and we know of one who even died in a stable. Others acted with more tenderness, when their nurses were taken sick they had proper care taken of them at their houses. We know of two instances of this.

It is even to this day a generally received opinion in this city, that our colour was not so liable to the sickness as the white. We hope our friends will pardon us for setting this matter in its true state.

The public were informed that in the West-Indies and other places where this terrible malady had been, it was observed the blacks were not affected with it—Happy would it have been for you, and much more so for us, if this observation had been verified by our experience.

When the people of colour had the sickness and died, we were imposed upon and told it was not with the prevailing sickness, until it became too notorious to be denied, then we were told some few died but not many. Thus were our services extorted *at the peril of our lives*, yet you accuse us of extorting *a little money from you*.

The bill of mortality for the year 1793, published by Matthew Whitehead, and John Ormrod, clerks, and Joseph Dolby, sexton, will convince any reasonable man that will examine it, that as many coloured people died in proportion as others. In 1792, there were 67 of our colour buried, and in 1793 it amounted to 305; thus the burials among us have increased more than fourfold, was not this to a great degree the effects of the services of the unjustly vilified black people?

Perhaps it may be acceptable to the reader to know how we found the sick affected by the sickness; our opportunities of hearing and seeing them have been very great. They were taken with a chill, a headach, a sick stomach, with pains in their limbs and back this is the way the sickness in general began, but all were not affected alike, some appeared but slightly affected with some of these symptoms, what confirmed us in the opinion of a person being smitten was the colour of their eyes. In some it raged more furiously than in others—some have languished for seven and ten days, and appeared to get better the day, or some hours before they died, while others were cut off in one, two, or three days, but their compliants were similar. Some lost their reason and raged with all the fury madness could produce, and died in strong convulsions. Others retained their reason to the last, and seemed rather to fall asleep than die. We could not help remarking that the former were of strong passions, and the latter of a mild temper. Numbers died in a kind of dejection, they concluded they must go, (so the phrase for dying was) and therefore in a kind of fixed determined state of mind went off.

It struck our minds with awe, to have application made by those in health, to take charge of them in their sickness, and of their funeral. Such applications have been made to us; many appeared as though they thought they must die, and not live, some have lain on the floor, to be measured for their coffin and grave. A gentleman called one evening, to request a good nurse might be got for him, when he was sick, and to superintend his funeral, and gave particular directions how he would have it conducted, it seemed a suprising circumstance, for the man appeared at the time, to be in perfect health, but calling two or three days after to see him, found a woman dead in the house, and the man so far gone, that to administer any thing for his recovery, was needless—he died that evening. We mention this, as an instance of the dejection and despondence, that took hold on the minds of thousands, and are of opinion, it aggravated the case of many, while others who bore up chearfully, got up again, that probably would otherwise have died.

When the mortality came to its greatest stage, it was impossible to procure sufficient assistance, therefore many whose friends, and relations had left them, died unseen, and unassisted. We have found them in various situations, some laying on the floor, as bloody as if they had been dipt in it, without any appearance of their having had, even a drink of water for their relief; others laying on a bed with their clothes on, as if they had came in fatigued, and lain down to rest; some appeared, as if they had fallen dead on the floor, from the position we found them in.

Truly our task was hard, yet through mercy, we were enabled to go on.

One thing we observed in several instances—when we were called, on the first appearance of the disorder to bleed, the person frequently, on the opening a vein before the operation was near over, felt a change for the better, and expressed a relief in their chief complaints; and we made it a practice to take more blood from them, than is usual in other cases; these in a general way recovered; those who did omit bleeding any considerable time, after being taken by the sickness, rarely expressed any change they felt in the operation.

We feel a great satisfaction in believing, that we have been useful to the sick, and thus publicly thank Doctor Rush, for enabling us to be so. We have bled upwards of eight hundred people, and do declare, we have not received to the value of a dollar and a half, therefor: we were willing to imitate the Doctor's benevolence, who sick or well, kept his house open day and night, to give that assistance he could in this time of trouble.

Several affecting instances occurred, when we were engaged in burying the dead. We have been called to bury some, who when we came, we found alive; at other places we found a parent dead, and none but little innocent babes to be seen, whose ignorance led them to think their parent was asleep; on account of their situation, and their little prattle, we have been so wounded and our feelings so hurt, that we almost concluded to withdraw from our undertaking, but seeing others so backward, we still went on.

An affecting instance.—A woman died, we were sent for to bury her, on our going into the house and taking the coffin in, a dear little innocent accosted us, with, mamma is asleep, don't wake her; but when she saw us put her in the coffin, the distress of the child was so great, that it almost overcame us; when she demanded why we put her mamma in the box? We did not know how to answer her, but committed her to the care of a neighbour, and left her with the heavy hearts. In other places where we have been to take the corpse of a parent, and have found a group of little ones alone, some of them in a measure capable of knowing their situation, their cries and the innocent confusion of the little ones, seemed almost too much for human nature to bear. We have picked up little children that were wandering they knew not where, whose (parents were cut off) and taken them to the orphan house, for at this time the dread that prevailed over people's minds was so general, that it was a rare instance to see one neighbour visit another, and even friends when they met in the streets were afraid of each other, much less would they admit into their houses the distressed orphan that had been where the sickness was; this extreme seemed in some instances to have the appearance of barbarity; with reluctance we call to mind the many opportunities there were in the power of individuals to be useful to their fellow-men, yet through the terror of the times was omited. A black man riding through the street, saw a man push a woman out of the house, the woman staggered and fell on her face in the gutter, and was not able to turn herself, the black man thought she was drunk, but observing she was in danger of suffocation alighted, and taking the woman up found her perfectly sober, but so far gone with the disorder that she was not able to help herself; the hard hearted man that threw her down, shut the door and left her—in such a situatuon she might have perished in a few minutes: we heard of it, and took her to Bush-hill. Many of the white people, that ought to be patterns for us to follow after, have acted in a manner that would make humanity shudder. We remember an instance of cruelty, which we trust, no black man would be guilty of: two sisters orderly, decent white women were sick with the fever, one of them recovered so as to come to the door; a neighbouring white man saw her, and in an angry tone asked her if her sister was dead or not? She answered no, upon which he replied, damn her, if she don't die before morning, I will make her die. The poor woman shocked at such an expression, from this monster of a man, made a modest reply, upon which he snatched up a tub of water, and would have dashed it over her, if he had not been prevented by a black man; he then went and took a couple of fowls out of a coop, (which had been given them for nourishment) and threw them into an open alley; he had his wish, the poor woman that he would make die, died the night. A white man threatened to shoot us, if we passed by his house with a corpse: we buried him three days after.

We have been pained to see the widows come to us, crying and wringing their hands, and in very great distress, on account of their husbands' death; having nobody to help them, they were obliged to come to get their husbands buried, their neighbours were afraid to go to their help or to condole with them, we ascribe such unfriendly conduct to the frailty of human nature, and not to wilful unkindness, or hardness of heart.

Notwithstanding the compliment Mr. Carey hath paid us, we have found reports spread, of our taking between one, and two hundred beds, from houses where people died; such slanderers as these, who propagate such wilful lies are dangerous, although unworthy notice. We wish if any person hath the least suspicion of us, they would endeavour to bring us to the punishment which such atrocious conduct must deserve; and by this means, the innocent will be cleared from reproach, and the guilty known.

We shall now conclude with the following old proverb, which we think applicable to those of our colour—who exposed their lives in the late afflicting dispensation:—

God and a soldier, all man do adore,
In time of war, and not before;
When the war is over, and all things righted,
God is forgotten, and the soldier slighted.

To Matthew Clarkson, EsQ.

Mayor of the City of Philadelphia

SIR,

For the personal respect we bear you, and for the satisfaction of the Mayor, we declare, that to the best of our remembrance we had the care of the following beds and no more.—

Two belonging to James Starr we buried; upon taking them up, we found one damaged; the blankets, &c. belonging to it were stolen; it was refused to be accepted of by his son Moses, it was buried again, and remains so for ought we know; the other was returned and accepted of.

We buried two belonging to Samuel Fisher, merchant, one of them was taken up by us, to carry a sick person on to Bush-hill, and there left; the other was buried in a grave, under a corpse.

Two beds were buried for Thomas Willing, one six feet deep in his garden, and lime and water trown upon it; the other was in the Potter's field, and further knowledge of it we have not.

We burned one bed with other furniture, and cloathing belonging to the late Mayor, Samuel Powel, on his farm on the west side of Schuylkill river;—we buried one of his beds.

For---------Dickenson, we buried a bed in a lot of Richard Allen; which we have a good cause to believe was stolen.

One bed was buried for a person in front street, whose name is unknown to us, it was buried in the Potter's field, by a person employed for the purpose; we told him he might take it up against after it had been buried a week, and apply it his own use, as he said he had lately been discharged from the hospital and had none to lay on.

Thomas Leiper's two beds were buried in the Potter's field, and remained there a week, and then taken up by us, for the use of the sick that we took to Bushhill, and left there.

We buried one for---------Smith, in the Potter's field, which was returned except the furniture, which we believe was stolen.

One other we buried for---------Davis, in Vine Street, it was buried near Schuylkill, and we believe continues so.

A bed from---------Guests in Second Streets, was buried in the Potter's field, and is there yet, for any thing we know.

One bed we buried in the Presbyterian burial ground the corner of Pine and Fourth Street, and we believe was taken up by the owner, Thomas Mitchel.

---------Millegan in Second Street, had a bed buried by us in the Potter's field—we have no futher knowledge of it.

This is a true state of matters respecting the beds, as far as we were concerned, we never undertook the charge of more than their burial, knowing they were liable to be taken away by evil minded persons. We think it beneath the dignity of an honest man, (although injured in his reputation by wicked and envious persons) to vindicate or support his character, by an oath or legal affirmation; we fear not our enemies, let them come forward with their charges, we will not flinch, and if they can fix any crime upon us, we refuse not to suffer.

Sir,

You have cause to believe our lives were endangered in more cases than one, in the time of the late mortality, and that we were so discouraged, that had it not been for your persuasion, we would would have relinquished our disagreeable and dangerous employment—and we hope there is no impropriety in soliciting a certificate of your approbation of our conduct, so far as it hath come to your knowledge.

With an affectionate regard and esteem,
We are your friends,
Absalom Jones.
Richard Allen.
January 7th 1794

****

Having, during the prevalence of the late malignant disorder, had almost daily opportunites of seeing the conduct of Absalom Jones and Richard Allen, and the people employed by them, to bury the dead—I with cheerfulness give this testimony of my approbation of their proceeedings, as far as the same came under my notice. Their diligence, attention and decency of deportment, afforded me, at the time, much satisfaction.

MATTHEW CLARKSON, Mayor.

Philadelphia, January 23, 1794

****

An Address to those who keep slaves, and approve the practice.

The judicious part of mankind will think it unreasonable, that a superior good conduct is looked for, from our race, by those who stigmatize us as men, whose baseness is incurable, and may therefore be held in a state of servitude, that a merciful man would not doom a beast to; yet you try what you can to prevent our rising from the state of barbarism, you represent us to be in, but we can tell you, from a degree of experience, that a black man, although reduced to the most abject state human nature is capable of, short of real madness, can think, reflect, and feel injuries, although it may not be with the same degree of keen resentment and revenge, that you who have been and are our greatest oppressors, would manifest if reduced to to pitiable condition of a slave. We believe if you would try the experiment of taking a few black children, and cultivate their minds with the same care, and let them have the same prospect in view, as to living in the world, as you would with for your own children, you would find upon the trail, they were not inferior in mental endowments.

We do not wish to make you angry, but excite your attention to consider, how hateful slavery is in the light of that God, who hath destroyed kings and princes, for their oppression of the poor slaves; Pharaoh and his princes with the posterity of king Saul, were destroyed by the protector and avenger of slaves. Would you not suppose the Israelites to be utterly unfit for freedom and that it was impossible for them to attain to any degree of excellence? Their history shews how slavery had debased their spirits. Men must be willfully blind and extremely partial, that cannot see the contrary effects of liberty and slavery upon the mind of man; we freely confess the vile habits often acquired in a state of sertitude, are not easily thown off; the example of the Israelites shews, who with all that Moses could do to reclaim them from it, still continued in their former habits more or less; and why will you look for better from us? Why will you look for grapes from thorns, or figs from thistles? It is in our posterity enjoying the same privileges with your own, that you ought to look for better things.

When you are pleaded with, do not you reply as Pharaoh did, "wherefore do ye Moses and Aaron, let the people from their work, behold the people of the land, now are many, and you make them rest from their burdens." We wish you to consider, that God himself was the first pleader of the cause of slaves.

That God who knows the hearts of all men, and the propensity of a slave to hate his oppressor, hath stictly forbidden it to his chosen people, "thou shalt not abhor an Egyptian, because thou wast a stanger in his land. Deut. xxiii. 7." The meek and humble Jesus, the great pattern of humanity, and every other virtue that can adorn and dignify men, hath commanded to love our enemies, to do good to them that hate and despitefully use us. We feel the obligations, we wish to impress them on the minds of our black brethren, and that we may all forgive you, as we wish to be forgiven; we think it a great mercy to have all anger and bitterness removed from our minds, we appeal to your own feelings, if it is not very disquieting to feel yourselves under the dominion of a wrathful disposition.

If you love your children, if you love your your country, if you love the God of love, clear your hands from slaves, burden not your children or country with them. Our hearts have been sorrowful for the late bloodshed of the oppressors, as well as the oppressed, both appear guilty of each others blood, in the sight of him who said, he that sheddeth man's blood, by man shall his blood be shed.

Will you, because you have reduced us to the unhappy condition our colour is in, plead our incapacity for freedom, and our contented condition under oppression, as a sufficient cause for keeping us under the grievous yoke? We have shewn the cause of our incapacity, we will also shew, why we appear contented; were we to attempt to plead with our masters, it would be deemed insolence, for which cause they appear as contented as they can in your sight, but the dreadful insurrections they have made, when opportunity has offered, is enough to convince a reasonable man, that great uneasiness and not contentment, is the inhabitant of their hearts.

God himself hath pleaded their cause, he hath from time to time raised up instruments for that purpose, sometimes mean and contemptible in your fight; at other times he hath used such as it hath pleased him with whom you have not thought it beneath your dignity to contend, many have been convinced of their error, condemned their former conduct, and become zealous advocates for the cause of those, whom you will not suffer to plead for themselves.

****

To the People of Colour

Feeling an engagement of mind for your welfare, we address you with an affectionate sympathy, having been ourselves slaves, and as desirous of freedom as any of you; yet the bands of bondage were so strong, that no way appeared for our release, yet at times a hope arose in our hearts that a way would open for it, and when our minds were mercifully visited with the feeling of the love of God, then these hopes increased, and a confidence arose that he would make way for our enlargement, and as a patient waiting was necessary, we were sometimes favoured with it, at other times we were very impatient, then the prospect of liberty almost vanished away, and we were in darkness and perplexity.

We mention our experience to you, that your hearts may not sink at the discouraging prospects you may have, and that you may put your truth in God, who sees your condition, and as a merciful father pitieth his children, so doth God pity them that love him; and as your hearts are inclined to serve God, you will feel an affectionate regard towards your masters and mistresses, and the whole family where you live, this will be seen by them, and tend to promote your liberty, especially with such as have feeling masters, and if they are otherwise you will have the favour and love of God dwelling in your hearts, which you will value more than anything else, which will be a consolation in the worst condition you can be in, and no master can deprive you of it; and as life is short and uncertain, and the chief end of our having a being in this world, is to be prepared for a better, we wish you to think of this more than any thing else: then will you have a view of that freedom which the sons of God enjoy; and if the troubles of your condition end with your lives, you will be admitted to the freedom which God hath prepared for those of all colours that love him; here the power of the most cruel master ends, and all sorrow and tears are wiped away.

To you who are favoured with freedom, let yor conduct manifest your gratitude toward the compassionate masters who have set you free, and let no rancour or ill—will lodge in your breasts for any bad treatment you may have received from any; if you do, you transgress against God, who will not hold you guiltless, he would not suffer it even in his beloved people Israel, and can you think he will allow it unto us?

There is much gratitude due from our colour towards the white people, very many of them are instruments in the hand of God for our good, even such as have held us in captivity, are now pleading our cause with earnestness and zeal; and we are sorry to say, that too many think more of the evil, than of the good they have received, and instead of taking the advice of their friends, turn from it with indifference; much depends upon us for the help of our colour more than many are aware; if we are lazy and idle, the enemies of freedom plead it as a cause why we ought not to be free, and say we are better in a state of servitude, and that giving us our liberty would be an injury to us, and by such conduct we strengthen the bands of oppression, and keep many in bondage who are more worthy than ourselves; we intreat you to consider the obligations we lay under, to help forward the cause of freedom, we who know how bitter the cup is of which the slave hath to drink, O how ought we to feel for those who yet remain in bondage? Will even our friends excuse, will God pardon us, for the part we act in making strong the hands of the enemies of our colour.

A short Address of the Friends of Him who hath no Helper.

We feel an inexpressible gratitude towards you, who have engaged in the cause of the African race; you have wrought a deliverance for many, from more than Egyptian bondage, your labours are unremitted for their complete redemption, from the cruel subjection they are in. You feel our afflictions—you sympathize with us in the heartrendering distress, when the husband is separated from the wife, and the parents from the children, who are never more to meet in this world. The tear of sensibility trickles from your eye, to see the sufferings that keep us from increasing—your righteous indignation is roused at the means taken to supply the place of the murdered babe. You see our race more effectually destroyed, then was in Pharaoh's power to effect, upon Israel's sons; you blow the trumpet against the mighty evil, you make the tyrants tremble; you strive to raise the slave, to the dignity of a man; you take our children by the hand, to lead them in the path of virtue, by your care of their education; you are not ashamed to call the most abject of our race, brethren, children of one father, who made of one blood all the nations of the earth: You ask for this, nothing for yourselves, nothing but what is worthy the cause you are engaged in; nothing but that we would be friends to ourselves, and not strengthen the bands of oppression, by an evil conduct, when led out of the house of bondage. May he, who hath arisen to plead our cause, and engaged you as volunteers in the service, add to your numbers, until the princes shall come forth from Egypt, and Ethiopia stretch out her hand unto God.

Absalom Jones
Richard Allen

Ye Ministers, that are call'd to preaching,
Teachers, and exhorters too;
Awake! behold your harvest wasting!
Arise! there is no rest for you.

To think upon that strict commandment,
That God has on his teachers laid,

The sinner's blood, who dies unwarned,
Shalt fall upon their Shepherd's head.

But oh! dear brethren, let's be doing,
Behold the nation's in distress,
The Lord of Hosts forbid their ruin,
Before the day of grace is past.

We read of wars and great commotions,
Before the great and dreadful day,
Oh, Sinners! turn your sinful courses
And trifle not your time away.

But Oh! dear sinners, that's not all that's dreadful!
You must before your God appear!
To give an account of your transactions,
And how you spent your time, when here.

[Manuscript note. leaf bound inside back cover]:
Died on the 14th of April 1813 a child of Daniel Sampson 6 mounths [months] old.no docter [doctor] attended it died of the belly complaint. Enteird [Interred?] in st. Thomas' African church burial ground

Absalom Jones

STATE OF THE UNION ADDRESS, 2001

President George W. Bush

Little more than a week after the terrorist attacks of September 11, 2001, President George W. Bush delivered his State of the Union Address. Speaking to the fear, anger, and confusion felt by many United States citizens, President Bush spoke with resolve as he presaged foreign and domestic policies that continue to be at the heart of "the war on terror." The occasion called for a powerful speech, and the 2001 State of the Union was understood as such. Consider what President Bush's language tells us about the demands of the rhetorical moment.

Mr. Speaker, Mr. President Pro Tempore, members of Congress, and fellow Americans, in the normal course of events, presidents come to this chamber to report on the state of the union. Tonight, no such report is needed; it has already been delivered by the American people.

We have seen it in the courage of passengers who rushed terrorists to save others on the ground. Passengers like an exceptional man named Todd Beamer. And would you please help me welcome his wife Lisa Beamer here tonight?

(APPLAUSE)

We have seen the state of our union in the endurance of rescuers working past exhaustion.

We've seen the unfurling of flags, the lighting of candles, the giving of blood, the saying of prayers in English, Hebrew and Arabic.

We have seen the decency of a loving and giving people who have made the grief of strangers their own.

My fellow citizens, for the last nine days, the entire world has seen for itself the state of union, and it is strong.

(APPLAUSE)

Tonight, we are a country awakened to danger and called to defend freedom. Our grief has turned to anger and anger to resolution. Whether we bring our enemies to justice or bring justice to our enemies, justice will be done.

(APPLAUSE)

I thank the Congress for its leadership at such an important time.

All of America was touched on the evening of the tragedy to see Republicans and Democrats joined together on the steps of this Capitol singing "God Bless America."

And you did more than sing. You acted, by delivering $40 billion to rebuild our communities and meet the needs of our military. Speaker Hastert, Minority Leader Gephardt, Majority Leader Daschle and Senator Lott, I thank you for your friendship, for your leadership and for your service to our country.

(APPLAUSE)

And on behalf of the American people, I thank the world for its outpouring of support.

America will never forget the sounds of our national anthem playing at Buckingham Palace, on the streets of Paris and at Berlin's Brandenburg Gate.

We will not forget South Korean children gathering to pray outside our embassy in Seoul, or the prayers of sympathy offered at a mosque in Cairo.

We will not forget moments of silence and days of mourning in Australia and Africa and Latin America.

Nor will we forget the citizens of 80 other nations who died with our own. Dozens of Pakistanis, more than 130 Israelis, more than 250 citizens of India, men and women from El Salvador, Iran, Mexico and Japan, and hundreds of British citizens.

America has no truer friend than Great Britain. (APPLAUSE) Once again, we are joined together in a great cause.

I'm so honored the British prime minister has crossed an ocean to show his unity with America.

Thank you for coming, friend.

(APPLAUSE)

On September the 11, enemies of freedom committed an act of war against our country. Americans have known wars, but for the past 136 years they have been wars on foreign soil, except for one Sunday in 1941. Americans have known the casualties of war, but not at the center of a great city on a peaceful morning.

Americans have known surprise attacks, but never before on thousands of civilians. All of this was brought upon us in a single day, and night fell on a different world, a world where freedom itself is under attack.

Americans have many questions tonight. Americans are asking, "Who attacked our country?"

The evidence we have gathered all points to a collection of loosely affiliated terrorist organizations known as al Qaeda. They are some of the murderers indicted for bombing American embassies in Tanzania and Kenya and responsible for bombing the *USS Cole.*

Al Qaeda is to terror what the Mafia is to crime. But its goal is not making money, its goal is remaking the world and imposing its radical beliefs on people everywhere.

The terrorists practice a fringe form of Islamic extremism that has been rejected by Muslim scholars and the vast majority of Muslim clerics; a fringe movement that perverts the peaceful teachings of Islam.

The terrorists' directive commands them to kill Christians and Jews, to kill all Americans and make no distinctions among military and civilians, including women and children. This group and its leader, a person named Osama bin Laden, are linked to many other organizations in different countries, including the Egyptian Islamic Jihad, the Islamic Movement of Uzbekistan.

There are thousands of these terrorists in more than 60 countries.

They are recruited from their own nations and neighborhoods and brought to camps in places like Afghanistan where they are trained in the tactics of terror. They are sent back to their homes or sent to hide in countries around the world to plot evil and destruction. The leadership of al Qaeda has great influence in Afghanistan and supports the Taliban regime in controlling most of that country. In Afghanistan we see al Qaeda's vision for the world. Afghanistan's people have been brutalized, many are starving and many have fled.

Women are not allowed to attend school. You can be jailed for owning a television. Religion can be practiced only as their leaders dictate. A man can be jailed in Afghanistan if his beard is not long enough. The United States respects the people of Afghanistan—after all, we are currently its largest source of humanitarian aid—but we condemn the Taliban regime.

(APPLAUSE)

It is not only repressing its own people, it is threatening people everywhere by sponsoring and sheltering and supplying terrorists.

By aiding and abetting murder, the Taliban regime is committing murder. And tonight the United States of America makes the following demands on the Taliban:

—Deliver to United States authorities all of the leaders of al Qaeda who hide in your land.

—Release all foreign nationals, including American citizens you have unjustly imprisoned.

—Protect foreign journalists, diplomats and aid workers in your country.

—Close immediately and permanently every terrorist training camp in Afghanistan. And hand over every terrorist and every person and their support structure to appropriate authorities.

—Give the United States full access to terrorist training camps, so we can make sure they are no longer operating.

These demands are not open to negotiation or discussion.

(APPLAUSE)

The Taliban must act and act immediately.

They will hand over the terrorists or they will share in their fate. I also want to speak tonight directly to Muslims throughout the world. We respect your faith. It's practiced freely by many millions of Americans and by millions more in countries that America counts as friends. Its teachings are good and peaceful, and those who commit evil in the name of Allah blaspheme the name of Allah.

(APPLAUSE)

The terrorists are traitors to their own faith, trying, in effect, to hijack Islam itself.

The enemy of America is not our many Muslim friends. It is not our many Arab friends. Our enemy is a radical network of terrorists and every government that supports them.

(APPLAUSE)

Our war on terror begins with al Qaeda, but it does not end there.

It will not end until every terrorist group of global reach has been found, stopped and defeated.

(APPLAUSE)

Americans are asking "Why do they hate us?"

They hate what they see right here in this chamber: a democratically elected government. Their leaders are self-appointed. They hate our freedoms: our freedom of religion, our freedom of speech, our freedom to vote and assemble and disagree with each other.

They want to overthrow existing governments in many Muslim countries such as Egypt, Saudi Arabia and Jordan. They want to drive Israel out of the Middle East. They want to drive Christians and Jews out of vast regions of Asia and Africa.

These terrorists kill not merely to end lives, but to disrupt and end a way of life. With every atrocity, they hope that America grows fearful, retreating from the world and forsaking our friends. They stand against us because we stand in their way.

We're not deceived by their pretenses to piety.

We have seen their kind before. They're the heirs of all the murderous ideologies of the 20th century. By sacrificing human life to serve their radical visions, by abandoning every value except the will to power, they follow in the path of fascism, Nazism and totalitarianism. And they will follow that path all the way to where it ends in history's unmarked grave of discarded lies. Americans are asking, "How will we fight and win this war?"

We will direct every resource at our command—every means of diplomacy, every tool of intelligence, every instrument of law enforcement, every financial influence, and every necessary weapon of war—to the destruction and to the defeat of the global terror network.

Now, this war will not be like the war against Iraq a decade ago, with a decisive liberation of territory and a swift conclusion. It will not look like the air war above Kosovo two years ago, where no ground troops were used and not a single American was lost in combat.

Our response involves far more than instant retaliation and isolated strikes. Americans should not expect one battle, but a lengthy campaign unlike any other we have ever seen. It may include dramatic strikes visible on TV and covert operations secret even in success.

We will starve terrorists of funding, turn them one against another, drive them from place to place until there is no refuge or no rest.

And we will pursue nations that provide aid or safe haven to terrorism. Every nation in every region now has a decision to make: Either you are with us or you are with the terrorists.

From this day forward, any nation that continues to harbor or support terrorism will be regarded by the United States as a hostile regime. Our nation has been put on notice, we're not immune from attack. We will take defensive measures against terrorism to protect Americans. Today, dozens of federal departments and agencies, as well as state and local governments, have responsibilities affecting homeland security.

These efforts must be coordinated at the highest level. So tonight, I announce the creation of a Cabinet-level position reporting directly to me, the Office of Homeland Security. And tonight, I also announce a distinguished American to lead this effort, to strengthen American security: a military veteran, an effective governor, a true patriot, a trusted friend, Pennsylvania's Tom Ridge.

He will lead, oversee and coordinate a comprehensive national strategy to safeguard our country against terrorism and respond to any attacks that may come. These measures are essential. The only way to defeat terrorism as a threat to our way of life is to stop it, eliminate it and destroy it where it grows.

Many will be involved in this effort, from FBI agents, to intelligence operatives, to the reservists we have called to active duty. All deserve our thanks, and all have our prayers. And tonight a few miles from the damaged Pentagon, I have a message for our military: Be ready. I have called the armed forces to alert, and there is a reason.

The hour is coming when America will act, and you will make us proud.

This is not, however, just America's fight. And what is at stake is not just America's freedom. This is the world's fight. This is civilization's fight. This is the fight of all who believe in progress and pluralism, tolerance and freedom.

We ask every nation to join us.

We will ask and we will need the help of police forces, intelligence service and banking systems around the world. The United States is grateful that many nations and many international organizations have already responded with sympathy and with support—nations from Latin America to Asia to Africa to Europe to the Islamic world.

Perhaps the NATO charter reflects best the attitude of the world: An attack on one is an attack on all. The civilized world is rallying to America's side.

They understand that if this terror goes unpunished, their own cities, their own citizens may be next. Terror unanswered can not only bring down buildings, it can threaten the stability of legitimate governments.

And you know what? We're not going to allow it.

(APPLAUSE)

Americans are asking, "What is expected of us?"

I ask you to live your lives and hug your children. I know many citizens have fears tonight, and I ask you to be calm and resolute, even in the face of a continuing threat.

I ask you to uphold the values of America and remember why so many have come here.

We're in a fight for our principles, and our first responsibility is to live by them. No one should be singled out for unfair treatment or unkind words because of their ethnic background or religious faith.

I ask you to continue to support the victims of this tragedy with your contributions. Those who want to give can go to a central source of information, Libertyunites.org, to find the names of groups providing direct help in New York, Pennsylvania and Virginia. The thousands of FBI agents who are now at work in this investigation may need your cooperation, and I ask you to give it. I ask for your patience with the delays and inconveniences that may accompany tighter security and for your patience in what will be a long struggle.

I ask your continued participation and confidence in the American economy. Terrorists attacked a symbol of American prosperity; they did not touch its source.

America is successful because of the hard work and creativity and enterprise of our people. These were the true strengths of our economy before September 11, and they are our strengths today.

And finally, please continue praying for the victims of terror and their families, for those in uniform and for our great country. Prayer has comforted us in sorrow and will help strengthen us for the journey ahead. Tonight I thank my fellow Americans for what you have already done and for what you will do.

And ladies and gentlemen of the Congress, I thank you, their representatives, for what you have already done and for what we will do together.

Tonight we face new and sudden national challenges. We will come together to improve air safety, to dramatically expand the number of air marshals on domestic flights and take new measures to prevent hijacking.

We will come together to promote stability and keep our airlines flying with direct assistance during this emergency.

(APPLAUSE)

We will come together to give law enforcement the additional tools it needs to track down terror here at home.

We will come together to strengthen our intelligence capabilities to know the plans of terrorists before they act and to find them before they strike.

(APPLAUSE)

We will come together to take active steps that strengthen America's economy and put our people back to work.

Tonight, we welcome two leaders who embody the extraordinary spirit of all New Yorkers, Governor George Pataki and Mayor Rudolph Giuliani.

As a symbol of America's resolve, my administration will work with Congress and these two leaders to show the world that we will rebuild New York City.

After all that has just passed, all the lives taken and all the possibilities and hopes that died with them, it is natural to wonder if America's future is one of fear.

Some speak of an age of terror. I know there are struggles ahead and dangers to face. But this country will define our times, not be defined by them.

As long as the United States of America is determined and strong, this will not be an age of terror. This will be an age of liberty here and across the world.

Great harm has been done to us. We have suffered great loss. And in our grief and anger we have found our mission and our moment.

Freedom and fear are at war. The advance of human freedom, the great achievement of our time and the great hope of every time, now depends on us.

Our nation, this generation, will lift the dark threat of violence from our people and our future. We will rally the world to this cause by our efforts, by our courage. We will not tire, we will not tire, we will not falter and we will not fail.

(APPLAUSE)

It is my hope that in the months and years ahead life will return almost to normal. We'll go back to our lives and routines and that is good.

Even grief recedes with time and grace.

But our resolve must not pass. Each of us will remember what happened that day and to whom it happened. We will remember the moment the news came, where we were and what we were doing.

Some will remember an image of a fire or story of rescue. Some will carry memories of a face and a voice gone forever.

And I will carry this. It is the police shield of a man named George Howard who died at the World Trade Center trying to save others.

It was given to me by his mom, Arlene, as a proud memorial to her son. It is my reminder of lives that ended and a task that does not end.

I will not forget the wound to our country and those who inflicted it. I will not yield, I will not rest, I will not relent in waging this struggle for freedom and security for the American people. The course of this conflict is not known, yet its outcome is certain. Freedom and fear, justice and cruelty, have always been at war, and we know that God is not neutral between them.

(APPLAUSE)

Fellow citizens, we'll meet violence with patient justice, assured of the rightness of our cause and confident of the victories to come.

In all that lies before us, may God grant us wisdom and may he watch over the United States of America. Thank you.

(APPLAUSE)

WHAT TO THE SLAVE IS THE FOURTH OF JULY?

Frederick Douglass

Frederick Douglass delivered the address, "What to the Slave is the Fourth of July?" on the fifth day of July in 1852. Douglass's rather pointed timing mirrors the interrogation of national values at the heart of his address. The questioning structure of the address continually exposes the distance between democratic virtue and the racial regime of the antebellum United States. As you read, notice Douglass's way of questioning the assumptions underlying the celebratory occasion of the national holiday.

What to the Slave is The Fourth of July?: An Address Delivered in Rochester, New York, on 5 July 1852

Frederick Douglass, *Oration, Delivered in Corinthian Hall, Rochester, July 5th, 1852* (Rochester, 1852). Other texts in *Frederick Douglass' Paper*, 9 July 1852; Douglass, *Bondage and Freedom*, 441–50; Woodson, *Negro Orators and Their Orations*, 197–223; James M. Gregory, *Frederick Douglass, the Orator* (New York, 1893), 103–06, misdated 4 July 1852; Foner, *Life and Writings*, 2: 181–204.

Between five and six hundred people paying 12 1/2 cents each gathered at Corinthian Hall to hear Douglass give a Fourth of July address on 5 July 1852. Douglass, who spoke at the invitation of the Rochester Ladies' Anti-Slavery Society, spent a great deal of time preparing this speech. "I have been engaged in writing a Speech," he wrote Gerrit Smith on 7 July 1852, "for the *4th*. July which has taken up much of my extra time for the last two or three weeks. You will readily think that the Speech ought to be good that has required So much time. Well, Some here think [it] was a good Speech—foremost among those who think So, is my friend Julia. She tells me it was *excellent!*" James Sperry presided until Lindley Murray Moore was elected to chair the meeting. The Reverend S. Ottman of Rush offered a prayer and the Reverend Robert R. Raymond of Syracuse read the Declaration of Independence. His recitation, said *Frederick Douglass' Paper*, was "eloquent and admirable, eliciting much applause throughout." Douglass delivered the principal address. Upon resuming his seat at the conclusion of his remarks, he was greeted by "a universal burst of applause." William C. Bloss then suggested a vote of thanks for Douglass. The vote was carried unanimously. "A request was . . . made, *that the Address be published in pamphlet form*, and seven hundred copies of it were subscribed on the spot." The meeting adjourned and Douglass subsequently published a pamphlet version of the speech. Douglass to Gerrit Smith, 7 July 1852, 14 July 1852, Gerrit Smith Papers, NSyU; *FDP*, 1, 16 July 1852.

M*r. President, Friends and Fellow Citizens:* He who could address this audience without a quailing sensation, has stronger nerves than I have. I do not remember ever to have appeared as a speaker before any assembly more shrinkingly, nor with greater distrust of my ability, than I do this day. A feeling has crept over me, quite unfavorable to the exercise of my limited powers of speech. The task before me is one which requires much previous thought and study for its proper performance. I know that apologies of this sort are generally considered flat and unmeaning. I trust, however, that mine will not be so considered. Should I seem at ease, my appearance would much misrepresent me. The little experience I have had in addressing public meetings, in country school houses, avails me nothing on the present occasion.

The papers and placards say, that I am to deliver a 4th [of] July oration. This certainly sounds large, and out of the common way, for me. It is true that I have often had the privilege to speak in this beautiful Hall, and to address many who now honor me with their presence. But neither their familiar faces, nor the perfect gage I think I have of Corinthian Hall, seems to free me from embarrassment.

The fact is, ladies and gentlemen, the distance between this platform and the slave plantation, from which I escaped, is considerable—and the difficulties to be overcome in getting from the latter to the former, are by no means slight. That I am here to-day is, to me, a matter of astonishment as well as of gratitude. You will not, therefore, be surprised, if in what I have to say, I evince no elaborate preparation, nor grace my speech with any high sounding exordium. With little experience and with less learning, I have been able to throw my thoughts hastily and imperfectly together; and trusting to your patient and generous indulgence, I will proceed to lay them before you.

This, for the purpose of this celebration, is the 4th of July. It is the birthday of your National Independence, and of your political freedom. This, to you, is what the Passover was to the emancipated people of God. It carries your minds back to the day, and to the act of your great deliverance; and to the signs, and to the wonders, associated with that act, and that day. This celebration also marks the beginning of another year of your national life; and reminds you that the Republic of America is now 76 years old. I am glad, fellow-citizens, that your nation is so young. Seventy-six years, though a good old age for a man, is but a mere speck in the life of a nation. Three score years and ten is the allotted time for individual men;[1] but nations number their years by thousands. According to this fact, you are, even now, only in the beginning of your national career, still lingering in the period of childhood. I repeat, I am glad this is so. There is hope in the thought, and hope is much needed, under the dark clouds which lower above the horizon. The eye of the reformer is met with angry flashes, portending disastrous times; but his heart may well beat lighter at the thought that America is young, and that she is still in the impressible stage of her existence. May he not hope that high lessons of wisdom, of justice and of truth, will yet give direction to her destiny? Were the nation older, the patriot's heart might be sadder, and the reformer's brow heavier. Its future might be shrouded in gloom, and the hope of its prophets go out in sorrow. There is consolation in the thought that America is young. Great

[1]Ps. 90:10.

streams are not easily turned from channels, worn deep in the course of ages. They may sometimes rise in quiet and stately majesty, and inundate the land, refreshing and fertilizing the earth with their mysterious properties. They may also rise in wrath and fury, and bear away, on their angry waves, the accumulated wealth of years of toil and hardship. They, however, gradually flow back to the same old channel, and flow on as serenely as ever. But, while the river may not be turned aside, it may dry up, and leave nothing behind but the withered branch, and the unsightly rock, to howl in the abyss-sweeping wind, the sad tale of departed glory. As with rivers so with nations.

Fellow-citizens, I shall not presume to dwell at length on the associations that cluster about this day. The simple story of it is that, 76 years ago, the people of this country were British subjects. The style and title of your "sovereign people" (in which you now glory) was not then born. You were under the British Crown. Your fathers esteemed the English Government as the home government; and England as the fatherland. This home government, you know, although a considerable distance from your home, did, in the exercise of its parental prerogatives, impose upon its colonial children, such restraints, burdens and limitations, as, in its mature judgement, it deemed wise, right and proper.

But, your fathers, who had not adopted the fashionable idea of this day, of the infallibility of government, and the absolute character of its acts, presumed to differ from the home government in respect to the wisdom and the justice of some of those burdens and restraints. They went so far in their excitement as to pronounce the measures of government unjust, unreasonable, and oppressive, and altogether such as ought not to be quietly submitted to. I scarcely need say, fellow-citizens, that my opinion of those measures fully accords with that of your fathers. Such a declaration of agreement on my part would not be worth much to anybody. It would, certainly, prove nothing, as to what part I might have taken, had I lived during the great controversy of 1776. To say *now* that America was right, and England wrong, is exceedingly easy. Everybody can say it; the dastard, not less than the noble brave, can flippantly discant on the tyranny of England towards the American Colonies. It is fashionable to do so; but there was a time when to pronounce against England, and in favor of the cause of the colonies, tried men's souls.[2] They who did so were accounted in their day, plotters of mischief, agitators and rebels, dangerous men. To side with the right, against the wrong, with the weak against the strong, and with the oppressed against the oppressor! *here* lies the merit, and the one which, of all others, seems unfashionable in our day. The cause of liberty may be stabbed by the men who glory in the deeds of your fathers. But, to proceed.

Feeling themselves harshly and unjustly treated by the home government, your fathers, like men of honesty, and men of spirit, earnestly sought redress. They petitioned and remonstrated; they did so in a decorous, respectful, and loyal manner. Their conduct was wholly unexceptionable. This, however, did not answer the purpose. They saw themselves treated with sovereign indifference, coldness and scorn. Yet they persevered. They were not the men to look back.

[2]Douglass paraphrases the opening line of Thomas Paine's first Crisis paper, 23 December 1776. The *Political Writings of Thomas Paine,* 2 vols. (Boston, 1859), 1:75.

As the sheet anchor takes a firmer hold, when the ship is tossed by the storm, so did the cause of your fathers grow stronger, as it breasted the chilling blasts of kingly displeasure. The greatest and best of British statesmen admitted its justice, and the loftiest eloquence of the British Senate came to its support. But, with that blindness which seems to be the unvarying characteristic of tyrants, since Pharoah and his hosts were drowned in the Red Sea, the British Government persisted in the exactions complained of.

The madness of this course, we believe, is admitted now, even by England; but we fear the lesson is wholly lost on our present rulers.

Oppression makes a wise man mad. Your fathers were wise men, and if they did not go mad, they became restive under this treatment. They felt themselves the victims of grievous wrongs, wholly incurable in their colonial capacity. With brave men there is always a remedy for oppression. Just here, the idea of a total separation of the colonies from the crown was born! It was a startling idea, much more so, than we, at this distance of time, regard it. The timid and the prudent (as has been intimated) of that day, were, of course, shocked and alarmed by it.

Such people lived then, had lived before, and will, probably, ever have a place on this planet; and their course, in respect to any great change, (no matter how great the good to be attained, or the wrong to be redressed by it), may be calculated with as much precision as can be the course of the stars. They hate all changes, but silver, gold and copper change! Of this sort of change they are always strongly in favor.

These people were called tories in the days of your fathers; and the appellation, probably, conveyed the same idea that is meant by a more modern, though a somewhat less euphonious term, which we often find in our papers, applied to some of our old politicians.[3]

Their opposition to the then dangerous thought was earnest and powerful; but, amid all their terror and affrighted vociferations against it, the alarming and revolutionary idea moved on, and the country with it.

On the 2d of July, 1776, the old Continental Congress, to the dismay of the lovers of ease, and the worshippers of property, clothed that dreadful idea with all the authority of national sanction. They did so in the form of a resolution; and as we seldom hit upon resolutions, drawn up in our day, whose transparency is at all equal to this, it may refresh your minds and help my story if I read it.

> "Resolved, That these united colonies *are*, and of right, ought to be free and Independent States; that they are absolved from all allegiance to the British

[3]Douglass probably refers to the term "Hunker," which was applied to conservative Democrats in New York state politics in the late 1840s. The label originally referred to the fiscally conservative faction of the state's Democratic party, but after an 1847 split over the Wilmot Proviso the term also differentiated Unionist followers of William L. Marcy and Daniel S. Dickinson from the antislavery "Barnburners." A study of the election of 1848 suggests that the word "was used to ridicule the conservatives' strenuous efforts to get a large 'hunk' of the spoils of office; others thought it was a corruption of the Dutch slang word *hanker,* freely translated as 'greedy.'" By the 1850s the "Hunker" designation was commonly applied to the great conservative Unionist majority of the Democratic party throughout the North. Rayback, *Free Soil,* 16n; Nichols, *Democratic Machine,* 18, 198–99.

Crown; and that all political connection between them and the State of Great Britain *is*, and ought to be, dissolved."[4]

Citizens, your fathers made good that resolution. They succeeded; and to-day you reap the fruits of their success. The freedom gained is yours; and you, therefore, may properly celebrate this anniversary. The 4th of July is the first great fact in your nation's history—the very ring-bolt in the chain of your yet undeveloped destiny.

Pride and patriotism, not less than gratitude, prompt you to celebrate and to hold it in perpetual remembrance. I have said that the Declaration of Independence is the RING-BOLT to the chain of your nation's destiny; so, indeed, I regard it. The principles contained in that instrument are saving principles. Stand by those principles, be true to them on all occasions, in all places, against all foes, and at whatever cost.

From the round top of your ship of state, dark and threatening clouds may be seen. Heavy billows, like mountains in the distance, disclose to the leeward huge forms of flinty rocks! That *bolt* drawn, that *chain* broken, and all is lost. *Cling to this day—cling to it*, and to its principles, with the grasp of a storm-tossed mariner to a spar at midnight.

The coming into being of a nation, in any circumstances, is an interesting event. But, besides general considerations, there were peculiar circumstances which make the advent of this republic an event of special attractiveness.

The whole scene, as I look back to it, was simple, dignified and sublime.

The population of the country, at the time, stood at the insignificant number of three millions. The country was poor in the munitions of war. The population was weak and scattered, and the country a wilderness unsubdued. There were then no means of concert and combination, such as exist now. Neither steam nor lightning had then been reduced to order and discipline. From the Potomac to the Delaware was a journey of many days. Under these, and innumerable other disadvantages, your fathers declared for liberty and independence and triumphed.

Fellow Citizens, I am not wanting in respect for the fathers of this republic. The signers of the Declaration of Independence were brave men. They were great men too—great enough to give fame to a great age. It does not often happen to a nation to raise, at one time, such a number of truly great men. The point from which I am compelled to view them is not, certainly, the most favorable; and yet I cannot contemplate their great deeds with less than admiration. They were statesmen, patriots and heroes, and for the good they did, and the principles they contended for, I will unite with you to honor their memory.

They loved their country better than their own private interests; and, though this is not the highest form of human excellence, all will concede that it is a rare virtue, and that when it is exhibited, it ought to command respect. He who will, intelligently, lay down his life for his country, is a man whom it is not in human nature to despise.

---

[4]A text of the quoted resolution, which indicates that the word "totally" appeared before the word "dissolved," may be found in W. C. Ford et al., eds., *Journal of the Continental Congress, 1774–1789,* 34 vols. (Washington, D.C., 1904–37), 5:507

Your fathers staked their lives, their fortunes, and their sacred honor, on the cause of their country. In their admiration of liberty, they lost sight of all other interests.

They were peace men; but they preferred revolution to peaceful submission mission to bondage. They were quiet men; but they did not shrink from agitating against oppression. They showed forbearance; but that they knew its limits. They believed in order; but not in the order of tyranny. With them, nothing was "*settled*" that was not right. With them, justice, liberty and humanity were "*final*;" not slavery and oppression. You may well cherish the memory of such men. They were great in their day and generation. Their solid manhood stands out the more as we contrast it with these degenerate times.

How circumspect, exact and proportionate were all their movements! How unlike the politicians of an hour! Their statesmanship looked beyond the passing moment, and stretched away in strength into the distant future. They seized upon eternal principles, and set a glorious example in their defence. Mark them!

Fully appreciating the hardship to be encountered, firmly believing in the right of their cause, honorably inviting the scrutiny of an on-looking world, reverently appealing to heaven to attest their sincerity, soundly comprehending the solemn responsibility they were about to assume, wisely measuring the terrible odds against them, your fathers, the fathers of this republic, did, most deliberately, under the inspiration of a glorious patriotism, and with a sublime faith in the great principles of justice and freedom, lay deep the corner-stone of the national superstructure, which has risen and still rises in grandeur around you.

Of this fundamental work, this day is the anniversary. Our eyes are met with demonstrations of joyous enthusiasm. Banners and pennants wave exultingly on the breeze. The din of business, too, is hushed. Even Mammon seems to have quitted his grasp on this day. The ear-piercing fife and the stirring drum unite their accents with the ascending peal of a thousand church bells. Prayers are made, hymns are sung, and sermons are preached in honor of this day; while the quick martial tramp of a great and multitudinous nation, echoed back by all the hills, valleys and mountains of a vast continent, bespeak the occasion one of thrilling and universal interest—a nation's jubilee.

Friends and citizens, I need not enter further into the causes which led to this anniversary. Many of you understand them better than I do. You could instruct me in regard to them. That is a branch of knowledge in which you feel, perhaps, a much deeper interest than your speaker. The causes which led to the separation of the colonies from the British crown have never lacked for a tongue. They have all been taught in your common schools, narrated at your firesides, unfolded from your pulpits, and thundered from your legislative halls, and are as familiar to you as household words. They form the staple of your national poetry and eloquence.

I remember, also, that, as a people, Americans are remarkably familiar with all facts which make in their own favor. This is esteemed by some as a national trait—perhaps a national weakness. It is a fact, that whatever makes for the wealth or for the reputation of Americans, and can be had *cheap!* will be found by Americans. I shall not be charged with slandering Americans, if I say I think the American side of any question may be safely left in American hands.

I leave, therefore, the great deeds of your fathers to other gentlemen whose claim to have been regularly descended will be less likely to be disputed than mine!

The Present

My business, if I have any here to-day, is with the present. The accepted time with God and his cause is the ever-living now.

> "Trust no future, however pleasant,
> Let the dead past bury its dead;
> Act, act in the living present,
> Heart within, and God overhead."[5]

We have to do with the past only as we can make it useful to the present and to the future. To all inspiring motives, to noble deeds which can be gained from the past, we are welcome. But now is the time, the important time. Your fathers have lived, died, and have done their work, and have done much of it well. You live and must die, and you must do your work. You have no right to enjoy a child's share in the labor of your fathers, unless your children are to be blest by your labors. You have no right to wear out and waste the hard-earned fame of your fathers to cover your indolence. Sydney Smith[6] tells us that men seldom eulogize the wisdom and virtues of their fathers, but to excuse some folly or wickedness of their own. This truth is not a doubtful one. There are illustrations of it near and remote, ancient and modern. It was fashionable, hundreds of years ago, for the children of Jacob to boast, we have "Abraham to our father," when they had long lost Abraham's faith and spirit.[7] That people contented themselves under the shadow of Abraham's great name, while they repudiated the deeds which made his name great. Need I remind you that a similar thing is being done all over this country to-day? Need I tell you that the Jews are not the only people who built the tombs of the prophets, and garnished the sepulchres of the righteous? Washington could not die till he had broken the chains of his slaves.[8]

---

[5]The stanza quoted is from Henry Wadsworth Longfellow's "A Psalm of Life." *Poems,* 22.

[6]Anglican minister Sydney Smith (1771–1845) was a master satirical essayist and lecturer. A highly partisan Whig, his barbed wit was employed to great effect in the causes of Catholic emancipation and parliamentary reform. *DNB,* 18: 527–31.

[7]Douglass appears to allude to a passage from Luke 3 : 8: "Bring forth therefore fruits worthy of repentance, and begin not to say within yourselves, We have Abraham to *our* father: for I say unto you, That God is able of these stones to raise up children unto Abraham."

[8]At the time of his death, George Washington owned or held claim to over three hundred slaves. His will provided that "upon the decease of my wife it is my . . . desire that all slaves whom I hold in my own right shall receive their freedom." Matthew T. Mellon, *Early American Views on Negro Slavery From the Letters and Papers of the Founders of the Republic* (1934; New York, 1969), 29–81; Walter H. Mazyck, *George Washington and the Negro* (Washington, D.C., 1932), 133–38; George Livermore, *An Historical Research Respecting the Opinions of the Founders of the Republic on Negroes as Slaves, as Citizens, and as Soldiers,* 4th ed. (1862; New York, 1968), 28–31; Paul F. Boller, "Washington, the Quakers, and Slavery," *JNH,* 46: 83–88 (April 1961).

Yet his monument is built up by the price of human blood, and the traders in the bodies and souls of men, shout—"We have Washington to *our father.*" Alas! that it should be so; yet so it is.

> "The evil that men do, lives after them,
> The good is oft' interred with their bones."[9]

Fellow-citizens, pardon me, allow me to ask, why am I called upon to speak here to-day? What have I, or those I represent, to do with your national independence? Are the great principles of political freedom and of natural justice, embodied in that Declaration of Independence, extended to us? and am I, therefore, called upon to bring our humble offering to the national altar, and to confess the benefits and express devout gratitude for the blessings resulting from your independence to us?

Would to God, both for your sakes and ours, that an affirmative answer could be truthfully returned to these questions! Then would my task be light, and my burden easy and delightful. For *who* is there so cold, that a nation's sympathy could not warm him? Who so obdurate and dead to the claims of gratitude, that would not thankfully acknowledge such priceless benefits? Who so stolid and selfish, that would not give his voice to swell the hallelujahs of a nation's jubilee, when the chains of servitude had been torn from his limbs? I am not that man. In a case like that, the dumb might eloquently speak, and the "lame man leap as an hart."

But, such is not the state of the case. I say it with a sad sense of the disparity between us. I am not included within the pale of this glorious anniversary! Your high independence only reveals the immeasurable distance between us. The blessings in which you, this day, rejoice, are not enjoyed in common. The rich inheritance of justice, liberty, prosperity and independence, bequeathed by your fathers, is shared by you, not by me. The sunlight that brought life and healing to you, has brought stripes and death to me. This Fourth [of] July is *yours*, not *mine*. *You* may rejoice, *I* must mourn. To drag a man in fetters into the grand illuminated temple of liberty, and call upon him to join you in joyous anthems, were inhuman mockery and sacrilegious irony. Do you mean, citizens, to mock me, by asking me to speak to-day? If so, there is a parallel to your conduct. And let me warn you that it is dangerous to copy the example of a nation whose crimes, towering up to heaven, were thrown down by the breath of the Almighty, burying that nation in irrecoverable ruin! I can to-day take up the plaintive lament of a peeled and woe-smitten people!

"By the rivers of Babylon, there we sat down. Yea! we wept when we remembered Zion. We hanged our harps upon the willows in the midst thereof. For there, they that carried us away captive, required of us a song; and they who wasted us required of us mirth, saying, Sing us one of the songs of Zion. How can we sing the Lord's song in a strange land? If I forget thee, O Jerusalem, let my right hand forget her cunning. If I do not remember thee, let my tongue cleave to the roof of my mouth."[10]

---

[9] *Julius Caesar,* act 3, sc. 2, line 76.

[10] Ps. 137 : 1–6.

Fellow-citizens; above your national, tumultous joy, I hear the mournful wail of millions! whose chains, heavy and grievous yesterday, are, to-day, rendered more intolerable by the jubilee shouts that reach them. If I do forget, if I do not faithfully remember those bleeding children of sorrow this day, "may my right hand forget her cunning, and may my tongue cleave to the roof of my mouth!" To forget them, to pass lightly over their wrongs, and to chime in with the popular theme, would be treason most scandalous and shocking, and would make me a reproach before God and the world. My subject, then fellow-citizens, is AMERICAN SLAVERY. I shall see, this day, and its popular characteristics, from the slave's point of view. Standing, there, identified with the American bondman, making his wrongs mine, I do not hesitate to declare, with all my soul, that the character and conduct of this nation never looked blacker to me than on this 4th of July! Whether we turn to the declarations of the past, or to the professions of the present, the conduct of the nation seems equally hideous and revolting. America is false to the past, false to the present, and solemnly binds herself to be false to the future. Standing with God and the crushed and bleeding slave on this occasion, I will, in the name of humanity which is outraged, in the name of liberty which is fettered, in the name of the constitution and the Bible, which are disregarded and trampled upon, dare to call in question and to denounce, with all the emphasis I can command, everything that serves to perpetuate slavery—the great sin and shame of America! "I will not equivocate; I will not excuse;"[11] I will use the severest language I can command; and yet not one word shall escape me that any man, whose judgement is not blinded by prejudice, or who is not at heart a slaveholder, shall not confess to be right and just.

But I fancy I hear some one of my audience say, it is just in this circumstance that you and your brother abolitionists fail to make a favorable impression on the public mind. Would you argue more, and denounce less, would you persuade more, and rebuke less, your cause would be much more likely to succeed. But, I submit, where all is plain there is nothing to be argued. What point in the anti-slavery creed would you have me argue? On what branch of the subject do the people of this country need light? Must I undertake to prove that the slave is a man? That point is conceded already. Nobody doubts it. The slaveholders themselves acknowledge it in the enactment of laws for their government. They acknowledge it when they punish disobedience on the part of the slave. There are seventy-two crimes in the State of Virginia, which, if committed by a black man, (no matter how ignorant he be), subject him to the punishment of death; while only two of the same crimes will subject a white man to the like punishment.[12] What is this but the acknowledgement that the slave is a moral, intellectual and responsible being? The manhood of the slave is conceded. It is admitted in the fact that Southern statute books are covered with enactments forbidding, under severe fines and penalties, the teaching of the slave to

[11]Douglass quotes from the first issue of the *Liberator,* in which William Lloyd Garrison promised, "I am in earnest—I will not equivocate—I will not excuse—I will not retreat a single inch—and *I will be heard.*" Lib., 1 January 1831; John L. Thomas, *The Liberator: William Lloyd Garrison* (Boston, 1963), 128.

[12]Douglass probably relies on [Weld], *American Slavery,* 149, which contrasts capital of fences in Virginia for slaves and whites.

read or to write. When you can point to any such laws, in reference to the beasts of the field, then I may consent to argue the manhood of the slave. When the dogs in your streets, when the fowls of the air, when the cattle on your hills, when the fish of the sea, and the reptiles that crawl, shall be unable to distinguish the slave from a brute, *then* will I argue with you that the slave is a man!

For the present, it is enough to affirm the equal manhood of the negro race. Is it not astonishing that, while we are ploughing, planting and reaping, using all kinds of mechanical tools, erecting houses, constructing bridges, building ships, working in metals of brass, iron, copper, silver and gold; that, while we are reading, writing and cyphering, acting as clerks, merchants and secretaries, having among us lawyers, doctors, ministers, poets, authors, editors, orators and teachers; that, while we are engaged in all manner of enterprises common to other men, digging gold in California, capturing the whale in the Pacific, feeding sheep and cattle on the hill-side, living, moving, acting, thinking, planning, living in families as husbands, wives and children, and, above all, confessing and worshipping the Christian's God, and looking hopefully for life and immortality beyond the grave, we are called upon to prove that we are men!

Would you have me argue that man is entitled to liberty? that he is the rightful owner of his own body? You have already declared it. Must I argue the wrongfulness of slavery? Is that a question for Republicans? Is it to be settled by the rules of logic and argumentation, as a matter beset with great difficulty, involving a doubtful application of the principle of justice, hard to be understood? How should I look to-day, in the presence of Americans, dividing, and subdividing a discourse, to show that men have a natural right to freedom? speaking of it relatively, and positively, negatively, and affirmatively. To do so, would be to make myself ridiculous, and to offer an insult to your understanding. There is not a man beneath the canopy of heaven, that does not know that slavery is wrong *for him*.

What, am I to argue that it is wrong to make men brutes, to rob them of their liberty, to work them without wages, to keep them ignorant of their relations to their fellow men, to beat them with sticks, to flay their flesh with the lash, to load their limbs with irons, to hunt them with dogs, to sell them at auction, to sunder their families, to knock out their teeth, to burn their flesh, to starve them into obedience and submission to their masters? Must I argue that a system thus marked with blood, and stained with pollution, is *wrong?* No! I will not. I have better employments for my time and strength, than such arguments would imply.

What, then, remains to be argued? Is it that slavery is not divine; that God did not establish it; that our doctors of divinity are mistaken? There is blasphemy in the thought. That which is inhuman, cannot be divine! *Who* can reason on such a proposition? They that can, may; I cannot. The time for such argument is past.

At a time like this, scorching irony, not convincing argument, is needed. O! had I the ability, and could I reach the nation's ear, I would, to-day, pour out a fiery stream of biting ridicule, blasting reproach, withering sarcasm, and stern rebuke. For it is not light that is needed, but fire; it is not the gentle shower, but thunder. We need the storm, the whirlwind, and the earthquake. The feeling of the nation must be quickened; the conscience of the nation must be roused; the propriety of the nation must be startled; the hypocrisy of the nation must be exposed; and its crimes against God and man must be proclaimed and denounced.

What, to the American slave, is your 4th of July? I answer: a day that reveals to him, more than all other days in the year, the gross injustice and cruelty to which he is the constant victim. To him, your celebration is a sham; your boasted liberty, an unholy license; your national greatness, swelling vanity; your sounds of rejoicing are empty and heartless; your denunciations of tyrants, brass fronted impudence; your shouts of liberty and equality, hollow mockery; your prayers and hymns, your sermons and thanksgivings, with all your religious parade, and solemnity, are, to him, mere bombast, fraud, deception, impiety, and hypocrisy—a thin veil to cover up crimes which would disgrace a nation of savages. There is not a nation on the earth guilty of practices, more shocking and bloody, than are the people of these United States, at this very hour.

Go where you may, search where you will, roam through all the monarchies and despotisms of the old world, travel through South America, search out every abuse, and when you have found the last, lay your facts by the side of the everyday practices of this nation, and you will say with me, that, for revolting barbarity and shameless hypocrisy, America reigns without a rival.

The Internal Slave Trade

Take the American slave-trade, which, we are told by the papers, is especially prosperous just now. Ex-Senator Benton[13] tells us that the price of men was never higher than now. He mentions the fact to show that slavery is in no danger. This trade is one of the peculiarities of American institutions. It is carried on in all the

---

[13]Thomas Hart Benton (1782–1858) served as a U.S. senator from Missouri from 1821 to 1851. Born near Hillsboro, North Carolina, Benton briefly studied at the University of North Carolina and at William and Mary College. Despite a promising start on a legal and political career in Tennessee, Benton migrated to Missouri after service in the War of 1812. Elected to the Senate upon Missouri's admission to the Union, he became an important Jacksonian Democrat and spokesman for western interests. When he failed to secure reelection to the Senate in 1850, Benton returned to Congress as a representative from 1853 to 1855 but lost his bid for a second term in 1854. Benton probably used his observation on slave prices to bolster his persistent denial that slaveholding interests were insecure in the Union. Although the remark does not appear in his published speeches attacking Calhoun's appeal for southern congressional unity in 1849 or in his major speeches delivered during the Senate debate on the 1850 compromise measures, Benton repeated this observation several years later when criticizing the 1850 secessionist movements in South Carolina and Mississippi: "[T]here is no danger to slavery in any slave State. Property is timid! and slave property above all: and the market is the test of safety and danger to all property. . . . Now, how is it with slave property, tried by this unerring standard? Has it been sinking in price since the year 1835? since the year of the first alarm manifesto in South Carolina, and the first of Mr. Calhoun's twenty years' alarm speeches in the Senate? On the contrary, the price has been constantly rising the whole time—and it is still rising although it has attained a height incredible to have been constantly rising the whole time—and it is still rising although it has attained a height incredible to have been predicted twenty years ago." Thomas Hart Benton, *Thirty Years' View,* 2 vols. (New York, 1854–56), 2: 782; Elbert B. Smith, *Magnificent Missourian: The Life of Thomas Hart Benton* (Philadelphia, 1958); William N. Chambers, *Old Bullion Benton: Senator from the West* (Boston, 1956); Theodore Roosevelt, Thomas H. Benton (Boston, 1899); *ACAB,* 1: 241–43; *DAB,* 2: 210–13.

large towns and cities in one-half of this confederacy; and millions are pocketed every year, by dealers in this horrid traffic. In several states, this trade is a chief source of wealth. It is called (in contradistinction to the foreign slave-trade) "*the internal slave-trade.*" It is, probably, called so, too, in order to divert from it the horror with which the foreign slave-trade is contemplated. That trade has long since been denounced by this government, as piracy. It has been denounced with burning words, from the high places of the nation, as an execrable traffic. To arrest it, to put an end to it, this nation keeps a squadron, at immense cost, on the coast of Africa. Everywhere, in this country, it is safe to speak of this foreign slave-trade, as a most inhuman traffic, opposed alike to the laws of God and of man. The duty to extirpate and destroy it, is admitted even by our DOCTORS OF DIVINITY. In order to put an end to it, some of these last have consented that their colored brethren (nominally free) should leave this country, and establish themselves on the western coast of Africa! It is, however, a notable fact that, while so much execration is poured out by Americans upon those engaged in the foreign slave-trade, the men engaged in the slave-trade between the states pass without condemnation, and their business is deemed honorable.

Behold the practical operation of this internal slave-trade, the American slave-trade, sustained by American politics and American religion. Here you will see men and women reared like swine for the market. You know what is a swine-drover? I will show you a man-drover. They inhabit all our Southern States. They perambulate the country, and crowd the highways of the nation, with droves of human stock. You will see one of these human flesh-jobbers, armed with pistol, whip and bowie-knife, driving a company of a hundred men, women, and children, from the Potomac to the slave market at New Orleans. These wretched people are to be sold singly, or in lots, to suit purchasers. They are food for the cotton-field, and the deadly sugar-mill. Mark the sad procession, as it moves wearily along, and the inhuman wretch who drives them. Hear his savage yells and his blood-chilling oaths, as he hurries on his affrighted captives! There, see the old man, with locks thinned and gray. Cast one glance, if you please, upon that young mother, whose shoulders are bare to the scorching sun, her briny tears falling on the brow of the babe in her arms. See, too, that girl of thirteen, weeping, *yes!* weeping, as she thinks of the mother from whom she has been torn! The drove moves tardily. Heat and sorrow have nearly consumed their strength; suddenly you hear a quick snap, like the discharge of a rifle; the fetters clank, and the chain rattles simultaneously; your ears are saluted with a scream, that seems to have torn its way to the centre of your soul! The crack you heard, was the sound of the slave-whip; the scream you heard, was from the woman you saw with the babe. Her speed had faltered under the weight of her child and her chains! that gash on her shoulder tells her to move on. Follow this drove to New Orleans. Attend the auction; see men examined like horses; see the forms of women rudely and brutally exposed to the shocking gaze of American slave-buyers. See this drove sold and separated forever; and never forget the deep, sad so as that arose from that scattered multitude. Tell me citizens, WHERE, under the sun, you can witness a spectacle more fiendish and shocking. Yet this is but a glance at the American slave-trade, as it exists, at this moment, in the ruling part of the United States.

I was born amid such sights and scenes. To me the American slave-trade is a terrible reality. When a child, my soul was often pierced with a sense of its horrors. I lived on Philpot Street, Fell's Point, Baltimore, and have watched from the wharves, the slave ships in the Basin, anchored from the shore, with their cargoes of human flesh, waiting for favorable winds to waft them down the Chesapeake. There was, at that time, a grand slave mart kept at the head of Pratt Street, by Austin Woldfolk.[14] His agents were sent into every town and county in Maryland, announcing their arrival, through the papers, and on flaming "*hand-bills*," headed CASH FOR NEGROES. These men were generally well dressed men, and very captivating in their manners. Ever ready to drink, to treat, and to gamble. The fate of many a slave has depended upon the turn of a single card; and many a child has been snatched from the arms of its mother by bargains arranged in a state of brutal drunkenness.

The flesh-mongers gather up their victims by dozens, and drive them, chained, to the general depot at Baltimore. When a sufficient number have been collected here, a ship is chartered, for the purpose of conveying the forlorn crew to Mobile, or to New Orleans. From the slave prison to the ship, they are usually driven in the darkness of night; for since the anti-slavery agitation, a certain caution is observed.

In the deep still darkness of midnight, I have been often aroused by the dead heavy footsteps, and the piteous cries of the chained gangs that passed our door. The anguish of my boyish heart was intense; and I was often consoled, when speaking to my mistress in the morning, to hear her say that the custom was very wicked; that she hated to hear the rattle of the chains, and the heart-rending cries. I was glad to find one who sympathised with me in my horror.

Fellow-citizens, this murderous traffic is, to-day, in active operation in this boasted republic. In the solitude of my spirit, I see clouds of dust raised on the highways of the South; I see the bleeding footsteps; I hear the doleful wail of fettered humanity, on the way to the slave-markets, where the victims are to be sold like *horses*, *sheep*, and *swine*, knocked off to the highest bidder. There I see the tenderest

---

[14]Actually Austin Woolfolk of Augusta, Georgia, who came to Baltimore in 1819 and became the best-known slave trader in the area in the 1820s and early 1830s. Attracted by the city's commercial shipping facilities, Woolfolk and his relatives made Baltimore the headquarters for their activities and annually transported between 230 and 460 slaves to New Orleans. Agents for Woolfolk were sent into counties throughout Maryland and his advertisements in local newspapers throughout the 1820s indicated that Woolfolk would pay "the highest prices and in cash" for young slaves. In his *Narrative,* Douglass noted that "if a slave was convicted of any high misdemeanor, became unmanageable, or evinced a determination to run away, he was brought immediately here [Lloyd's home plantation], severely whipped, put on board the sloop, carried to Baltimore, and sold to Austin Woolfolk, or some other slave trader, as a warning to the slaves remaining." Woolfolk's slave-trading activities declined in the early 1830s owing to increased competition from larger firms, a decrease in the number of slaves available for sale to traders as owners who left the area took the slaves into the western territories or manumitted them, and the increased opposition of Marylanders to slave trading within the state. Douglass, *Narrative,* 32; William Calderhead, "The Role of the Professional Slave Trader in a Slave Economy: Austin Woolfolk, A Case Study," *Civil War History,* 23: 195–211 (September 1977).

ties ruthlessly broken, to gratify the lust, caprice and rapacity of the buyers and sellers of men. My soul sickens at the sight.

> "Is this the land your Fathers loved,
> The freedom which they toiled to win?
> Is this the earth whereon they moved?
> Are these the graves they slumber in?"[15]

But a still more inhuman, disgraceful, and scandalous state of things remains to be presented.

By an act of the American Congress, not yet two years old, slavery has been nationalized in its most horrible and revolting form. By that act, Mason & Dixon's line has been obliterated; New York has become as Virginia; and the power to hold, hunt, and sell men, women, and children as slaves remains no longer a mere state institution, but is now an institution of the whole United States. The power is co-extensive with the star-spangled banner and American Christianity. Where these go, may also go the merciless slave-hunter. Where these are, man is not sacred. He is a bird for the sportsman's gun. By that most foul and fiendish of all human decrees, the liberty and person of every man are put in peril. Your broad republican domain is hunting ground for *men. Not* for thieves and robbers, enemies of society, merely, but for men guilty of no crime. Your lawmakers have commanded all good citizens to engage in this hellish sport. Your President, your Secretary of State, your *lords, nobles*, and ecclesiastics, enforce, as a duty you owe to your free and glorious country, and to your God, that you do this accursed thing. Not fewer than forty Americans have, within the past two years, been hunted down and, without a moment's warning, hurried away in chains, and consigned to slavery and excruciating torture. Some of these have had wives and children, dependent on them for bread; but of this, no account was made. The right of the hunter to his prey stands superior to the right of marriage, and to *all* rights in this republic, the rights of God included! For black men there are neither law, justice, humanity, nor religion. The Fugitive Slave *Law* makes MERCY TO THEM, A CRIME; and bribes the judge who tries them. An American JUDGE GETS TEN DOLLARS FOR EVERY VICTIM HE CONSIGN to slavery, and five, when he fails to do so. The oath of any two villains is sufficient, under this hell-black enactment, to send the most pious and exemplary black man into the remorseless jaws of slavery! His own testimony is nothing. He can bring no witnesses for himself. The minister of American justice is bound by the law to hear but *one* side; and *that* side, is the side of the oppressor.[16] Let this damning

---

[15]Douglass slightly alters the first four lines of John Greenleaf Whittier's "Stanzas for the Times." Whittier, *Poetical Works,* 3: 35.

[16]Although the 1850 Fugitive Slave Law did not specify the number of witnesses needed to establish that an individual was a fugitive slave, it did provide that "in no trial or hearing . . . shall the testimony of such alleged fugitive be admitted in evidence." No provision was made for the alleged fugitive to bring forth witnesses who might dispute the claims of the court transcript or warrant, but the commissioner or judge did have to be convinced that the person brought before him was indeed the escaped slave described in the transcript. *The Public Statutes at Large and Treaties of the United States of America, 1789–1873,* 17 vols. (Boston, 1845–73), 9: 462–65; Campbell, *Slave Catchers,* 110–15.

fact be perpetually told. Let it be thundered around the world, that, in tyrant-killing, king-hating, people-loving, democratic, Christian America, the seats of justice are filled with judges, who hold their offices under an open and palpable *bribe*, and are bound, in deciding in the case of a man's liberty, *to hear only his accusers!*

In glaring violation of justice, in shameless disregard of the forms of administering law, in cunning arrangement to entrap the defenceless, and in diabolical intent, this Fugitive Slave Law stands alone in the annals of tyrannical legislation. I doubt if there be another nation on the globe, having the brass and the baseness to put such a law on the statute-book. If any man in this assembly thinks differently from me in this matter, and feels able to disprove my statements, I will gladly confront him at any suitable time and place he may select.

Religious Liberty

I take this law to be one of the grossest infringements of Christian Liberty, and, if the churches and ministers of our country were not stupidly blind, or most wickedly indifferent, they, too, would so regard it.

At the very moment that they are thanking God for the enjoyment of civil and religious liberty, and for the right to worship God according to the dictates of their own consciences, they are utterly silent in respect to a law which robs religion of its chief significance, and makes it utterly worthless to a world lying in wickedness. Did this law concern the *"mint, anise* and *cummin"*[17] —abridge the right to sing psalms, to partake of the sacrament, or to engage in any of the ceremonies of religion, it would be smitten by the thunder of a thousand pulpits. A general shout would go up from the church, demanding *repeal, repeal, instant repeal!* And it would go hard with that politician who presumed to solicit the votes of the people without inscribing this motto on his banner. Further, if this demand were not complied with, another Scotland would be added to the history of religious liberty, and the stern old Covenanters would be thrown into the shade. A John Knox would be seen at every church door, and heard from every pulpit, and Fillmore[18] would have no more quarter than was shown by Knox, to the beautiful, but treacherous Queen Mary of Scotland.[19] The fact that the church of our country, (with fractional exceptions), does not esteem "the Fugitive Slave Law" as a declaration of war against religious liberty, implies that that church regards religion simply as a form of worship, an empty ceremony, and *not* a vital principle, requiring active benevolence, justice, love and good will towards man. It esteems sacrifice above mercy; psalm-singing above right doing; solemn meetings above practical righteousness. A worship that can be conducted by persons who refuse to give shelter to the houseless, to give bread to the hungry, clothing to the naked, and who enjoin obedience to a law forbidding these acts of mercy, is a curse,

[17]Matt. 23: 23: "Woe unto you, scribes and Pharisees, hypocrites! For ye pay tithe of mint, anise and cummin, and have omitted the weightier *matters* of the law, judgment, mercy and faith; these ought ye to have done, and not to leave the other undone."

[18]President Millard Fillmore.

[19]Mary Stuart (1542–87).

not a blessing to mankind. The Bible addresses all such persons as "scribes, pharisees, hypocrites, who pay tithe of *mint, anise*, and *cummin*, and have omitted the weighter matters of the law, judgement, mercy and faith."

The Church Responsible

But the church of this country is not only indifferent to the wrongs of the slave, it actually takes sides with the oppressors. It has made itself the bulwark of American slavery, and the shield of American slave-hunters. Many of its most eloquent Divines, who stand as the very lights of the church, have shamelessly given the sanction of religion and the Bible to the whole slave system. They have taught that man may, properly, be a slave; that the relation of master and slave is ordained of God; that to send back an escaped bondman to his master is clearly the duty of all the followers of the Lord Jesus Christ; and this horrible blasphemy is palmed off upon the world for Christianity.

For my part, I would say, welcome infidelity! welcome atheism! welcome anything! in preference to the gospel, *as preached by those Divines!* They convert the very name of religion into an engine of tyranny, and barbarous cruelty, and serve to confirm more infidels, in this age, than all the infidel writings of Thomas Paine, Voltaire, and Bolingbroke,[20] put together, have done! These ministers make religion a cold and flinty-hearted thing, having neither principles of right action, nor bowels of compassion. They strip the love of God of its beauty, and leave the throne of religion a huge, horrible, repulsive form. It is a religion for oppressors, tyrants, man-stealers, and *thugs.* It is not that *"pure and undefiled religion"* which is from above, and which is *"first pure, then peaceable, easy to be entreated,* full of mercy and good fruits, *without partiality, and without hypocrisy."*[21] But a religion which favors the rich against the poor; which exalts the proud above the humble; which divides mankind into two classes, tyrants and slaves; which says to the man in chains, *stay there;* and to the oppressor, *oppress on;* it is a religion which may be professed and enjoyed by all the robbers and enslavers of mankind; it makes God a respecter of persons, denies his fatherhood of the race, and tramples in the dust the great truth of the brotherhood of man. All this we affirm to be true of the popular church, and the popular worship of our land and nation—a religion, a church, and a worship which, on the authority of inspired wisdom, we pronounce to be an abomination in the sight of God. In the language of Isaiah, the American church might be well

---

[20]Thomas Paine (1737–1809), American revolutionary writer; Francois Marie Arouet de Voltaire (1694–1778), French essayist, playwright, and philosopher; and Henry St. John, Viscount Bolingbroke (1678–1751), English statesman, orator, and essayist, criticized the established Protestant and Catholic churches, and espoused a form of "natural religion" or Deism, for which they often received the opprobrium of supporters of orthodox Christianity in the eighteenth and nineteenth centuries. *Biographie Universelle,* 49: 464–512; *DNB,* 17 : 618–33 *DAB,* 14 : 159–66.

[21]Douglass quotes from James 1 : 27: "Pure religion and undefiled . . . is this . . .," and 3 : 17, "But the wisdom that is from above is first pure, then peaceable, gentle, and easy to be intreated, full of mercy and good fruits, without partiality and without hypocrisy."

addressed, "Bring no more vain oblations; incense is an abomination unto me: the new moons and Sabbaths, the calling of assemblies, I cannot away with; it is iniquity, even the solemn meeting. Your new moons and your appointed feasts my soul hateth. They are a trouble to me; I am weary to bear them; and when ye spread forth your hands I will hide mine eyes from you. Yea! when ye make many prayers, I will not hear. YOUR HANDS ARE FULL OF BLOOD; cease to do evil, learn to do well; seek judgement; relieve the oppressed; judge for the fatherless; plead for the widow."[22]

The American church is guilty, when viewed in connection with what it is doing to uphold slavery; but it is superlatively guilty when viewed in connection with its ability to abolish slavery.

The sin of which it is guilty is one of omission as well as of commission. Albert Barnes but uttered what the common sense of every man at all observant of the actual state of the case will receive as truth, when he declared that "There is no power out of the church that could sustain slavery an hour, if it were not sustained in it."[23]

Let the religious press, the pulpit, the Sunday school, the conference meeting, the great ecclesiastical, missionary, Bible and tract associations of the land array their immense powers against slavery and slave-holding; and the whole system of crime and blood would be scattered to the winds; and that they do not do this involves them in the most awful responsibility of which the mind can conceive.

In prosecuting the anti-slavery enterprise, we have been asked to spare the church, to spare the ministry; but *how,* we ask, could such a thing be done? We are met on the threshold of our efforts for the redemption of the slave, by the church

---

[22]Isa. 1 : 13–17.

[23]Presbyterian minister Albert Barnes (1798–1870) was born in Rome, New York, and graduated from Hamilton College, Clinton, New York, in 1820 and Princeton Theological Seminary in 1823. Appointed to the Presbyterian Church in Morristown, New Jersey, in 1824, Barnes in 1830 accepted an appointment at the First Presbyterian Church in Philadelphia, where he remained for almost forty years. One of the leaders of the "New School" movement within the Presbyterian Church, supporting joint religious missionary activities with other denominations and more flexible interpretations of church doctrine, Barnes appeared "dangerous" to many Old School Presbyterians. In 1837 he was tried for heresy, though later acquitted. During the mid-1830s Barnes encountered a runaway slave at his church door. Using as his argument St. Paul's epistle that urged slaves to be dutiful to their masters, Barnes refused to assist the fugitive and told him to return to his owner. The slave rejected the minister's suggestion and fled. After this attempt to uphold and justify the institution of slavery in the United States, Barnes became an "implacable foe of slavery," although he never officially affiliated with any anti-slavery organization. Douglass quotes from Barnes's *An Inquiry into the Scriptural Views of Slavery* (Philadelphia, 1846), 383, in which Barnes argued that "the principles laid down by the Savior and his apostles, are such as are opposed to slavery, and if carried out would secure its universal abolition." In a later work, *The Church and Slavery* (Philadelphia, 1857), Barnes examined "What the church is doing, and what it ought to do, in reference to an evil so vast, and so perilous to all our institutions." E. Bradford Davis, "Albert Barnes, 1798–1870: An Exponent of New School Presbyterianism" (Doctor of Theology diss., Princeton Theological Seminary, 1961), 276–330; C. Bruce Steiger, "Abolitionism and the Presbyterian Schism of 1837–1838," MVHR, 36: 391–414 (December 1949); *NCAB,* 7: 360; *DAB,* 1: 627–629.

and ministry of the country, in battle arrayed against us; and we are compelled to fight or flee. From what *quarter*, I beg to know, has proceeded a fire so deadly upon our ranks, during the last two years, as from the Northern pulpit? As the champions of oppressors, the chosen men of American theology have appeared—men, honored for their so-called piety, and their real learning. The LORDS[24] of Buffalo, the SPRINGS[25] of New York, the LATHROPS[26] of Auburn, the COXES[27] and SPENCERS[28] of Brooklyn, the GANNETS[29] and SHARPS[30] of Boston, the DEWEYS[31] of Washington, and other great religious lights of the land, have, in utter denial of the authority of *Him*, by whom they professed to be called to the ministry, deliberately taught us, against the example of the Hebrews and against the remonstrance of the Apostles, they teach "*that we ought to obey man's law before the law of God.*"

---

[24]John Chase Lord.

[25]Gardiner Spring.

[26]Leonard Elijah Lathrop.

[27]In a sermon preached in Brooklyn, New York, on Thanksgiving Day of 1850, the Reverend Samuel Hanson Cox reiterated his disapproval of slavery but urged obedience to the recently enacted Fugitive Slave Law. Taking as one of his texts 1 Pet. 2: 13–16, "Submit yourself to every ordinance of man for the Lord's sake," Cox denounced as "wicked and unchristian" those who urged northern blacks to resist the Fugitive Slave Law, and warned that "blood would flow in the streets" if the law were defied. At the same time, however, Cox expressed sympathy for the "colored population" and affirmed his conviction that "black and white have one common origin." The duty of all Christians, as Cox saw it, was "to pray for the freedom of the slave, but not to force that freedom against principles of justice and in the face of the most fearful consequences." Visiting the South had given Cox a fuller appreciation of the "difficulties under which the slaveholders labored" in dealing with a "brutified, barbarous race" of "halfsavages." Convinced that "If the colored race is to be freed, it must be by their own masters," Cox personally favored purchasing the freedom of all southern slaves and was ready to impose a "heavy tax" for the purpose. New York Herald, 15 December 1850.

[28]Ichabod Smith Spencer.

[29]Rev. Ezra Stiles Gannett (1801–71), pastor of the Federal Street Church in Boston, often castigated radical abolitionists for their defiance of the law and their call for "immediate emancipation" because he believed such measures would lead to disunion. Born in Cambridge, Massachusetts, to a longtime steward of Harvard College and the daughter of a former president of Yale College, Gannett attended Phillips Academy, Andover, and was graduated with honors from Harvard College in 1820. He completed Harvard Divinity School in 1823 and the following year accepted an appointment as assistant to Dr. William Ellery Channing of the Federal Street Church in Boston; after Channing's death in 1842, Gannett assumed the pastorate of the church and remained there the rest of his life. Gannett became one of the leaders of "old-fashioned Unitarianism" and exercised great influence through the editorship of several religious journals, including the *Scriptural Interpreter* (1831–35), *Monthly Miscellany of Religion and Letters* (1839–43), and *Christian Examiner* (1844–49). In a Thanksgiving Day sermon published in 1850 Gannett proclaimed, "God save us from disunion! I know that Slavery is a political and moral evil, a sin and curse; but disunion seems to me to be treason, not so much against the country, as against humanity." William C. Gannett, *Ezra Stiles Gannett, Unitarian Minister in Boston: A Memoir* (1875; Port Washington, N. Y., 1971), 287–88; Ezra Stiles Gannett, *Thanksgiving For the Union: A Discourse Delivered in the Federal Meeting House, November 28, 1850* (Boston, 1850), 17; DAB, 7: 122–23.

[30]Daniel Sharp.

[31]Orville Dewey.

My spirit wearies of such blasphemy; and how such men can be supported, as the "standing types and representatives of Jesus Christ," is a mystery which I leave others to penetrate. In speaking of the American church, however, let it be distinctly understood that I mean the *great mass* of the religious organizations of our land. There are exceptions, and I thank God that there are. Noble men may be found, scattered all over these Northern States, of whom Henry Ward Beecher[32] of Brooklyn, Samuel J. May of Syracuse, and my esteemed friend* on the platform, are shining examples; and let me say further, that upon these men lies the duty to inspire our ranks with high religious faith and zeal, and to cheer us on in the great mission of the slave's redemption from his chains.

Religion in England and Religion in America

One is struck with the difference between the attitude of the American church towards the anti-slavery movement, and that occupied by the churches in England towards a similar movement in that country. There, the church, true to its mission of ameliorating, elevating, and improving the condition of mankind, came forward promptly, bound up the wounds of the West Indian slave, and restored him to his liberty. There, the question of emancipation was a high[ly] religious question. It was demanded, in the name of humanity, and according to the law of the living God. The Sharps,[33] the Clarksons,[34] the Wilberforces,[35] the

---

[32]Henry Ward Beecher (1813–87), the fourth son of Presbyterian clergyman Lyman Beecher and brother of anti-slavery novelist Harriet Beecher Stowe, was the noted pastor of Brooklyn's Plymouth Church for forty years. After his graduation from Amherst College in 1834, Beecher studied at Lane Theological Seminary and served as pastor of Presbyterian churches in Lawrenceburg and Indianapolis, Indiana, before becoming minister at Plymouth Church in 1847. Committed to making the church an active instrument of social reform, Beecher in his sermons addressed the major social and political issues of his time with a force and drama that established him as one of the century's major orators. Though he denounced the evil of slavery, on occasion staging mock slave auctions in his church to impress his congregation with slavery's injustices, he denied that a constitutional basis existed for interfering with the institution in states where it already existed. Instead he urged that its exclusion from the territories would achieve abolition gradually and peacefully. His theology, minimizing doctrinal differences, stressed the religious worth of personal loyalty to Christ, and in 1882 he led his church out of the Congregational denomination. In addition to writing extensively for the secular press, Beecher edited the widely read religious journals New York *Independent* (1861–63) and *Christian Union* (1870–81). His reputation survived five years of public discussion that preceded the 1875 court trial and a subsequent Congregational council's examination of New York Congregational journalist. Theodore Tilton's charge that an adulterous relation existed between his wife and Beecher. Marie Caskey, *Chariot of Fire: Religion and the Beecher Family* (New Haven, 1978), 208–48; Sydney E. Ahlstrom, *A Religious History of the American People* (New Haven, 1972), 739; *NCAB,* 3: 129–30; *DAB,* 2: 129–35.

*Rev. R. R. Raymond.

[33]Granville Sharp.

[34]Thomas Clarkson.

[35]William Wilberforce.

Buxtons,[36] and Burchells[37] and the Knibbs,[38] were alike famous for their piety, and for their philanthropy. The anti-slavery movement *there* was not an anti-church movement, for the reason that the church took its full share in prosecuting that movement: and the anti-slavery movement in this country will cease to be an anti-church movement, when the church of this country shall assume a favorable, instead of a hostile position towards that movement.

Americans! your republican politics, not less than your republican religion, are flagrantly inconsistent. You boast of your love of liberty, your superior civilization, and your pure Christianity, while the whole political power of the nation (as embodied in the two great political parties), is solemnly pledged to support and perpetuate the enslavement of three millions of your countrymen. You hurl your anathemas at the crowned headed tyrants of Russia and Austria, and pride yourselves on your Democratic institutions, while you yourselves consent to be the mere *tools* and *bodyguards* of the tyrants of Virginia and Carolina. You invite to your shores fugitives of oppression from abroad, honor them with banquets, greet them with ovations, cheer them, toast them, salute them, protect them, and pour out your money to them like water; but the fugitives from your own land you advertise, hunt, arrest, shoot and kill. You glory in your refinement and your universal education; yet you maintain a system as barbarous and dreadful as ever stained the character of a nation—a system begun in avarice, supported in pride, and perpetuated in cruelty. You shed tears over fallen Hungary, and make the sad story of her wrongs the theme of your poets, statesmen and orators, till your gallant sons are ready to fly to arms to vindicate her cause against her oppressors,[39] but, in regard to the ten

---

[36]Thomas Fowell Buxton (1786–1845), politician, philanthropist, and successor to Wilberforce in the parliamentary struggle to end British slavery and the slave trade, was born in Essex County, England, and educated at Trinity College, Dublin. Buxton entered Parliament in 1818 and achieved prominence for his support of various reform measures, including education of the poor and equitable criminal laws. In the late 1820s he exposed the practice of slave trading in Mauritius, Trinidad, and Jamaica, and between 1831 and 1833 led the abolition campaign in Parliament. Buxton wrote *The African Slave Trade and Its Remedy* (London, 1839) and supported several unsuccessful explorations of the Niger River. Mathieson, *British Slavery and its Abolition,* 115–27, 194–98, 222–24; Klingberg, *Anti-Slavery Movement in England,* 187–212; Taylor, *British and American Abolitionists,* 33–34, 73–74; *DNB,* 3: 559–61.

[37]Thomas Burchell.

[38]William Knibb.

[39]Douglass here refers to the turmoil in Hungary following the invasion of the country by Russian and Austrian troops in August 1849. The Magyar-dominated Hungarian Diet in the spring of 1848, after the outbreak of revolution in Austria, seized the opportunity to enact a series of internal reforms, the "April Laws," which among other things created an independent Hungarian ministry. The ministry, however, was viewed as a direct threat to Austrian control, and in September 1848, with the support of Austrian King Ferdinand, Croatian troops invaded Hungary under the leadership of Josip Jelacic. The new ministry fled, leaving in charge Magyar nationalist Louis Kossuth, who was eventually able to rout the Croatian forces. Francis Joseph, nephew of King Ferdinand of Austria, assumed the throne of Hungary in December 1848 and revoked the "April Laws." At this point the Hungarian Diet proclaimed its independence and Louis Kossuth became governor. The Hungarian republic was short-lived, however, and Francis Joseph, with the assistance of Russian troops, marched on Hungary and defeated the republican army in August 1849. The country was dismembered and brought under the control of Vienna. Janos Pragay, *The*

thousand wrongs of the American slave, you would enforce the strictest silence, and would hail him as an enemy of the nation who dares to make those wrongs the subject of public discourse! You are all on fire at the mention of liberty for France or for Ireland; but are as cold as an iceberg at the thought of liberty for the enslaved of America. You discourse eloquently on the dignity of labor; yet, you sustain a system which, in its very essence, casts a stigma upon labor. You can bare your bosom to the storm of British artillery to throw off a threepenny tax on tea; and yet wring the last hard-earned farthing from the grasp of the black laborers of your country. You profess to believe "that, of one blood, God made all nations of men to dwell on the face of all the earth,"[40] and hath commanded all men, everywhere to love one another; yet you notoriously hate, (and glory in your hatred), all men whose skins are not colored like your own. You declare, before the world, and are understood by the world to declare, that you "*hold these truths to be self evident, that all men are created equal; and are endowed by their Creator with certain inalienable rights; and that, among these are, life, liberty, and the pursuit of happiness;*"[41] and yet, you hold securely, in a bondage which, according to your own Thomas Jefferson, *"is worse than ages of that which your fathers rose in rebellion to oppose,"*[42] *a seventh part* of the inhabitants of your country.

Fellow-citizens! I will not enlarge further on your national inconsistencies. The existence of slavery in this country brands your republicanism as a sham, your humanity as a base pretence, and your Christianity as a lie. It destroys your moral power abroad; it corrupts your politicians at home. It saps the foundation of religion; it makes your name a hissing, and a byword to a mocking earth. It is the antagonistic force in your government, the only thing that seriously disturbs and endangers your *Union*. It fetters your progress; it is the enemy of improvement, the deadly foe of education; it fosters pride; it breeds insolence; it promotes vice; it shelters crime; it is a curse to the earth that supports it; and yet, you cling to it, as if it were the sheet anchor of all your hopes. Oh! be warned! be warned! a horrible reptile is coiled up in your nation's bosom; the venomous creature is nursing at the tender breast of your youthful republic; *for the love of God, tear away*, and fling from you the hideous monster, and *let the weight of twenty millions crush and destroy it forever!*

Hungarian Revolution: Outlines of the Prominent Circumstances Attending the Hungarian Struggle for Freedom (New York, 1850); B. F. Tefft, *Hungary and Kossuth: An American Exposition of the late Hungarian Revolution* (Philadelphia, 1852); Edwin L. Godkin, *The History of Hungary and the Magyars From the Earliest Period to the Close of the Late War* (London, 1856), 324–69.

[40]A paraphrase of Acts 17 : 26: "And [God] hath made of one blood all nations of men for to dwell on all the face of the earth."

[41]Douglass quotes the American Declaration of Independence.

[42]Writing to Jean Nicholas Démeunier on 26 June 1786, Thomas Jefferson observed: "What a stupendous, what an incomprehensible machine is man! Who can endure toil, famine, stripes, imprisonment or death itself in vindication of his own liberty, and the next moment be deaf to all those motives whose power supported him thro' his trial, and inflict on his fellow men a bondage, one hour of which is fraught with more misery than ages of that which he rose in rebellion to oppose." Boyd, *Papers of Thomas Jefferson,* 10 : 63.

The Constitution

But it is answered in reply to all this, that precisely what I have now denounced is, in fact, guaranteed and sanctioned by the Constitution of the United States; that the right to hold and to hunt slaves is a part of that Constitution framed by the illustrious Fathers of this Republic.

Then, I dare to affirm, notwithstanding all I have said before, your fathers stooped, basely stooped

"To palter with us in a double sense:
And keep the word of promise to the ear,
But break it to the heart."[43]

And instead of being the honest men I have before declared them to be, they were the veriest imposters that ever practised on mankind. *This* is the inevitable conclusion, and from it there is no escape. But I differ from those who charge this baseness on the framers of the Constitution of the United States. *It is a slander upon their memory*, at least, so I believe. There is not time now to argue the constitutional question at length; nor have I the ability to discuss it as it ought to be discussed. The subject has been handled with masterly power by Lysander Spooner, Esq.,[44] by William Goodell,[45] by Samuel E. Sewall, Esq.,[46] and last, though not least, by Gerritt Smith, Esq.[47] These gentlemen have, as I think, fully and clearly vindicated the Constitution from any design to support slavery for an hour.

Fellow-citizens! there is no matter in respect to which, the people of the North have allowed themselves to be so ruinously imposed upon, as that of the pro-slavery character of the Constitution. In *that* instrument I hold there is neither warrant, license, nor sanction of the hateful thing; but, interpreted as it *ought* to be interpreted, the Constitution is a GLORIOUS LIBERTY DOCUMENT. Read its preamble, consider its purposes. Is slavery among them? Is it at the gateway? or is it in the temple? It is neither. While I do not intend to argue this question on the present

---

[43]Douglass paraphrases *Macbeth*, act 5, sc. 8, lines 20–22.

[44]Lysander Spooner (1808–87), lawyer, writer, and uncompromising foe of slavery, first published his famous work, *The Unconstitutionality of Slavery*, in Boston, in 1845. An expanded version appeared in 1847, and it became one of the major sources of campaign literature used by the Liberty party in the 1840s. *ACAB*, 5: 634–35; *DAB*, 17: 466–67.

[45]Douglass probably refers to William Goodell, *Views of American Constitutional Law, Its Bearing upon American Slavery* (Utica, 1844), and idem, *Slavery and Anti-Slavery*.

[46]Attorney Samuel E. Sewall (1799–1888) published in 1827 his *Remarks on Slavery in the United States*, which had first appeared in the *Christian Examiner*. Although he wrote no lengthy legal analysis of American slavery, Sewall was active in the defense of fugitive slaves captured in Massachusetts and in 1843 ran for governor of the state on the Liberty party ticket. Nina Moore Tiffany, *Samuel E. Sewall: A Memoir* (Boston, 1898), 33–81.

[47]Among Gerrit Smith's many letters, tracts, and pamphlets denying the constitutionality of slavery are *Letter of Gerrit Smith to Henry Clay* (New York, 1839); *Letter of Gerrit Smith to S. P. Chase on the Unconstitutionality of Every Part of American Slavery* (Albany, 1847); *Abstract of the Argument on the Fugitive Slave Law, Made by Gerrit Smith in Syracuse, June, 1852 on the Trial of Henry W. Allen, U.S. Deputy Marshal, for Kidnapping* (Syracuse, 1852).

occasion, let me ask, if it be not somewhat singular that, if the Constitution were intended to be, by its framers and adopters, a slave-holding instrument, why neither *slavery, slaveholding,* nor *slave* can anywhere be found in it. What would be thought of an instrument, drawn up, *legally* drawn up, for the purpose of entitling the city of Rochester to a track of land, in which no mention of land was made? Now, there are certain rules of interpretation, for the proper understanding of all legal instruments. These rules are well established. They are plain, common-sense rules, such as you and I, and all of us, can understand and apply, without having passed years in the study of law. I scout the idea that the question of the constitutionality or unconstitutionality of slavery is not a question for the people. I hold that every American citizen has a right to form an opinion of the constitution, and to propagate that opinion, and to use all honorable means to make his opinion the prevailing one. Without this right, the liberty of an American citizen would be as insecure as that of a Frenchman. Ex-Vice-President Dallas[48] tells us that the constitution is an object to which no American mind can be too attentive, and no American heart too devoted. He further says, the constitution, in its words, is plain and intelligible, and is meant for the home-bred, unsophisticated understandings of our fellow-citizens. Senator Berrien[49] tells us that the Constitution is the fundamental law, that which controls all others. The charter of our liberties, which every citizen has a personal interest in

[48]George Mifflin Dallas (1792–1864), Philadelphia-born lawyer and Democratic politician, served as U.S. vice-president (1845–49) under James Polk. Other political offices Dallas held during his public career included U.S. attorney for the Eastern District of Pennsylvania (1829–31), U.S. senator (1831–33), Pennsylvania attorney general (1833–35), and U.S. minister to Russia (1837–39). Although retired to private law practice in 1849, he expressed his support for the Compromise of 1850 and its provisions for the return of fugitive slaves in a letter to Guy M. Bryan published in the New York Times, 13 October 1851. Denouncing "the self-slaughter of intermeddling with the institutions and rights exclusively of state creation, state responsibility, and state control," Dallas observed that "the act for the extradition of fugitives is the pretext for protracted and persevering war upon the guarantees of the Constitution." As a candidate for the Democratic presidential nomination in 1852, Dallas was asked whether he would enforce the Fugitive Slave Law and he answered unequivocally "Yes, I would!" George Mifflin Dallas to Guy M. Bryan, 25 July 1851, in New York *Daily Times,* 13 October 1851; New York *Daily Times,* 31 May 1852; John M. Belohlavek, *George Mifflin Dallas: Jacksonian Patrician* (University Park, Pa., 1977), 138–43; *NCAB,* 6: 268; *BDAC,* 772, *DAB,* 5: 38–39.

[49]Georgia senator John MacPherson Berrien (1781–1856), known as the "American Cicero" because of his magnificent oratory, was also regarded as one of the ablest constitutional lawyers in the U.S. Senate during the 1840s. Born near Princeton, New Jersey, in 1781, he grew up in Savannah, Georgia, was graduated from Princeton at age fourteen, returned to Savannah to study law, and was admitted to the bar in 1798. From 1809 until 1821 he served as solicitor and then as judge of the eastern circuit. A member of the Georgia state senate (1822–23) and the U.S. Senate (1823–25) and U.S. attorney general under Andrew Jackson in 1829, Berrien was returned to the Senate as a Whig in 1841 after a decade's retirement from public life. In 1849 Berrien's *Address to the People of the United States* pleaded for compromise on the slavery question. He later voted in favor of the Fugitive Slave Law and opposed the abolition of the slave trade in the District of Columbia and the admission of California as a free state. Defeated in his bid for reelection in November 1851, he spent his final years organizing the American or Know-Nothing party. Josephine Mellichamp, *Senators from Georgia* (Huntsville, Ala., 1976), 99–103; Richard H. Shryock, *Georgia and the Union in 1850* (Durham, N.C., 1926), 157–63, 267–69, 358; *BDAC,* 548; *DAB,* 2: 225–26.

understanding thoroughly. The testimony of Senator Breese,[50] Lewis Cass, and many others that might be named, who are everywhere esteemed as sound lawyers, so regard the constitution. I take it, therefore, that it is not presumption in a private citizen to form an opinion of that instrument.

Now, take the constitution according to its plain reading, and I defy the presentation of a single pro-slavery clause in it. On the other hand it will be found to contain principles and purposes, entirely hostile to the existence of slavery.

I have detained my audience entirely too long already. At some future period I will gladly avail myself of an opportunity to give this subject a full and fair discussion.

Allow me to say, in conclusion, notwithstanding the dark picture I have this day presented of the state of the nation, I do not despair of this country. There are forces in operation, which must inevitably work the downfall of slavery. "*The arm of the Lord is not shortened*,"[51] and the doom of slavery is certain. I, therefore, leave off where I began, with *hope*. While drawing encouragement from the Declaration of Independence, the great principles it contains, and the genius of American Institutions, my spirit is also cheered by the obvious tendencies of the age. Nations do not now stand in the same relation to each other that they did ages ago. No nation can now shut itself up from the surrounding world, and trot round in the same old path of its fathers without interference. The time *was* when such could be done. Long established customs of hurtful character could formerly fence themselves in, and do their evil work with social impunity. Knowledge was then confined and enjoyed by the privileged few, and the multitude walked on in mental darkness. But a change has now come over the affairs of mankind. Walled cities and empires have become unfashionable. The arm of commerce has borne away the gates of the strong city. Intelligence is penetrating the darkest corners of the globe. It makes its pathway over and under the sea, as well as on the earth. Wind, steam, and lightning are its chartered agents. Oceans no longer divide, but link nations together. From Boston to London is now a holiday excursion. Space is comparatively annihilated. Thoughts expressed on one side of the Atlantic are distinctly heard on the other.

The far off and almost fabulous Pacific rolls in grandeur at our feet. The Celestial Empire, the mystery of ages, is being solved. The fiat of the Almighty, "*Let there be Light*,"[52] has not yet spent its force. No abuse, no outrage whether in taste, sport or avarice, can now hide itself from the all-pervading light. The iron

---

[50]Sidney Breese (1800–78), Democrat from Illinois, served in the U.S. Senate for only one term (1843–49) and generally supported the positions of his fellow midwestern senator, Lewis Cass, of Michigan, on such issues as the constitutionality of slavery, popular sovereignty, and limited congressional authority over slavery. Born into a wealthy family in Whitesboro, New York, and a graduate of Union College, Breese headed west to study in Illinois and was admitted to the bar in 1820. In 1857 he was elected to the Illinois Supreme Court and was reelected in 1861 and 1870, from which position he gained a reputation as one of the leading American jurists of the era. Melville W. Fuller, "Biographical Memoir of Sidney Breese," in Sidney Breese, *The Early History of Illinois, From Its Discovery by the French, in 1763 . . .* ,ed. Thomas Hoyne (Chicago, 1884), 3–60; *ACAB,* 1: 367; *NCAB,* 8: 122; *DAB,* 3: 14–16.

[51]Douglass paraphrases Isa. 59 : 1: "Behold, the Lord's hand is not shortened, that it cannot save, neither His ear heavy, that it cannot hear."

[52]Gen. 1 : 3.

shoe, and crippled foot of China must be seen, in contrast with nature. *Africa must rise and put on her yet unwoven garment. "Ethiopia shall stretch out her hand unto God."*[53] In the fervent aspirations of William Lloyd Garrison, I say, and let every heart join in saying it:

God speed the year of jubilee
    The wide world o'er!
When from their galling chains set free,
Th' oppress'd shall vilely bend the knee,
And wear the yoke of tyranny
    Like brutes no more.
That year will come, and freedom's reign,
To man his plundered rights again
    Restore.

God speed the day when human blood
    Shall cease to flow!
In every clime be understood,
The claims of human brotherhood,
And each return for evil, good,
    Not blow for blow;
That day will come all feuds to end,
And change into a faithful friend
    Each foe.

God speed the hour, the glorious hour,
    When none on earth
Shall exercise a lordly power,
Nor in a tyrant's presence cower;
But all to manhood's stature tower,
    By equal birth!
THAT HOUR WILL COME, to each, to all,
And from his prison-house, the thrall
    Go forth.

Until that year, day, hour, arrive,
With head, and heart, and hand I'll strive,
To break the rod, and rend the gyve,
The spoiler of his prey deprive—
    So witness Heaven!
And never from my chosen post,
Whate'er the peril or the cost,
    Be driven.[54]

[53]An allusion to Ps. 68 : 31: "Princes shall come out of Egypt; Ethiopia shall soon stretch out her hands unto God."

[54] William Lloud Garrison, "The Triumph of Freedom," in *Lib.,* 10 Jaunary 1845.

TO THE PUBLIC

William Lloyd Garrison

William Lloyd Garrison, perhaps the most well-known and certainly one of the most influential nineteenth-century abolitionists, waged much of his war of words in his newspaper, *The Liberator*. "To the Public," which appeared in the inaugural issue of *The Liberator* in 1831, announced Garrison's moral and political principles, which ones he had derived largely from the African American abolitionists who preceded him. Garrison's statement still stands today as an affirmation of an uncompromising commitment to justice.

In the month of August, I issued proposals for publishing "THE LIBERATOR" in Washington city; but the enterprise, though hailed in different sections of the country, was palsied by public indifference. Since that time, the removal of the Genius of Universal Emancipation[1] to the Seat of Government has rendered less imperious the establishment of a similar periodical in that quarter.

During my recent tour for the purpose of exciting the minds of the people by a series of discourses on the subject of slavery, every place that I visited gave fresh evidence of the fact, that a greater revolution in public sentiment was to be effected in the free states—*and particularly in New-England*—than at the south. I found contempt more bitter, opposition more active, detraction more relentless, prejudice more stubborn and apathy more frozen, than among slave owners themselves. Of course, there were individual exceptions to the contrary. This state of things afflicted, but did not dishearten me. I determined, at every hazard, to lift up the standard of emancipation in the eyes of the nation, *within sight of Bunker Hill*[2] *and in the birth place of liberty*. That standard is now unfurled; and long may it float, unhurt by the spoliations of time or the missiles of a desperate foe—yea, till every chain be broken, and every bondman set free! Let southern oppressors tremble—let their secret abettors tremble—let their northern apologists tremble—let all the enemies of the persecuted blacks tremble.

I deem the publication of my original Prospectus unnecessary, as it has obtained a wide circulation. The principles therein inculcated will be steadily pursued in this paper, excepting that I shall not array myself as the political partisan of any man. In defending the great cause of human rights, I wish to derive the assistance of all religions and of all parties.

[1]Benjamin Lundy's paper, *The Genius of Universal Emancipation*, with which Garrison had been associated and which had been based in Baltimore.

[2]Site of an important early battle (in fact, however, the battle took place on Breed's Hill) in the American Revolution, fought in Boston on June 17, 1775. The cornerstone for the Bunker Hill Monument was laid in a ceremony on June 17, 1825, and the completion of it celebrated on June 17, 1843.

Assenting to the "self-evident truth" maintained in the American Declaration of Independence, "that all men are created equal, and endowed by their Creator with certain inalienable rights—among which are life, liberty and the pursuit of happiness," *I shall strenuously contend for the immediate enfranchisement of our slave population.*

In Park-street Church, on the Fourth of July, 1829, in an address on slavery, I unreflectingly assented to the popular but pernicious doctrine of *gradual* abolition. I seize this opportunity to make a full and unequivocal recantation, and thus publicly to ask pardon of my God, of my country, and of my brethren the poor slaves, for having uttered a sentiment so full of timidity, injustice and absurdity. A similar recantation, from my pen, was published in the Genius of Universal Emancipation at Baltimore, in September, 1829. My conscience is now satisfied.

I am aware, that many object to the severity of my language; but is there not cause for severity? I *will be* as harsh as truth, and as uncompromising as justice. On this subject, I do not wish to think, or speak, or write, with moderation. No! no! Tell a man whose house is on fire, to give a moderate alarm; tell him to moderately rescue his wife from the hands of the ravisher; tell the mother to gradually extricate her babe from the fire into which it has fallen;—but urge me not to use moderation in a cause like the present. I am in earnest—I will not equivocate—I will not excuse—I will not retreat a single inch—AND I WILL BE HEARD. The apathy of the people is enough to make every statue leap from its pedestal, and to hasten the resurrection of the dead.

It is pretended, that I am retarding the cause of emancipation by the coarseness of my invective, and the precipitancy of my measures. The charge is not true. On this question my influence,—humble as it is,—is felt at this moment to a considerable extent, and shall be felt in coming years—not perniciously, but beneficially—not as a curse, but as a blessing; and posterity will bear testimony that I was right. I desire to thank God, that he enables me to disregard "*the fear of man which bringeth a snare*," and to speak his truth in its simplicity and power. And here I close with this fresh dedication:

Oppression! I have seen thee, face to face,
And met they cruel eye and cloudy brow;
But thy soul-withering glance I fear not now—
For dread to prouder feelings doth give place
Of deep abhorrence! *Scoring the disgrace*
Of slavish knees that at they footstool bow,
I also kneel—but with far other vow
Do hail thee and thy hord of hirelings base:—
I swear, while life-blood warms my throbbing veins,
Still to oppose and thwart, with heart and hand,
Thy brutalising sway—till Africa's chains
Are burst, and Freedom rules the rescued land,—
Trampling Oppression and his iron rod:
Such is the vow I take—SO HELP ME GOD!

PART I: IX/XI

From Norman Mailer, *Why Are We at War?*

Norman Mailer is widely regarded as one of America's best writers. He has published more than 30 works of fiction and non-fiction. Mailer's work has always engaged American ideals and culture, and the selection reprinted here recounts his response to the horrible events of 9/11. The text consists largely of the transcript of a discussion between Mailer and writer Dotsun Rader.

1

DOTSON RADER: I was at home in my apartment on East Eighty-fifth Street in Manhattan when the first of the Twin Towers was hit by one of the planes. But at the time I didn't know it had happened. Later that morning I tried to make a phone call, and my phone was dead. So I got dressed and went outside. I live four blocks from Gracie Mansion, the official residence of the mayor. None of the pay phones on the street worked. People were wandering oddly about, sort of dazed, as if kind of lost. It was very strange. I started walking downtown—it was a bright, almost hot day in New York. I was supposed to have lunch with a friend on Fifty-seventh Street, and I was walking down Third Avenue to meet him at the restaurant. When I reached Sixty-fourth Street, I noticed this huge, bubbling cloud in the sky above Manhattan south of me. The rest of the sky was blue and clear. I didn't know what it was. And then, looking down Third Avenue, six or seven blocks away, as far as I could see, I suddenly noticed a vast throng of people, a flood of humanity, like a slow wave rolling north up the avenue. Many of them were men in white shirts. They were the office workers from Wall Street, fleeing the disaster. This quiet mass of people, tens of thousands, was walking up the island like a funeral procession and turning at Fifty-seventh Street and then moving as one toward the 59th Street Bridge to cross over out of the island. And I thought, "Jesus! Is this Christ's Second Coming?" Because they were in white, covered in dust, and they looked stunned, and they were speaking in whispers, like kids in church. I thought it was the Rapture and Jesus was calling his saints home, and that I was being left behind. That was my initial feeling.

NORMAN MAILER: Wouldn't that be it? Jesus had come and everybody has gone to meet him by crossing the bridge from Manhattan to Queens. That does capture my pessimism concerning cosmic matters. [*laughter*]

DOTSON RADER: Okay. Where were you on September 11? How did you learn about the terrorist attacks, and what was your initial reaction?

NORMAN MAILER: I was in my house up here in Provincetown. I remember a phone call telling me to turn on the TV. While I was watching I called my youngest daughter, Maggie. I have an apartment in Brooklyn Heights, and she was staying there with a friend. You can see lower Manhattan and the Twin Towers from that apartment. Our windows look across the East River. So Maggie had witnessed the first attack and was terribly affected by it. Then, while we were on the phone, the second plane hit the other building. I'm still watching on TV. In Brooklyn, Maggie and her friend are both seeing it through the window as well as viewing it on TV. That was a considerable shock. Why? Because the one thing TV always promises us is that, deep down, what we see on television is not real. It's why there's always that subtle numbness to TV. The most astonishing events, even terrifying events, nonetheless have a touch of nonexistence when seen on the tube. They don't terrify us. We see something that's hideous, but we're not shocked proportionally. It's why we can watch anything on TV.

Now, there are exceptions. The shooting of Lee Harvey Oswald by Jack Ruby was one; the second plane striking the second Tower; the collapse of the Towers. TV at that moment was no longer a coat of insulation between us and the horrific. When broken, the impact is enormous.

DOTSON RADER: What struck me, what I'll never forget, is the silence. Everyone was just silent. Or if they spoke, they whispered. It was like everyone was at a funeral. And this went on for hours and hours. Occasionally, the silence was broken by an ambulance or police siren. And what I'd never seen in New York before—military jets started flying over the island, because they started closing Manhattan down. The military started showing up in the streets. I thought, What in God's name is happening?

2

What in God's name was happening? It is one thing to hear a mighty explosion. It is another to recognize some time after the event that one has been deafened by it. The United States was going through an identity crisis. Questions about our nature as a country were being asked that most good American men and women had never posed to themselves before. Questions such as, Why are we so hated? How could anyone resent us that much? We do no evil. We believe in goodness and freedom. Who are we, then? Are we not who we think we are? More pressing, who are "they?" What does it all mean?

Simple questions. Blank as white and empty pages. We were going through an identity crisis, and that is an incomparable experience. The ego has been disrupted. It has been pre-empted. Most of us look to command an ego that will keep us reasonably efficient while we carry out our personal projects. We see ourselves as husbands or wives, as brave or prudent, reliable or decent, or certain egos may depend on the right to excuse themselves—as flighty, or in search of friendship, which, once found, will take care of all else.

In that sense, it hardly matters what kind of firm notion the ego attaches to itself. That, from the need of the ego, is less important than the ongoing expectation that the notion will rest reasonably stable. Upon that depends our identity, that firm seat which offers the psyche an everyday working notion of who we are (good-looking or good-looking enough—whatever serves).

An identity crisis builds slowly, or it can strike like a thunderclap, but the effect is unmistakable. One can no longer offer a firm declaration of who one is. The seat upon which the ego depends has been slipped out from under. The psyche is in a sprawl. The simplest questions become difficult to answer.

A mass identity crisis for all of America descended upon us after 9/11, and our response was wholly comprehensible. We were plunged into a fever of patriotism. If our long-term comfortable and complacent sense that America was just the greatest country ever had been brought into doubt, the instinctive reflex was to reaffirm ourselves. We had to overcome the identity crisis—hell, overpower it, wave a flag.

We had had a faith. The ship of the United States was impregnable and had been on a great course. We were steering ourselves into a great future. All of a sudden, not to be able to feel like that was equal to seeing oneself as a traitor to the grand design. So we gathered around George W. Bush. That he had not been elected by a majority even became a species of new strength for him. The transient, still-forming, fresh national identity could not for a moment contemplate the fact that maybe Bush should not even be in the White House. Why? Because now the country had to be saved. A horror had come upon us. There were people on earth so eager to destroy us that they were ready to immolate themselves. That went right to the biblical root. Samson had pulled down the pillars of the Temple. Now there were all these Muslim Samsons. A ripple went through the country, a determining wind. In its wake, flags rippled everywhere. Nearly everyone in America was waving a flag.

For a few of us, this great indiscriminate wave of patriotism was not a joy to behold. "Patriotism," after all, "is the last refuge of a scoundrel." So said H. L. Mencken, or was it Samuel Johnson? One could argue over the source but not the sentiment.

3

DOTSON RADER: Are they even waving flags up in Provincetown?

NORMAN MAILER: They are. We had a parade in Provincetown on the Fourth of July, 2002. A rather nice looking, pleasant fellow—he looked to me like a young liberal lawyer—came up and smiled and handed me a small American flag. And I looked at him and just shook my head. And he walked on. It wasn't an episode in any way. He came over with a half-smile and walked away with a half-smile. But I was furious at myself afterward for not saying, "You don't have to wave a flag to be a patriot." By July 2002, it bothered me a good deal. Free-floating patriotism seemed like a direct measure of our free-floating anxiety.

Take the British for contrast. The British have a love of their country that is profound. They can revile it, tell dirty stories about it, give you dish on all the imperfects who are leading the country. But their patriotism is deep. In America it's as if we're playing musical chairs, and you shouldn't get caught without a flag or you're out of the game. Why do we need all this reaffirmation? It's as if we're a three-hundred-pound man who's seven feet tall, superbly shaped, absolutely powerful, and yet every three minutes he's got to reaffirm the fact that his armpits have a wonderful odor. We don't need compulsive, self-serving patriotism.

It's odious. When you have a great country, it's your duty to be critical of it so it can become even greater. But culturally, emotionally, we are growing more arrogant, more vain. We're losing a sense of the beauty not only of democracy but also of its peril.

Democracy is built upon a notion that is exquisite and dangerous. It virtually states that if the will of the populace is freely expressed, more good than bad will result. When America began, it was the first time in the history of civilization that a nation dared to make an enormous bet founded on this daring notion—that there is more good than bad in people. Until then, the prevailing assumption had been that the powers at the top knew best; people were no good and had to be controlled. Now we have to keep reminding ourselves that just because we've been a great democracy, it doesn't guarantee we're going to continue to be one. Democracy is existential. It changes. It changes all the time. That's one reason why I detest promiscuous patriotism. You don't take democracy for granted. It is always in peril. We all know that any man or woman can go from being a relatively good person to a bad one. We can all become corrupted, or embittered. We can be swallowed by our miseries in life, become weary, give up. The fact that we've been a great democracy doesn't mean we will automatically keep being one if we keep waving the flag. It's ugly. You take a monarchy for granted, or a fascist state. You have to. That's the given. But a democracy changes all the time.

4

The fear that waved the flag in every hand was our nightmare of terrorism. Nightmares tell us that life is absurd, unreasonable, unjust, warped, crazy, and ridiculously dangerous. Terrorism suggests that your death will have no relation to your life, as if your death will also produce an identity crisis.

Implicit in our attitude toward our own end is that, for most of us, there is a logic within it. We spend much of our lives searching for that logic. We live in a certain manner. We act out some of our virtues and vices; we restrain others. From the sum of all those actions and abstentions will come our final disease. That is our assumption, at least for most of us. It can even be seen as a logical conclusion. We pay with our bodies for the sins and excesses of our minds and hearts. It is almost as if we want it that way. Our psyches are jarred, even tortured, by absurdity, and confirmed, sometimes soothed even, by a reasonable recognition of consequence.

Terrorism, however, shatters this equation. The comprehension of our death that we have worked to obtain is lost. Our ability to find meaning in our lives is lost.

5

DOTSON RADER: So, do you hate terrorism?

NORMAN MAILER: I hate it; I loathe it. Since I believe in reincarnation, I think the character of your death is tremendously important to you. One wants to be able to meet one's death with a certain seriousness. To me, it is horrible to be killed without warning. Because you can't prepare yourself in any last way for your next existence. So your death contributes to absurdity. Terrorism's ultimate tendency is to make life absurd.

When I consider the nearly three thousand people who died in the Twin Towers disaster, it's not the ones who were good fathers and good mothers and good daughters, good brothers and good husbands or sons, that I mourn most. It's the ones who came from families that were less happy. When a good family member dies, there's a tenderness and a sorrow that can restore life to those who are left behind. But when someone dies who's half loved and half hated by his own family, whose children, for example, are always trying to get closer to that man or to that woman and don't quite succeed, then the aftereffect is obsessive. Those are the ones who are hurt the most. I won't call them dysfunctional families, but it's into the less successful families that terrorism bites most deeply. Because there is that terrible woe that one can't speak to the dead parent or the dead son or daughter or dead mate; one can't set things right anymore. One was planning to, one was hoping to, and now it's lost forever. That makes it profoundly obsessive.

DOTSON RADER: Would you define terrorism as wickedness, as an evil?

NORMAN MAILER: To me there's a great difference between doing evil and being wicked. I don't use the words interchangeably. People who are wicked are always raising the ante without knowing quite what they're doing. Most of us are wicked to a good degree. Most of us who are game players or adventurous in any way are wicked. We raise the ante all the time without knowing what the results might be. We're mischievous, if you will.

Evil, however, is to have a pretty good idea of the irreparable damage you're going to do and then proceed to do it. In that sense, yes, terrorism is evil.

However, it's worth trying to understand terrorism in the context by which the terrorists see it. They feel they're gouging out an octopus that's looking to destroy their world. They feel virtuous. The individual terrorist might be violating every single rule in Islam—he might, for example, be a drug addict or booze a lot—but at the end, he still believes he will find redemption through immolation. He is one small shard in the spiritual wreckage of the world right now. After all, in America there are a great many people on the right who are going around saying, Let's kill all the Muslims; let's simplify the world. You think Islam has a special purchase on terrorism?

DOTSON RADER: What I think is that we are facing a war of civilizations between an Islamic cult of death—

NORMAN MAILER: Wait a minute. Cult of death? You're going too far. For every Muslim who believes in your cult of death, thousands don't. People who are ready to sacrifice their lives form a very special group. They don't need big numbers.

DOTSON RADER: But millions cheer them in the streets.

NORMAN MAILER: Oh, it's easy to cheer. I can cheer athletes who score winning touchdowns when I don't know the first thing about them. I'm cheering for an idea, my team! That's one thing. It's another to shed your own blood. There's a gulf between the two. Many a Muslim who hates us is nowhere near to being a terrorist.

Still, so many of them do hate us.

DOTSON RADER: Okay, recognizing that, why? Why are we so hated?

NORMAN MAILER: To some degree it's envy. Some human emotions are obvious. But we're also hated for more intrusive reasons. Corporate capitalism does have this tendency to take over large parts of the economies of other countries. Often we are the next thing to cultural barbarians. We don't always pay attention to what we are trampling. What intensifies the anger is how often we are successful in these commercial invasions. You go into a McDonald's in Moscow and there are marble floors. The Russian equivalent of young corporate executives are phoning each other across the room on their cell phones. They're proud of that. I spoke once at Moscow State University to a class that was studying American literature. One of the students asked me, "Is there anything in our economy that compares to American economy?" I said, "Yes. Your McDonald's are better than ours." And they loved it. They were delighted. They had something they could do that was better than us. It was as if Brooklyn College were playing the University of Nebraska in football. The score had been one hundred to nothing, but then they kicked a field goal—it's now one hundred to three. And the Brooklyn College stands went crazy. So, by the same token, those are the people—and these are the young people in Moscow—who are reacting positively to American corporate culture.

Now think of all the other people in Russia who hate the very thought that not only were they bankrupted by the United States, not only were they betrayed by a communism that many of them had believed in, but now on top of it they're being culturally invaded by these people with their money-grubbing notions of food. And, worse, the young love it. The young are leaving them. So the hatred toward America intensifies.

Now, take the West's cultural invasion into Islam. The Muslim reaction is that Islam is endangered by modern technology and corporate capitalism. They see everything in America as aiming to destroy the basis of Islam. The huge freedom given to women in American culture is seen as an outrage by orthodox Muslims. American TV they find licentious in the extreme. They feel all that Islam stands for is going to be eroded by American culture. So, to repeat: The core of the hatred of Muslims toward us is the fear that they're going to lose their own people to Western values. Maybe half the people in Muslim countries may want secretly to be free of Islam. And so the ones who retain the old religion become extreme in response. Many Muslims can put Christian fundamentalists to shame by the intensity of their belief. It's an interesting belief, after all.

There is one fascinating element in Islam, which is the idea that all Muslims are equal before God, a tremendous egalitarian concept. Like all organized religion, Islam ends up being the perversion of itself in practice. Just as in

Christianity, compassion is supposed to be the greatest good, but its present exercise in the world seems to be a study in military power and greed. In Islam, no Muslim has the right to consider himself superior to another Muslim. What happens in reality is that you have oppressive societies run for the wealthy, with the poor getting less and less—tremendous economic inequalities in many a Muslim society. And tyrannical people in the seats of power.

Now, of course, the Koran, like the Old and New Testaments, has something in it for everyone. You can run north, run south, blow east, you can blow west. But there have been numerous revolutions within Islam over the centuries to restore its original beliefs. There is no understanding of Islam until one recognizes that Muslims who are truly devoted feel they are in a direct relationship with God. Their Islamic culture is the most meaningful experience of their lives, and their culture is being infiltrated. They feel the kind of outrage toward us that, let's say, a good Catholic would know if a black mass were performed in his church.

DOTSON RADER: But if that's true, if that's what the motivation is about, then there's no fixing it.

NORMAN MAILER: There's no quick fix. In fact, I'll go so far as to say that this is a war between those who believe the advance of technology is the best solution for human ills and those who believe that we got off the track somewhere a century ago, two centuries ago, five centuries ago, and we've been going in the wrong direction ever since, that the purpose of human beings on earth is not to obtain more and more technological power but to refine our souls. This is the deep divide that now goes on, even with many Americans. You know, what does it profit me if I gain the entire world and lose my soul?

Now, I don't want to paint myself into a corner where I am defending Islam. I'm sure they have as many sons of bitches as we have, maybe more. They probably have more in that they suffer lousier living conditions and they're under more tension. Muslims also bear a huge sense of shame, because they were a superior civilization around 1200, 1300 A.D., the most advanced culture then, and now they lag behind. There is a deep sense of failure among them. Think of those periods in your life when you felt you were a failure, and recall the bitterness, the anger, the disturbance. Multiply that by the followers of a faith, and that gives some sense of how bad it can get.

We in the West have this habit of looking for solutions. Part of the spirit of technology is to assume that there's always a solution to a problem, or something damn close to one. There may be no solution this time. This may be the beginning of an international cancer we cannot cure. What's in the mind of a cancer cell? Doubtless, its basic desire is to kill as many cells and invade as many organs as it can. So, too, the greater number of people the terrorists can wipe out, the happier they're going to be. Before you feel too righteous and outraged, however, let me ask: Did Harry Truman shiver in his bed at the thought that a hundred thousand people had been killed in Hiroshima and another hundred thousand in Nagasaki two days later, or was he proud that he had won the war?

COULD WE TRACE THE RECORD OF EVERY HUMAN HEART

Frances Ellen Watkins Harper

Frances Ellen Watkins Harper was a poet, lecturer, novelist, and journalist, and all of her language work was devoted to abolitionism, women's rights, peace advocacy and other social movements. Over the course of her long career, Harper remained a dogged critic of the social influence of greed and prejudice. Harper delivered "Could We Trace the Record of Every Human Heart," at the Fourth Anniversary Meeting of the New York City Anti-Slavery Society in May of 1857. The address is characteristic of Harper's way of arguing, juxtaposing as it does the crimes of slavery and spiritual values that would surely resonate with her audience.

Could we trace the record of every human heart, the aspirations of every immortal soul, perhaps we would find no man so imbruted and degraded that we could not trace the word liberty either written in living characters upon the soul or hidden away in some nook or corner of the heart. The law of liberty is the law of God, and is antecedent to all human legislation. It existed in the mind of Deity when He hung the first world upon its orbit and gave it liberty to gather light from the central sun.

Some people say, set the slaves free. Did you ever think, if the slaves were free, they would steal everything they could lay their hands on from now till the day of their death—that they would steal more than two thousand millions of dollars? (applause) Ask Maryland, with her tens of thousands of slaves, if she is not prepared for freedom and hear her answer: "I help supply the cofflegangs of the South." Ask Virginia, with her hundreds of thousands of slaves, if she is not weary with her merchandise of blood and anxious to shake the gory traffic from her hands, and hear her reply: "Though fertility has covered my soil, though a genial sky bends over my hills and vales, though I hold in my hand a wealth of water-power enough to turn the spindles to clothe the world, yet, with all these advantages, one of my chief staples has been the sons and daughters I send to the human market and human shambles." (applause) Ask the farther South, and all the cotton growing states chime in, "We have need of fresh supplies to fill the ranks of those whose lives have gone out in unrequited toil on our distant plantations."

A hundred thousand new-born babes are annually added to the victims of slavery; twenty thousand lives are annually sacrificed on the plantations of the South. Such a sight should send a thrill of horror, through the nerves of civilization and impel the heart of humanity to lofty deeds. So it might, if men had not found a fearful alchemy by which this blood can be transformed into gold. Instead of listening to the cry of agony, they listen to the ring of dollars and stoop down to pick up the coin. (applause)

But a few months since a man escaped from bondage and found a temporary shelter almost beneath the shadow of Bunker Hill. Had that man stood upon the deck of an Austrian ship, beneath the shadow of the house of the Hapsburgs, he would have found protection. Had he been wrecked upon an island or colony of Great Britain, the waves of the tempest-lashed ocean would have washed him deliverance. Had he landed upon the territory of vine-encircled France and a Frenchman had reduced him to a thing and brought him here beneath the protection of our institutions and our laws, for such a nefarious deed that Frenchman would have lost his citizenship in France. Beneath the feebler light which glimmers from the Koran, the Bey of Tunis would have granted him freedom in his own dominions. Beside the ancient pyramids of Egypt he would have found liberty, for the soil laved by the glorious Nile is now consecrated to freedom. But from Boston harbour, made memorable by the infusion of three-penny taxed tea, Boston in its proximity to the plains of Lexington and Concord, Boston almost beneath the shadow of Bunker Hill and almost in sight in Plymouth Rock, he is thrust back from liberty and manhood and reconverted into a chattel. You have heard that, down South, they keep bloodhounds to hunt slaves. Ye bloodhounds, go back to your kennels! When you fail to catch the flying fugitive, when his stealthy tread is heard in the place where the bones of the revolutionary sires repose, the ready North is base enough to do your shameful service. (applause)

Slavery is mean because it tramples on the feeble and weak. A man comes with his affidavits from the South and hurries me before a commissioner; upon that evidence *ex parte* and alone he hitches me to the car of slavery and trails my womanhood in the dust. I stand at the threshold of the Supreme Court and ask for justice, simple justice. Upon my tortured heart is thrown the mocking words, "You are a negro; you have no rights which white men are bound to respect!" (long and loud applause) Had it been my lot to have lived beneath the Crescent instead of the Cross, had injustice and violence been heaped upon my head as a Mohammedan woman, as a member of a common faith, I might have demanded justice and been listened to by the Pasha, the Bey or the Vizier; but when I come here to ask justice, men tell me, "We have no higher law than the Constitution." (applause)

But I will not dwell on the dark side of the picture. God is on the side of freedom; and any cause that has God on its side, I care not how much it may be trampled upon, how much it may be trailed in the dust, is sure to triumph. The message of Jesus Christ is on the side of Freedom, "I come to preach deliverance to the captives, the opening of the prison doors to them that are bound." The truest and noblest hearts in the land are on the side of freedom. They may be hissed at by slavery's minions, their names cast out as evil, their characters branded with fanaticism, but O,

"To side with Truth is noble when we share her humble crust Ere the cause bring fame and profit and it's prosperous to be just."

May I not, in conclusion, ask every honest, noble heart, every seeker after truth and justice, if they will not also be on the side of freedom. Will you not resolve that you will abate neither heart nor hope till you hear the deathknell of human bondage sounded, and over the black ocean of slavery shall be heard a song more exulting than the song of Miriam when it floated o'er Egypt's dark sea, the requiem of Egypt's ruined hosts and the anthem of the deliverance of Israel's captive people? (great applause)

ONE GREAT BUNDLE OF HUMANITY

Frances Ellen
Watking Harpr

Harper delivered this address in May of 1866 at the National Woman's Rights Convention. With the end of Civil War and the emerging political battles of Reconstruction, Harper had to carefully negotiate her allegiances to the politics of African American liberation and the women's rights movement. The national prominence of the initiative for "universal manhood suffrage," which would culminate in the Fourteenth Amendment angered many white feminists who believed the rights of women were being disregarded. Harper's address to the Women's Rights Convention uncompromisingly makes the case for the particular struggles of African American women. As you read, notice how Harper grounds her reasoning in premises about the interconnectedness of all people, a strategy that should not surprise us given the divisiveness of the moment.

We Are All Bound up Together

I feel I am something of a novice upon this platform. Born of a race whose inheritance has been outrage and wrong, most of my life had been spent in battling against those wrongs. But I did not feel as keenly as others, that I had these rights, in common with other women, which are now demanded. About two years ago, I stood within the shadows of my home. A great sorrow had fallen upon my life. My husband had died suddenly, leaving me a widow, with four children, one my own, and the others step-children. I tried to keep my children together. But my husband died in debt; and before he had been in his grave three months, the administrator had swept the very milk-crocks and wash tubs from my hands. I was a farmer's wife and made butter for the Columbus market; but what could I do, when they had swept all away? They left me one thing—and that was a looking-glass! Had I died instead of my husband, how different would have been the result! By this time he would have had another wife, it is likely; and no administrator would have gone into his house, broken up his home, and sold his bed, and taken away his means of support.

I took my children in my arms, and went out to seek my living. While I was gone; a neighbor to whom I had once lent five dollars, went before a magistrate and swore that he believed I was a non-resident, and laid an attachment on my very bed. And I went back to Ohio with my orphan children in my arms, without a single feather bed in this wide world, that was not in the custody of the law. I say, then, that justice is not fulfilled so long as woman is unequal before the law.

We are all bound up together in one great bundle of humanity, and society cannot trample on the weakest and feeblest of its members without receiving the curse in its own soul. You tried that in the case of the negro. You pressed him down for two centuries; and in so doing you crippled the moral strength and paralyzed the spiritual energies of the white men of the country. When the hands of the black were fettered, white men were deprived of the liberty of speech and the freedom of the press. Society cannot afford to neglect the enlightenment of any class of its members. At the South, the legislation of the country was in behalf of the rich slaveholders, while the poor white man was neglected. What is the consequence to-day? From that very class of neglected poor white men, comes the man who stands to-day with his hand upon the helm of the nation. He fails to catch the watchword of the hour, and throws himself, the incarnation of meanness, across the pathway of the nation. My objection to Andrew Johnson is not that he has been a poor white man; my objection is that he keeps "poor whits" all the way through. (Applause.) That is the trouble with him.

This grand and glorious revolution which has commenced, will fail to reach its climax of success, until throughout the length and brea[d]th of the American Republic, the nation shall be so color-blind, as to know no man by the color of his skin or the curl of his hair. It will then have no privileged class, trampling upon and outraging the unprivileged classes, but will be then one great privileged nation, whose privilege will be to produce the loftiest manhood and womanhood that humanity can attain.

I do not believe that giving the woman the ballot is immediately going to cure all the ills of life. I do not believe that white women are dewdrops just exhaled from the skies. I think that like men they may be divided into three classes, the good, the bad, and the indifferent. The good would vote according to their convictions and principles; the bad, as dictated by preju[d]ice or malice; and the indifferent will vote on the strongest side of the question, with the winning party.

You white women speak here of rights. I speak of wrongs. I, as a colored woman, have had in this country an education which has made me feel as if I were in the situation of Ishmael, my hand against every man, and every man's hand against me. Let me go to-morrow morning and take my seat in one of your street cars—I do not know that they will do it in New York, but they will in Philadelphia—and the conductor will put up his hand and stop the car rather than let me ride.

A Lady—They will not do that here.

Mrs. Harper—They do in Philadelphia. Going from Washington to Baltimore this Spring, they put me in the smoking car. (Loud Voices—"Shame.") Aye, in the capital of the nation, where the black man consecrated himself to the nation's defence, faithful when the white man was faithless, they put me in the smoking car! They did it once; but the next time they tried it, they failed; for I would not go in. I felt the fight in me; but I don't want to have to fight all the time. To-day I am puzzled where to make my home. I would like to make it in Philadelphia, near my own friends and relations. But if I want to ride in the streets of Philadelphia, they send me to ride on the platform with the driver. (Cries of "Shame.") Have women nothing to do with this? Not long since, a colored woman took her seat in an Eleventh Street car in Philadelphia, and the conductor stopped the car, and told the rest of the passengers to get out, and left the car with her in it alone, when they took it back to the station. One day I took my seat in a car, and the conductor came to me and told me to take another seat. I just screamed "murder." The man said if I was black I ought to behave myself. I knew that if he was white he was not behaving himself. Are there not wrongs to be righted?

THE PHILOSOPHY OF THE ABOLITION MOVEMENT

Wendell Phillips

Wendell Phillips must be remembered as one of the most radical voices of the abolitionist era. Phillips not only championed the cause of abolitionism, but he also spoke and organized for the equal rights of women and Native Americans. Known for his powerful oration and sophisticated political and philosophical arguments, Phillips was a rhetorical force to be reckoned with. "The Philosophy of the Abolition Movement," delivered before the Massachusetts Anti-Slavery Society, in Boston on January 27, 1853, is a careful defense of abolitionist rhetorical practice. Phillips answers to the charges of moderate anti-slavery reformers who were uneasy with the aggressive and passionate language of radicals such as Phillips. Notice Phillips's critique of the politics of moderation, and the pathos that grounds his reasoning.

MR. CHAIRMAN: I have to present, from the business committee, the following resolution:—

"*Resolved,* That the object of this society is now, as it has always been, to convince our countrymen, by arguments addressed to their hearts and consciences, that slaveholding is a heinous crime, and that the duty, safety, and interest of all concerned demand its immediate abolition, without expatriation."

I wish, Mr. Chairman, to notice some objections that have been made to our course ever since Mr. Garrison began his career, and which have been lately urged again, with considerable force and emphasis, in the columns of the London Leader, the able organ of a very respectable and influential class in England. I hope, Sir, you will not think it waste of time to bring such a subject before you. I know these objections have been made a thousand times, that they have been often answered, though we generally submitted to them in silence, willing to let results speak for us. But there are times when justice to the slave will not allow us to be silent. There are many in this country, many in England, who have had their attention turned, recently, to the antislavery cause. They are asking, "Which is the best and most efficient method of helping it?" Engaged ourselves in an effort for the slave, which time has tested and success hitherto approved, we are very properly desirous that they should join us in our labors, and pour into this channel the full tide of their new zeal and great resources. Thoroughly convinced ourselves that our course is wise, we can honestly urge others to adopt it. Long experience gives us a right to advise. The fact that our course, more than all other efforts, has caused that agitation which has awakened those new converts, gives us a right to counsel them. They are our spiritual children: for their sakes, we would free the cause we love and trust from every seeming defect and plausible objection. For the slave's sake, we reiterate our explanations, that he may lose no tittle of help by the mistakes or misconceptions of his friends.

All that I have to say on these points will be to you, Mr. Chairman, very trite and familiar; but the facts may be new to some, and I prefer to state them here, in Boston, where we have lived and worked, because, if our statements are incorrect, if we claim too much, our assertions can be easily answered and disproved.

The charges to which I refer are these: that, in dealing with slaveholders and their apologists, we indulge in fierce denunciations, instead of appealing to their reason and common sense by plain statements and fair argument;—that we might have won the sympathies and support of the nation, if we would have submitted to argue this question with a manly patience; but, instead of this, we have outraged the feelings of the community by attacks, unjust and unnecessarily severe, on its most valued institutions, and gratified our spleen by indiscriminate abuse of leading men, who were often honest in their intentions, however mistaken in their views;—that we have utterly neglected the ample means that lay around us to convert the nation, submitted to no discipline, formed no plan, been guided by no foresight, but hurried on in childish, reckless, blind, and hot-headed zeal,—bigots in the narrowness of our views, and fanatics in our blind fury of invective and malignant judgment of other men's motives.

There are some who come upon our platform, and give us the aid of names and reputations less burdened than ours with popular odium, who are perpetually urging us to exercise charity in our judgments of those about us, and to consent to argue these questions. These men are ever parading their wish to draw a line between themselves and us, because *they must be permitted* to wait,—to trust more to reason than feeling,—to indulge a generous charity,—to rely on the sure influence of simple truth, uttered in love, &c., &c. I reject with scorn all these implications that *our* judgments are uncharitable,—that *we* are lacking in patience,—that *we* have any other dependence than on the simple truth, spoken with Christian frankness, yet with Christian love. These lectures, to which you, Sir, and all of us, have so often listened, would be impertinent, if they were not rather ridiculous for the gross ignorance they betray of the community, of the cause, and of the whole course of its friends.

The article in the Leader to which I refer is signed "ION," and may be found in the Liberator of December 17, 1852. The writer is cordial and generous in his recognition of Mr. Garrison's claim to be the representative of the antislavery movement, and does entire justice to his motives and character. The criticisms of "Ion" were reprinted in the Christian Register, of this city, the organ of the Unitarian denomination. The editors of that paper, with their usual Christian courtesy, love of truth, and fairdealing, omitted all "Ion's" expressions of regard for Mr. Garrison and appreciation of his motives, and reprinted only those parts of the article which undervalue his sagacity and influence, and indorse the common objections to his method and views. You will see in a moment, Mr. President, that it is with such men and presses "Ion" thinks Mr. Garrison has not been sufficiently wise and patient, in trying to win their help for the antislavery cause. Perhaps, were he on the spot, it would tire even his patience, and puzzle even his sagacity, to make any other use of them than that of the drunken Helot,—a warning to others how disgusting is mean vice. Perhaps, were he here, he would see that the best and only use to be made of them is to let them unfold their own characters, and then show the world how rotten our politics and religion are, that they naturally bear such fruit. "Ion" quotes Mr. Garrison's original declaration, in the Liberator:—

> "I am aware that many object to the severity of my language; but is there not cause for severity? I *will* be as harsh as truth, and as uncompromising as justice. I am in earnest,—I will not equivocate,—I will not excuse,—I will not retreat a single inch,—AND I WILL BE HEARD.
>
> "It is *pretended* that I am retarding the cause of emancipation by the coarseness of my invective and the precipitancy of my measures. *The charge is not true.* On this question, my influence, humble as it is, is felt at this moment to a considerable extent, and shall be felt in coming years,—not perniciously, but beneficially,—not as a curse, but as a blessing; and posterity will bear testimony that I was right. I desire to thank God that he enables me to disregard 'the fear of man, which bringeth a snare,' and to speak his truth in its simplicity and power."

"Ion" then goes on to say:—

> "This is a defence which has been generally accepted on this side of the Atlantic, and many are the Abolitionists among us whom it has encouraged in honesty and impotence, and whom it has converted into conscientious hinderances. . . .
>
> "We would have Mr. Garrison to say, 'I will be as harsh as *progress*, as uncompromising as *success*.' If a man speaks for his own gratification, he may be as 'harsh' as he pleases; but if he speaks for the down-trodden and oppressed, he must be content to put a curb upon the tongue of holiest passion, and speak only as harshly as is compatible with the amelioration of the evil he proposes to redress. Let the question be again repeated: Do you seek for the slave vengeance or redress? If you seek retaliation, go on denouncing. But distant Europe honors William Lloyd Garrison because it credits him with seeking for the slave simply redress. We say, therefore, that 'uncompromising' policy is not to be measured by absolute justice, but by practical amelioration of the slave's condition. Amelioration as fast as you can get it,—absolute justice as soon as you can reach it."

He quotes the sentiment of Confucius, that he would choose for a leader "a man who would maintain a steady vigilance in the direction of affairs, who was capable of forming plans, and of executing them," and says:—

> "The philosopher was right in placing wisdom and executive capacity above courage; for, down to this day, our popular movements are led by heroes who *fear* nothing, and who *win* nothing . . . .
>
> "There is no question raised in these articles as to the work to be done, but only as to the mode of *really* doing it. The platform resounds with announcements of principle, which is but *asserting* the right, while nothing but contempt is showered on policy, which is the *realization* of right. The air is filled with all high cries and spirited denunciations; indignation is at a premium; and this is called advocacy. . . . But to calculate, to

> make sure of your aim, is to be descried as one who is too cold to feel, too genteel to strike."

Further on, he observes:—

> "If an artillery officer throws shell after shell which never reach the enemy, he is replaced by some one with a better eye and a surer aim. But in the artillery battle of opinion, *to mean* to hit is quite sufficient: and if you have a certain grand indifference as to whether you hit or not you may want on public applause . . . .
>
> "A man need be no less militant, as the soldier of facts, than as the agent of swords. But the arena of argument needs discipline, no less than that of arms. It is this which the antislavery party seem to me not only to overlook, but to despise. They do not put their valor to drill. Neither on the field nor the platform has courage any inherent capacity of taking care of itself."

The writer then proceeds to make a quotation from Mr. Emerson, the latter part of which I will read:—

> "Let us withhold every *reproachful*, and, if we can, every *indignant* remark. In this cause, we must renounce our temper, and the risings of pride. If there be any man who thinks the ruin of a race of men a small matter compared with the last decorations and completions of his own comfort,—who would not so much as part with his ice-cream to save them from rapine and manacles,—I think I must not hesitate to satisfy *that* man that also his cream and vanilla are safer and cheaper by placing the negro nation on a fair footing, than by robbing them. If the Virginian piques himself on the picturesque luxury of his vassalage, on the heavy Ethiopian manners of his house-servants, their silent obedience, their hue of bronze, their turbaned heads, and would not exchange them for the more intelligent but precarious hired services of whites, I shall not refuse to show *him* that, when their free papers are made out, it will still be their interest to remain on his estates; and that the oldest planters of Jamaica are convinced that it is cheaper to pay wages than to own slaves."

The critic takes exception to Mr. Garrison's approval of the denunciatory language in which Daniel O'Connell rebuked the giant sin of America, and concludes his article with this sentence:—

> "When William Lloyd Garrison praises the great Celtic monarch of invective for this dire outpouring, he acts the part of the boy who fancies that the terror is in the war-whoop of the savage, unmindful of the quieter muskets of the civilized infantry, whose unostentatious execution blows whoop and tomahawk to the Devil."

Before passing to a consideration of these remarks of "Ion," let me say a word in relation to Mr. Emerson. I do not consider him as indorsing any of these criticisms on the Abolitionists. His services to the most radical antislavery movement have been generous and marked. He has never shrunk from any odium which lending his name and voice to it would incur. Making fair allowance for his peculiar taste, habits, and genius, he has given a generous amount of aid to the antislavery movement, and never let its friends want his cordial "God-speed."

"Ion's" charges are the old ones, that we Abolitionists are hurting our own cause,—that, instead of waiting for the community to come up to our views, and endeavoring to remove prejudice and enlighten ignorance by patient explanation and fair argument, we fall at once, like children, to abusing everything and everybody,—that we imagine zeal will supply the place of common sense,—that we have never shown any sagacity in adapting our means to our ends, have never studied the national character, or attempted to make use of the materials which lay all about us to influence public opinion, but by blind, childish, obstinate fury and indiscriminate denunciation, have become "honestly impotent, and conscientious hinderances."

These, Sir, are the charges which have uniformly been brought against all reformers in all ages. "Ion" thinks the same faults are chargeable on the leaders of all the "popular movements" in England, which, he says, "are led by heroes who *fear* nothing and who *win* nothing." If the leaders of popular movements in Great Britain for the last fifty years have been *losers,* I should be curious to know what party, in "Ion's" opinion, have won? My Lord Derby and his friends seem to think Democracy has made, and is making, dangerous headway. If the men who, by popular agitation, outside of Parliament, wrung from a powerful oligarchy Parliamentary Reform, and the Abolition of the Test Acts, of High Post Rates, of Catholic Disability, of Negro Slavery and the Corn Laws, did "not win anything," it would be hard to say what winning is. If the men who, without the ballot, made Peel their tool and conquered the Duke of Wellington, are considered unsuccessful, pray what kind of a thing would success be? Those who now, at the head of that same middle class, demand the separation of Church and State, and the Extension of the Ballot, may well guess, from the fluttering of Whig and Tory dove-cotes, that soon they will "win" that same "nothing." Heaven grant they may enjoy the same *ill success* with their predecssors! On our side of the ocean, too, we ought deeply to sympathize with the leaders of the temperance movement in their entire want of success! If "Ion's" mistakes about the antislavery cause lay as much on the surface as those I have just noticed, it would be hardly worth while to reply to him; for as to these, he certainly exhibits only "the extent and variety of his misinformation."

His remarks upon the antislavery movement are, however, equally inaccurate. I claim, before you who know the true state of the case,—I claim for the antislavery movement with which this society is identified, that, looking back over its whole course, and considering the men connected with it in the mass, it has been marked by sound judgment, unerring foresight, the most sagacious adaptation of means to ends, the strictest self-discipline, the most thorough research, and an amount of patient and manly argument addressed to the conscience and intellect of the nation, such as no other cause of the kind, in England or this country, has ever offered. I claim, also, that its course has been marked by a cheerful surrender of all individual claims to merit or leadership,—the most cordial welcoming of the slightest effort, of every honest attempt, to lighten or to break the chain of the slave. I need not waste time by repeating the superfluous confession that we are men, and therefore do not claim to be perfect. Neither would I be understood as denying that we use denunciation, and ridicule, and every other weapon that the human mind knows. We must plead guilty, if there be guilt in not knowing how to separate the sin from the sinner. With all the fondness for abstractions attributed to us, we are not yet capable of that. We are fighting a momentous battle at desperate odds,—one against a thousand. Every weapon that ability or ignorance, wit, wealth, prejudice, or fashion can command, is pointed against us. The guns are shotted to their lips. The arrows are poisoned. Fighting against such an array, we cannot afford to confine ourselves to any one weapon. The cause is not ours, so that we might, rightfully, postpone or put in peril the victory by moderating our demands, stifling our convictions, or filing down our rebukes, to gratify any sickly taste of our own, or to spare the delicate nerves of our neighbor. Our clients are three millions of Christian slaves, standing dumb suppliants at the threshold of the Christian world. They have no voice but ours to utter their complaints, or to demand justice. The press, the pulpit, the wealth, the literature, the prejudices, the political arrangements, the present self-interest of the country, are all against us. God has given us no weapon but the truth, faithfully uttered, and addressed, with the old prophers' directness, to the conscience of the individual sinner. The elements which control public opinion and mould the masses are against us. We can but pick off here and there a man from the triumphant majority. We have facts for those who think, arguments for those who reason; but he who cannot be reasoned out of his prejudices must be laughed out of them; he who cannot be argued out of his selfishness must be shamed out of it by the mirror of his hateful self held up relentlessly before his eyes. We live in a land where every man makes broad his phylactery, inscribing thereon, "All men are created equal,"—"God hath made of one blood all nations of men." It seems to us that in such a land there must be, on this question of slavery, sluggards to be awakened, as well as doubters to be convinced. Many more, we verily believe, of the first than of the last. There are far more dead hearts to be quickened, than confused intellects to be cleared up,—more dumb dogs to be made to speak, than doubting consciences to be enlightened. [Loud cheers.] We have use, then, sometimes, for something beside argument.

What is the denunciation with which we are charged? It is endeavoring, in our faltering human speech, to declare the enormity of the sin of making merchandise of men,—of separating husband and wife,—taking the infant from its mother, and selling the daughter to prostitution,—of a professedly Christian nation denying, by statute, the Bible to every sixth man and woman of its population, and making it illegal for "two or three" to meet together, except a white man be present! What is this harsh criticism of motives with which we are charged? It is simply holding the intelligent and deliberate actor responsible for the character and consequences of his acts. Is there anything inherently wrong in such denunciation or such criticism? This we may claim,—we have never judged a man but out of his own mouth. We have seldom, if ever, held him to account, except for acts of which he and his own friends were proud. All that we ask the world and thoughtful men to note are the principles and deeds on which the American pulpit and American public men plume themselves. We always allow our opponents to paint their own pictures.

Our humble duty is to stand by and assure the spectators that what they would take for a knave or a hypocrite is really, in American estimation, a Doctor of Divinity or Secretary of State.*

The South is one great brothel, where half a million of women are flogged to prostitution, or, worse still, are degraded to believe it honorable. The public squares of half our great cities echo to the wail of families torn asunder at the auction-block; no one of our fair rivers that has not closed over the negro seeking in death a refuge from a life too wretched to bear; thousands of fugitives skulk along over highways, afraid to tell their names, and trembling at the sight of a human being; free men are kidnapped in our streets, to be plunged into that hell of slavery; and now and then one, as if by mirracle, after long years, returns to make men aghast with his tale. The press says, "It is all right"; and the pulpit cries, "Amen." They print the Bible in every tongue in which man utters his prayers; and get the money to do so by agreeing never to give the book, in money to do so by agreeing never to give the book, in the language our mothers taught us, to any negro, free or bond, south of Mason and Dixon's line. The press says, "It is all right"; and the pulpit cries, "Amen." The slave lifts up his imploring eyes, and sees in every face but ours the face of an enemy. Prove to me

---

*A paragraph from the New England Farmer, of this city, has gone the rounds of the press, and is generally believed. It says:—

"We learn, on reliable authority, that Mr. Webster coufessed to a warm political friend, a short time before his death, that the great mistake of his life was the famous Seventh of March Speech, in which, it will be remembered, he defended the Fugitive Slave Law, and fully committed himself to the Compromise Measures. Before taking his stand on that occasion, he is said to have corresponded with Professor Stuart, and other eminent divines, to ascertain how far the religious sentiment of the North would sustain him in the position he was about to assume."

Some say this "warm political friend" was a clergyman! Consider a moment the language of this statement, the form it takes on every lip and in every press. "The great mistake of his life"! Seventy years old, brought up in New England churches, with all the culture of the world at his command, his soul method by the repeated loss of those dearest to him, a great statesman, with a heart, according to his admires, yet tender and fresh,—one who beat in such agony over the death-best of his first daughter,—he looks back on this speech, which his friends say changed the feelings of ten millions of people, and made it possible to exact and execute the Fugitive Slave Law. He sees that is seaside the hearth-stones of thousands of egloral man with wretchedness and despair,—crazed the mother, and broke the heart of the wife—paradise the virtue of woman and the liberty man is the power of the vilest, — and all, as he at least now saw, nothing. Yet one who, according to his worshippers, was "the grandest growth of our soil and our institutions," looked back on such an act, and said—what? With one foot in the grave, said what of it? "I did wrong"? "I committed a foul outrage on my brother man"? moral chord in that heart, "the grandest growth of our soil and our institutions"? No! He said, "I made a mistake!" Not, "I was false in my stewardship of these great talents and this high position!" No! But on the chess-board of the political game, I made a bad move! I threw away my chances! A gambler, I did not understand my cards! And to whom does he offer this acknowledgement? To a clergyman! the representative of the moral sense of the community! What a picture! We laugh at the lack of heart in Talleyrand, when he says, "It is worse than a crime, a blunder." Yet all our New-Englander can call this momentous crime of his life is—a *mistake!*

Whether this statement be entirely true or not, we all know it is exactly the tone in which all about us talk of that speech. If the statment be true, what an entire want of right feeling and moral sensibility it shows in Mr. Webster! If it be unfounded, still the welcome it has received, and the ready belief it has gained, show the popular appreciation of him, and of such a crime. Such is the public with which Abolitionists have to deal.

now that harsh rebuke, indignant denunciation, scathing sarcasm, and pitiless ridicule are wholly and always injustifiable; else we dare not, in so desperate a case, throw away any weapon which never broke up the crust of an ignorant prejudice, roused a slumbering conscience, shamed a proud sinner, or changed, in any way, the conduct of a human being. Our aim is to alter public opinion. Did we live in a market, our talk should be of dollars and cents, and we would seek to prove only that slavery was an unprofitable investment. Were the nation one great, pure church, we would sit down and reason of "righteousness, temperance, and judgment to come." Had slavery fortified itself in a college, we would load our cannons with cold facts, and wing our arrows with arguments. But we happen to live in the world,—the world made up of thought and impulse, of self-conceit and self-interest, of weak men and wicked. To conquer, we must reach all. Our object is not to make every man a Christian or a philosopher, but to induce every one to aid in the abolition of slavery. We expect to accomplish our object long before the nation is made over into saints or elevated into philosophers. To change public opinion, we use the very tools by which it was formed. That is, all such as an honest man may touch.

All this I am not only ready to allow, but I should be ashamed to think of the slave, or to look into the face of my fellow-man, if it were otherwise. It is the only thing which justifies us to our own consciences, and makes us able to say we have done, or at least tried to do, our duty.

So far, however you distrust my philosophy, you will not doubt my statements. That we have denounced and rebuked with unsparing fidelity will not be denied. Have we not also addressed ourselves to that other duty, of arguing our question thoroughly?—of using due discretion and fair sagacity in endeavoring to promote our cause? Yes, we have. Every statement we have made has been doubted. Every principle we have laid down has been denied by overwhelming majorities against us. No one step has ever been gained but by the most laborious research and the most exhausting argument. And no question has ever, since Revolutionary days, been so thoroughly investigated or argued here, as that of slavery. Of that research and that argument, of the whole of it, the old-fashioned, fanatical, crazy Garrisonian antislavery movement has been the author. From this band of men has proceeded every important argument or idea which has been broached on the antislavery question from 1830 to the present time. [Cheers.] I am well aware of the extent of the claim I make. I recognize, as fully as any one can, the ability of the new laborers,—the eloquence and genius with which they have recommended this cause to the nation, and flashed conviction home on the conscience of the community. I do not mean, either, to assert that they have in every instance borrowed from our treasury their facts and arguments. Left to themselves, they would probably have looked up the one and originated the other. As a matter of fact, however, they have generally made use of the materials collected to their hands. But there are some persons about us, sympathizers to a great extent with "Ion," who pretend that the antislavery movement has been hitherto mere fanaticism, its only weapon angry abuse. They are obliged to assert this, in order to justify their past indifference or hostility. At present, when it suits their purpose to give it some attention, they endeavor to explain the change by alleging that now it has been taken up by men of thoughtful minds, and its claims are urged by fair discussion and able argument.

My claim, then, is this: that neither the charity of the most timid of sects, the sagacity of our wisest converts, nor the culture of the ripest scholars, though all have been aided by our twenty years' experience, has yet struck out any new argument or train of thought, or discovered any new or discovered any new fact bearing on the question. When once brought fully into the struggle, they have found it necessary to adopt the same means, to rely on the same arguments, to hold up the same men and the same measures to public reprobation, with the same bold rebuke and unsparing invective that we have used. All their conciliatory bearing, their painstaking moderation, their constant and anxious endeavor to draw a broad line between their camp and ours, have been thrown away. Just so far as they have been effective laborers, they have found, as we have, their hands against every man, and every man's hand against them. The most experienced of them are ready to acknowledge that our plan has been wise, our course efficient, and that our unpopularity is no fault of ours, but flows necessarily and unavoidably from our position. "I should suspect," says old Fuller, "that his preaching had no salt in it, if no galled horse did wince." Our friends find, after all, that men do not so much hate us as the truth we utter and the light we bring. They find that the community are not the honest seekers after truth which they fancied, but selfish politicians and sectarian bigots, who shiver, like Alexander's butler, whenever the sun shines on them. Experience has driven these new laborers back to our method. We have no quarrel with them,—would not steal one wreath of their laurels. All we claim is, that, if they are to be complimented as prudent, moderate, Christian, sagacious, statesmanlike reformers, we deserve the same praise; for they have done nothing that we, in our measure, did not attempt before. [Cheers.]

I claim this, that the cause, in its recent aspect, has put on nothing but timidity. It has taken to itself no new weapons of recent years; it has become more compromising,—that is all. It has become neither more persuasive, more learned, more Christian, more charitable, nor more effective than for the twenty years preceding. Mr. Hale, the head of the Free Soil movement, after a career in the Senate that would do honor to any man,—after a six years' course which entiles him to the respect and confidence of the antislavery public,—can put his name, within the last month, to an appeal from the city of Washington, signed by a Houston and a Cass, for a monument to be raised to Henry Clay! If that be the test of charity and courtesy, we cannot give it to the world. [Loud cheers.] Some of the leaders of the Free Soil party of Massachusetts, after exhausting the whole capacity of our language to paint the treachery of Daniel Webster to the cause of liberty, and the evil they thought he was able and seeking to do,—after that, could feel it in their hearts to parade themselves in the funeral procession got up to do him honor! In this we allow we cannot follow them. The deference which every gentleman owes to the proprieties of social life, that self-respect and regard to consistency which is every man's duty,—these, if no deeper feelings, will ever prevent us from giving such proofs of this newly-invented Christian courtesy. [Great cheering.] We do not *play* politics; antislavery is no half-jest with us; it is a terrible earnest, with life or death, worse than life or death, on the issue. It is no lawsuit, where it matters not to the good feeling of opposing counsel which way the verdict goes, and where advocates can shake hands after the decision as pleasantly as before. When we think of such a man as Henry Clay, his long life, his mighty influence cast always into the scale against the slave,—of that irresistible fascination with which he moulded every one to his will; when we remember that, his conscience acknowledging the justice of our cause, and his heart open on every other side to the gentlest impulses, he could sacrifice so remorsely his convictions and the welfare of millions to his low ambition; when we think how the slave trembled at the sound of his voice, and that, from a multitude of breaking hearts there went up nothing but gratitude to God when it pleased him to call that great sinner from this world,—we cannot find it in our hearts, we could not shape our lips to ask any man to do him honor. [Great sensation.] No amount of eloquence, no sheen of official position, no loud grief of partisan friends, would ever lead us to ask monuments or walk in fine processions for pirates; and the sectarian zeal or selfish ambition which gives up, deliberately and in full knowledge of the facts, three million of human beings to hopeless ignorance, daily robbery, systematic prostitution, and murder, which the law is neither able nor undertakes to prevent or avenge, is more monstrous, in our eyes, than the love of gold which takes a score of lives with merciful quickness on the high seas. Haynau on the Danube is no more hateful to us than Haynau on the Potomac. Why give mobs to one, and monuments to the other?

If these things be necessary to courtesy, I cannot claim that we are courteous. We seek only to be honest men, and speak the same of the dead as of the living. If the grave that hides their bodies could swallow also the evil they have done and the example they leave, we might enjoy at least the luxury of forgetting them. But the evil that men do lives after them, and example acquires tenfold authority when it speaks from the grave. History, also, is to be written. How shall a feeble minority, without weight or influence in the country, with no jury of millions to appeal to,—denounced, vilified, and contemned,—how shall we make way against the overwhelming weight of some colossal reputation, if we do not turn from the idolatrous present, and appeal to the human race? saying to your idols of to-day. "Here we are defeated: but we will write our judgment with the iron pen of a century to come, and it shall never be forgotten, if we can help it, that you were false in your generation to the claims of the slave!" [Loud cheers.]

At present, our leading men, strong in the support of large majorities, and counting safely on the prejudices of the community, can afford to despise us. They know they can overawe or cajole the Present; their only fear is the judgment of the Future. Strange fear, perhaps, considering how short and local their fame! But however little, it is their all. Our only hold upon them is the thought of that bar of posterity, before which we are all to stand. Thank God! there is the elder brother of the Saxon race across the water,—there is the army of honest men to come! Before that jury we summon you. We are weak here,—out-talked, out-voted. You load our names with infamy, and shout us down. But our words bide their time. We warn the living that we have terrible memories, and that their sins are never to be forgotten. We will gibbet the name of every apostate so black and high that his children's children shall blush to bear it. Yet we bear no malice,—cherish no resentment. We thank God that the love of fame, "that last infirmity of noble mind," is shared by the ignoble. In our necessity, we seize this weapon in the slave's behalf, and teach caution to the living by meting out relentless justice to the dead. How strange the change death produces in the way a man is talked about here! While leading men live, they avoid as much as possible all mention of slavery, from fear of being thought Abolitionists. The moment they are dead, their friends rake up every word they ever contrived to whisper in a corner for liberty, and parade it before the world; growing angry, all the while, with us, because we insist on explaining these chance expressions by the tenor of a long and base life. While drunk with the temptations of the present hour, men are willing to bow to any Moloch. When their friends bury them, they feel what bitter mockery, fifty years hence, any epitaph will be, if it cannot record of one living in this era some service rendered to the slave! These, Mr. Chairman, are the reasons why we take care that "the memory of the wicked shall rot."

I have claimed that the antislavery cause has, from the first, been ably and dispassionately argued, every objection candidly examined, and every difficulty or doubt anywhere honestly entertained treated with respect. Let me glance at the literature of the cause, and try not so much, in a brief hour, to prove this assertion, as to point out the sources from which any one may satisfy himself of its truth.

I will begin with certainly the ablest and perhaps the most honest statesman who has ever touched the slave question. Any one who will examine John Quincy Adams's speech on Texas, in 1838, will see that he was only seconding the full and able exposure of the Texas plot, prepared by Benjamin Lundy, to one of whose pamphlets Dr. Channing, in his "Letter to Henry Clay," has confessed his obligation. Every one acquainted with those years will allow that the North owes its earliest knowledge and first awakening on that subject to Mr. Lundy, who made long journeys and devoted years to the investigation. His labors have this attestation, that they quickened the zeal and strengthened the hands of such men as Adams and Channing. I have been told that Mr. Lundy prepared a brief for Mr. Adams, and furnished him the materials for his speech on Texas.

Look next at the right of petition. Long before any member of Congress had opened his mouth in its defence, the Abolition presses and lecturers had examined and defended the limits of this right with profound historical research and eminent constitutional ability. So thoroughly had the work been done, that all classes of the people had made up their minds about it long before any speaker of eminence had touched it in Congress. The politicians were little aware of this. When Mr. Adams threw himself so gallantly into the breach, it is said he wrote anxiously home to know whether he would be supported in Massachusetts, little aware of the outburst of popular gratitude which the Northern breeze was even then bringing him, deep and cordial enough to wipe away the old grudge Massachusetts had borne him so long. Mr. Adams himself was only in favor of receiving the petitions, and advised to refuse their prayer, which was the abolition of slavery in the District. He doubted the power of Congress to abolish. His doubts were examined by Mr. William Goodell, in two letters of most acute logic, and of masterly ability. If Mr. Adams still retained his doubts, it is certain at least that he never expressed them afterward. When Mr. Clay paraded the same objections, the whole question of the power of Congress over the district was treated by Theodore D. Weld in the fullest manner, and with the widest research,—indeed, leaving nothing to be added: an argument which Dr. Channing characterized as "demonstration," and pronounced the essay "one of the ablest pamphlets from the American press." No answer was ever attempted. The best proof of its ability is, that no one since has presumed to doubt the power. Lawyers and statesmen have tacitly settled down into its full acknowledgment.

The influence of the Colonization Society on the welfare of the colored race was the first question our movement encountered. To the close logic, eloquent appeals, and fully sustained charges of Mr. Garrison's Letters on that subject no answer was ever made. Judge Jay followed with a work full and able, establishing every charge by the most patient investigation of facts. It is not too much to say of these two volumes, that they left the Colonization Society hopeless at the North. It dares never show its face before the people, and only lingers in some few nooks of sectarian pride, so secluded from the influence of present ideas as to be almost fossil in their character.

The practical working of the slave system, the slave laws, the treatment of slaves, their food, the duration of their lives, their ignorance and moral condition, and the influence of Southern public opinion on their fate, have been spread out in a detail and with a fulness of evidence which no subject has ever received before in this country. Witness the works of Phelps, Bourne, Rankin, Grimke, the "Antislavery Record," and, above all, that encyclopædia of facts and storehouse of arguments, the "Thousand Witnesses" of Mr. Theodore D. Weld. He also prepared that full and valuable tract for the World's Convention called "Slavery and the Internal Slave-Trade in the United States," published in London, 1841. Unique in antislavery literature is Mrs. Child's "Appeal," one of the ablest of our weapons, and one of the finest efforts of her rare genius.

The Princeton Review, I believe, first challenged the Abolitionists to an investigation of the teachings of the Bible on slavery. That field had been somewhat broken by our English predecessors. But in England, the proslavery party had been soon shamed out of the attempt to drag the Bible into their service, and hence the discussion there had been short and somewhat superficial. The proslavery side of the question has been eagerly sustained by theological reviews and doctors of divinity without number, from the half-way and timid faltering of Wayland up to the unblushing and melancholy recklessness of Stuart. The argument on the other side has come wholly from the Abolitionists; for neither Dr. Hague nor Dr. Barnes can be said to have added anything to the wide research, critical acumen, and comprehensive views of Theodore D. Weld, Beriah Green, J. G. Fee, and the old work of Duncan.

On the constitutional questions which have at various times arisen,—the citizenship of the colored man, the soundness of the "Prigg" decision, the constitutionality of the old Fugitive Slave Law, the true construction of the slave-surrender clause,—nothing has been added, either in the way of fact or argument, to the works of Jay, Weld, Alvan Stewart, E. G. Loring, S. E. Sewall, Richard Hildreth, W. I. Bowditch, the masterly essays of the Emancipator at New York and the Liberator at Boston, and the various addresses of the Massachusetts and American Societies for the last twenty years. The idea of the antislavery character of the Constitution,—the opiate with which Free Soil quiets its conscience for voting under a proslavery government,—I heard first suggested by Mr. Garrison in 1838. It was elaborately argued that year in all our antislavery gatherings, both here and in New York, and sustained with great ability by Alvan Stewart, and in part by T. D. Weld. The antislavery construction of the

Constitution was ably argued in 1836, in the "Antislavery Magazine," by Rev. Samuel J. May, one of the very first to seek the side of Mr. Garrison, and pledge to the slave his life and efforts.—a pledge which thirty years of devoted labors have nobly redeemed. If it has either merit or truth, they are due to no legal learning recently added to our ranks, but to some of the old and well-known pioneers. This claim has since received the fullest investigation from Mr. Lysander Spooner, who has urged it with all his unrivalled ingenuity, laborious research, and close logic. He writes as a lawyer, and has no wish, I believe, to be ranked with any class of antislavery men.

The influence of slavery on our government has received the profoundest philosophical investigation from the pen of Richard Hildreth, in his invaluable essay on "Despotism in America,"—a work which deserves a place by the side of the ablest political disquisitions of any age.

Mrs. Chapman's survey of "Ten Years of Antislavery Experience," was the first attempt at a philosophical discussion of the various aspects of the antislavery cause, and the problems raised by its struggles with sect and party. You, Mr. Chairman, [Edmund Quincy, Esq.,] in the elaborate Reports of the Massachusetts Antislavery Society for the last ten years, have followed in the same path, making to American literature a contribution of the highest value, and in a department where you have few rivals and no superior. Whoever shall write the history either of this movement, or any other attempted under a republican government, will find nowhere else so clear an insight and so full an acquaintance with the most difficult part of his subject.

Even the vigorous mind of Rantoul, the ablest man, without doubt, of the Democratic party, and perhaps the ripest politician in New England, added little or nothing to the storehouse of antislavery argument. The grasp of his intellect and the fulness of his learning every one will acknowledge. He never trusted himself to speak on any subject till he had dug down to its primal granite. He laid a most generous contribution on the altar of the antislavery cause. His speeches on our question, too short and too few, are remarkable for their compact statement, iron logic, bold denunciation, and the wonderful light thrown back upon our history. Yet how little do they present which was not familiar for years in our antislavery meetings!

Look, too, at the last great effort of the idol of so many thousands, Mr. Senator Sumner,—the discussion of a great national question, of which it has been said that we must go back to Webster's Reply to Hayne, and Fisher Ames on the Jay Treaty, to find its equal in Congress,—praise which we might perhaps qualify, if any adequate report were left us of some of the noble orations of Adams. No one can be blind to the skilful use he has made of his materials, the consummate ability with which he has marshalled them, and the radiant glow which his genius has thrown over all. Yet, with the exception of his reference to the antislavery debate in Congress, in 1817, there is hardly a train of thought or argument, and no single fact in the whole speech, which has not been familiar in our meetings and essays for the last ten years.

Before leaving the halls of Congress, I have great pleasure in recognizing one exception to my remarks, Mr. Giddings. Perhaps he is no real exception, since it would not be difficult to establish his claim to be considered one of the original Abolition party. But whether he would choose to be so considered or not, it is certainly true that his long presence at the seat of government, his whole souled devotedness, his sagacity and unwearied industry, have made him a large contributor to our anti-slavery resources.

The relations of the American Church to slavery, and the duties of private Christians,—the whole casuistry of this portion of the question, so momentous among descendants of the Puritans,—have been discussed with great acuteness and rare common-sense by Messrs. Garrison, Goodell, Gerritt Smith, Pillsbury, and Foster. They have never attempted to judge the American Church by any standard except that which she has herself laid down,—never claimed that she should be perfect, but have contented themselves by demanding that she should be consistent. They have never judged her except out of her own mouth, and on facts asserted by her own presses and leaders. The sundering of the Methodist and Baptist denominations, and the universal agitation of the religious world, are the best proof of the sagacity with which their measures have been chosen, the cogent arguments they have used, and the indisputable facts on which their criticisms have been founded.

In nothing have the Abolitionists shown more sagacity or more thorough knowledge of their countrymen than in the course they have pursued in relation to the Church. None but a New-Englander can appreciate the power which church organizations wield over all who share the blood of the Puritans. The influence of each sect over its own members is overwhelming, often shutting out, or controlling, all other influences. We have Popes here, all the more dangerous because no triple crown puts you on your guard. The Methodist priesthood brings the Catholic very vividly to mind. That each local church is independent of all others, we have been somewhat careful to assert, in theory and practice. The individual's independence of all organizations which place themselves between him and his God, some few bold minds have asserted in theory, but most even of those have stopped there.

In such a land, the Abolitionists early saw, that, for a moral question like theirs, only two paths lay open: to work through the Church,—that failing, to join battle with it. Some tried long, like Luther, to be Protestants, and yet not come out of Catholicism; but their eyes were soon opened. Since then we have been convinced that, to come out from the Church, to hold her up as the bulwark of slavery, and to make her shortcomings the main burden of our appeals to the religious sentiment of the community, was our first duty and best policy. This course alienated many friends, and was a subject of frequent rebuke from such men as Dr. Channing. But nothing has ever more strengthened the cause, or won it more influence; and it has had the healthiest effect on the Church itself. British Christians have always sanctioned it, whenever the case has been fairly presented to them. Mr. John Quincy Adams, a man far better acquainted with his own times than Dr. Channing, recognized the soundness of our policy. I do not know that he ever uttered a word in public on the delinquency of the churches; but he is said to have assured his son, at the time the Methodist Church broke asunder, that other men might be more startled by the *éclat* of political success, but nothing, in his opinion, promised more good, or showed more clearly the real strength of the antislavery movement, than that momentous event.*

*Henry Clay attached the same importance to the ecclesiastical influence and divisions. See his "Interview with Rev. Dr. Hill, of Louisville. Ky." *Antislavery Standard,* July 14, 1860.

In 1838, the British Emancipation in the West Indies opened a rich field for observation, and a full harvest of important facts. The Abolitionists, not willing to wait for the official reports of the government, sent special agents through those islands, whose reports they scattered, at great expense and by great exertion, broadcast through the land. This was at a time when no newspaper in the country would either lend or sell them the aid of its columns to enlighten the nation on an experiment so vitally important to us. And even now, hardly a press in the country cares or dares to bestow a line or communicate a fact toward the history of that remarkable revolution. The columns of the Antislavery Standard, Pennsylvania Freeman, and Ohio Bugle have been for years full of all that a thorough and patient advocacy of our cause demands. And the eloquent lips of many whom I see around me, and whom I need not name here, have done their share toward pressing all these topics on public attention. There is hardly any record of these labors of the living voice. Indeed, from the nature of the case, there cannot be any adequate one. Yet, unable to command a wide circulation for our books and journals, we have been obliged to bring ourselves into close contact with the people, and to rely mainly on public addresses. These have been our most efficient instrumentality. For proof that these addresses have been full of pertinent facts, sound sense, and able arguments, we must necessarily point to results, and demand to be tried by our fruits. Within these last twenty years it has been very rare that any fact stated by your lecturers has been disproved, or any statement of theirs successfully impeached. And for evidence of the soundness, simplicity, and pertinency of their arguments we can only claim that our converts and co-laborers throughout the land have at least the reputation of being specially able "to give a reason for the faith that is in them."

I remember that when, in 1845, the present leaders of the Free Soil party, with Daniel Webster in their company, met to draw up the Anti-Texas Address of the Massachusetts Convention, they sent to Abolitionists for antislavery facts and history, for the remarkable testimonies of our Revolutionary great men which they wished to quote. [Hear! hear!] When, many years ago, the Legislature of Massachusetts wished to send to Congress a resolution affirming the duty of immediate emancipation, the committee sent to William Lloyd Garrison to draw it up, and it stands now on our statute-book as he drafted it.

How vigilantly, how patiently, did we watch the Texas plot from its commencement! The politic South felt that its first move had been too bold, and thenceforward worked underground. For many a year, men laughed at us for entertaining any apprehensions. It was impossible to rouse the North to its peril. David Lee Child was thought crazy, because he would not believe there was no danger. His elaborate "Letters on Texan Annexation" are the ablest and most valuable contribution that has been made towards a history of the whole plot. Though we foresaw and proclaimed our conviction that annexation would be, in the end, a fatal step for the South, we did not feel at liberty to relax our opposition, well knowing the vast increase of strength it would give, at first, to the Slave Power. I remember being one of a committee which waited on Abbott Lawrence, a year or so only before annexation, to ask his countenance to some general movement, without distinction of party, against the Texas scheme. He smiled at our fears, begged us to have no apprehensions; stating that his correspondence with leading men at Washington enabled him to assure us annexation was impossible, and that the South itself was determined to defeat the project. A short time after, Senators and Representatives from Texas took their seats in Congress!

Many of these services to the slave were done before I joined his cause. In thus referring to them, do not suppose me merely seeking occasion of eulogy on my predecessors and present co-laborers. I recall these things only to rebut the contemptuous criticism which some about us make the excuse for their past neglect of the movement, and in answer to "Ion's" representation of our course as reckless fanaticism, childish impatience, utter lack of good sense, and of our meetings as scenes only of excitement, of reckless and indiscriminate denunciation. I assert that every social, moral, economical, religious, political, and historical aspect of the question has been ably and patiently examined. And all this has been done with an industry and ability which have left little for the professional skill, scholarly culture, and historical learning of the new laborers to accomplish. If the people are still in doubt, it is from the inherent difficulty of the subject, or a hatred of light, not from want of it.

So far from the antislavery cause having lacked a manly and able discussion, I think it will be acknowledged hereafter that this discussion has been one of the noblest contributions to a literature really American. Heretofore, not only has our tone been but an echo of foreign culture, but the very topics discussed and the views maintained have been too often pale reflections of European politics and European philosophy. No matter what dress we assumed, the voice was ever "the voice of Jacob." At last we have stirred a question thoroughly American; the subject has been looked at from a point of view entirely American; and it is of such deep interest, that it has called out all the intellectual strength of the nation. For once, the nation speaks its own thoughts, in its own language, and the tone also is all its own. It will hardly do for the defeated party to claim that, in this discussion, all the ability is on their side.

We are charged with lacking foresight, and said to exaggerate. This charge of exaggeration brings to my mind a fact I mentioned, last month, at Horticultural Hall. The theatres in many of our large cities bring out, night after night, all the radical doctrines and all the startling scenes of "Uncle Tom." They preach immediate emancipation, and slaves shoot their hunters to loud applause. Two years ago, sitting in this hall, I was myself somewhat startled by the assertion of my friend, Mr. Pillsbury, that the theatres would receive the gospel of antislavery truth earlier than the churches. A hiss went up from the galleries, and many in the audience were shocked by the remark. I asked myself whether I could indorse such a statement, and felt that I could not. I could not believe it to be true. Only two years have passed, and what was then deemed rant and fanaticism, by seven out of ten who heard it, has proved true. The theatre, bowing to its audience, has preached immediate emancipation, and given us the whole of "Uncle Tom"; while the pulpit is either silent or hostile, and in the columns of the theological papers the work is subjected to criticism, to reproach, and its author to severe rebuke. Do not, therefore, friends, set down as extravagant every statement which your experience does not warrant. It may be that you and I have not studied the signs of the times quite as accurately as the speaker. Going up and down the land, coming into close contact with the feelings and prejudices of the community, he is sometimes a better judge than you are of its present state. An Abolitionist has more motives for watching and more means of finding out the true state of public opinion, than most of those careless critics who jeer at his assertions to-day, and are the first to cry, "Just what *I* said," when his prophecy becomes fact to-morrow.

Mr. "Ion" thinks, also, that we have thrown away opportunities, and needlessly outraged the men and parties about us. Far from it. The antislavery movement was a patient and humble suppliant at every door whence any help could possibly be hoped. If we now repudiate and denounce some of our institutions, it is because we have faithfully tried them, and found them deaf to the claims of justice and humanity. Our great Leader, when he first meditated this crusade, did not

"At once, like a sunburst, his banner unfurl."

O no! he sounded his way warily forward. Brought up in the strictest reverence for church organizations, his first effort was to enlist the clergymen of Boston in the support of his views. On their aid he counted confidently in his effort to preach immediate repentance of all sin. He did not go, with *malice prepense*, as some seem to imagine, up to that "attic" where Mayor Otis with difficulty found him. He did not court hostility or seek exile. He did not sedulously endeavor to cut himself off from the sympathy and countenance of the community about him. O no! A fervid disciple of the American Church, he conferred with some of the leading clergy of the city, and laid before them his convictions on the subject of slavery.* He painted their responsibility, and tried to induce them to take from his shoulders the burden of so mighty a movement. He laid himself at their feet. He recognized the colossal strength of the Clergy; he knew that against their opposition it would be almost desperate to attempt to relieve the slave. He entreated them, therefore, to take up the cause. But the Clergy turned away from him! They shut their doors upon him! They bade him compromise his convictions,—smother one half of them, and support the colonization movement, making his own auxiliary to that, or they would have none of him. Like Luther, he said: "Here I stand; God help me; I can do nothing else!" But the men who joined him were not persuaded that the case was so desperate. They returned, each to his own local sect, and remained in them until some of us, myself among the number,—later converts to the antislavery movement,—thought they were slow and faltering in their obedience to conscience, and that they ought to have cut loose much sooner than they did. But a patience, which old sympathies would not allow to be

*"The writer accompanied Mr. Garrison, in 1829, in calling upon a number of prominent ministers in Boston, to secure their co-operation in this case. Our expectations of important assistance from them were, at that time, very acquired." —Testimony of William Goodell, in a recent work entitled "Slavery and Antislavery."

In an address on Slavery and Colonization, delivered by Mr. Garrison in the Park Street Church, Boston, July 4, 1829, (which was subsequently published in the National Philanthropist) he said: "I call on the ambassadors of Christ anywhere, to make known this proclamation. Thus saith the Lord God of the Affairs. Let this people go, that they may serve me.' I ask them to 'proclaim liberty to the captive, and the opening of the prison to them that are bound.' I call on the churches of the living God to LEAD in this great enterprise."

exhausted, and associations, planted deeply in youth, and spreading over a large part of manhood, were too strong for any mere argument to dislodge them. So they still persisted in remaining in the Church. Their zeal was so fervent, and their labors so abundant, that in some towns large societies were formed, led by most of the clergymen, and having almost all the church-members on their lists. In those same towns now you will not find one single Abolitionist, of any stamp whatever. They excuse their falling back by alleging that we have injured the cause by our extravagance and denunciation, and by the various other questions with which our names are associated. This might be a good reason why they should not work with us, but does it excuse their not working at all? These people have been once awakened, thoroughly instructed in the momentous character of the movement, and have acknowledged the rightful claim of the slave on their sympathy and exertions. It is not possible that a few thousand persons, however extravagant, could prevent devoted men from finding some way to help such a cause, or at least manifesting their interest in it. But they have not only left us, they have utterly deserted the slave, in the hour when the interests of their sects came across his cause. Is it uncharitable to conjecture the reason? At the early period, however, to which I have referred, the Church was much exercised by the persistency of the Abolitionists in not going out from her. When I joined the antislavery ranks, sixteen years ago, the voice of the clergy was: "Will these *pests* never leave us? Will they still remain to trouble us? If you do not like us, there is the door!" When our friends had exhausted all entreaty, and tested the Christianity of that body, they shook off the dust of their feet, and came out of her.

At the outset, Mr. Garrison called on the head of the Orthodox denomination,—a man compared with whose influence on the mind of New England that of the statesman whose death you have just mourned was, I think, but as dust in the balance,—a man who then held the Orthodoxy of Boston in his right hand, and who has since taken up the West by its four corners, and given it so largely to Puritanism,—I mean the Rev. Dr. Lyman Beecher. Mr. Garrison was one of those who bowed to the spell of that matchless eloquence which then fulmined over our Zion. He waited on his favorite divine, and urged him to give to the new movement the incalculable aid of his name and countenance. He was patiently heard. He was allowed to unfold his plans and array his facts. The reply of the veteran was, "Mr. Garrison, I have too many irons in the fire to put in another." My friend said, "Doctor, you had better take them all out and put this one in, if you mean well either to the religion or to the civil liberty of our country." [Cheers.]

The great Orthodox leader did not rest with merely refusing to put another iron in his fire; he attempted to limit the irons of other men. As President of Lane Theological Seminary, he endeavored to prevent the students from investigating the subject of slavery. The result, we all remember, was a strenuous resistance on the part of a large number of the students, led by that remarkable man, Theodore D. Weld. The right triumphed, and Lane Seminary lost her character and noblest pupils at the same time. She has languished ever since, even with such a President. Why should I follow Dr. Beecher into those ecclesiastical conventions where he has been tried, and found wanting, in fidelity to the slave? He has done no worse, indeed he has done much better, than most of his class. His opposition has always been open and manly.

But, Mr. Chairman, there is something in the blood which, men tell us, brings out virtues and defects, even when they have lain dormant for a generation. Good and evil qualities are hereditary, the physicians say. The blood whose warm currents of eloquent aid my friend solicited in vain in that generation has sprung voluntarily to his assistance in the next,—both from the pulpit and the press,—to rouse the world by the vigor and pathos of its appeals. [Enthusiastic cheers.] Even on that great triumph I would say a word. Marked and unequalled as has been that success, remember, in explanation of the phenomenon,—for "Uncle Tom's Cabin" is rather an event than a book,—remember this: if the old antislavery movement had not roused the sympathies of Mrs. Stowe, the book had never been written; if that movement had not raised up hundreds of thousands of hearts to sympathize with the slave, the book had never been read. [Cheers.] Not that the genius of the author has not made the triumph all her own; not that the unrivalled felicity of its execution has not trebled, quadrupled, increased tenfold, if you please, the number of readers; but there must be a spot even for Archimedes to rest his lever upon, before he can move the world, [cheers,] and this effort of genius, consecrated to the noblest purpose, might have fallen dead and unnoticed in 1835. It is the antislavery movement which has changed 1835 to 1852. Those of us familiar with antislavery literature know well that Richard Hildreth's "Archy Moore," now "The White Slave," was a book of eminent ability; that it owed its want of success to no lack of genius, but only to the fact that it was a work born out of due time; that the antislavery cause had not then aroused sufficient numbers, on the wings of whose enthusiasm even the most delightful fiction could have risen into world-wide influence and repute. To the cause which had changed 1835 to 1852 is due somewhat of the influence of "Uncle Tom's Cabin."

The Abolitionists have never overlooked the wonderful power which the wand of the novelist was yet to wield in their behalf over the hearts of the world. Fredrika Bremer only expressed the common sentiment of many of us, when she declared that "the fate of the negro is the romance of our history." Again and again, from my earliest knowledge of the cause, have I heard the opinion, that in the debatable land between Freedom and Slavery, in the thrilling incidents of the escape and sufferings of the fugitive, and the perils of his friends, the future Walter Scott of America would find the "border-land" of his romance, and the most touching incidents of his "sixty years since"; and that the literature of America would gather its freshest laurels from that field.

So much, Mr. Chairman, for our treatment of the Church. We clung to it as long as we hoped to make it useful. Disappointed in that, we have tried to expose its paltering and hypocrisy on this question, broadly and with unflinching boldness, in hopes to purify and bring it to our aid. Our labors with the great religious societies, with the press, with the institutions of learning, have been as untiring, and almost as unsuccessful. We have tried to do our duty to every public question that has arisen, which could be made serviceable in rousing general attention. The Right of Petition, the Power of Congress, the Internal Slave-Trade. Texas, the Compromise Measures, the Fugitive Slave Law, the motions of leading men, the tacties of parties, have all been watched and used with sagacity and effect as means to produce a change in public opinion. Dr. Channing has thanked the Abolition party, in the name of all the lovers of free thought and free speech, for having vindicated that right, when all others seemed ready to surrender it,—vindicated it at the cost of reputation, case, property, even life itself. The only blood that has ever been shed, on this side the ocean, in defence of the freedom of the press, was the blood of Lovejoy, one of their number. In December, 1836, Dr. Channing spoke of their position in these terms:—

> "Whilst, in obedience to conscience, they have refrained from opposing force to force, they have still persevered, amidst menace and insult, in bearing their testimony against wrong, in giving utterance to their deep convictions. Of such men, I do not hesitate to say, that they have rendered to freedom a more essential service than any body of men among us. The defenders of freedom are not those who claim and exercise rights which no one assails, or who win shouts of applause by well-turned compliments to Liberty in the days of her triumph. They are those who stand up for rights which mobs, conspiracies, or single tyrants put in jeopardy; who contend for liberty in that particular form which is threatened at the moment by the many or the few. To the Abolitionists this honor belongs. The first systematic effort to strip the citizen of freedom of speech they have met with invincible resolution. From my heart I thank them. I am myself their debtor. I am not sure that I should this moment write in safety, had they shrunk from the conflict, had they shut their lips, imposed silence on their presses, and hid themselves before their ferocious assailants. I know not where these outrages would have stopped, had they not met resistance from their first destined victims. The newspaper press, with a few exceptions, uttered no genuine indignant rebuke of the wrongdoers, but rather countenanced by its gentle censures the reign of force. The mass of the people looked supinely on this new tyranny, under which a portion of their fellow-citizens seemed to be sinking. A tone of denunciation was beginning to proscribe all discussion of slavery; and had the spirit of violence, which selected associations as its first objects, succeeded in this preparatory enterprise, it might have been easily turned against any and every individual, who might presume to agitate the unwelcome subject. It is hard to say to what outrage the fettered press of the country might not have been reconciled. I thank the Abolitionists that, in this evil day, they were true to the rights which the multitude were ready to betray. Their purpose to suffer, to die, rather than surrender their dearest liberties, taught the lawless that they had a foe to contend with whom it was not safe to press, whilst, like all manly appeals, it called forth reflection and sympathy in the better portion of the community. In the name of freedom and humanity, I thank them."

No one, Mr. Chairman, deserves more of that honor than he whose chair you now occupy. Our youthful city can boast of but few places of historic renown; but I know of no one which Francis Jackson offered to the antislavery women of Boston, when Mayor Lyman confessed he was unable to protect their meeting, and when the only protection the laws could afford Mr. Garrison was the shelter of the common jail.

Sir, when a nation sets itself to do evil, and all its leading forces, wealth, party, and piety, join in the career, it is impossible but that those who offer a constant opposition should be hated and maligned, no matter how wise, cautious, and well planned their course may be. We are peculiar sufferers in this way. The community has come to hate its reproving Nathan so bitterly, that even those whom the relenting part of it is beginning to regard as standard-bearers of the antislavery host think it unwise to avow any connection or sympathy with him. I refer to some of the leaders of the political movement against slavery. They feel it to be their mission to marshal and use as effectively as possible the present convictions of the people. They cannot afford to encumber themselves with the odium which twenty years of angry agitation have engendered in great sects sore from unsparing rebuke, parties galled by constant defeat, and lending men provoked by unexpected exposure. They are willing to confess, privately, that our movement produced theirs, and that its continued existence is the very breath of their life. But, at the same time, they would fain walk on the road without being soiled by too close contact with the rough pioneers who threw it up. They are wise and honorable, and their silence is very expressive.

When I speak of their eminent position and acknowledged ability, another thought strikes me. Who converted these men and their distinguished associates? It is said we have shown neither sagacity in plans, nor candor in discussion, nor ability. Who, then, or what, converted Burlingame and Wilson, Sumner and Adams, Palfrey and Mann, Chase and Hale, and Phillips and Giddings? Who taught the Christian Register, the Daily Advertiser, and that class of prints, that there were such things as a slave and a slaveholder in the land, and so gave them some more intelligent basis than their mere instincts to hate William Lloyd Garrison? [Shouts and laughter.] What magic wand was it whose touch made the toadying servility of the land start up the real demon that it was, and at the same time gathered into the slave's service the professional ability, ripe culture, and personal integrity which grace the Free Soil ranks? We never argue! These men, then, were converted by simple denunciation! They were all converted by the "hot," "reckless," "ranting," "bigoted," "fanatic" Garrison, who never troubled himself about facts, nor stopped to argue with an opponent, but straightway knocked him down! [Roars of laughter and cheers.] My old and valued friend, Mr. Sumner, often boasts that he was a reader of the Liberator before I was. Do not criticise too much the agency by which such men were converted. That blade has a double edge. Our reckless course, our empty rant, our fanaticism, has made Abolitionists of some of the best and ablest men in the land. We are inclined to go on, and see if even with such poor tools we cannot make some more. [Enthusiastic applause.] Antislavery zeal and the roused conscience of the "godless comeouters" made the trembling South demand the Fugitive Slave Law, and the Fugitive Slave Law "provoked" Mrs. Stowe to the good work of "Uncle Tom." That is something! [Cheers.] Let me say, in passing, that you will nowhere find an earlier or more generous appreciation, or more flowing eulogy, of these men and their labors, than in the columns of the Liberator. No one, however feeble, has ever peeped or muttered, in any quarter, that the vigilant eye of the Pioneer has not recognized him. He has stretched out the right hand of a most cordial welcome the moment any man's face was turned Zionward. [Loud cheers.]

I do not mention these things to praise Mr. Garrison, I do not stand here for that purpose. You will not deny—if you do, I can prove it—that the movement of the Abolitionists converted these men. Their constituents were converted by it. The assault upon the right of petition, upon the right to print and speak of slavery, the denial of the right of Congress over the District, the annexation of Texas, the Fugitive Slave Law, were measures which the antislavery movement provoked, and the discussion of which has made all the Abolitionists we have. The antislavery cause, then, converted these men; it gave them a constituency; it gave them an opportunity to speak, and it gave them a public to listen. The antislavery cause gave them their votes, got them their offices, furnished them their facts, gave them their audience. If you tell me they cherished all these principles in their own breasts before Mr. Garrison appeared, I can only say, if the antislavery movement did not give them their ideas, it surely gave the courage to utter them.

In such circumstances, is it not singular that the name of William Lloyd Garrison has never been pronounced on the floor of the United States Congress linked with any epithet but that of contempt! No one of those men who owe their ideas, their station, their audience, to him, have ever thought it worth their while to utter one word in grateful recognition of the power which called them into being. When obliged, by the course of their argument, to treat the question historically, they can go across the water to Clarkson and Wilberforce,—yes, to a safe salt-water distance. [Laughter.] As Daniel Webster, when he was talking to the farmers of Western New York, and wished to contrast slave labor and free labor, did not dare to compare New York with Virginia,—sister States, under the same government, planted by the same race, worshipping at the same altar, speaking the same language,—identical in all respects, save that one in which he wished to seek the contrast; but no; he compared it with Cuba,—[cheers and laughter,]—the contrast was so close! [Renewed cheers.] Catholic—Protestant; Spanish—Saxon; despotism—municipal institutions; readers of Lope de Vega and of Shakespeare; mutterers of the Mass—children of the Bible! But Virginia is too near home! So is Garrison! One would have thought there was something in the human breast which would sometimes break through policy. These noble-hearted men whom I have named must surely have found quite irksome the constant practice of what Dr. Gardiner used to call "that despicable virtue, prudence"! [Laughter.] One would have thought, when they heard that name spoken with contempt, their ready eloquence would have leaped from its scabbard to avenge even a word that threatened him with insult. But it never came,—never! [Sensation.] I do not say I blame them. Perhaps they thought they should serve the cause better by drawing a broad black line between themselves and him. Perhaps they thought the Devil could be cheated;—I do not think he can. [Laughter and cheers.]

We are perfectly willing—I am, for one—to be the dead lumber that shall make a path for these men into the light and love of the people. We hope for nothing better. Use us freely, in any way, for the slave. When the temple is finished, the tools will not complain that they are thrown aside, let who will lead up the nation to "put on the topstone with shoutings." But while so much remains to be done, while our little camp is beleaguered all about, do nothing to weaken his influence, whose sagacity, more than any other single man's, has led us up hither, and whose name is identified with that movement which the North still heeds, and the South still fears the most. After all, Mr. Chairman, this is no hard task. We know very well, that, notwithstanding this loud clamor about our harsh judgment of men and things, our opinions differ very little from those of our Free Soil friends, or of intelligent men generally, when you really get at them. It has even been said, that one of that family which has made itself so infamously conspicuous here in executing the Fugitive Slave Law, a judge, whose earnest defence of that law we all heard in Faneuil Hall, did himself, but a little while before, arrange for a fugitive to be hid till pursuit was over. I hope it is true,—it would be an honorable inconsistency. And if it be not true of him, we know it is of others. Yet it is base to incite others to deeds, at which, whenever we are hidden from public notice, our own hearts recoil! But thus we see that when men lay aside the judicial ermine, the senator's robe, or the party collar, and sit down in private life, you can hardly distinguish their tones from ours. Their eyes seem as anointed as our own. As in Pope's day,—

"At all we laugh they laugh, no doubt;
The only difference is, we dare *laugh out.*"

Caution is not always good policy in a cause like ours. It is said that, when Napoleon saw the day going against him, he used to throw away all the rules of war, and trust himself to the hot impetuosity of his soldiers. The masses are governed more by impulse than conviction; and even were it not so, the convictions of most men are on our side, and this will surely appear, if we can only pierce the crust of their prejudice or indifference. I observe that our Free Soil friends never stir their audience so deeply as when some individual leaps beyond the platform, and strikes upon the very heart of the people. Men listen to discussions of laws and tactics with ominous patience. It is when Mr. Sumner, in Faneuil Hall, avows his determination to disobey the Fugitive Slave Law, and cries out, "I was a man before I was a Commissioner,"—when Mr. Giddings says of the fall of slavery, quoting Adams, "Let it come; if it must come in *blood,* yet I say let it come!"—that their associates on the platform are sure they are wrecking the party,—while many a heart beneath beats its first pulse of antislavery life.

These are brave words. When I compare them with the general tone of Free Soil men in Congress, I distrust the atmosphere of Washington and of politics. These men move about, Sauls and Goliaths among us, taller by many a cubit. There they lose port and stature. Mr. Sumner's speech in the Senate unsays no part of his Faneuil Hall pledge. But, though discussing the same topic, no one would gather from any word or argument that the speaker ever took such ground as he did in Faneuil Hall. It is all through, the *law,* the *manner* of the surrender, not the surrender itself, of the slave, that he objects to. As my friend Mr. Pillsbury so forcibly says, so far as anything in the speech shows, he puts the slave behind the jury trial, behind the *habeas corpus* act, and behind the new interpretation of the Constitution, and says to the slave claimant: "You must get through all these, before you reach him; but if you *can* get through all these, you may have him!" It was no tone like this which made the old Hall rock! Not if he got through twelve jury trials, and forty *habeas corpus* acts, and constitutions built high as yonder monument, would he permit so much as the shadow of a little finger of the slave claimant to touch the slave! [Loud applause.] At least, so he was understood. In an elaborate discussion, by the leader of the political antislavery party, of the whole topic of fugitive slaves, you do not find one protest against the surrender itself, one frank expression on the constitutional clause, or any indication of the speaker's final purpose, should any one be properly claimed under that provision. It was under no such uncertain trumpet that the antislavery host was originally marshalled. The tone is that of the German soldiers whom Napoleon routed. They did not care, they said, for the defeat, but only that they were not beaten according to rule. [Laughter and cheers.] Mr. Mann, in his speech of February 15, 1850, says: "*The States being separated*, I would as soon return my own brother or sister into bondage, as I would return a fugitive slave. Before God, and Christ, and all Christian men, they are my brothers and sisters." What a condition! from the lips, too, of a champion of the Higher Law! Whether the States be separate or united, neither my brother nor any other man's brother shall, with my consent, go back to bondage. [Enthusiastic cheers.] So speaks the *heart*,—Mr. Mann's version is that of the politician.

Mr. Mann's recent speech in August, 1852, has the same non-committal tone to which I have alluded in Mr. Sumner's. While professing, in the most eloquent terms, his loyalty to the Higher Law, Mr. Sutherland asked: "Is there, in Mr. Mann's opinion, any conflict between that Higher Law and the Constitution? If so, what is it? If not so, why introduce an irrelevant topic into the debate?" Mr. Mann avoided any reply, and asked not to be interrupted! Is that the frankness which becomes an Abolitionist? Can such concealment help any cause? The design of Mr. Sutherland is evident. If Mr. Mann had allowed there was no conflict between the Higher Law and the Constitution, all his remarks were futile and out of order. But if he asserted that any such conflict existed, how did he justify himself in swearing to support that instrument?—a question our Free Soil friends are slow to meet. Mr. Mann saw the dilemma, and avoided it by silence!

The same speech contains the usual deprecatory assertions that Free-Soilers have no wish to interfere with slavery in the States; that they "consent to let slavery remain where it is." If he means that he, Horace Mann, a moral and accountable being, "consents to let slavery remain where it is," all the rest of his speech is sound and fury, signifying nothing. If he means that he, Horace Mann, as a politician and party man, consents to that, but, elsewhere and otherwise, will do his best to abolish this "all-comprehending wickedness of slavery, in which every wrong and every crime has its natural home," then he should have plainly said so. Otherwise, his disclaimer is unworthy of him, and could have deceived no one. He must have known that all the South care for is the action, not in what capacity the deed is done.

Mr. Giddings is more careful in his statement; but, judged by his speech on the "Platforms," how little does he seem to understand either his own duty or the true philosophy of the cause he serves! He says:—

> "We, Sir, would drive the slave question from discussion in this hall. It never had a constitutional existence here. Separate this government from all interference with slavery: let the Federal power wash its hands from that institution; let us purify ourselves from its contagion; leave it with the States, who alone have the power to sustain it,—then, Sir, will agitation cease in regard to it here; then we shall have nothing more to do with it; our time will be no more occupied with it; and, like a band of freemen, a band of brothers, we could meet here, and legislate for the prosperity, the improvement of mankind, for the elevation of our race."

Mr. Sumner speaks in the same strain. He says:—

> "The time will come when courts or Congress will declare, that nowhere under the Constitution can man hold property in man. For the republic, such a decree will be the way of peace and safety. As slavery is banished from the national jurisdiction, it will cease to vex our national politics. It may linger in the States as a local institution, but it will no longer endanger national animosities when it no longer demands national support . . . . For himself, he knows no better aim under the Constitution than to bring the government back to the precise position which it occupied" when it was launched.

This seems to me a very mistaken strain. Whenever slavery is banished from our national jurisdiction, it will be a momentous gain, a vast stride. But let us not mistake the half-way house for the end of the journey. I need not say that it matters not to Abolitionists under what special law slavery exists. Their battle lasts while it exists anywhere, and I doubt not Mr. Sumner and Mr. Giddings feel themselves enlisted for the whole war. I will even suppose, what neither of these gentlemen states, that their plan includes, not only that slavery shall be abolished in the District and Territories, but that the slave basis of representation shall be struck from the Constitution, and the slave-surrender clause construed away. But even then, does Mr. Giddings or Mr. Sumner really believe that slavery, existing in its full force in the States, "will cease to vex our national politics"? Can they point to any State where a powerful oligarchy, possessed of immense wealth, has ever existed, without attempting to meddle in the government? Even now, does not manufacturing, banking, and commercial capital perpetually vex our politics? Why should not slave capital exert the same influence? Do they imagine that a hundred thousand men, possessed of two thousand millions of dollars, which they feel the spirit of the age is seeking to tear from their grasp, will not eagerly catch at all the support they can obtain by getting the control of the government? In a land where the dollar is almighty, "where the sin of not being rich is only atoned for by the effort to become so," do they doubt that such an oligarchy will generally succeed? Besides, banking and manufacturing stocks are not urged by despair to seek a controlling influence in politics. They know they are about equally safe, whichever party rules,—that no party wishes to legislate their rights away. Slave property knows that its being allowed to exist depends on its having the virtual control of the government. Its constant presence in politics is dictated, therefore, by despair, as well as by the wish to secure fresh privileges. Money, however, is not the only strength of the Slave Power. That, indeed, were enough, in an age when capitalists are our feudal barons. But, though driven entirely from national shelter, the slaveholders would have the strength of old associations, and of peculiar laws in their own States, which gives those States wholly into their hands. A weaker prestige, fewer privileges, and less comparative wealth, have enabled the British aristocracy to rule England for two centuries, though the root of their strength was cut at Naseby. It takes ages for deeply-rooted institutions to die; and driving slavery into the States will hardly be our Naseby. Whoever, therefore, lays the flattering unction to his soul, that, while slavery exists anywhere in the States, our legislators will sit down "like a band of brothers,"—unless they are all slaveholding brothers,—is doomed to find himself wofully mistaken. Mr. Adams, ten years ago, refused to sanction this doctrine of his friend, Mr. Giddings, combating it ably and eloquently in his well-known reply to Ingersoll. Though Mr. Adams touches on but one point, the principle he lays down has many other applications.

But is Mr. Giddings willing to sit down with slaveholders, "like a band of brothers," and not seek, knowing all the time that they are tyrants at home, to use the common strength to protect their victims? Does he not know that it is impossible for Free States and Slave States to unite under any form of Constitution, no matter how clean the parchment may be, without the compact resulting in new strength to the slave system? It is the unimpaired strength of Massachusetts and New York, and the youthful vigor of Ohio, that, even now, enable bankrupt Carolina to hold up the institution. Every nation must maintain peace within her limits. No government can exist which does not fulfil that function. When we say the Union will maintain peace in Carolina, that being a Slave State, what does "peace" mean? It means keeping the slave beneath the heel of his master. Now, even on the principle of two wrongs making a right, if we put this great weight of a common government into the scale of the slaveholder, we are bound to add something equal to the slave's side. But no, Mr. Giddings is content to give the slaveholder the irresistible and organic help of a common government, and bind himself to utter no word, and move not a finger, in his civil capacity, to help the slave! An Abolitionist would find himself not much at home, I fancy, in that "band of brothers"!

And Mr. Sumner "knows no better aim, under the Constitution, than to bring back the government" to where it was in 1789! Has the voyage been so very honest and prosperous a one, in his opinion, that his only wish is to start again with the same ship, the same crew, and the same sailing-orders? Grant all he claims as to the state of public opinion, the intentions of leading men, and the form of our institutions at that period; still, with all these checks on wicked men, and helps to good ones, here we are, in 1853, according to his own showing, ruled by slavery, tainted to the core with slavery, and binding the infamous Fugitive Slave Law like an honorable frontlet on our brows! The more accurate and truthful his glowing picture of the public virtue of 1789, the stronger my argument. If even all those great patriots, and all that enthusiasm for justice and liberty, did not avail to keep us safe in such a Union, what will? In such desperate circumstances, can his statesmanship devise no better aim than to try the same experiment over again, under precisely the same conditions? What new guaranties does he propose to prevent the voyage from being again turned into a piratical slave-trading cruise? None! Have sixty years taught us nothing? In 1660, the English thought, in recalling Charles II., that the memory of that scaffold which had once darkened the windows of Whitehall would be guaranty enough for his good behavior. But, spite of the spectre, Charles II. repeated Charles I., and James outdid him. Wiser by this experience, when the nation, in 1689, got another chance, they trusted to no guaranties, but so arranged the very elements of their government that William III. *could not* repeat Charles I. Let us profit by the lesson. These mistakes of leading men merit constant attention. Such remarks as those I have quoted, uttered from the high places of political life, however carefully guarded, have a sad influence on the rank and file of the party. The antislavery awakening has cost too many years and too much labor to risk letting its energy be turned into a wrong channel, or balked by fruitless experiments. Neither the slave nor the country must be cheated a second time.

Mr. Chairman, when I remember the grand port of these men elsewhere, and witness this confusion of ideas, and veiling of their proud crests to party necessities, they seem to me to lose in Washington something of their old giant proportions. How often have we witnessed this change! It seems the inevitable result of political life under any government, but especially under ours; and we are surprised at it in these men, only because we fondly hoped they would be exceptions to the general rule. It was Chamfort, I think, who first likened a republican senate-house to Milton's Pandemonium;—another proof of the rare insight French writers have shown in criticising republican institutions. The Capitol at Washington always brings to my mind that other Capitol, which in Milton's great epic "rose like an exhalation" "from the burning marl,"—that towering palace, "with starry lamps and blazing cressets" hung,—with "roof of fretted gold" and stately height, its hall "like a covered field." You remember, Sir, the host of archangels gathered round it, and how thick the airy crowd

> "Swarmed and were straitened; till, the signal given,
> Behold a wonder! They but now who seemed
> In bigness to surpass earth's giant sons,
> Now less than smallest dwarfs, in narrow room
> Throng numberless, like that pygmean race
> Beyond the Indian mount; or fairy elves,
> Whose midnight revels, by a forest side
> Or fountain, some belated peasant sees.
>
> Thus incorporeal spirits to smallest forms
> Reduced their shapes immense, and were at large,
> Though without number still, amid the hall
> Of that infernal court."

Mr. Chairman, they got no further than the hall [Cheers.] They were not, in the current phrase, *"a healthy party"*! The healthy party—the men who made no compromise in order to come under that arch—Milton describes further on, where he says:

> "But far within,
> And in their own dimensions, like themselves,
> The great seraphic lords and cherubim,
> In close recess and secret conclave, sat;
> A thousand demigods on golden seats
> Frequent and full."

These were the healthy party! [Loud applause.] These are the Casses and the Houstons, the Footes and the Soulés, the Clays, the Websters, and the Douglases, that bow no lofty forehead in the dust, but can find ample room and verge enough under the Constitution. Our friends go down there, and must be dwarfed into pygmies before they can find space within the lists! [Cheers.]

It would be superfluous to say that we grant the entire sincerity and true-heartedness of these men. But in critical times, when a wrong step entails most disastrous consequences, to "mean well" is not enough. Sincerity is no shield for any man from the criticism of his fellow-laborers. I do not fear that such men as these will take offence at our discussion of their views and conduct. Long years of hard labor, in which we have borne at least our share, have resulted in a golden opportunity. How to use it, friends differ. Shall we stand courteously silent, and let these men play out the play, when, to our thinking, their plan will slacken the zeal, balk the hopes, and waste the efforts of the slave's friends? No! I know Charles Sumner's love for the cause so well, that I am sure he will welcome my criticism whenever I deem his counsel wrong; that he will hail every effort to serve our common client more efficiently. [Great cheering.] It is not his honor nor mine that is at issue; not his feeling nor mine that is to be consulted. The only question for either of us is, What in these golden moments can be done? where can the hardest blow be struck? [Loud applause.] I hope I am just to Mr. Summer; I have known him long, and honor him. I know his genius, I honor his virtues; yet if, from his high place, he sends out counsels which I think dangerous to the cause, I am bound to raise my voice against them. I do my duty in a private communication to him first, then in public to his friends and mine. The friendship that will not bear this criticism is but the frost-work of a winter's morning, which the sun looks upon and it is gone. His friendship will survive all that I say of him, and mine will survive all that he shall say of me; and this is the only way in which the antislavery cause can be served. Truth, success, victory, triumph over the obstacles that beset us,—this is all either of us wants. [Cheers.]

If all I have said to you is untrue, if I have exaggerated, explain to me this fact. In 1831, Mr. Garrison commenced a paper advocating the doctrine of immediate emancipation. He had against him the thirty thousand churches and all the clergy of the country,—its wealth, its commerce, its press. In 1831, what was the state of things? There was the most entire ignorance and apathy on the slave question. If men knew of the existence of slavery, it was only as a part of picturesque Virginia life. No one preached, no one talked, no one wrote about it. No whisper of it stirred the surface of the political sea. The Church heard of it occasionally, when some colonization agent asked funds to send the blacks to Africa. Old school-books tainted with some antislavery selections had passed out of use, and new ones were compiled to suit the times. Soon as any dissent from the prevailing faith appeared, every one set himself to crush it. The pulpits preached at it; the press denounced it; mobs tore down houses, threw presses into the fire and the stream, and shot the editors; religious conventions tried to smother it; parties arrayed themselves against it. Daniel Webster boasted in the Senate, that he had never introduced the subject of slavery to that body, and never would. Mr. Clay, in 1839, makes a speech for the Presidency, in which he says, that to discuss the subject of slavery is moral treason, and that no man has a right to introduce the subject into Congress. Mr. Benton, in 1844, laid down his platform, and he not only denies the right, but asserts that he never has and never will discuss the subject. Yet Mr. Clay, from 1839 down to his death, hardly made a remarkable speech of any kind, except on slavery. Mr. Webster, having indulged now and then in a little easy rhetoric, as at Niblo's and elsewhere, opens his mouth in 1840, generously contributing his aid to both sides, and stops talking about it only when death closes his lips. Mr. Benton's six or eight speeches in the United States Senate have all been on the subject of slavery in the Southwestern section of the country, and form the basis of whatever claim he has to the character of a statesman, and he owes his seat in the next Congress somewhat, perhaps, to antislavery pretensions! The Whig and Democratic parties pledged themselves just as emphatically against the antislavery discussion,—against agitation and free speech. These men said: "It sha'n't be talked about, it won't be talked about!" These are *your statesmen!*—men who understand the present, that is, and mould the future! The man who understands his own time, and whose genius moulds the future to his views, he is a statesman, is he not? These men devoted themselves to banks, to the tariff, to internal improvements, to constitutional and financial questions. They said to slavery: "Back! no entrance here! We pledge ourselves against you." And then there came up a humble printer-boy, who whipped them into the traces, and made them talk, like Hotspur's starling, nothing BUT slavery. He scattered all these gigantic shadows,—tariff, bank, constitutional questions, financial questions,—and slavery, like the colossal head in Walpole's romance, came up and filled the whole political horizon! [Enthusiastic applause.] Yet you must remember he is not a statesman; he is a "fanatic." He has no discipline,—Mr. "Ion" says so; he does not understand the "discipline that is essential to victory"! This man did not understand his own time,—he did not know what the future was to be,—he was not able to shape it,—he had no "prudence,"—he had no "foresight"! Daniel Webster says, "I have never introduced this subject, and never will,"—and died broken-hearted because he had not been able to talk enough about it. Benton says, "I will never speak of slavery," and lives to break with his party on this issue! Mr. Clay says it is "moral treason" to introduce the subject into Congress, and lives to see Congress turned into an antislavery debating-society, to suit the purpose of one "too powerful individual"!

These were statesmen, mark you! Two of them have gone to their graves covered with eulogy; and our national stock of eloquence is all insufficient to describe how profound and far-reaching was the sagacity of Daniel Webster! Remember who it was that said, in 1831, "I am in earnest,—I will not equivocate,—I will not excuse,—I will not retreat a single inch,—*and I will be heard!*" [Repeated cheers.] That speaker has lived twenty-two years, and the complaint of twenty-three millions of people is, "Shall we never hear of anything but slavery?" [Cheers.] I heard Dr. Kirk, of Boston, say in his own pulpit, when he returned from London,—where he had been as a representative to the "Evangelical Alliance,"—"I went up to London, and they asked me what I thought of the question of immediate emancipation. They examined us all. Is an American never to travel anywhere in the world but men will throw this troublesome question in his face?" Well, it is all HIS fault [pointing to Mr. Garrison]. [Enthusiastic cheers.]

Now, when we come to talk of statesmanship, of sagacity in choosing time and measures, of endeavor, by proper means, to right the public mind, of keen insight into the present and potent sway over the future, it seems to me that the Abolitionists, who have taken—whether for good or for ill, whether to their discredit or to their praise—this country by the four corners, and shaken it until you can hear nothing but slavery, whether you travel in railroad or steamboat, whether you enter the hall of legislation or read the columns of a newspaper,—it seems to me that such men may point to the present aspect of the nation, to their originally avowed purpose, to the pledges and efforts of all your great men against them, and then let you determine to which side the credit of sagacity and statesmanship belongs. Napoleon busied himself, at St. Helena, in showing how Wellington ought not to have conquered at Waterloo. The world has never got time to listen to the explanation. Sufficient for it that the Allies entered Paris. In like manner, it seems hardly the province of a defeated Church and State to deny the skill of measures by which they have been conquered.

It may sound strange to some, this claim for Mr. Garrison of a profound statesmanship. Men have heard him styled a mere fanatic so long, that they are incompetent to judge him fairly. "The phrases men are accustomed," says Goethe, "to repeat incessantly, end by becoming convictions, and ossify the organs of intelligence." I cannot accept you, therefore, as my jury. I appeal from Festus to Caesar; from the prejudice of our streets to the common sense of the world, and to your children.

Every thoughtful and unprejudiced mind must see that such an evil as slavery will yield only to the most radical treatment. If you consider the work we have to do, you will not think us needlessly aggressive, or that we dig down unnecessarily deep in laying the foundations of our enterprise. A money power of two thousand millions of dollars, as the prices of slaves now range, held by a small body of able and desperate men; that body raised into a political aristocracy by special constitutional provisions; cotton, the product of slave labor, forming the basis of our whole foreign commerce, and the commercial class thus subsidized; the press bought up, the pulpit reduced to vassalage, the heart of the common people chilled by a bitter prejudice against the black race; our leading men bribed, by ambition, either to silence or open hostility;—in such a land, on what shall an Abolitionist rely? On a few cold prayers, mere lip-service, and never from the heart? On a church resolution, hidden often in its records, and meant only as a decent cover for servility in daily practice? On political parties, with their superficial influence at best, and seeking ordinarily only to use existing prejudices to the best advantage? Slavery has deeper root here than any aristocratic institution has in Europe; and politics is but the common pulse-beat, of which revolution is the fever-spasm. Yet we have seen European aristocracy survive storms which seemed to reach down to the primal strata of European life. Shall we, then, trust to mere politics, where even revolution has failed? How shall the stream rise above its fountain? Where shall our church organizations or parties get strength to attack their great parent and moulder, the Slave Power? Shall the thing formed say to him that formed it, Why hast thou made me thus? The old jest of one who tried to lift himself in his own basket, is but a tame picture of the man who imagines that, by working solely through existing sects and parties, he can destroy slavery. Mechanics say nothing but an earthquake, strong enough to move all Egypt, can bring down the Pyramids.

Experience has confirmed these views. The Abolitionists who have acted on them have a "short method" with all unbelievers. They have but to point to their own success, in contrast with every other man's failure. To waken the nation to its real state, and chain it to the consideration of this one duty, is half the work.

So much we have done. Slavery has been made the question of this generation. To startle the South to madness, so that every step she takes, in her blindness, is one step more toward ruin, is much. This we have done. Witness Texas and the Fugitive Slave Law. To have elaborated for the nation the only plan of redemption, pointed out the only exodus from this "sea of troubles," is much. This we claim to have done in our motto of IMMEDIATE, UNCONDITIONAL EMANCIPATION ON THE SOIL. The closer any statesmanlike mind looks into the question, the more favor our plan finds with it. The Christian asks fairly of the infidel, "If this religion be not from God, how do you explain its triumph, and the history of the first three centuries?" Our question is similar. If our agitation has not been wisely planned and conducted, explain for us the history of the last twenty years! Experience is a safe light to walk by, and he is not a rash man who expects success in future from the same means which have secured it in times past.

AR'N'T I A WOMAN?

Sojourner Truth

Born in slavery around 1797, Isabella Baumfree took the name Sojourner Truth in 1843 with the conviction that God had called her for the work of preaching abolitionism, women's rights, religious tolerance, and pacifism. The transcribed version of her, landmark speech, "Ar'n't I a Woman," demonstrates the power of ethical arguments. The ethos Truth created on the speaker's platform of the Ohio Women's Rights Convention in May of 1851 called into question the racial and gender codes of the antebellum period with memorable force. Truth has become an icon of the power of character against formidable odds.

The leaders of the movement trembled on seeing a tall, gaunt black woman in a gray dress and white turban, surmounted with an uncouth sun-bonnet, march deliberately into the church, walk with the air of a queen up the aisle, and take her seat upon the pulpit steps. A buzz of disapprobation was heard all over the house, and there fell on the listening ear, "An abolition affair!" "Woman's rights and niggers!" "I told you so!" "Go it, darkey!"

I chanced on that occasion to wear my first laurels in public life as president of the meeting. At my request order was restored, and the business of the Convention went on. Morning, afternoon, and evening exercises came and went. Through all these sessions old Sojourner, quiet and reticent as the "Lybian Statue," sat crouched against the wall on the corner of the pulpit stairs, her sun-bonnet shading her eyes, her elbows on her knees, her chin resting upon her broad, hard palms. At intermission she was busy selling the "Life of Sojourner Truth," a narrative of her own strange and adventurous life. Again and again, timorous and trembling ones came to me and said, with earnestness, "Don't let her speak, Mrs. Gage, it will ruin us. Every newspaper in the land will have our cause mixed up with abolition and niggers, and we shall be utterly denounced." My only answer was, "We shall see when the time comes."

The second day the work waxed warm. Methodist, Baptist, Episcopal, Presbyterian, and Universalist ministers came in to hear and discuss the resolutions presented. One claimed superior rights and privileges for man, on the ground of "superior intellect;" another, because of the "manhood of Christ; if God had desired the equality of woman, He would have given some token of His will through the birth, life, and death of the Saviour." Another gave us a theological view of the "sin of our first mother."

There were very few women in those days who dared to "speak in meeting"; and the august teachers of the people were seemingly getting the better of us, while the boys in the galleries, and the sneerers among the pews, were hugely enjoying the discomfiture, as they supposed, of the "strong-minded." Some of the tender-skinned friends were on the point of losing dignity, and the atmosphere betokened a storm. When, slowly from her seat in the corner rose Sojourner Truth, who, till now, had scarcely lifted her head. "Don't let her speak!" gasped half a dozen in my ear. She moved slowly and solemnly to the front, laid her old bonnet at her feet, and turned her great speaking eyes to me. There was a hissing sound of disapprobation above and below. I rose and announced "Sojourner Truth," and begged the audience to keep silence for a few moments.

The tumult subsided at once, and every eye was fixed on this almost Amazon form, which stood nearly six feet high, head erect, and eyes piercing the upper air like one in a dream. At her first word there was a profound hush. She spoke in deep tones, which, though not loud, reached every ear in the house, and away through the throng at the doors and windows.

"Wall, chilern, what dar is so much racket dar must be somethin' out o' kilter. I tink dat 'twixt de niggers of de Souf and de womin at de Norf, all talkin' 'bout rights, de white men will be in a fix pretty soon. But what's all dis here talkin' 'bout?

"Dat man ober dar say dat womin needs to be helped into carriages, and lifted ober ditches, and to hab de best place everywhar. Nobody eber helps me into carriages, or ober mud-puddles, or gibs me any best place!" And raising herself to her full height, and her voice to a pitch like rolling thunder; she asked. "And a'n't I a woman? Look at me! Look at my arm! (and she bared her right arm to the shoulder, showing her tremendous muscular power). I have ploughed, and planted, and gathered into barns, and no man could head me! And a'n't I a woman? I could work as much and eat as much as a man—when I could get it—and bear de lash as well! And a'n't I a woman? I have borne thirteen chilern, and seen 'em mos' all sold off to slavery, and when I cried out with my mother's grief none but Jesus heard me! And a'n't I a woman?

"Den dey talks 'bout dis ting in de head; what dis dey call it?" ("Intellect," whispered some one near.) "Dat's it, honey. What's dat got to do wid womin's rights or nigger's rights? If my cup won't hold but a pint, and yourn holds a quart, wouldn't ye be mean not to let me have my little half-measure full?" And she pointed her significant finger, and sent a keen glance at the minister who had made the argument. The cheering was long and loud.

"Den dat little man in black dar, he say women can't have as much rights as men, cause Christ wan't a woman! Whar did your Christ come from?" Rolling thunder couldn't have stilled that crowd, as did those deep, wonderful tones, as she stood there with outstretched arms and eyes of fire. Raising her voice still louder, she repeated; "Whar did your Christ come from? From God and a woman! Man had nothin' to do wid Him." Oh, what a rebuke that was to that little man.

Turning again to another objector, she took up the defense of Mother Eve. I can not follow her through it all. It was pointed, and witty, and solemn; eliciting at almost every sentence deafening applause; and she ended by asserting: "If de fust woman God ever made was strong enough to turn de world upside down all alone, dese women togedder (and she glanced her eye over the platform) ought to be able to turn it back, and get it right side up again! And now dey is asking to do it, de men better let 'em." Long-continued cheering greeted this. "'Bleeged to ye for hearin' on me, and now ole Sojourner han't got nothin' more to say."

Amid roars of applause, she returned to her corner, leaving more than one of us with streaming eyes, and hearts beating with gratitude. She had taken us up in her strong arms and carried us safely over the slough of difficulty turning the whole tide in our favor. I have never in my life seen anything like the magical influence that subdued the mobbish spirit of the day, and turned the sneers and jeers of an excited crowd into notes of respect and admiration. Hundreds rushed up to shake hands with her, and congratulate the glorious old mother, and bid her God-speed on her mission of "testifyin' agin concerning the wickedness of this 'ere people."

One of the most unique and interesting speeches of the Convention was made by Sojourner Truth, an emancipated slave. It is impossible to transfer it to paper, or convey any adequate idea of the effect it produced upon the audience. Those only can appreciate it who saw her powerful form, her whole-souled, earnest gesture, and listened to her strong and truthful tones. She came forward to the platform and addressing the President said with great simplicity: "May I say a few words?" Receiving an affirmative answer, she proceeded:

> I wanted to say a few words about this matter. I am a woman's rights. I have as much muscle as any man, and can do as much work as any man. I have plowed and reaped and husked and chopped and mowed, and can any man do more than that? I have heard much about the sexes being equal. I can carry as much as any man, and can eat as much too, if I can get it. I am as strong as any man that is now. As for intellect, all I can say is, if woman have a pint and a man a quart—why can't she have her little pint full? You need not be afraid to give us our rights for fear we will take too much,—for we can't take more than our pint'll hold. The poor men seem to be all in confusion, and don't know what to do. Why children, if you have woman's rights, give it to her and you will feel better. You will have your own rights, and they won't be so much trouble. I can't read, but I can hear. I have heard the bible and learned that Eve caused man to sin. Well, if woman upset the world, do give her a chance to set it right side up again. The Lady has spoken about Jesus, how he never spurned woman from him, and she was right. When Lazarus died, Mary and Martha came to him with faith and love and besought him to raise their brother. And Jesus wept and Lazarus came forth. And how came Jesus into the world? Through God who created him and a woman who bore him. Man, where is your part? But the women are coming up blessed by God and a few of the men are coming up with them. But man is in a tight place, the poor slave is on him, woman is coming on him, he is surely between a hawk and a buzzard.

Sojourner Truth, a tall colored woman, well known in anti-slavery circles, and called the Lybian Sybil, made her appearance on the platform. This was the signal for a fresh outburst from the mob; for at every session every man of them was promptly in his place, at twenty-five cents a head. And this was the one redeeming feature of this mob—it paid all expenses, and left a surplus in the treasury. Sojourner combined in herself, as an individual, the two most hated elements of humanity. She was black, and she was a woman, and all the insults that could be cast upon color and sex were together hurled at her; but there she stood, calm and dignified, a grand, wise woman, who could neither read nor write, and yet with deep insight could penetrate the very soul of the universe about her. As soon as the terrible turmoil was in a measure quelled.

She said:

Is it not good for me to come and draw forth a spirit, to see what kind of spirit people are of? I see that some of you have got the spirit of a goose, and some have got the spirit of a snake. I feel at home here. I come to you, citizens of New York, as I suppose you ought to be. I am a citizen of the State of New York; I was born in it, and I was a slave in the State of New York; and now I am a good citizen of this State. I was born here, and I can tell you I feel at home here. I've been lookin' round and watchin' things, and I know a little mite 'bout Woman's Rights, too. I come forth to speak 'bout Woman's Rights, and want to throw in my little mite, to keep the scales a-movin'. I know that it feels a kind o' hissin' and ticklin' like to see a colored woman get up and tell you about things, and Woman's Rights. We have all been thrown down so low that nobody thought we'd ever get up again; but we have been long enough trodden now; we will come up again, and now I am here.

I was a-thinkin', when I see women contendin' for their rights, I was a-thinkin' what a difference there is now, and what there was in old times. I have only a few minutes to speak; but in the old times the kings of the earth would hear a woman. There was a king in the Scriptures; and then it was the kings of the earth would kill a woman if she come into their presence; but Queen Esther[1] come forth, for she was oppressed, and felt there was a great wrong, and she said I will die or I will bring my complaint before the king. Should the king of the United States be greater, or more crueler, or more harder? But the king, he raised up his sceptre and said: "Thy request shall be granted unto thee—to the half of my kingdom will I grant it to thee!" Then he said he would hang Haman on the gallows he had made up high. But that is not what women come forward to contend. The women want their rights as Esther. She only wanted to explain her rights. And he was so liberal that he said, "the half of my kingdom shall be granted to thee," and he did not wait for her to ask, he was so liberal with her.

[1]The Old Testament King Ahasuerus offered to fulfill any request made by his Jewish wife Esther, even if she asked for half of his kingdom. Esther asked for justice for her people because he believed he had been insulted by the king's adviser, Mordecai. King Ahasuerus hanged Haman on the gallows Haman had built for Mordecai.

FROM *A RED RECORD*: TABULATED STATISTICS AND ALLEGED CAUSES OF LYNCHINGS IN THE UNITED STATES, 1892-1893-1894

Ida B. Wells

The brutal murder of African Americans by vigilantes after the Civil War operated as an unofficial but undeniable form of social control in an era when "equal rights" had ostensibly been accomplished. No other single person was as integral to exposing the inner workings and massive scale of "lynch law" than Ida B. Wells. As a journalist and activist, Wells gathered information from newspapers, eyewitnesses, legal records, and other sources to produce exposés such as *A Red Record*.

Preface

Hon. Frederick Douglass' Letter[1]

Dear Miss Wells:

Let me give you thanks for your faithful paper on the lynch abomination now generally practiced against colored people in the South. There has been no word equal to it in convincing power. I have spoken, but my word is feeble in comparison. You give us what you know and testify from actual knowledge. You have dealt with the facts with cool, painstaking fidelity, and left those naked and uncontradicted facts to speak for themselves.

Brave woman! you have done your people and mine a service which can neither be weighed nor measured. If the American conscience were only half alive, if the American church and clergy were only half Christianized, if American moral sensibility were not hardened by persistent infliction of outrage and crime against colored people, a scream of horror, shame, and indignation would rise to Heaven wherever your pamphlet shall be read.

But alas! even crime has power to reproduce itself and create conditions favorable to its own existence. It sometimes seems we are deserted by earth and Heaven—yet we must still think, speak and work, and trust in the power of a merciful God for final deliverance

Very truly and gratefully yours,
FREDERICK DOUGLASS.

Cedar Hill, Anacostia, D.C.

Contents

[1]This letter was originally written for *Southern Horrors;* Wells reprinted it in *A Red Record.*

Chapter I. The Case Stated

The student of American sociology will find the year 1894 marked by a pronounced awakening of the public conscience to a system of anarchy and outlawry which had grown during a series of ten years to be so common, that scenes of unusual brutality failed to have any visible effect upon the humane sentiments of the people of our land.

Beginning with the emancipation of the Negro, the inevitable result of unbribled power exercised for two and a half centuries, by the white man over the Negro, began to show itself in acts of conscienceless outlawry. During the slave regime, the Southern white man owned the Negro body and soul. It was to his interest to dwarf the soul and preserve the body. Vested with unlimited power over his slave, to subject him to any and all kinds of physical punishment, the white man was still restrained from such punishment as tended to injure the slave by abating his physical powers and thereby reducing his financial worth. While slaves were scourged mercilessly, and in countless cases inhumanly treated in other respects, still the white owner rarely permitted his anger to go so far as to take a life, which would entail upon him a loss of several hundred dollars. The slave was rarely killed, he was too valuable; it was easier and quite as effective, for discipline or revenge, to sell him "Down South."

But Emancipation came and the vested interests of the white man in the Negro's body were lost. The white man had no right to scourge the emancipated Negro, still less has he a right to kill him. But the Southern white people had been educated so long in that school of practice, in which might makes right, that they disdained to draw strict lines of action in dealing with the Negro. In slave times the Negro was kept subservient and submissive by the frequency and severity of the scourging, but, with freedom, a new system of intimidation came into vogue; the Negro was not only whipped and scourged; he was killed.

Not all nor nearly all of the murders done by white men, during the past thirty years in the South, have come to light, but the statistics as gathered and preserved by white men, and which have not been questioned, show that during these years more than ten thousand Negroes have been killed in cold blood, without the formality of judicial trial and legal execution. And yet, as evidence of the absolute impunity with which the white man dares to kill a Negro, the same record shows that during all these years, and for all these murders only three white men have been tried, convicted, and executed. As no white man has been lynched for the murder of colored people, these three executions are the only instances of the death penalty being visited upon white men for murdering Negroes.

Naturally enough the commission of these crimes began to tell upon the public conscience, and the Southern white man, as a tribute to the nineteenth century civilization, was in a manner compelled to give excuses for his barbarism. His excuses have adapted themselves to the emergency, and are aptly outlined by that greatest of all Negroes, Frederick Douglass, in an article of recent date, in which he shows that there have been three distinct eras of Southern barbarism, to account for which three distinct excuses have been made.

The first excuse given to the civilized world for the murder of unoffending Negroes was the necessity of the white man to repress and stamp out alleged "race riots." For years immediately succeeding the war there was an appalling slaughter of colored people, and the wires usually conveyed to northern people and the world the intelligence, first, that an insurrection was being planned by Negroes, which, a few hours later, would prove to have been vigorously resisted by white men, and controlled with a resulting loss of several killed and wounded. It was always a remarkable feature in these insurrections and riots that only Negroes were killed during the rioting, and that all the white men escaped unharmed.

From 1865 to 1872, hundreds of colored men and women were mercilessly murdered and the almost invariable reason assigned was that they met their death by being alleged participants in an insurrection or riot. But this story at last wore itself out. No insurrection ever materialized; no Negro rioter was ever apprehended and proven guilty, and no dynamite ever recorded the black man's protest against oppression and wrong. It was too much to ask thoughtful people to believe this transparent story, and the southern white people at last made up their minds that some other excuse must be had.

Then came the second excuse, which had its birth during the turbulent times of reconstruction. By an amendment to the Constitution the Negro was given the right of franchise, and, theoretically at least, his ballot became his invaluable emblem of citizenship. In a government "of the people, for the people, and by the people," the Negro's vote became an important factor in all matters of state and national politics. But this did not last long. The southern white man would not consider that the Negro had any right which a white man was bound to respect, and the idea of a republican form of government in the southern states grew into general contempt. It was maintained that "This is a white man's government," and regardless of numbers the white man should rule. "No Negro domination" became the new legend on the sanguinary banner of the sunny South, and under it rode the Ku Klux Klan, the Regulators, and the lawless mobs, which for any cause chose to murder one man or a dozen as suited their purpose best. It was a long, gory campaign; the blood chills and the heart almost loses faith in Christianity when one thinks of Yazoo, Hamburg, Edgefield, Copiah, and the countless massacres of defenseless Negroes, whose only crime was the attempt to exercise their right to vote.

But it was a bootless strife for colored people. The government which had made the Negro a citizen found itself unable to protect him. It gave him the right to vote, but denied him the protection which should have maintained that right. Scourged from his home, hunted through the swamps; hung by midnight raiders, and openly murdered in the light of day, the Negro clung to his right of franchise with a heroism which would have wrung admiration from the hearts of savages. He believed that in that small white ballot there was a subtle something which stood for manhood as well as citizenship, and thousands of brave black men went to their graves, exemplifying the one by dying for the other.

The white man's victory soon became complete by fraud, violence, intimidation and murder. The franchise vouchsafed to the Negro grew to be a "barren ideality," and regardless of numbers, the colored people found themselves voiceless in the councils of those whose duty it was to rule. With no longer the fear of "Negro Domination" before their eyes, the white man's second excuse became valueless. With the Southern governments all subverted and the Negro actually eliminated from all participation in state and national elections, there could be no longer an excuse for killing Negroes to prevent "Negro Domination."

Brutality still continued; Negroes were whipped, scourged, exiled, shot and hung whenever and wherever it pleased the white man so to treat them, and as the civilized world with increasing persistency held the white people of the South to account for its outlawry, the murderers invented the third excuse—that Negroes had to be killed to avenge their assaults upon women. There could be framed no possible excuse more harmful to the Negro and more unanswerable if true in its sufficiency for the white man.

Humanity abhors the assailant of womanhood, and this charge upon the Negro at once placed him beyond the pale of human sympathy. With such unanimity, earnestness and apparent candor was this charge made and reiterated that the world has accepted the story that the Negro is a monster which the Southern white man has painted him. And to-day, the Christian world feels, that while lynching is a crime, and lawlessness and anarchy the certain precursors of a nation's fall, it can not by word or deed, extend sympathy or help to a race of outlaws, who might mistake their plea for justice and deem it an excuse for their continued wrongs.

The Negro has suffered much and is willing to suffer more. He recognizes that the wrongs of two centuries can not be righted in a day, and he tries to bear his burden with patience for to-day and be hopeful for to-morrow. But there comes a time when the veriest worm will turn, and the Negro feels to-day that after all the work he has done, all the sacrifices he has made, and all the suffering he has endured, if he did not, now, defend his name and manhood from this vile accusation, he would be unworthy even of the contempt of mankind. It is to this charge he now feels he must make answer.

If the Southern people in defense of their lawlessness, would tell the truth and admit that colored men and women are lynched for almost any offense, from murder to a misdemeanor, there would not now be the necessity for this defense. But when they intentionally, maliciously and constantly belie the record and bolster up these falsehoods by the words of legislators, preachers, governors and bishops, then the Negro must give to the world his side of the awful story.

A word as to the charge itself. In considering the third reason assigned by the Southern white people for the butchery of blacks, the question must be asked, what the white man means when he charges the black man with rape. Does he mean the crime which the statutes of the civilized states describe as such? Not by any means.

With the Southern white man, any mesalliance existing between a white woman and a colored man is a sufficient foundation for the charge of rape. The Southern white man says that it is impossible for a voluntary alliance to exist between a white woman and a colored man, and therefore, the fact of an alliance is a proof of force. In numerous instances where colored men have been lynched on the charge of rape, it was positively known at the time of lynching, and indisputably proven after the victim's death, that the relationship sustained between the man and woman was voluntary and clandestine, and that in no court of law could even the charge of assault have been successfully maintained.

It was for the assertion of this fact, in the defense of her own race, that the writer hereof became an exile; her property destroyed and her return to her home forbidden under penalty of death, for writing the following editorial which was printed in her paper, the Free Speech, in Memphis, Tenn., May 21, 1892:

"Eight Negroes lynched since last issue of the 'Free Speech' one at Little Rock, Ark., last Saturday morning where the citizens broke (?) into the penitentiary and got their man; three near Anniston, Ala., one near New Orleans; and three at Clarksville, Ga., the last three for killing a white man, and five on the same old racket—the new alarm about raping white women. The same programme of hanging, then shooting bullets into the lifeless bodies was carried out to the letter. Nobody in this section of the country believes the old threadbare lie that Negro men rape white women. If Southern white men are not careful, they will over-reach themselves and public sentiment will have a reaction; a conclusion will then be reached which will be very damaging to the moral reputation of their women."

But threats cannot suppress the truth, and while the Negro suffers the soul deformity, resultant from two and a half centuries of slavery, he is no more guilty of this vilest of all vile charges than the white man who would blacken his name.

During all the years of slavery, no such charge was ever made, not even during the dark days of the rebellion, when the white man, following the fortunes of war went to do battle for the maintenance of slavery. While the master was away fighting to forge the fetters upon the slave, he left his wife and children with no protectors save the Negroes themselves. And yet during those years of trust and peril, no Negro proved recreant to his trust and no white man returned to a home that had been dispoiled.

Likewise during the period of alleged "insurrection," and alarming "race riots," it never occurred to the white man, that his wife and children were in danger of assault. Nor in the Reconstruction era, when the hue and cry was against "Negro Domination," was there ever a thought that the domination would ever contaminate a fireside or strike to death the virtue of womanhood. It must appear strange indeed, to every thoughtful and candid man, that more than a quarter of a century elapsed before the Negro began to show signs of such infamous degeneration.

In his remarkable apology for lynching, Bishop Haygood,[2] of Georgia, says: "No race, not the most savage, tolerates the rape of woman, but it may be said without

[2]Atticus G. Haygood was president of Emory University when he was named a bishop of the Methodist Church in 1890.

reflection upon any other people that the Southern people are now and always have been most sensitive concerning the honor of their women—their mothers, wives, sisters and daughters." It is not the purpose of this defense to say one word against the white women of the South. Such need not be said, but it is their misfortune that the chivalrous white men of that section, in order to escape the deserved execration of the civilized world, should shield themselves by their cowardly and infamously false excuse, and call into question that very honor about which their distinguished priestly apologist claims they are most sensitive. To justify their own barbarism they assume a chivalry which they do not possess. True chivalry respects all womanhood, and no one who reads the record, as it is written in the faces of the million mulattoes in the South, will for a minute conceive that the southern white man had a very chivalrous regard for the honor due the women of his own race or respect for the womanhood which circumstances placed in his power. That chivalry which is "most sensitive concerning the honor of women" can hope for but little respect from the civilized world, when it confines itself entirely to the women who happen to be white. Virtue knows no color line, and the chivalry which depends upon complexion of skin and texture of hair can command no honest respect.

When emancipation came to the Negroes, there arose in the northern part of the United States an almost divine sentiment among the noblest, purest and best white women of the North, who felt called to a mission to educate and Christianize the millions of southern exslaves. From every nook and corner of the North, brave young white women answered that call and left their cultured homes, their happy associations and their lives of ease, and with heroic determination went to the South to carry light and truth to the benighted blacks. It was a heroism no less than that which calls for volunteers for India, Africa and the Isles of the sea. To educate their unfortunate charges; to teach them the Christian virtues and to inspire in them the moral sentiments manifest in their own lives, these young women braved dangers whose record reads more like fiction than fact. They became social outlaws in the South. The peculiar sensitiveness of the southern white men for women, never shed its protecting influence about them. No friendly word from their own race cheered them in their work; no hospitable doors gave them the companionship like that from which they had come. No chivalrous white man doffed his hat in honor or respect. They were "Nigger teachers"—unpardonable offenders in the social ethics of the South, and were insulted, persecuted and ostracised, not by Negroes, but by the white manhood which boasts of its chivalry toward women.

And yet these northern women worked on, year after year, unselfishly, with a heroism which amounted almost to martyrdom. Threading their way through dense forests, working in schoolhouse, in the cabin and in the church, thrown at all times and in all places among the unfortunate and lowly Negroes, whom they had come to find and to serve, these northern women, thousands and thousands of them, have spent more than a quarter of a century in giving to the colored people their splendid lessons for home and heart and soul. Without protection, save that which innocence gives to every good woman, they went about their work, fearing no assault and suffering none. Their chivalrous protectors were hundreds of miles away in their northern homes, and yet they never feared any "great dark faced mobs," they dared night or day to "go beyond their own roof trees." They never complained of assaults, and no mob was ever called into existence to avenge crimes against them. Before the world adjudges the Negro a moral monster, a vicious assailant of womanhood and a menace to the sacred precincts of home, the colored people ask the consideration of the silent record of gratitude, respect, protection and devotion of the millions of the race in the South, to the thousands of northern white women who have served as teachers and missionaries since the war.

The Negro may not have known what chivalry was, but he knew enough to preserve inviolate the womanhood of the South which was entrusted to his hands during the war. The finer sensibilities of his soul may have been crushed out by years of slavery, but his heart was full of gratitude to the white women of the North, who blessed his home and inspired his soul in all these years of freedom. Faithful to his trust in both of these instances, he should now have the impartial ear of the civilized world, when he dares to speak for himself as against the infamy wherewith he stands charged.

It is his regret, that, in his own defense, he must disclose to the world that degree of dehumanizing brutality which fixes upon America the blot of a national crime. Whatever faults and failings other nations may have in their dealings with their own subjects or with other people, no other civilized nation stands condemned before the world with a series of crimes so peculiarly national. It becomes a painful duty of the Negro to reproduce a record which shows that a large portion of the American people avow anarchy, condone murder and defy the contempt of civilization.

These pages are written in no spirit of vindictiveness, for all who give the subject consideration must concede that far too serious is the condition of that civilized government in which the spirit of unrestrained outlawry constantly increases in violence, and casts its blight over a continually growing area of territory. We plead not for the colored people alone, but for all victims of the terrible injustice which puts men and women to death without form of law. During the year 1894, there were 132 persons executed in the United States by due form of law, while in the same year, 197 persons were put to death by mobs who gave the victims no opportunity to make a lawful defense. No comment need be made upon a condition of public sentiment responsible for such alarming results.

The purpose of the pages which follow shall be to give the record which has been made, not by colored men, but that which is the result of compilations made by white men, of reports sent over the civilized world by white men in the South. Out of their own mouths shall the murderers be condemned. For a number of years the Chicago Tribune, admittedly one of the leading journals of America, has made a specialty of the compilation of statistics touching upon lynching. The data compiled by that journal and published to the world January 1st, 1894, up to the present time has not been disputed. In order to be safe from the charge of exaggeration, the incidents hereinafter reported have been confined to those vouched for by the Tribune.

INTRODUCTION: THE AMERICAN IDEOLOGY.

Howard Zinn, From *Declarations of Independence: Cross-Examining American Ideology*

Howard Zinn is a student of American belief and culture. His most famous work may be *A People's History of America*, in which he tells the stories of people whose lives and actions are not typically chronicled by historians. The selection reprinted here, from a different work, presents Zinn's argument about the importance of shared ideas as motivators of community action.

The idea, which entered Western consciousness several centuries ago, that black people are less than human, made possible the Atlantic slave trade, during which perhaps 40 million people died. Beliefs about racial inferiority, whether applied to blacks or Jews or Arabs or Orientals, have led to mass murder.

The idea, presented by political leaders and accepted by the American public in 1964, that communism in Vietnam was a threat to our "national security" led to policies that cost a million lives, including those of 55,000 young Americans.

The belief, fostered in the Soviet Union, that "socialism" required a ruthless policy of farm collectivization, as well as the control of dissent, brought about the deaths of countless peasants and large numbers of political prisoners.

Other ideas—leave the poor on their own ("laissez-faire") and help the rich ("economic growth")—have led the U.S. government for most of its history to subsidize corporations while neglecting the poor, thus permitting terrible living and working conditions and incalculable suffering and death. In the years of the Reagan presidency, "laissez-faire" meant budget cutting for family care, which led to high rates of infant mortality in city ghettos.

We can reasonably conclude that how we *think* is not just mildly interesting, not just a subject for intellectual debate, but a matter of life and death.

If those in charge of our society—politicians, corporate executives, and owners of press and television—can dominate our ideas, they will be secure in their power. They will not need soldiers patrolling the streets. We will control ourselves.

Because force is held in reserve and the control is not complete, we can call ourselves a "democracy." True, the openings and the flexibility make such a society a more desirable place to live. But they also create a more effective form of control. We are less likely to object if we can feel that we have a "pluralist" society, with two parties instead of one, three branches of government instead of one-man rule, and various opinions in the press instead of one official line.

A close look at this pluralism shows that it is very limited. We have the kinds of choices that are given in multiple-choice tests, where you can choose *a, b, c,* or *d.* But *e, f, g,* and *h* are not even listed.

And so we have the Democratic and Republican parties (choose *a* or *b*), but no others are really tolerated or encouraged or financed. Indeed, there is a law limiting the nationally televised presidential debates to the two major parties.

We have a "free press," but big money dominates it; you can choose among *Time, Newsweek,* and *U.S. News & World Report.* On television, you can choose among NBC, CBS, and ABC. There is a dissident press, but it does not have the capital of the great media chains and cannot get the rich corporate advertising, and so it must strain to reach small numbers of people. There is public television, which is occasionally daring, but also impoverished and most often cautious.

We have three branches of government, with "checks and balances," as we were taught in junior high school. But one branch of government (the presidency) gets us into wars and the other two (Congress and the Supreme Court) go sheepishly along.

There is the same limited choice in public policy. During the Vietnam War, the argument for a long time was between those who wanted a total bombing of Indochina and those who wanted a limited bombing. The choice of withdrawing from Vietnam altogether was not offered. Daniel Ellsberg, working for Henry Kissinger in 1969, was given the job of drawing a list of alternative policies on Vietnam. As one possibility on his long list he suggested total withdrawal from the war. Kissinger looked at the possibilities and crossed that one off before giving the list to President Richard Nixon.

In debates on the military budget there are heated arguments about whether to spend $300 billion or $290 billion. A proposal to spend $100 billion (thus making $200 billion available for human needs) is like the *e* or *f* in a multiple-choice test—it is missing. To propose zero billion makes you a candidate for a mental institution.

On the question of prisons there is debate on how many prisons we should have. But the idea of *abolishing* prisons is too outrageous even to be discussed.

We hear argument about *how much* the elderly should have to pay for health care, but the idea that they should not have to pay *anything*, indeed, that no one should have to pay for health care, is not up for debate.

Thus we grow up in a society where our choice of ideas is limited and where certain ideas dominate: We hear them from our parents, in the schools, in the churches, in the newspapers, and on radio and television. They have been in the air ever since we learned to walk and talk. They constitute an American *ideology*—that is, a dominant pattern of ideas. Most people accept them, and if we do, too, we are less likely to get into trouble.

The dominance of these ideas is not the product of a conspiratorial group that has devilishly plotted to implant on society a particular point of view. Nor is it an accident, an innocent result of people thinking freely. There is a process of natural (or, rather *unnatural*) selection, in which certain orthodox ideas are encouraged, financed, and pushed forward by the most powerful mechanisms of our culture. These ideas are preferred because they are safe; they don't threaten established wealth or power.

For instance:

> "Be realistic; this is the way things *are*; there's no point thinking about how things *should be*."
>
> "People who teach or write or report the news should be *objective*; they should not try to advance their own opinions."

"There are unjust wars, but also just wars."

"If you disobey the law, even for a good cause, you should accept your punishment."

"If you work hard enough, you'll make a good living. If you are poor, you have only yourself to blame."

"Freedom of speech is desirable, but not when it threatens national security."

"Racial equality is desirable, but we've gone far enough in that direction."

"Our Constitution is our greatest guarantee of liberty and justice."

"The United States must intervene from time to time in various parts of the world with military power to stop communism and promote democracy."

"If you want to get things changed, the only way is to go through the proper channels."

"We need nuclear weapons to prevent war."

"There is much injustice in the world but there is nothing that ordinary people, without wealth or power, can do about it."

These ideas are not accepted by all Americans. But they are believed widely enough and strongly enough to dominate our thinking. And as long as they do, those who hold wealth and power in our society will remain secure in their control.

In the year 1984 *Forbes* magazine, a leading periodical for high finance and big business, drew up a list of the wealthiest individuals in the United States. The top 400 people had assets totaling $60 billion. At the bottom of the population there were 60 million people who had *no* assets at all.

Around the same time, the economist Lester Thurow estimated that 482 very wealthy individuals controlled (without necessarily owning) over $2,000 billion ($2 trillion).

Consider the influence of such a very rich class—with its inevitable control of press, radio, television, and education—on the *thinking* of the nation.

Dissident ideas can still exist in such a situation, but they will be drowned in criticism and made disreputable, because they are outside the acceptable choices. Or they may be allowed to survive in the corners of the culture—emaciated, but alive—and presented as evidence of our democracy, our tolerance, and our pluralism.

A sophisticated system of control that is confident of its power can permit a measure of dissidence. However, it watches its critics carefully, ready to overwhelm them, intimidate them, and even suppress them should they ever seriously threaten the system, or should the establishment, in a state of paranoia, *think* they do. If readers think I am exaggerating with words such as "*watching . . . overwhelm . . . suppress . . .paranoia*," they should read the volumes of reports on the FBI and the CIA published in 1975 by the Senate Select Committee on Government Operations.

However, government surveillance and threats are the exception. What normally operates day by day is the quiet dominance of certain ideas, the ideas we are expected to hold by our neighbors, our employers, and our political leaders; the ones we quickly learn are the most acceptable. The result is an obedient, acquiescent, passive citizenry—a situation that is deadly to democracy.

If one day we decide to reexamine these beliefs and realize they do not come naturally out of our innermost feelings or our spontaneous desires, are not the result of independent thought on our part, and, indeed, do not match the real world as we experience it, then we have come to an important turning point in life. Then we find ourselves examining, and confronting, American ideology.

There is in orthodox thinking a great dependence on experts. Because modern technological society has produced a breed of experts who understand technical matters that bewilder the rest of us, we think that in matters of social conflict, which require *moral* judgments, we must also turn to experts.

There are two false assumptions about experts. One is that they see more clearly and think more intelligently than ordinary citizens. Sometimes they do, sometimes not. The other assumption is that these experts have the same *interests* as ordinary citizens, want the same things, hold the same values, and, therefore, can be trusted to make decisions for all of us.

To depend on great thinkers, authorities, and experts is, it seems to me, a violation of the spirit of democracy. Democracy rests on the idea that, except for technical details for which experts may be useful, the important decisions of society are within the capability of ordinary citizens. Not only *can* ordinary people make decisions about these issues, but they *ought* to, because citizens understand their own interests more clearly than any experts.

In John Le Carré's novel *The Russia House*, a dissident Russian scientist is assured that his secret document has been entrusted "to the authorities. People of discretion. Experts." He becomes angry:

> I do not *like* experts. They are our jailers. I despise experts more than anyone on earth . . . . They solve nothing! They are servants of whatever system hires them. They perpetuate it. When we are tortured, we shall be tortured by experts. When we are hanged, experts will hang us . . . . When the world is destroyed, it will be destroyed not by its madmen but by the sanity of its experts and the superior ignorance of its bureaucrats.

We are expected to believe that great thinkers—experts—are *objective*, that they have no axes to grind and no biases, and that they make pure intellectual judgments. However, the minds of all human beings are powerfully influenced (though not totally bound) by their backgrounds, by whether they are rich or poor, male or female, black or white or Asian, in positions of power, or in lowly circumstances. Even scientists making "scientific" observations know that what they see will be affected by their *position*.

Why should we cherish "objectivity," as if ideas were innocent, as if they don't serve one interest or another? Surely, we want to be objective if that means telling the truth as we see it, not concealing information that may be embarrassing to our point of view. But we don't want to be objective if it means pretending that ideas don't play a part in the social struggles of our time, that we don't take sides in those struggles.

Indeed, it is impossible to be neutral. In a world already moving in certain directions, where wealth and power are already distributed in certain ways, neutrality means accepting the way things are now. It is a world of clashing interests—war against peace, nationalism against internationalism, equality against greed, and democracy against elitism—and it seems to me both impossible and undesirable to be neutral in those conflicts.

Writing this book, I do not claim to be neutral, nor do I want to be. There are things I value, and things I don't. I am not going to present ideas objectively if that means I don't have strong opinions on which ideas are right and which are wrong. I will try to be fair to opposing ideas by accurately representing them. But the reader should know that what appear here are my own views of the world as it is and as it should be.

I do want to influence the reader. But I would like to do this by the strength of argument and fact, by presenting ideas and ways of looking at issues that are outside the orthodox. I am hopeful that given more possibilities people will come to wiser conclusions.

In my years of teaching, I never listened to the advice of people who said that a teacher should be objective, neutral, and professional. All the experiences of my life, growing up on the streets of New York, becoming a shipyard worker at the age of eighteen, enlisting in the Air Force in World War II, participating in the civil rights movement in the Deep South, cried out against that.

It seems to me we should make the most of the fact that we live in a country that, although controlled by wealth and power, has openings and possibilities missing in many other places. The controllers are gambling that those openings will pacify us, that we will not really *use* them to make the bold changes that are needed if we are to create a decent society. We should take that gamble.

We are not starting from scratch. There is a long history in this country of rebellion against the establishment, of resistance to orthodoxy. There has always been a commonsense perception that there are things seriously wrong and that we can't really depend on those in charge to set them right.

This perception has led Americans to protest and rebel. I think of the Boston Bread Rioters and Carolina antitax farmers of the eighteenth century; the black and white abolitionists of slavery days; the working people of the railroads, mines, textile mills, steel mills, and auto plants who went on strike, facing the clubs of policemen and the machine guns of soldiers to get an eight-hour workday and a living wage; the women who refused to stay in the kitchen and marched and went to jail for equal rights; the black protesters and antiwar activists of the 1960s; and the protesters against industrial pollution and war preparations in the 1980s.

In the heat of such movements brains are set stirring with new ideas, which live on through quieter times, waiting for another opportunity to ignite into action and change the world around us.

Dissenters, I am aware, can create their own orthodoxy. So we need a constant reexamination of our thinking, using the evidence of our eyes and ears and the realities of our experience to think freshly. We need declarations of independence from all nations, parties, and programs—all rigid dogmas.

The experience of our century tells us that the old orthodoxies, the traditional ideologies, the neatly tied bundles of ideas—capitalism, socialism, democracy—need to be untied, so that we can play and experiment with all the ingredients, add others, and create new combinations in looser bundles. We know as we come to the twenty-first century that we desperately need to develop new, imaginative approaches to the human problems of our time.

For citizens to do this on their own, to listen with some skepticism to the great thinkers and the experts, and to think for themselves about the great issues of today's world, is to make democracy come alive.

CREDITS

Text Credits: *The 9/11 Commission Report,* 2004. www.9-11commission.gov; Excerpt from Ameerah Al-Islam. By permission; Christian Appy, from "Military Families May Once Again Lead Us Out of War," 2005, from www.tomsdispatch.com. Reprinted by permission of the author; Aristotle, *Rhetoric* II, 1393b; Kristin Breitweiser, from speech accepting The Ridenhour Truth Award, April 19, 2005. Reprinted as "Are We Safer" in *The Nation.* Used by permission of Inkwell Management on behalf on the author; George W. Bush, President's Address to the Nation, September 11, 2001; George W. Bush, from "Address to a Joint Session of Congress and the American People," September 20, 2001; George W. Bush, from "State of the Union Address" January 2005; George W. Bush, "State of the Union Address," 2001; Excerpt from Rosa Casas. By permission; Excerpt from Kellen Chavez. By permission; Reprinted with the permission of The Free Press, a Division of Simon & Schuster Adult Publishing Group, from *Against All Enemies: Inside America's War on Terror* by Richard Clarke. Copyright © 2004 by RAC Enterprises, Inc. All rights reserved;.Crumley, Bruce. "The French Correction: America Behind 9/11!" *Time,* May 20, 2002. Copyright © 2002, Time, Inc. All rights reserved. Reprinted by permission; Frederick Douglass, from "What to the Slave Is the Fourth of July?" An address delivered in Rochester, New York, July 5, 1852; Thomas Eager and Christopher Musso, "Why Did the World Trade Center Collapse? Science, Engineering, and Speculation," *JOM: Journal of the Society of Minerals, Metals, and Materials,* 53.12: 2001; "Earth Charter Preamble." Used by permission of the Earth Charter Center of Education for Sustainable Development, University for Peace Campus, Costa Rica. www.earthcharter.org; Frances D. Gage, *Reminiscences by Frances D. Gage of Sojourner Truth,* 1881; William Lloyd Garrison, from "To the Public," an editorial from *The Liberator,* January 1, 1831; David Ray Griffin, *The 9:11 Commission Report: Omissions and Distortions.* Northampton, Mass: Olive Branch Press, 2005; Frances Ellen Watkins Harper, from speech "Could We Trace the Record of Every Human Heart." An address to the New York City Anti-Slavery Society, May 13, 1857 and published in *National Anti-Slavery Standard,* May 23, 1857; Frances Ellen Watkins Harper, from speech "We Are All Bound Up Together" from Proceedings of the Eleventh Woman's Rights Convention, May 1866; E.D. Hirsch, *Cultural Literacy: What Every American Needs to Know.* Boston: Houghton Mifflin, 1987; Excerpt from Michael Irei. By permission; Heather Johnson. Letter to the *New York Times,*October 2004. By permission of Heather Johnson; Lyndon B. Johnson, from "To Fulfill These Rights," Commencement Address, Howard University, Washington, DC. June 4, 1965. Austin, TX: LBJ Library and Museum; Heather Johnson, "Letter to the Editor of *The New York Times,*";October 2004. By permission; Absalom Jones and Richard Allen, *A Narrative of the Proceedings of the Black People During the Late Awful Calamity in Philadelphia, In the Year 1793: And a Refutation of Some Censures, Thrown Upon Them in Some Late Publications,* 1794; Excerpt from Tom LeGault. By permission; Norman Mailer, from *Why Are We At War?* © 2003 by Norman Mailer. By permission of The Wylie Agency; Excerpt from Kevin Marshall. By permission; Letter by Jared Miller. By permission; Excerpt from Edwin Molina. By permission; MSNBC.com, excerpt from "Report: 9/11-Iraq Link Refuted Days After Attack," November 22, 2005. Copyright 2005 by MSNBC Interactive news, LLC. Reproduced with permission of MSNBC Interactive News, LLC in the format Textbook via Copyright Clearance Center; Offley, G.W, *A Narrative of the Life and Labors of the Rev. G.W. Offley,* 1859; Wendell Phillips, from "The Philosophy of the Abolition Movement," a speech before the Massachusetts Antislavery Society, Boston, January 27, 1853; James Robbins, "9/11 Denial: The French Bestseller and Its Company." *National Review OnLine,* April 9, 2002; Phil Scraton, *Beyond September 11: An Anthology of Dissent.* London: Pluto Press, 2002; Sojourner Truth, "Ain't I a Woman" a speech delivered in Akron, Ohio (May 1851), reprinted by Frances D. Gage as *Reminiscences by Frances D. Gage of Sojourner Truth,* 1881; Ida B. Wells, A *Crusade for Justice: The Autobiography of Ida B. Wells,* ed. by Alfreda M. Duster. Chicago: University of Chicago Press, 1970; Ida B. Wells, *A Red Record,* 1895; James Wolcott, "Caution: Women Seething," *Vanity Fair,* June 2005; James Wolcott, from "Dwight MacDonald at 100." *New York Times* (Book Review), April 16, 2006. © 2006 The New York Times Co. Reprinted by permission; From *Declarations of Independence* by Howard Zinn. Copyright © 1990 by Howard Zinn. Reprinted by permission of Harper-Collins Publishers.

Photo Credits: Page 9: © Mary Altaffer/AP Photo; **15:** © Library of Congress; **19:** © St. John Fisher College; **20:** ©Library of Congress; **22:** © Gulnara Samoilova/AP Photo; **31:** © Schomburg Center for Research in Black Culture/Art Resource; **32:** © Library of Congress; **33:** © Khue Bui/AP Photo; **35:** © Peter Turnley/Corbis; **38:** © Oxford University Press, Inc.; from "The New York City Draft Riots: Their Significance for American Society and Politics in the Age of Civil War," 1990, by Iver Bernstein; **39, 40:** © University of Pennsylvania Press, "The Philadelphia Negro" by W.E.B. Dubois, 1995, s 61, 62, 63; **49:** © pbpgalleries/Alamy; **49:** © Ric Feld/AP Photo; **61:** © Library of Congress; **82:** © Castoria/Corbis Sygma; **83:** © Mary Altaffer/AP Photo **87:** Courtesy of the National Library of Medicine; **95:** © 1Apix/Alamy; **110:** © Steve Pope/AP Photo; **114:** © Russell Tate/Istock; **116 top:** © Dawn Johnston/Istock; **116 bottom:** © Jude Maceren/Getty Images; **129:** © NASA; **124:** © Library of Congress; **165:** © Library of Congress; **187 top:** © Jason Reed/Reuters/Corbis; **187 bottom:** © David J. Phillip/AP Photo; **175:** © The Granger Collection; **204:** © The Granger Collection.

INDEX

Page numbers with an *f* indicate figures.

D